W9-DAZ-355

AND THE CROOKED

SHALL BE MADE STRAIGHT

AND THE CROOKED SHALL BE MADE STRAIGHT

The Eichmann Trial, the Jewish Catastrophe,
and Hannah Arendt's Narrative

Jacob Robinson

THE JEWISH PUBLICATION SOCIETY
OF AMERICA, PHILADELPHIA, 5725-1965

CONTENTS

CONTENTS

PREFACE

The trial of Adolf Eichmann before an Israel District Court in Jerusalem aroused worldwide interest. The court proceedings brought before the public eye a portion of Jewish history called "the Catastrophe," extending from 1933 to 1945 and encompassing all parts of the world dominated or menaced by Nazi Germany. Eichmann, as head of the department that directed and supervised most of the anti-Jewish activities of the Nazi regime, had a major part in the annihilation of thousands of Jewish communities throughout Europe and in the murder of six million human beings— men and women, aged and young, healthy and sick, and little children.

From the time when the German program to exterminate the Jews became known, scholars and research institutions began to devote themselves to a study of Nazi oppression of Jews in Germany and the countries she dominated. The study is still continuing. Mountains of material have been amassed—official documents, writings buried by Jewish victims, reports made by survivors of concentration and extermination camps, eyewitness accounts by non-Jews, and records of postwar trials for war crimes and for crimes of Nazi violence.

The Eichmann trial in Jerusalem provoked both public and scholarly interest. Much evidence was submitted to the Israeli court on the savagery perpetrated by the Nazis in their extermination program against the Jews as it related to Eichmann's work. And the elucidation of the legal basis of the trial had significant implications for the development of international criminal law.

The trial led to the publication of many articles and books. The publication that had the greatest popular appeal came from the pen of Hannah Arendt.

Miss Arendt's discussion of the Eichmann trial first appeared in February and March, 1963, in five successive issues of *The New*

Yorker under the title "Eichmann in Jerusalem." In May, 1963, these articles were published by the Viking Press in a book titled *Eichmann in Jerusalem: A Report on the Banality of Evil.* The articles and the book do not differ much in content. In January, 1965, Viking published the same title in a paperback edition (Compass Books). This new edition is called "revised and enlarged," but in a Note to the Reader Miss Arendt states: "the revisions . . . concern about a dozen technical errors, none of which has any bearing on the analysis or argument of the original text"; "most of the additions are also of a technical nature"; and "the character of the book as a whole is completely unaltered."

The comprehensive nature of Miss Arendt's account has perhaps led many readers to accept her conclusions. But scholars who have studied the Catastrophe in the myriad original sources have rejected her presentation. Miss Arendt does not convey reliable information. She has misread many of the documents and books referred to in her text and bibliography. She has not equipped herself with the necessary background for an understanding and analysis of the trial.

The purpose of the present volume is to give the reader accurate information—about Adolf Eichmann and his work as SS officer in charge of Nazi activities against the Jews; about the trial in the light of international criminal law; about the court's high standards of justice; and about conditions that prevailed among the Jews of Europe and the way they faced disaster. The facts show up the historical falsities in Miss Arendt's narrative. Her errors demand correction.

In the present volume, references to Miss Arendt's articles in *The New Yorker* are called "serial version" and are indicated by Roman numerals (followed by page numbers) as follows: I stands for the issue of February 16; II for February 23; III for March 2; IV for March 9; and V for March 16. References to her book are indicated only by page numbers in parentheses. References to her later paperback edition are indicated by the words "paperback edition" and page numbers. All italics are mine, unless otherwise indicated.

To enable both the professional historian and the layman to gain access to the source material I have drawn upon, extensive references are provided in Notes for each chapter and in the Bibliography. I have also made English translations of passages from scores of relevant documents written in eighteen different languages. Though more research is needed before we can obtain a truly synoptic view of the Jewish Catastrophe, the details offered in the present volume can give an idea of the nature of the tragedy that overtook the Jewish people and all of mankind.

JACOB ROBINSON

New York
April 30, 1965

1

Adolf Eichmann:
The Man and His Work

HANNAH ARENDT's account of Adolf Eichmann's background and character, his authority and activities, his attitude toward his work, and the functioning of his conscience—in her book titled *Eichmann in Jerusalem*—portrays him as a powerless product of a totalitarian system which could corrupt any "average person" with an "innate repugnance toward crime" (pp. 87-88). The present chapter reveals in detail how Miss Arendt has ignored evidence concerning Eichmann, and how in so doing she ends up with a portrait of the man in no way resembling reality.

Background and Character

Adolf Eichmann was born on March 19, 1906, to a Protestant family in Solingen, Germany. After the death of his mother and his father's remarriage the family moved to Linz, Austria, where Adolf completed his studies in public school and attended high school (*Oberrealschule*). He did not graduate, but enrolled in a school for machine-building, which he left after two years, also without graduating. After being unemployed for a few years, he became a salesman for an Austrian firm in 1925. Two years later he was a traveling salesman for the Vacuum Oil Company, a position he retained till 1933. He joined the National Socialist Party in 1932, and the Elite Guard (SS) at the same time. Following a period of military training and service in Dachau, he was attached on October 1, 1934, to the Main Office of the Security Service (*Sicherheitsdienst*, or SD), where he remained until the end of the war. By November 1941 he had reached the rank of *Obersturmbann-führer* (Lieutenant Colonel, in the SS). His department, designated in turn by the symbols II-112, IVD4, IVB4, and IVA4(b), had the

1

principal jurisdiction in Jewish Affairs (*Judenangelegenheiten*). As head of this office he was in charge of activities against Jews, beginning with intelligence, subsequently going over to compulsory emigration, and culminating with the physical destruction of most of European Jewry.[1]

According to Miss Arendt, the story of Adolf Eichmann is "a hard-luck story, if there ever was one" (p. 67; see also pp. 45, 255), the story of a "life . . . beset with frustrations" (p. 30). But when she comes to recite its details, they seem ordinary, especially in the early days, which she stresses. The only misfortune that she specifies in Eichmann's boyhood is his failure to graduate from high school (p. 24); a page later this misfortune is described as something "ordinary" (p. 25). His later "hard luck" ranges from his having become a member of the Security Service (SD) through a "misunderstanding" (pp. 32 f.) to such events as the collapse of his "cherished" plans for a Jewish territory in Nisko and Madagascar[2] (pp. 29 f.), or the loss of satisfaction with his job (*Arbeitsfreude*, which he seems to have recovered with remarkable rapidity) on receiving the *Führer's* order for the physical extermination of the Jews (p. 27). As further evidence of bad fortune, Miss Arendt adduces Eichmann's statement at the conclusion of his trial that he was "the victim of a fallacy"—the nature of which is never indicated—and that he "must suffer for the acts of others" (p. 226). The final disappointment mentioned is Eichmann's lack of "time for a last meal" before his execution (p. 228).

She describes his "unhappy existence of a refugee" (p. 30; a strange characterization of a fugitive from justice) and his "dreary life" in Argentina (p. 216); how in court "not once does he face the audience" (p. 3); how "for the most part [he] successfully maintains his self-control" (p. 3) in the face of what she says he referred to as "a cross-examination that lasted longer than any known before" (p. 203); and how he was able "to look upon death with remarkable equanimity" (p. 221).

In speaking of Eichmann's abilities, Miss Arendt is careful to belittle his intelligence. Comparing him with General Alfred Jodl (the German Chief of Operations, one of the defendants in the trial of the major war criminals), she writes that he was "much less intelligent and without any education to speak of" (p. 133). She considers Eichmann's reading of Adolf Böhm's *Die zionistische Bewegung* (*The Zionist Movement*—not, as she calls it, *History of*

Zionism) "a considerable achievement" for someone unaccustomed to reading books (p. 37). She discounts his ability to read Yiddish newspapers "haltingly" as "not a very difficult accomplishment, since Yiddish, basically an old German dialect written in Hebrew letters, can be understood by any German-speaking person who has mastered a few dozen Hebrew words" (pp. 36 f.).[3] Although she believes Eichmann's claim to have read Kant's *Critique of Practical Reason*, and even admits that he "came up with an approximately correct definition of the categorical imperative" (p. 121), she finds him incapable of understanding "the [Foreign Office] method" which "though simple, was somewhat subtle, and was certainly quite beyond Eichmann's mental grasp and political apprehension" (p. 144).[4]

Despite her low opinion of Eichmann's intelligence, Miss Arendt asserts that "he was recognized not merely as an expert on 'the Jewish question,' the intricacies of Jewish organizations and Zionist parties, but as an 'authority' on emigration and evacuation, as the 'master' who knew how to make people move" (p. 60). In addition, we are told that "there were two things he could do well, better than others: he could organize and he could negotiate" (p. 40)—considerable talents which we would hardly expect to find in an average man. She also asserts that "now [at his trial] he knew how to read documents, something he had not known during the police examination, and he could do it better than his lawyer" (p. 202). For this half-educated "déclassé" (p. 28) to do in eight months what students of law and history spend years to attain is no small achievement.

Miss Arendt devotes a good deal of time to an examination of Eichmann's manner of expressing himself. She accepts his claim that "officialese [*Amtssprache*] is my only language" (pp. 43-44) and goes on to generalize that he "was genuinely incapable of uttering a single sentence that was not a cliché" (p. 44). Later she adds, "this horrible gift for consoling himself with clichés did not leave him in the hour of his death" (p. 50). But, of the many examples offered of Eichmann's expressions, virtually none can be considered as governmental *Amtssprache*, and only some of them as "clichés." For example, the following specimens, brought out in Miss Arendt's book, hardly qualify as "officialese": "I will jump into my grave laughing" (p. 42); Europe would be "combed from West to East" for Jews (p. 123), an expression used for the first time in the minutes of the Wannsee Conference, which had been prepared by Eichmann; "forest of difficulties" (p. 144); "yawning emptiness" (p. 62); "death whirl" (p. 102); "the old song and dance" (p. 30), in his words *die alte Tour*; "apathy of an ox being led to his stall" (p. 52); "allowed his tongue to run away with him" (p. 74); "drunkenness of their power" (p. 74); "like pulling teeth" (p. 61); and Eichmann's claim that he had been "grilled until the steak was done" (p. 203). Expressions like "this [extermination] must be done in a more elegant way," attributed by Eichmann to the circles of the Ministry for the Occupied Eastern Territories;[5] "I have to clean the Jewish filth out of the provinces" (*Ich muss diesen jüdischen Dreck aus der Provinz ausräumen*), told to Kasztner and repeated more than once[6]—are these expressions clichés? Is his courtroom use of cardplayers' jargon (*Skat*), referred to by Miss Arendt on page 43, "officialese"? In the Sassen Papers (see Chapter 3, Note 52), we find phrases such as "material for heating ovens," referring to people burned in the gassing installations,[7] and "the only good 'enemy of the Reich' [Jew, in this context] is a dead one."[8] Are these common sayings? A German author, Joachim Schwelien, in his study *Jargon of Violence*, has presented a far more discerning analysis of Eichmann's language:

Eichmann does not suspect that he is actually revealing the full truth whenever, obstinately or with sly cunning, he tries to falsify the truth about events or deeds by lying, glossing, or concealing. Not *what* he says is important, but *how* he says it, for just as language itself mirrors the truth buried in thought, so the jargon of violence unavoidably reflects sinister inhumanity in spite of all attempts to hide it. Let us, therefore, listen to Eichmann—"heartily merry and lively . . . at any rate open and honest" (*frisch-fröhlich und munter . . . jedenfalls offen und ehrlich*)[9]—as he tries to whitewash himself and his kind. No defendant provided with all possible legal means ever condemned himself and his era more clearly than did Adolf Eichmann through his revealing jargon. For every accusation (*Vorhalt*) he had a ready answer, but he was unable to rid himself of the vocabulary of the murder trade practiced by him and by his sinister accomplices.[10]

Miss Arendt hops back and forth between Eichmann the modest and trustworthy man and Eichmann the forgetful braggart. Those of his admissions which contradict her version of his activities she invalidates as bragging, while she explains away his sudden reticences as "faulty memory" (p. 57). "Bragging," she says, "had always been one of his cardinal vices" (p. 25). Eichmann had a great inclination "to deck himself in borrowed plumes" (p. 40). "Bragging was the vice that was Eichmann's undoing" (p. 41)— as if not what he did, but what he said, had brought him to the gallows. Miss Arendt continues: "What eventually led to his capture was his compulsion to talk big—he was 'fed up with being an anonymous wanderer between the worlds'—and this compulsion must have grown considerably stronger . . . because the postwar era had bestowed so much unexpected 'fame' upon him" (pp. 42-43).[11] This bragging, offered as an alibi, is, however, incompatible with another quality she bestows on Adolf Eichmann when she asserts that in relation to higher Nazi officials "he was . . . ruined by modesty" (p. 101).

Miss Arendt frequently finds him trustworthy where there is evidence to the contrary. She explicitly denies that Eichmann was "a clever, calculating liar" (p. 49). Elsewhere she exclaims "Alas, nobody believed him" (p. 23), and proceeds to analyze in psychological terms why the prosecutor, the counsel for defense, and the judges did not take his word: ". . . the judges did not believe him, because they were too good, and perhaps also too conscious of the very foundations of their profession, to admit that an average, normal' person, neither feeble-minded nor indoctrinated nor cynical, could be perfectly incapable of telling right from wrong.[12] They preferred to conclude from occasional lies that he was a liar— and missed the greatest moral and even legal challenge of the whole case" (p. 23).

On the other hand, Miss Arendt also charges Eichmann with distorting the truth. She writes about his own statement on his trustworthiness: "His own convictions in this matter were far from modest: 'One of the few gifts fate bestowed upon me is a capacity for truth insofar as it depends on myself'" (p. 49). She condemns as an "outright lie" his claim made in the period 1937-1945 that "his birthplace was Palestine and that he was fluent in Hebrew and Yiddish" (p. 25). Eichmann's statement that he was dismissed from the Vacuum Oil Company because unmarried employees were losing their jobs is presented by her as "not the truth either" (p. 25) and she goes on to suggest that "one need not believe his saying that he had been 'very happy' about his dismissal" (p. 27). She charges him with lying about his profession (p. 25), with not telling the whole truth in his biography (p. 25), with contradictions in "several important entries in all his official Nazi records" (p. 25). She notes the contradiction between his statement to Police Superintendent Avner Less in the pretrial interrogation that he had "asked to be sent to active military duty" in order "to attain a higher grade in the S.S.," and the court testimony that "he had asked to be transferred because he wanted to escape his murderous duties" (p. 44).[13] Relating the story of Eichmann's alleged effort to direct German Jews to Lodz instead of Russia, she brands his version as "not true" (p. 89). She refers to Eichmann's "foolish and stubborn contention that he had saved the lives of hundreds of thousands of Jews through 'forced emigration'" (p. 172). The account he gave, during the pretrial interrogation, of his appointment to the Jewish department is characterized by Miss Arendt as "distorted, of course, but not wholly devoid of truth" (p. 36). She also states that "he once said his only alternative would have been suicide," but she calls this "a lie" and adds, "he did not mean to be taken literally" (p. 86). She says that Eichmann "repeatedly visited Auschwitz" (p. 84), though he admitted after some hedging to only five or six times.[14] One more instance of lying is offered by Miss Arendt: During the discussion of the so-called *Erschiessen* episode (see Chapter 5, under Yugoslavia), Eichmann categorically denied that he ever killed or gave an order to kill. Here she comes up with a euphemism: his denial was "very ineffective" (pp. 19-20).

Nevertheless, despite her repeated admission of Eichmann's lying, Miss Arendt frequently accepts his version of disputed events. Thus she finds that he told his version of the reasons for his involvement in the "blood for goods" episode[15] "quite truthfully" (p. 21), and, discussing his version of Nisko—embellished by herself—she claims that "Eichmann's version of the Nisko adventure is true . . . there is no reason not to believe him" (p. 68). She finds Eichmann's Storfer story[16] "presumably true enough" (p. 45) and considers it a "normal human encounter" (p. 46). She even promotes Eichmann to "the rank of the most cooperative defendant ever," though he needed the aid of "irrefutable documents" (p. 24) to be reminded of the truth, as in the case of his visit to Bratislava (p. 76).

The Jerusalem District Court considered Eichmann untruthful, for reasons spelled out in the judgment. There the court said:

> The evidence of the defendant in this case was not truthful evidence, in spite of his repeated declarations that he was reconciled to his fate, knowing the gravity of the deeds to which he had confessed of his own

free will, and that now his only desire was to reveal the truth in order to set straight in the eyes of his countrymen and of the whole world the wrong impression that had been created, in the course of time, concerning his activities. Throughout this judgment we have pointed out a variety of instances in which the defendant was discovered to have been testifying falsely. We now add that his entire testimony was nothing else than a consistent, continuous effort to contradict the truth in order to deny his proper share of responsibility, or at least to reduce it as much as possible. He maintained this effort not without skill, with the aid of the same characteristics in which he excelled during the time he had been active: an alert mind; the ability to find his bearings in any difficult situation; cunning; and a smooth tongue. But he did not have the courage to admit the truth, not about the way things had really occurred and not about his inner feelings toward what he had done. We saw him over and over again weaving back and forth under the pressure of cross-examination, retreating from complete denial to partial denial and, when no alternative was left, to admission; but of course always falling back on the explicit order he was obeying, as it were, every time he did anything, great or small.

The question arises: Why did the defendant confess before Superintendent Less to a number of incriminating matters for which, on the face of it, no proof could have been provided except for his confession—in particular, his trips to the East, where he saw the atrocities with his own eyes? We cannot investigate the mazes of the defendant's soul now, when he is in confinement, in order to find out what moved him to do so. It is possible to make a variety of speculations in explanation of these partial admissions, but there is no point in doing this for the sake of a juridical evaluation of his evidence. Suffice it to say that these admissions did not lend credibility in our eyes to his testimony before us concerning matters about which he was found to be lying.[17]

Miss Arendt argues that the whole of German society had become so practiced in self-deception, so "shielded against reality and factuality" that "the same self-deception, lies, and stupidity . . . had now become ingrained in Eichmann's mentality" (p. 47). This self-deception, she continues, had become so embedded in Germans during the Nazi era that she finds it hard even now not to believe that "mendacity has become an integral part of the German national character" (p. 47). She concludes: "Eichmann's astounding willingness, in Argentina as well as in Jerusalem [where? certainly not in court], to admit his crimes was due less to his own criminal capacity for self-deception than to the aura of systematic mendacity that had constituted the general, and generally accepted, atmosphere of the Third Reich" (p. 47). She nowhere explains how his alleged willingness to admit his crimes follows from his mendacity, whatever its origin.

An interesting exhibition of her reliance on preconceptions is her discussion of Eichmann's "extraordinarily faulty memory" (pp. 49, 56, 57, 79, 88, 93, 183). Only in a few cases was the excuse of forgetfulness used by Eichmann; in the majority of cases it is used by Miss Arendt on Eichmann's behalf. The question arises: How does she know that Adolf Eichmann "forgot"? She states, for example, that Eichmann would readily forget his routine activities. All his actions against Jews were routine and thus forgotten (p. 137), but not so his meetings with persons of higher status. Let us examine a case in point.

Eichmann visited the Slovak Minister of the Interior, Sano Mach, in Bratislava, in 1942. When first questioned about this visit, he described vividly how he was invited to bowl with Mach. He insisted this was merely a social visit, absolutely no business was discussed. Later, when confronted with documents that showed he had been sent to Bratislava to talk over "the current evacuation action against Jews from Slovakia," he replied: "Clear, clear,[18] that was an order from Berlin, they did not send me there to go bowling" (p. 76). Instead of drawing the obvious conclusion in regard to Eichmann's credibility, Miss Arendt considers that the first statement was an error on his part and continues: "Had he lied twice, with great consistency? Hardly. To evacuate and deport Jews had become routine business; what stuck in his mind was bowling, being the guest of a minister, and hearing of the attack on Heydrich" (p. 76). Two years after this incident, in July 1944, when Hungary's ruler Admiral Horthy ordered all deportations of Jews to be discontinued—a perfect opportunity for Eichmann to stop his activities—Eichmann managed, by duplicity, to apprehend and deport to Auschwitz the 1,500 Jews from the Kistarcsa camp. This act is well remembered not only by Jewish leaders[19] but also by Nazi Foreign Office officials such as Horst Grell.[20] Eichmann, however, while not denying the fact, pretended that he could not remember. Miss Arendt has this to say: "Although the judges were 'convinced that the accused remembers his victory over Horthy very well,' this is doubtful, since to Eichmann Horthy was not such a great personage" (p. 183). (This explanation is offered not by Eichmann but by Miss Arendt, who does not reveal her source.) She apparently finds it reasonable that Sano Mach, a Cabinet Minister in Slovakia, was a memorable person to Eichmann, while Horthy, the ruler of Hungary, was of little account.

Miss Arendt says that Eichmann even forgot facts "that might have supported" his story (p. 56). As an example, she notes that he "had forgotten in Jerusalem, much to his disadvantage" that Heydrich allegedly told him in a personal interview in 1941 "that the whole enterprise [the actual killing process] had been 'put under the authority of the S.S. Head Office for Economy and Administration' [WVHA]—that is, not of his own R.S.H.A." (p. 79). Eichmann knew well the division of functions between the WVHA and the RSHA. Had Miss Arendt consulted Raul Hilberg's *The Destruction of the European Jews*,[21] listed in her Bibliography, she would have discovered on page 572 that the extermination camps of Chełmno, Bełżec (not "Belzek," as she has it on pp. 96, 265), Sobibór, and Treblinka were under the jurisdiction of the Higher SS and Police Leaders, while only Lublin and Auschwitz, which were extermination *and* labor camps, were under the jurisdiction of the WVHA. The Pohl trial cleared up the responsibility of the WVHA. Pohl himself, chief of the WVHA, was condemned to death, but not for the murder of victims of concentration camps. In the words of the judgment delivered at the Pohl trial: "Neither Pohl nor any other member of the WVHA had authority to order the execution of concentration camp prisoners. Nor is there any evidence that he, or they, attempted to exercise any such prerogative. The order for executions originated between the Secret State Police and Himmler personally."[22] The department responsible for the "executions" was IVB4 under Adolf Eichmann, the competent *Referent* ("Specialist"). No wonder Eichmann "forgot" the statement of Heydrich; in light of the realities of the situation, it could never have been made.

The fact is, Eichmann had an unusually good memory for autobiographical details. He remembered, when he wanted to remember, in minutest detail, names, dates, and occurrences. Only when he was questioned about having taken part in important conferences and activities concerning the Final Solution (the euphemism for the murder of the Jews) did he plead lack of memory, and here his recollections could be refreshed only when the relevant documents were shown to him.

The first seventy pages of his statement to the police are a demonstration of Eichmann's excellent memory. A quarter of a century after the events described he could remember details of conversations. He was able, without any notes or other aids, to give a detailed picture of his service in the Nazi movement up to the period of extermination. He could describe in detail the offices and the furniture, documents, and files. He remembered well hundreds of persons, their appearance and character. He even remembered—twenty-three years afterward—his salary in Dachau, and the title of the Hebrew textbook from which he studied. But he did not remember the facts of his involvement in the supply of gas for the extermination camps, the date when he was told about the Final Solution, the liquidation of the ghettos, whether he inspected the loading of the deportees in the cars, what he did in the East, and other similar data. Eichmann's memory, it would appear, served him well in trivial matters but failed him in significant ones. It just happened that the significant ones were unfavorable to him.

Miss Arendt writes: "Had his memory served him better, he would never have told the Theresienstadt story at all. For all this happened when the time of 'political solutions' had passed and the era of the 'physical solution' had begun" (p. 76). It is interesting to observe her concern with Eichmann's defense. But here she omits one detail: Eichmann's part in the foundation and supervision of Theresienstadt had been established beforehand by irrefutable documentary proof, and the record of the decisive conference in this connection, which took place in Prague on October 10, 1941, in which both Heydrich and Eichmann are mentioned as active participants,[23] had already been shown to Eichmann during his pretrial interrogation.[24] Eichmann, therefore, had no choice but to remember.

Perhaps the best examples of Miss Arendt's efforts to tell the Eichmann story according to her preconceptions are the numerous instances where she freely supplements his evidence in court with her own interpretations, and even fashions a mental state for him from her own imagination. According to her, Eichmann "had been an ambitious young man who was fed up with his job as traveling salesman" (p. 29). "Thus bored to distraction, he heard that the Security Service of the Reichsführer S.S. . . . had jobs open, and applied immediately" (p. 31). But, alas, "the trouble was that things were again very, very boring, and he was greatly relieved when . . . he was put into the brand-new department concerned with Jews" (p. 33). Orthodox Jews "bored him" (p. 37). After the end of the war, when he stayed in the Lüneburger Heide for four years, "he was probably bored to death" (p. 215). All these interpretations emanate not from Adolf Eichmann but from Miss Arendt.

She goes on: "Would he [Adolf Eichmann] then have pleaded guilty if he had been indicted as an accessory to murder?" (p. 21); Adolf Eichmann did not like "dispatching people to their death by the trainload" (p. 29); "he might still have preferred . . . to be hanged as *Obersturmbannführer a. D.* . . . rather than living out his life . . . as a traveling salesman" (p. 30). She also asserts (p. 160) that "he was told—and believed" the fantastic story of fifteen thousand Jews hiding in Monaco, without naming her source. She knows too that Adolf Eichmann "was not serious when he threatened that he would refuse to answer any more questions" (p. 203), but the source of this information also remains a mystery. In another telepathic reading, Miss Arendt says "it is more than likely that he saw himself as the future Governor General, like Hans Frank in Poland, or the future Protector, like Heydrich in Czechoslovakia, of a 'Jewish State'" (p. 70). This, and the reference to the unprecedented case of "repatriation," are almost all she has to say concerning the notorious Nisko episode.

The Nisko operation (October 1939 to the spring of 1940), a brainchild of Eichmann's, began with the first mass expulsion of Jews from their native region (Czechoslovakia) to another (the Government-General, formerly part of Poland). What happened to these people, who were transported with complete disregard for their life and health, we learn from the succinct summary presented in the judgment:

Of the one thousand people who departed . . . from Moravska Ostrava, 300 returned. The others were expelled or fled across the demarcation line into the Soviet zone, and most of them were caught there by the Germans after the German-Russian war broke out. . . .[25]

The same, if not a worse, fate befell the subsequent transports. Miss Arendt is too busy explaining the reasons for the origin and failure of the project (pp. 68-70) to pay much attention to the Jews, the victims. She does, however, mention the fact that "some [of the Jews] were even repatriated," adding that Eichmann's order to camouflage the returnees in the police records as "returning from vocational training" (*Umschichtung*) was "a curious relapse into the pro-Zionist stage of the [Nazi] movement" (p. 70). The fact is that the camouflage of the status of returnees from the Nisko project was not motivated by any desire to protect them; it was a result of the fact that the entire operation had been undertaken by Eichmann and Stahlecker without authorization, as Miss Arendt herself realizes (p. 70).

At every turn Miss Arendt explains what Eichmann *really* meant, what we should believe and what we should not believe of what he says, as if she had looked into his mind and could see through to a meaning contradicting much that he had said previously, that was said of him, or that he did.

Authority and Activities

The limits Miss Arendt arbitrarily imposes on Eichmann's authority and activities lead her to exclude Eichmann from the class of major war criminals. She writes: "Only the 'major war criminals' had acted without territorial limitations, and Eichmann certainly was not one of them" (p. 237). Immediately afterward she adds a contradictory statement: "If Eichmann's activities had spread all over occupied Europe, this was so not because he was so important that territorial limits did not apply to him but because it was in the nature of his task, the collection and deportation of all Jews, that he and his men had to roam the continent" (p. 237). Even though she herself writes that "he [Eichmann] was to play such an important role" in the Final Solution (p. 27), she is ready to characterize his mission as not a major one. We know, however, that if Eichmann had been found, he would have stood trial before the Nuremberg Military Tribunals as a major war criminal (in the sense of the statute of the International Military Tribunal and the Control Council Law No. 10). In this connection, Telford Taylor, United States Chief of Counsel at the Subsequent Trials, had the following to say: "After the victory, when his [Eichmann's] apparent role in the business of mass extermination became known, Eichmann's name rose nearly to the top of the allied 'wanted' list, beneath only those of Martin Bormann, who is now believed to have survived Hitler by only a few hours, and 'Gestapo Mueller,' Eichmann's superior, whose fate is still unknown."[26] The Deputy Chief of Counsel, Robert M. W. Kempner, also stated clearly that "Eichmann would have certainly been indicted for war crimes against humanity. The boundless nature of his crime made him a major war criminal under the Nuremberg Charter."[27] In fact, a large number of Nuremberg defendants and witnesses had been questioned on the whereabouts of Eichmann for the purpose of locating him for prosecution as a major war criminal.[28]

Miss Arendt presents her own list of Eichmann's criminal deeds and activities on the strength of which alone he "would not have escaped capital punishment" (p. 199). She declares that "after the tape-recorder [playing back the pretrial interrogation] had addressed the court, the death sentence was a foregone conclusion" (p. 87); and that "there was more than enough, as he [Eichmann] occasionally pointed out, to hang him" (p. 85). The following are some comments she makes on Adolf Eichmann's position and activities:

1. His work is characterized as "work of evacuation and transportation" (II, 92; left out on p. 87).

2. His function was "to ship millions of men, women, and children to their death," which he carried out "with great zeal and the most meticulous care" (p. 22).

3. About the planned deportation of the Serbian Jews, she states that "Eichmann was informed, since it was a matter of deportation" (p. 20), "and this was precisely his job" (I, 60; left out on p. 20).

4. "Eichmann's position was that of the most important conveyor belt in the whole operation, because it was always up to him and his men how many Jews could or should be transported from any given area, and it was through his office that the ultimate destination of the shipment was cleared, though that destination was not determined by him" (p. 137). "All deportations from West to East were organized and coordinated by Eichmann and his associates" (p. 142).

5. His statement, if he "had not transported them, they would not have been delivered to the butcher" (p. 47), is not challenged by her, and she later adds: "Eichmann had to coordinate all these 'efforts' . . ." (p. 136).

6. Concerning his attitude toward his work, she says that "he had been doing his best right along to help with the Final Solution" (p. 101); that "Eichmann had at all times done his best to make the Final Solution final" (p. 130).

7. "He had . . . always done his best to aggravate 'the consequences of the offense,' rather than to reduce them" (pp. 86-87).

8. "He was quite capable of sending millions of people to their death" (p. 129).

9. "The enormity of the [his] crime" is expressly admitted (p. 87).

This is a formidable indictment. To be sure, the emphasis on transportation creates the impression that Eichmann's was the technical job of supplying the means of transportation, whereas this was actually the function of his assistant Franz Novak.[29] Eichmann's "main work lay," as the judgment made clear, "not in obtaining the railroad cars, but in obtaining the Jews with whom he would fill the railroad cars, in order to transport them to their extermination—and in doing everything connected with that."[30] But even the part of his work that dealt with transportation was far from innocent. As the judgment put it:

It is no exaggeration to say that the very transportation under such conditions had the elements of a first step in the process of exterminating the deportees. And indeed it happened more than once that when a transport reached its destination, or at one of the stations along the way, corpses of people who had died en route were removed from the railroad cars. This applies not only to the stage of the Final Solution, but also to the second [i.e., previous] stage, in which the Jews were deported from the Warthe District, etc., and from Stettin under murderous conditions of transportation.[31]

Yet, in keeping with her belittlement of Eichmann's abilities, Miss Arendt takes pains, even in undisputed cases, to minimize his role, his sphere of influence, his personal responsibilities, and his function. Thus, when mentioning his earlier service in Dachau, she observes that "he had nothing to do with the concentration camp there" (pp. 30-31). Indicating that the Mobile Killing Units (*Einsatzgruppen*) "were under the command of Heydrich and the R.S.H.A." (p. 65), she adds "which, of course, does not mean that Eichmann necessarily had anything to do with them." Mentioning the violent outbreaks against Jews in Germany during the night of November 9-10, 1938—the so-called *Kristallnacht* (the Crystal Night pogrom)—she points out that Eichmann had nothing to do with it (p. 206). She writes that in the period of the Final Solution "his department had become merely instrumental," and continues: "Hence he had every reason to be very 'embittered and disappointed' . . ." (p. 74).

The range of his experience is narrowed by Miss Arendt. She writes that "Eichmann did not see much" (p. 84); that in Auschwitz, "Höss . . . spared him the gruesome sights" (p. 84). But this statement is not compatible with Eichmann's own admission that on one of his visits in Auschwitz he witnessed with his own eyes the burning of bodies in an iron grating within a pit 100 or even 180 meters long.[32] Mentioning his visit to Treblinka, she states: "Well, he had been lucky, for he had still seen only the preparations for the future carbon-monoxide chambers at Treblinka" (p. 82). This statement is belied by Eichmann's pretrial interrogation. Reporting on his visit to Treblinka he says:

I saw how a column of naked Jews went across the gangplanks, which were walled in with barbed wire, into a house . . . into a large—not a house, a hall-like structure, to be gassed, as I was told . . . with potassium cyanide.[33]

This was not the only time Eichmann watched "the gassing process." During the cross-examination he admitted that he was in the extermination camp of Chełmno (Kulmhof) where he "saw people being gassed."[34] Describing his visit to the shooting area at Minsk, Miss Arendt says, "it seemed as though he would be lucky, for by the time he arrived . . . 'the affair had almost been finished,' which pleased him very much" (p. 83). But Eichmann himself admitted to the contrary. In a part of his pretrial interrogation that was played back in the District Court, he said:

Müller told me in Linz . . . : "In Minsk they are shooting the Jews; I want a report as to how they are doing it." So I went to Minsk . . . . I saw young riflemen shooting into a pit . . . and I saw a woman, her arms stretched backward, and then my knees went weak and I left.[35]

In Lwów he saw a trench "which was already filled, and there was a spring of blood, like a geyser, gushing from it."[36]

Miss Arendt also limits his responsibility for action in the East. She sees the "trouble" in discussing the connection of Eichmann with the Jewish Catastrophe in the East in the fact that the evidence on this score was ("admittedly, as the Judgment said"; IV, 116) "scanty" (p. 188). She is convinced that "Eichmann had next to nothing to do with what happened to Jews in Poland and the Baltic countries, in White Russia and the Ukraine" (p. 199). Thus, at a stroke, she dismisses his status as *Referent* for Jewish questions, his functions in regard to the Special Operations Units (Mobile Killing Units), and his complicity in the procurement and the use of gas for extermination purposes.

The Jerusalem District Court looked carefully into the question "whether, and to what extent, it has been proved that the defendant was active in connection with all the crimes committed by the Germans in Eastern Europe."[37] With regard to the Government-General area of Poland, the court concluded that there too "the defendant and his department were authorized to deal with matters concerning the Final Solution and, as has been proved, on occasion actually did deal with these matters . . . although there existed in the area other channels of command in which the defendant was not involved."[38] The judgment goes into great detail concerning Eichmann's role in the occupied territories of the Soviet Union, in particular in regard to the famous Brown Folder (Braune Mappe),[39] which contained, inter alia, instructions for treatment of Jews in these territories.

Miss Arendt maintains that the Wannsee Conference of January 20, 1942, attended by Eichmann and representatives of several government departments for the purpose of mapping out the destruction of European Jewry, made no decisions concerning the Jews in the East, including the Government-General (p. 198). To secure her point, she explains the presence there of State Secretary Bühler, highest Government-General official under Frank, by the delicate phrase, "for purposes of coordination" (p. 197; not in IV, 130). Referring to General Lahousen's testimony before the International Military Tribunal, she alleges that "the massacre of Polish Jewry had been decided on by Hitler not in May or June, 1941, but in September, 1939" (p. 198). An examination of the International Military Tribunal record reveals that Miss Arendt misinterpreted the sources. Responding to a question of the Soviet prosecutor concerning the Ukrainian population of Poland, Lahousen stated that during the conference in Hitler's train on September 12, 1939 (two weeks before the fall of Warsaw, when the war in Poland was still going on) Ribbentrop had instructed the German Army Intelligence to promote an uprising of the Ukrainian nationalists in which the Poles and Jews were to be killed. Lahousen makes no reference to Hitler in this statement, and he mentions the killing of the Jews not as a chief objective but only in connection with what he calls "simply a preparation for military sabotage."[40]

It is true that Jews were murdered in Poland from the very start of the German occupation; but, in contrast to the mass deportations to the extermination centers carried out within the framework of the Final Solution, these killings were not the result of a planned, concerted effort. Miss Arendt errs when she implies that the Jews of Poland, and of Eastern Europe in general, were not affected by the Final Solution because they were being killed anyway. The flimsiness of this argument, and of the explanation of Bühler's presence at the Wannsee Conference, is demonstrated by the fact that the statistical table which Heydrich presented at Wannsee lists 8,000,000 Eastern European Jews (then still alive)—including 2,284,000 for the Government-General alone—out of a total of 11,000,000 earmarked for the Final Solution in all of Europe. That Heydrich's figures were wrong is beside the point. What is important here is the fact that the Final Solution was a project for the future, the master plan for the killing of all the Jews in Europe, including those in England, Switzerland, Turkey, and other countries not under Nazi control. And, as Heydrich, after the Conference, informed Martin Luther of the Foreign Office, Eichmann was his "competent specialist" (*zuständiger Referent*) for this entire operation.[41]

Miss Arendt denies that Eichmann had a function in the ghetto of Lodz (p. 195), despite the evidence cited by the court:

As to the Lodz Ghetto, the second largest of all the ghettos, also situated in the Warthe District, we have mentioned Kaltenbrunner's telegram dated June 30, 1943 (from the files of the Düsseldorf Gestapo), in which he gives notice of a visit by the defendant to the Lodz Ghetto, in connection with removing the Jews from there. Then, at a later stage, apparently at the beginning of 1944, the defendant is mentioned by name as Kaltenbrunner's representative, as a participant in discussions concerning liquidation of the Lodz Ghetto and its conversion to a concentration camp, and its transfer to the Head Office for Administration and Economy (T/247). Similarly we read in another document (T/248) that the defendant cooperated in submitting a report on the economic enterprises in the Lodz Ghetto—a report drawn up by him, together with [Dr. Max] Horn, the manager of "Osti." From these documents we learn that the defendant had a governing voice in the affairs of the Lodz Ghetto, being the person in charge of Jewish affairs on behalf of the RSHA.[42]

Eichmann himself admitted that the Lodz Ghetto and the Warthe District as a whole were under his authority insofar as they had to do with Jewish matters.[43]

In her discussion of the "deportation of Jews from Polish ghettos to the nearby killing centers" (pp. 194-195), Miss Arendt deals with Eichmann's part in the transportation of Jews from the East to the extermination camps. Believing Eichmann, she denies that he played a role in this action, and even makes the serious charge that the court acted *in dubio contra reum* (p. 195)—that is, that the court violated the rule that the defendant always gets the benefit of the doubt. In addition she asserts that the judgment "finally fell back on testimony given by a witness at the Höss trial that some Jews from the General Government area had arrived in Auschwitz together with Jews from Bialystok, a Polish city that had been incorporated into the German province of East Prussia, and hence fell within Eichmann's jurisdiction" (p. 195). In fact, the judgment relied on a considerable body of evidence, summarized in the following words:

Evidence was also submitted in connection with the deportation of Jews living in the Government-General area by train to the extermination camps, including an exchange of letters between Ganzenmüller, Secretary of State in the German Ministry of Transport, and Wolff, head of Himmler's personal staff. On July 28, 1942, Ganzenmüller lets Wolff know the schedule of trains from Warsaw to Treblinka (one train per day, carrying 5,000 Jews each), and from Przemyśl to Bełżec (one train per week, carrying 5,000 Jews each). He adds that the routes of these trains have been agreed upon with the Commander of the Security Police in Cracow, and that Globocnik too has been notified (T/251). To this Wolff replies on August 13, 1942, expressing joy—on Himmler's behalf too—at the fact that each day a train is going to Treblinka with 5,000 of "the chosen people," and he requests the continued assistance of Ganzenmüller in the matter (T/252). As the defendant himself testifies (Session 100, p. 17 and top of p. 18), this was after the death of Heydrich, when Himmler himself was acting as Head of the Security Police and the SD. It is likely that on this occasion Himmler was acting in this capacity and that this matter too passed therefore through the RSHA.

On the other hand, we have before us the minutes of the Berlin conference held on September 26 and 28, 1942, on the removal of 600,000 Jews in the Government-General area and of 200,000 Romanian Jews to the Government-General area (T/1284). A list of those who participated in the conference is not included. The conference dealt with urgent shipments proposed by the Chief of the Security Police and the SD from Warsaw to Treblinka, from the Radom District to Treblinka, from Cracow to Bełżec, and from Lemberg to Bełżec. In his statement to Superintendent Less the defendant says (T/37, p. 3545) that it is probable that Novak, a member of his department, participated in this conference, but almost in the same breath he contends (pp. 3540, 3544) that his department did not deal with shipments in the Government-General area, and in his testimony in court he reiterates this most forcefully (Session 100, pp. 15 *et seq.*). But we do not believe this denial, for in our opinion the fact that the Chief of the Security Police and the SD was involved in the matter is decisive, and makes it eminently reasonable that someone from the defendant's department, the department authorized to deal with Jewish affairs, participated in the conference on behalf of the RSHA. And the defendant was right in assuming, in his statement to Superintendent Less, that the suitable person was Novak, the transportation expert in Department IVB4. It should be noted that the discussion on the establishment of general policy took place in Berlin and not in Cracow, which was the seat of the Eastern Railways Administration, and that transfers in the Government-General area are discussed at the same conference as transfers from Romania, which all parties agree to have been within the authority of the defendant's department. The commander of the Security Police in Cracow, mentioned in letter T/251, was also a member of the RSHA. The defendant's conjecture, made in his statement to Superintendent Less, that transport matters of this kind were within Globocnik's authority, is unfounded. In T/251 we see that Globocnik was merely notified of what had been agreed upon by others, and it is clear that it was necessary to notify him, since he was the one who received the shipments of Jews in the extermination camps.

Novak himself, in evidence given on behalf of the defense, taken for this trial in Vienna (p. 8), admits that he had dealings with the Eastern Railways Administration too, although he denies having had anything to do with the authorities of the Government-General.

Ludwig Rajevski, who gave evidence at the trial of Höss in Poland, worked in the Office of Vital Statistics at Auschwitz. In his evidence (T/1356), he said that Jews from the Government-General area, too, arrived at Auschwitz, and in his account he lumps together these shipments with shipments from Białystok. This fact is of some importance, since there is no doubt that the defendant's department dealt with the Jews of Białystok. This provides proof that the defendant's department had a hand also in the deportation of Jews from the Government-General area to Auschwitz. We learn about the shipment of Jews from the Government-General area (from Cracow) to Auschwitz also from the evidence of Mrs. Rivka Kupper (Session 26).[44]

As has been indicated earlier, Miss Arendt denies that "Eichmann necessarily had anything to do with" the *Einsatzgruppen* (p. 65), but somewhat later she states: "To be sure, he had also sent people into the area of the *Einsatzgruppen*" (p. 96). The court, after discarding all uncorroborated evidence and relying only upon evidence not disputed by Eichmann or contradicted by documents, reached the following conclusion:

We find, therefore, that the defendant was in contact with the Special Operations Units from the commencement of their activities. Beginning with the spring of 1942 the defendant was active in connection with the issuing of operational directives to these groups; he assembled material relating to the extermination of Jews and drew up summaries of this material. The preparation of summaries was of itself a kind of assistance to those into whose hands was given the authority to make decisions, on occasion, concerning the continued activities of the Special Operations Units. Further activity on the part of the defendant with regard to the Special Operations Units can be discerned in a later period, that of the letter T/310, dated March 5, 1943, which we have already mentioned in discussing the Government-General area. This letter, which deals, as will be remembered, with the fate of Jews having foreign nationality, has Special Operations Units B and D among its addressees. This is evidence that at that period the defendant's department was concerned also with transmitting instructions to the Special Operations Units. Instructions in the letter T/784, dated September 23, 1943, on the same subject, are also addressed, *inter alia,* to the commander of Special Operations Unit B.[45]

Miss Arendt, however, states that ". . . all that was left was evidence that Eichmann was well informed of what was going on in the East, which had never been in dispute, and the judgment, surprisingly, concluded that this evidence was sufficient to constitute proof of actual participation" (p. 194). The issuance of operational directives, the preparation of summaries, the transmission of instructions to Special Operations Units B and D, all referred to in the above-cited excerpt from the judgment—all this is considered by Miss Arendt as nothing more than evidence that "Eichmann was well informed."[46]

Miss Arendt also concerns herself with the problem of Adolf Eichmann's responsibility for the supply and use of gas. Referring to Eichmann's discussion with Höss on "details" for expanding the lethal capacity of Auschwitz, including the use of gas, she writes that Eichmann was "probably right" in "strenuously" denying his complicity, "for all other sources contradict Höss's story" (p. 81). Appropriating Eichmann's words,[47] she then states categorically:

"And with the use of gas Eichmann had nothing whatever to do"
(p. 81). In the serial version (II, 82) she says that Eichmann
"probably" had nothing to do with the use of gas. Elsewhere, she
declares that Eichmann's involvement in what she calls *Gasgeschichten* "is unlikely, . . . though one of his men, Rolf Günther,
might have become interested of his own accord" (p. 95). Günther's
involvement is a matter of record,[48] and it is difficult to understand
how anyone can seriously maintain that in Nazi Germany Günther,
Eichmann's deputy, could have undertaken an assignment of such
magnitude as ordering and supplying poison gas for the murder
of millions of people "of his own accord," without the knowledge
of the man in charge. Even Eichmann never stated that the use
of gas was kept a secret from him. Miss Arendt's own Bibliography
lists a book by Rudolf Höss, the commandant of Auschwitz, which
contains the following passage: "Eichmann told me about the
method of killing people with exhaust gases in trucks . . . Killing
with showers of carbon monoxide while bathing, as was done with
mental patients in some places in the Reich, would necessitate too
many buildings. . . We left the matter unresolved. Eichmann decided to try and find a gas which was in ready supply, and which
would not entail special installations for its use."[49]

Miss Arendt states that "the extermination program in the
Eastern gas factories grew out of Hitler's euthanasia program, and
it is deplorable that the Eichmann trial, so concerned with 'historical truth,' paid no attention to this factual connection. This
would have thrown some light on . . . whether Eichmann . . . was
involved in *Gasgeschichten*" (p. 95). This statement calls for three
corrections: (1) The Final Solution, as a program, did not "grow"
out of the euthanasia program; the latter only supplied the Final
Solution with personnel and with certain technical procedures,
which were later perfected in the extermination process. (2) The
connection with euthanasia *is* mentioned, both in documents submitted in evidence[50] and in two passages in the judgment.[51] (3)
"Light" *was* thrown on Eichmann's involvement in *Gasgeschichten*
by substantive documentation.[52]

In general, Miss Arendt maintains throughout her book that
Eichmann was merely a passive receiver of orders (e.g., pp. 57,
101, 120). This evaluation overlooks the hierarchical setup in the
RSHA[53] (particularly the administrative regulations governing its

activities[54]), the extent of Eichmann's initiative and responsibility, and his extreme zeal in the execution of the Final Solution. In the structural hierarchy of Nazi Germany, Eichmann, as *Referent* for the Jewish question *in its totality*, was co-responsible for the destruction of Jews in all of Europe. In a letter concerning the "Brown Folder for the Ukraine," dated January 10, 1942, Heydrich informed the Reich Minister for the Occupied Eastern Territories that the police was officially in charge (*federführend*) of matters concerning Jews (*Judenangelegenheiten*) and that within the RSHA the competent specialist (*Sachbearbeiter*) was Eichmann.[55] Indeed, after numerous evasive replies, Eichmann himself admitted during the cross-examination that in the whole of the RSHA he was the only *Referent* in charge of Jewish Affairs.[56] And notwithstanding his absurd claim before the court that as *Referent* he never made recommendations to Müller, his direct superior, or, for that matter, was never asked to make such recommendations,[57] there is ample evidence that he was anything but the file clerk he claimed to be. Agencies outside the RSHA were well aware of his authority in Jewish affairs. Thus, on one occasion, the German Foreign Office formally apologized to Eichmann for having given instructions on measures to be taken within the framework of the Final Solution to its own Embassy in Paris without consulting him beforehand. The letter explained that this had happened because Eichmann had been away on an official trip and the matter, being most urgent, could not wait for his return.[58]

In connection with foreign affairs, Miss Arendt writes on page 144 that "it was the task of the experienced diplomats of the Foreign Service" to find ways of making "use of foreign Jews in German territory to test the general atmosphere in their home countries." And she adds: "The method by which this was done, though simple, was somewhat subtle, and was certainly quite beyond Eichmann's mental grasp and political apprehension. (This was borne out by the documentary evidence; letters that his department addressed to the Foreign Office in these matters were signed by Kaltenbrunner or Müller.)"

Let us look at some of these "letters that his department addressed to the Foreign Office in these matters." On June 22, 1942, Eichmann wrote a letter to the Under Secretary of State for Foreign Affairs, Martin Luther, informing him that citizens of the British Empire, the United States, and the Latin American countries were to be exempted from the deportation from France, Belgium, and The Netherlands.[59] Later, in January 1943, Eichmann and Hunsche prepared a nine-page memorandum detailing plans for the treatment of Jews having foreign citizenship.[60] On July 5, 1943, Eichmann again wrote to the Foreign Office on this matter, this time to Eberhard von Thadden.[61] In this letter he suggested that the Foreign Office inform the governments of Italy, Switzerland, Spain, Portugal, Denmark, Sweden, Finland, Hungary, Romania, and Turkey that the final date for obtaining exit visas for their Jewish nationals would be July 31, 1943, and that those Jews who had not left Germany by August 3, 1943, would be on the same footing as Jews in the areas under German control. Characteristic of Eichmann's attitude is the concluding sentence of the letter: "Finally, it is requested that in the interest of the final solution of the Jewish question all possible scruples be set aside in view of the fact that the Reich has shown generous consideration to these foreign governments." The Foreign Office accepted Eichmann's suggestion with slight modification.[62] In a circular letter signed by Müller, official notification was given that the procedure had been accepted, with a somewhat later deadline.[63] Thus the chief architect of German policy toward foreign Jews was Eichmann, at all times.

As for the signatures appearing on letters sent from the RSHA to the Foreign Office, due account must be taken of the fact that there existed in Germany rules about the signatures that had to appear on official letters.[64] Letters written to von Thadden or to Franz Rademacher, whose rank in the Foreign Office corresponded to that of Eichmann in the RSHA, were generally signed by Eichmann,[65] while Müller's or Heydrich's signatures had to appear on letters directed to the heads of departments. But this was a mere formality, and in his pretrial interrogation Eichmann admitted that although these letters carried the signatures of his superiors, they were in fact written by him, as is evident from the IVB4 symbol appearing at the head of the stationery.[66]

In other passages minimizing Eichmann's role, Miss Arendt depicts him as merely one of an "army of 'Jewish experts'" (p. 67) who competed with him, and she speaks of "innumerable intrigues ... among ... offices that were busy 'solving the Jewish question'" (p. 135). She complains on behalf of Eichmann about the "never ending interference from other offices" (p. 72), and about the "perpetual conflict over jurisdiction in Jewish matters" (p. 146). All these excuses are based on Eichmann's testimony in the trial, which reads in part as follows:

. . . In regard to the Jewish question, there existed so many instructions and orders, and there were so many, I might say, points of common interest [*Anstosspunkte*] between all the central authorities and all the party agencies that it was exceedingly difficult for the Gestapo somehow to coordinate all these elements and wishes and to carry them out the way they were requested and ordered. Many things came rushing in [*überschlugen sich*]—there was overlapping and there were contradictions—because everyone, but everyone, mixed into the thing and interfered and made demands. That is probably the reason why we hardly needed to make recommendations—the department not at all, and Müller hardly ever. All we did was comply with the requests of others who prodded, made demands, and gave numerous suggestions.[67]

On this statement the court rightly commented:

There is no doubt that other authorities too in the Third Reich sought to show their ability in the handling of Jewish affairs. But this explanation, according to which the RSHA as a whole was only the servant of others, does not appear to us to have been advanced seriously, and we reject it.[68]

If interoffice conflicts really existed, Eichmann's responsibility is enhanced, not lessened, for he carried out virtually all his plans despite any conflicts. Attempts at "interference" directed toward the rescue of individual Jews are known,[69] but it is regrettable that so few interferences took place, and that even fewer were crowned with success, because of Eichmann's implacable lust for annihilation.

The following examples suffice to show how groundless the excuse of "interference" was, and how widely recognized in the Third Reich Eichmann's authority and power were in matters pertaining to Jews.

1. Dieter Wisliceny, awaiting trial in Bratislava in 1946, traced in twenty-one handwritten pages[70] the various stages of Eichmann's career until Eichmann reached a position of undisputed power with respect to the Final Solution, a position from which he maintained direct contact with Globocnik, Höss, Müller, Heydrich, Kaltenbrunner, and Himmler. Miss Arendt's explanation that Wisliceny tried to put the blame on Eichmann in order to save his own neck (p. 130) leaves the following question unanswered: Why should

Wisliceny pick on Eichmann, instead of blaming their common superiors?

2. According to a sworn declaration of a personal friend of Eichmann, Rudolf Mildner, dated November 16, 1945, *Obersturmbannführer* Eichmann was adviser to Himmler, Kaltenbrunner, and Müller in all matters regarding Jews (*in allen Judenfragen*) and commissioned by Himmler (*Beauftragter des RFSS*) to carry out the deportations to the camps, to negotiate with the governments of occupied countries the "evacuation" of the Jews from those countries, and to act as liaison to the Higher SS and Police Leaders in matters regarding Jews.[71]

3. Georg-Konrad Morgen carried out toward the end of the war, in his capacity as judge in the SS, an investigation into alleged cases of corruption in the management of concentration camps. The SS had its own judiciary, which was empowered to investigate and judge members of the SS for violations of the law. Morgen initiated an investigation "against the executors of murder orders (*Blutbefehle*)," among them such "prominent (*markante*) personalities" as *Obersturmbannführer* Eichmann (who heads the list), Höss (commandant of Auschwitz), SS *Oberführer* Hans Loritz (commandant of Dachau and Oranienburg), and SS *Untersturmführer* Maximilian Grabner (head of the political department in Auschwitz).[72] He testified before the International Military Tribunal, and described in two affidavits[73] the whole elaborate system for the arrest, deportation, and annihilation of the Jews. He characterized the "Eichmann-Organization"[74] as responsible for moving the European Jews into the concentration or extermination camps.

4. Dr. Six, a witness for the defense, testified:

. . . It was known that Eichmann personally had all the details in regard to the Jews. It was clear to me that Eichmann was the man from whom I could receive the details of the murdering of Jews and all the other particulars.[75]

5. Dr. G. M. Gilbert, the psychologist of the International Military Tribunal, kept a day-by-day diary of his conversations with the war criminals, and submitted to the Jerusalem court the full manuscript of this diary.[76] He quotes Göring as saying: "We weren't a band of criminals meeting in the woods in the dead of night to plan mass murders like figures in a dime novel. After all, the four real conspirators are missing. The Führer, Himmler, Bormann, and

Goebbels—and Heydrich too; that's five. That Wisliceny is just a little swine who looks like a big one because Eichmann isn't here. . . ."[77] In testimony before the court Gilbert quoted Höss to the effect that "Eichmann was the only SS officer who was permitted to keep lists with regard to the aforesaid operations [extermination in Auschwitz], and this in pursuance of orders given him by the *Reichsführer-SS*."[78] Gilbert testified that Höss repeatedly mentioned "Eichmann as the man who was the kingpin in the machinery, or you might say the driving shaft in the whole machinery, without which the machinery could not work." Miss Arendt's theory (p. 66) that Höss obviously had no hope of saving his own life and wanted to exculpate his own outfit, the Head Office for Economy and Administration, at the expense of the RSHA, does not stand up. If that was his intention, why should he have invented detailed stories about his friend Adolf Eichmann, instead of blaming Eichmann's commanders, like Gestapo chief Müller, who had also disappeared, or Heydrich and Kaltenbrunner, the heads of the RSHA, who were dead?

6. László Endre and László Baky, two notorious anti-Semites who were high officials of the Hungarian Ministry of the Interior, both stated before they were hanged that Eichmann was the man chiefly responsible for the murder of Hungarian Jewry.[79] Although we can suspect these two men of trying to shift the blame from the Hungarian Fascists to the Nazis, the question still remains: Why charge Eichmann, with whom they had most friendly relations? Why not pick on Veesenmayer, who was far superior in rank? Why not mention Winkelmann, the Higher SS and Police Leader in Hungary and Himmler's personal representative there? Gábor Vajna, Hungarian Minister of the Interior in the Szalasi Government, described the impertinent way in which Eichmann tried to force the pace during the final stages of deportation, claiming that he had the full authority of Kaltenbrunner behind him.[80] Vajna, though mentioning Kaltenbrunner and Winkelmann as well, made a point of stressing Eichmann's extreme demands and impertinence.

Miss Arendt raises the following objection to these charges: "No doubt one of the chief objective mistakes of the prosecution at Jerusalem was that its case relied too heavily on sworn or unsworn affidavits of former high-ranking Nazis, dead or alive; it did not see, and perhaps could not be expected to see, how dubious these documents were" (p. 67). The majority of documents bearing on Eichmann's responsibility were not affidavits but incriminating documents signed by him. Affidavits were used only when other sources corroborated them. The court emphasized that the Nazi witnesses had been criminals and accomplices of the defendant, and that it could not be expected to decide an important point of fact on their uncorroborated evidence. The judgment stressed that "the statements of these witnesses [Nazis] must be examined carefully, for at least some of them were accomplices, and their statements, therefore, require corroboration, and not merely as a formality."[81] Thus, discussing Eichmann's responsibility for the Hungarian Jewish Catastrophe, the court points out that it reached its conclusions "without having recourse to the evidence of Veesenmayer and Winkelmann [both Nazis], since for obvious reasons they are trying to remove themselves as far as possible from any connection with anti-Jewish actions."[82] A survey of the court's use of evidence reveals that where high-ranking Nazis consistently and independently of one another related certain facts regarding the defendant, facts of which in the nature of things they had more intimate knowledge than anyone else, and where their testimony was borne out by documentary and other evidence, then (and only then) did the court accept the testimony as credible.[83] This policy of the court rested on the belief that it was hardly plausible to imagine that high-ranking Nazis or pro-Nazis, imprisoned in separate prisons and often in different countries—in Germany, Poland, Hungary, and Czechoslovakia—should all conspire to throw the blame on Eichmann, a "minor" official of the Gestapo.

There are also comments of neutral observers that deal with Eichmann's position and importance. In one case, a Dutch lawyer, Mrs. van Taalingen-Dols, was asked by friends of Edward Mauritz Meyers, the eminent Dutch jurist who was threatened with deportation to the East, to intervene on his behalf and seek permission for him to emigrate to Switzerland. She went to Berlin and sought an interview with Eichmann, whom she described in the following terms: "They always hinted to me that he was the supreme chief of department IV (the group of 'Jewish departments' in the RSHA in Berlin). As such they also described him to me as an important and extremely influential man."[84] A book by Mrs. van Taalingen-Dols quotes a member of the SS as calling Eichmann the "supreme chief for Jewish affairs."[85]

Two other neutral observers, emissaries of the Red Cross, visited

Eichmann in Theresienstadt on April 6 and again on April 21, 1945. They had the following to say: "Eichmann is there introduced as 'specialist for all Jewish questions' . . . He had played a leading role in the concentration camps of Lublin and Auschwitz. According to his own word, he was the direct plenipotentiary of the *Reichsführer-SS* for all Jewish questions." At the same time Eichmann had also stated to them his dissatisfaction with Himmler's desire for "humane methods."[86]

Eichmann stated, and Miss Arendt agrees, that he had no power to initiate any program relating to the annihilation of the Jews. This evaluation is incompatible with her own account elsewhere. In reference to Nisko and Madagascar she says: "For the first (and almost the last) time in his life in the S.S. he was compelled by circumstances to take the initiative, to see if he could not 'give birth to an idea'" (p. 67). She follows with two contradictory statements: First we are told that Stahlecker and Eichmann went off "on their own initiative, without orders from anybody" (p. 69), but twenty-one lines later she retreats and claims that their initiative "amounted to no more than a concrete plan for carrying out Heydrich's directives."[87] Later the same "initiative" is described as "private" (p. 70). On subsequent pages we read that "the last time Eichmann recalled having tried something on his own was in September, 1941" (p. 74); that Eichmann "'for the first and last time' took an initiative contrary to orders" (p. 88); that Eichmann "began, once more, taking initiatives—for instance, he organized the foot marches of Jews from Budapest to the Austrian border after Allied bombing had knocked out the transportation system" (p. 122). Behind this statement lies one of the most brutal crimes committed by Eichmann, described in the judgment as follows:

In the middle of October 1944 the wheel of fate turned again: The Germans intervened anew in order to prevent Horthy's surrender to the Allies, and forced him to appoint Szalasi, the extremist leader of the "Arrow Cross," as Prime Minister. With this, the way was again open for deporting the Jews from the country. Horthy gave in to the Germans on October 16 (evidence of von dem Bach-Zelewski, p. 13), and two days later the defendant returns to Budapest and starts negotiations for the surrender of more Jews to the Germans. Veesenmayer's telegram sent on the same day to the German Foreign Ministry states that the defendant "started negotiations with the Hungarian authorities for the deportation of 50,000 able-bodied male Jews on foot (*im Fusstreck*) to work in Germany" (T/1234). On the same day Veesenmayer wires again

(T/1235) reporting the results of the negotiations between the defendant and the Hungarian Minister of the Interior: the Minister will try to obtain approval for the surrender of the 50,000 male Jews. Veesenmayer adds that "according to top secret information, Eichmann intends after successful completion of the aforementioned forced march to demand another 50,000 Jews, in order to achieve the final aim of completely emptying out the Hungarian region, with due regard for Szalasi's basic position." (Szalasi's basic position, as appears from the same telegram, was that the Arrow Cross men themselves should deal with the Jews within Hungary proper.)

The idea of marching the Jews from Budapest to the Austrian frontier, some 220 kilometers distance, was conceived as a result of Allied bombing, which had destroyed the railway line.

This forced march of thousands of Budapest Jews began on November 10, 1944. We heard about the events that marked this operation from Mrs. Aviva Fleischmann, who took part in it (Session 61) and from Dr. Arieh Breslauer, who was employed by the Swiss Embassy in Budapest—a person who saw the marchers en route and who wrote at the time a report on the subject (Session 61; T/1237). The Arrow Cross men assembled the Jews from the quarters set aside specially for Jews. Those taken were not exclusively adults—for the most part women, since many men were away from home on Labor Service—but also children and old people. Thousands of Jews were crammed into the yard of a brick factory which was used as the assembly point for the marchers. There they were kept, terribly crowded, under the open sky, during rainy weather. From there the march started, in large groups. The witness Fleischmann spent only one night at the factory, but others stayed there two or three days before they started on their way. The escort consisted of Arrow Cross men, who abused the Jews, robbed them of all their valuables, clothes, blankets, and the provisions they had taken with them for the way. Thus they marched for seven or eight days, without food entering their mouths for days. They slept in stables, in pigsties, or even under the open sky in the cold of the November nights. No medical assistance was given to them. Those who fell from exhaustion on the way were shot by the Arrow Cross men or died on the wayside. The survivors were handed over to German SS men at the Austrian frontier.

In this way 25,000 Jews had been dispatched by November 22, 1944. Veesenmayer estimated the total number of Jews thus brought to the frontier to be no more than 30,000 (T/1242). Mr. Breslauer testified to 50,000 (Session 61).

The forced march was considered an atrocity even by SS officers, who saw the marchers en route. Krumey, the defendant's assistant, discussed the march with him. The defendant's reply was simply: "You saw nothing," that is, he passed over it, and ordered Krumey to close his eyes to it too (evidence of Krumey on pp. 15, 16). The witness Jüttner, who was an SS General, describes the appearance of the marchers as shocking. He approached Winkelmann, the Higher SS and Police Leader in Hungary, but Winkelmann said that in this matter he was helpless, since it was in the hands of the defendant's unit and the defendant was not under his (Winkelmann's) command. Jüttner then turned to the defendant's office, whence a young officer was sent to him to inform him that he, Jüttner, was not to intervene in the affair, since the defendant's unit took orders from the RSHA exclusively (affidavit T/692 and the testimony by Jüttner in this case). Finally the march was stopped by order of Himmler. The credit for this is claimed by a number of German witnesses (Becher, Jüttner, Winkelmann). It is no concern of ours to decide whether one of them or someone else was responsible for the issuance of the order to stop the march. But it should be stated that Szalasi, on his part, also ordered the stopping of the march (see Veesenmayer's telegram of November 21, 1944, T/1242).[88]

By Miss Arendt the story is presented (p. 183) to mean that Veesenmayer negotiated with the Hungarians and that the latter were responsible for the forced march. Insofar as Eichmann is concerned, she only quotes Veesenmayer to the effect that Eichmann "hoped to send 50,000 more" (p. 183). She ignores his statement to Sassen that he wished to prove to the Allies that he could continue the deportations despite the destruction of the railway,[89] and she makes no mention of the drink he had with Endre in celebration of the "brilliant action."[90] She also overlooks Eichmann's statement to Dr. Kasztner: "The Budapest Jews will be deported, and this time they will walk."[91]

Much is made by Miss Arendt of the fact that Eichmann was always "outranked" by Higher SS and Police Leaders (pp. 65, 135)—from whom, however, he did not take orders (see the case of Winkelmann, just quoted)—and by the *Einsatzgruppen* commanders (p. 65). But she admits that he did negotiate "agreements" with "the local commanders" (p. 89). There are dozens of instances of Eichmann's initiative for which undisputed evidence was submitted to the District Court.[92]

One of the most striking illustrations of Eichmann's power, zeal, and initiative is the following infamous case. During the period of the annihilation of Hungarian Jewry in 1944, Hitler, in order to obtain Horthy's consent to the deportation of the Jews from Budapest, permitted 8,700 families, comprising about 40,000 persons, to leave Hungary, apparently via Romania.[93] The final destination of these would-be emigrants was not fixed, but it appears that the only realistic destination was Palestine.[94] The judgment summarized the episode in these words:

And here the extremism of the defendant in his struggle against the rescue efforts reaches its peak. This is what Veesenmayer writes in a cable dated July 25, 1944 (T/1215, par. 2): SS-*Obersturmbannführer* Eichmann, head of the Special Jewish Kommando of the SD here, has taken the position that, as far as he knows, in no circumstances does the *Reichsführer-SS* agree to the emigration of Hungarian Jews to Palestine. The Jews in question are without exception biologically valuable material, many of them veteran Zionists, whose emigration to Palestine is most undesirable. Having regard to the *Führer's* decision, *of which he had been informed,* he intends to submit a report to the *Reichsführer-SS* and, if necessary, seek a new decision from the *Führer*. Furthermore, it has been agreed with Eichmann that to the extent that additional evacuations of Jews from Budapest will be approved, they are to be started as suddenly as possible and carried out with such speed that the Jews in question will already have been deported before the formalities have been completed.

It is also stated there that, in the event of permission being given for emigration to the West, the defendant is considering preventing the emigrants from continuing their journey—for example, by taking appropriate steps on French territory.

And what has the defendant to say upon this matter, as telling against him as a hundred witnesses? Apart from rambling comments, to the effect that Veesenmayer reported the matter incorrectly, he gives an excuse— that the *Führer's* order was not before him in writing, whereas Himmler's order [forbidding emigration to Palestine] had been given to him in writing. The Attorney General proved this excuse unfounded by pointing out that the all-embracing extermination order, to exterminate the Jews, was also made known to the defendant only by word of mouth, and yet all his actions were guided by it. This incident is characteristic of the defendant's attitude.[95]

The quoted cable and other documents that were introduced by the prosecution in conjunction with it,[96] constituted unequivocal proof that Eichmann felt himself able to question even Hitler's orders and to appeal for a reconsideration.

Let us now see how Miss Arendt deals with this incident. She writes: "When Himmler's [*sic*] order to stop the evacuation of Hungarian Jews arrived in Budapest, Eichmann threatened, according to a telegram from Veesenmayer, 'to seek a new decision from the Führer,' and this telegram the judgment found 'more damning than a hundred witnesses could be.' Eichmann lost his fight against the 'moderate wing,' headed by the Reichsführer S.S. . . . In Jerusalem, confronted with documentary proof of his extraordinary loyalty to Hitler and the Führer's order [sic], Eichmann tried a number of times to explain that during the Third Reich 'the Führer's words had the force of law' . . . which meant, among other things, that if the order came directly from Hitler, it did not have to be in writing" (pp. 131-132).

Miss Arendt has switched the roles of Hitler and Himmler in the entire affair, though the document quoted in the judgment leaves no doubt that it was Hitler who gave the order to permit the emigration of these Jews and that Eichmann was prepared to ask him to reconsider this order, or, alternatively, to cajole Veesenmayer into evading these orders by trickery. Nothing could more effectively knock the bottom out of all the "small cog" theories offered by the defense.

How ironical that Miss Arendt should illustrate the binding force of the Führer's oral orders by an example where a *written* text was required by Eichmann, and that she should present Eichmann's hesitation in carrying out Hitler's order as an example of his "extraordinary loyalty" to the Führer.

Eichmann clearly could have saved the lives of those Jews by simply obeying an order issued by the Führer himself. Yet, he was not prepared to, and he fell back on the excuse that the Reichsführer-SS, Himmler, did not agree to the emigration of Jews to Palestine.

It is not hard to understand why the court and the prosecution attached such importance to these documents.

According to Miss Arendt, Eichmann was a law-abiding citizen (Chapter VIII of her book is titled "Duties of a Law-Abiding Citizen"); the Führer's words were the law of the land, and the Führer ordered the destruction of the Jews. "Eichmann . . . at least dimly realized that it was not an order but a law which had turned them all into criminals" (p. 133). Eichmann himself, however, told Sassen that the extermination of the Jews "was after all outside the law, or, one should say, outside the norm of authority (*ausserhalb der behördlichen Norm*)."[97] In the cross-examination, Eichmann insisted that he used to receive clear orders from his immediate superiors, and that it was they who had to worry about their orders and the law. He admitted, however, that he knew there was no law empowering the commandants of extermination camps to destroy human beings; that he did not know whether there was a law empowering him to carry out deportations from the Reich and the occupied and satellite territories; but that "people" (*die Leute*) used to invoke the phrase "The words of the *Führer* have the force of law."[98] Miss Arendt interprets this expression to mean that "every order contrary in letter or spirit to a word spoken by Hitler was, by definition, unlawful" (p. 132)—though even Nazi theoreticians refrained from such a wide-ranging interpretation. The farthest they would go was to attach the authority of "source of law" to Hitler's *public* pronouncements.[99]

On Eichmann's attitude toward superior orders, Miss Arendt further asserts that, in the fall of 1944, "it must have been a shattering experience for Eichmann" to find Himmler "giving orders right and left that the Jews be treated well" (p. 123), and that Eichmann considered these orders to be "criminal" (p. 133). She presents Eichmann's position as showing "a most unpleasant resemblance to that of the often-cited soldier who, acting in a normal legal framework, refuses to carry out orders that run counter to his ordinary experience of lawfulness and hence can be recognized by him as criminal" (p. 132). Eichmann's persistence in continuing with the Final Solution even after Himmler's "criminal" counter-order is explained away as follows: ". . . the old 'radical' orders . . . still reached Eichmann through Müller and Kaltenbrunner, his immediate superiors in the R.S.H.A." (p. 128). Thus she says that Himmler's orders were disregarded by his own immediate subordinates, Müller and Kaltenbrunner. Miss Arendt does not reveal her source for this statement.

Eichmann himself had testified that he was aware of the criminal nature of the Final Solution. Miss Arendt does not explain how Eichmann could regard as "criminal" both the Final Solution and Himmler's order to stop it.

Attitude Toward His Work

According to Miss Arendt, Eichmann was a bureaucrat of the Final Solution, a man of *Kadavergehorsam* (corpse-like, i.e., robot-like, obedience) completely devoid of any particular interest in carrying out his assignment (p. 120).

Eichmann offered a partial self-portrait in the Sassen Papers, in a section that was authenticated by both defense and prosecution and admitted in evidence by the court:

And so the Jews are actually right. To tell the truth, I was working relentlessly to kindle the fire wherever I thought there was a sign of resistance. Had I been just a recipient of orders, then I would have been a simpleton. I was thinking matters over. I was an idealist. When I reached the conclusion that it was necessary to do to the Jews what we did, I worked with the fanaticism a man can expect from himself. No doubt they considered me the right man in the right place. . . . I always acted 100 per cent, and in the giving of orders I certainly was not lukewarm.[100]

He was no less conscious of his zeal and authority in 1943. This appears from an incident reported by him concerning Karl Wolff, head of Himmler's personal staff, who held the rank of general. An almost grotesque situation developed when Eichmann became involved in a telephone argument with Wolff, a man as arrogant as himself. Wolff insisted that the life of a certain Jew should be spared; Eichmann was equally insistent that it should not be. As the argument became more intense, Wolff shouted: "Do you realize that you are talking to a general of the SS?" Eichmann replied: "Do you realize that you are talking to a lieutenant colonel of the Gestapo—Adolf Eichmann?" Wolff thereupon slammed down the receiver, an affront which so enraged Eichmann that he challenged the general to a duel. Only through the personal intervention of Himmler was the duel called off.[101]

Some statements by Eichmann that reveal the way he felt about his work are summarized in the judgment:

To conclude this chapter, in which we are concerned with the defendant's inner approach to his work, we shall mention a few more comments made by him on various occasions—comments that reveal how he felt in his heart:

(a) The Attorney General questioned the defendant about a passage in the Sassen Papers where the rate of shipment from various countries is discussed:

I am speaking of all the countries: we had the same thing in Slovakia, and we had the same in France, although things there looked very promising (sehr hoffnungsvoll) in the beginning. We had the same thing in Holland where in the beginning the transports were rolling so well that it was simply magnificent (es war eine Pracht), and later difficulties piled up upon difficulties (T/1432, p. 21).

And this is how the defendant reacted to this passage and to its continuation in the Sassen Papers:

> I said, you cannot take that literally, for in part it has no meaning, but the content is in substance correct; I cannot say otherwise (Session 104).

Thus it is "in substance" correct, this attitude of complete identification with his work—this delight in the activity of shipping Jews to their death. Such is not the manner of speech of a person who was performing this terrible occupation with any inner revulsion, or even indifference.

(b) In the memoirs he wrote while under arrest in Israel, he relates what he said at the time to his superior, Müller:

> I remember, when discussing the subject of victory, I said [to Müller] that I believed that, acting as we did, we were bound to lose the war: For what right do we have to kill the Jews, I said, while tens of thousands of German scoundrels, criminal and political ones, are not being killed. Such an injustice would surely have to be paid for.

In line with this, during a conversation with Müller, he proposed to resort to the trusted remedy of the Gestapo: "To line up against a wall" 100,000 Germans (Session 95).

We quote these words here only to point out how the defendant felt about the extermination of the Jews. He has no inner reservations about the act itself; instead, the wrong that will in the end avenge itself on the German people consists solely in the failure of exterminating, together with the Jews, 100,000 Germans, whose crime was their opposition to the Nazi regime.

(c) And finally, the defendant's statement at the end of the war that he is ready to "jump into the grave." In this matter, the proper version must first be established, because there is a sharp difference of opinion about it. In his statement to Superintendent Less, the defendant described the matter in the following way:

During the last days of the war, a feeling of depression seized the men of his department, and in order to improve their morale, he told them that he was looking forward joyfully to the final battle for Berlin, because it was his intention that "if I do not meet death, at least I will seek it out." He quotes his own words:

> "Millions of German women, children and old people"—I said to my men—"lost their lives in this war," I said to the men and to the soldiers. "For five years millions of enemies have attacked Germany. Millions of enemies have also lost their lives, and I believe the war has also cost five million Jews. Now it's all over; the Reich is lost. And if the end is to come now," I said, "I shall also jump into the grave" (T/37, p. 308).

And in his evidence before us, in answer to his counsel (Session 88), he gave this version:

> And then I told the officers who were also present that in my opinion the thing was indeed over with, that the Reich had collapsed, and that I admit . . . I would gladly jump into the grave knowing that in the same grave are five million enemies of the Reich.

He asserts categorically that when mentioning at this gathering "the enemies of the Reich" he did not have the Jews in mind, but

> the enemy knocking on the gates of the Reich—the Russians, or the fleet of United States bombers; these were the enemies meant in those words.

He gave the same explanation in his comments on the article in *Life* Magazine (T/51, passage 1).

In our opinion, this explanation is nothing but a lie. To Superintendent Less, and then again in his evidence in court (Session 105), the accused explicitly mentioned the five million Jews killed—according to his estimate—in one and the same breath with his expressed readiness to "jump into the grave." It has not been explained to us on what grounds the defendant could at that time have estimated the number of the Allied victims just exactly at five million. Reason dictates that the defendant spoke at that gathering about the front on which he was active and on which his listeners were active—namely, the battlefront against the Jews. This is what was likely to raise fallen spirits. And we know that the Jews were considered enemies of the Reich in the language of Nazi propaganda, which the defendant adopted in its entirety.

This was not the only occasion on which the defendant voiced such sentiments. The witness Grell, who during 1944 was in charge of Jewish affairs in the German Embassy in Budapest, and who in this capacity was in continuous contact with the defendant, says in his evidence at this trial (pp. 7/8):

> In the late autumn of 1944, Eichmann once told me that he was regarded by the enemy powers as war criminal No. 1 and that he had some six million people on his conscience. In this connection, he did not speak of Jews but of enemies of the Reich. I interpreted this remark of Eichmann's in the sense of "the more enemies, the greater the honor," and I remembered it only when the American prosecution brought it up. As far as I was concerned, this remark was part of his effort to magnify his status or himself personally.

According to the affidavit of Dr. Wilhelm Hoettl (T/157), which was placed in evidence at Nuremberg as Document 2738-PS (Exhibit USA-296), the defendant spoke with him in Budapest at the end of August 1944, and told him too that

> he knew that the United Nations regarded him as one of the major

war criminals, because he had millions of Jewish lives on his conscience.

And when Hoettl asked the defendant what the exact number was, the latter revealed that about four million had been killed in extermination camps, and an additional two million in other ways, most of them by the Special Operations Units of the Security Police.

In his testimony [before the District Court of Bad Aussee of June 19, 20, and 21, 1961] submitted in the [Eichmann] trial, Hoettl reiterated that the defendant had mentioned the number of six million victims, but he partially retracted the above-mentioned affidavit by stating that the defendant had not said "that he felt personally guilty of the deaths of those six million Jews" (p. 61).

The most incriminating version is found in the affidavit of Wisliceny given at Nuremberg on November 24, 1945 (T/56, section 10 of the affidavit):

> He [the defendant] said to me on the occasion of our last meeting in February 1945, at which time we were discussing our fates upon losing the war: "I [shall] laugh when I jump into the grave, because of the feeling that I have killed five million Jews. That gives me a lot of satisfaction and pleasure." (See also the evidence of Wisliceny at Nuremberg, T/58, p. 22.)

Let us be guarded and assume for the benefit of the defendant that he did not at the time confess to personal responsibility for the death of five or six million Jews. But there remains the fact—undisputed in our opinion—that at the end of the war he expressed satisfaction at the death of millions of Jews, and declared that the thought of this would make it easier for him to "jump into the grave." His expressed satisfaction was at the overwhelming blow delivered to "the enemy of the Reich" on the front where the defendant had been active during the war years and earlier. This "spiritual stocktaking" by the defendant at a time of general despair is sufficient to reveal to us his true feelings toward the occupation of murder in which he had been engaged.[102]

In addition to Eichmann's own words, and the facts adduced by the court, we have the evidence of others who knew or met Eichmann, concerning his zeal in work. Thus, Kurt Becher (an SS Colonel stationed in Hungary), in evidence given immediately after the end of the war in a Nuremberg prison, attested that "Eichmann was the zealous henchman [of the Final Solution]; he was not the guiding spirit, though."[103] Heinrich Müller (head of the Gestapo), gave the following evaluation of Eichmann (of which Eichmann was proud[104]): "If we only had fifty Eichmanns, we would have won the war."[105] Dr. Bernhard Loesener, specialist on race problems in the Nazi Ministry of the Interior, who died in 1952, described Eichmann in his memoirs.[106] He analyzed all the stages of the persecution of the Jews and the characters of the leading actors involved. Of Eichmann, he says that of all the people he knew "next to Heydrich, his chief, he was the strongest personification of satanic principles." While Miss Arendt mentions Loesener, referring to him as "the Ministry of the Interior's expert on Jewish affairs" (p. 113), she fails to include Loesener's vivid description of Eichmann's character.

Miss Arendt finds it strange that Eichmann "was not confronted with his utterances to Captain Less, whom he also told that he had hoped to be nominated for the *Einsatzgruppen*, the mobile killing units in the East" (p. 45). Her reproach is without foundation. The issue did come up, when the Attorney General questioned him on his connection with the *Einsatzgruppen*. Eichmann did not deny that he had applied for assignment to this unit, but he claimed that at that time he did not know of the task to be performed, even though he had been present at a meeting in which the leaders of the *Einsatzgruppen-Kommandos* involved in the so-called Barbarossa Jurisdiction order (to shoot all suspects without judicial procedure) discussed their previously received assignments.[107]

Miss Arendt reports that "his was obviously . . . no case of insane hatred of Jews, of fanatical anti-Semitism or indoctrination of any kind" (p. 23), and she accepts Eichmann's claim that "he had never harbored any ill feelings against his victims" (p. 26). She speaks of the Jews in his stepmother's family (p. 26) to whom he showed favors that might have resulted in the rescue of those persons, although, as she notes, he soon recanted and "confessed his sins" to his superiors (p. 122). She even mentions that during the cross-examination Eichmann felt uncomfortable about these favors and became "openly apologetic" (p. 122). But there was no need for this, she says; his "uncompromising attitude towards the performances of his murderous duties" was "in his own eyes . . . precisely what justified him" (p. 122). The judges are reproached for believing that Eichmann's activities in the Final Solution were proof of his fanaticism. It was not "fanaticism," says Miss Arendt, but "boundless and immoderate admiration for Hitler" (p. 133).

In the Third Reich, the older governmental and social anti-Semitism had become obsolete—*ein überwundener Standpunkt*, a point of view already surpassed. The attitude of the Nazi regime toward Jews was for the most part that felt toward a species that simply has to be physically destroyed. This attitude was the moving force behind Eichmann's deeds. With all his enthusiasm he was engaged in "cleansing" Europe of its Jews and carrying them swiftly to their death, though it is true that at the same time he professed a philosophy of pre-Nazi anti-Semitism.

Let us see how the District Court approached the question:

From what has been said so far, it follows that the door has been firmly closed on the defendant's attempts to fall back on orders he had received as a justification for his actions, or even in mitigation of his punishment. . . . Since the orders were manifestly unlawful, they cannot avail him. Nevertheless, we shall go on to examine what the inner approach of the defendant was to the orders which provided the framework for his actions: Did these orders cause him to struggle with his conscience, so that he was acting only because of coercion from which he saw no escape; or did he carry out his functions because he was personally indifferent, like an obedient automaton; or did he perhaps in his heart identify himself with the contents of the order? Although this inquiry does not affect the question of the defendant's guilt, it is important in order to determine the degree of moral responsibility the defendant bears for his acts. For this reason the Attorney General rightly requested of us that already at this juncture we draw up our conclusions on these matters too on the basis of the evidence before us.

What is in essence the defendant's version concerning this matter? He spoke a great deal both before the court and in statements he made outside the court, but when all is said and done we do not find in his words any clear and consistent version. Besides repeating in essence that he acted under orders, and that the oaths of loyalty which he had taken as a member of the SS and the SD strengthened even further his absolute duty to obey every order given to him, he says over and over that up to a certain time he was doing his work willingly and with inner rejoicing. This was the situation—he says—as long as he was working at the Emigration Centers in Vienna and Prague, for he regarded this work as beneficial to both sides—his side and the Jewish side. That, too, was his attitude toward the Madagascar Plan, on which he labored so hard, for this too was still a "political solution." But when this plan too was shelved, his world fell to pieces and his feelings about his work changed from one extreme to the other. He lost interest in his work, and he decided that from then on he would act like just another bureaucrat, doing exactly what he was told and no more. Up to this point the version is more or less clear, but from this point on the picture becomes increasingly blurred. How does he describe his reaction to the atrocities he would witness from time to time during his visits to the East—the slaughter of masses of Jews, men, women, and infants, shot near the pit that was to be their grave; the geyser of blood spurting from a common grave; loading Jews into the gas vans in Chełmno; the cremation of corpses there; conveying Jews to the gas chambers? According to him, this is what he said to Müller when he would return from such trips:

"Terrible, I tell you, the inferno, this I cannot bear" I told him (T/37, p. 177).

"Please don't send me there. Send someone else, send someone more robust (*jemand robusteren*). Look, I was never allowed to go to the front. I was never a soldier. . . . They do not collapse. I cannot look at it," I said, "I cannot sleep at night! I have dreams—I cannot, *Gruppenführer*" (T/37, p. 218).

Elsewhere in his statement to Superintendent Less he explains his desire to change to some other kind of work as stemming from different reasons, namely, an opportunity for promotion and—from the very beginning, from the time of his transfer to Berlin in 1939 (T/37, p. 250)—a lack of interest in police work as such.

And in the same vein, in his testimony, replying to the Attorney General (Session 94, pp. 13-14):

I repeatedly asked my immediate superior, SS-*Gruppenführer* and Lieutenant General of the Police Müller—at first, that I would not have to come to Berlin at all, that I could stay where I had my family. This was the first time. And then, the second time, I asked him urgently and I pleaded with him, telling him, when I returned from the trip to the East on which he had sent me, that I could hardly stand it physically. And then after each following trip, Müller was well aware of the condition I was in.

It is therefore clear that according to his own contention he requested a change to some other kind of work for reasons of convenience, to obtain a promotion, and also—according to his own words—because physically he was not sufficiently robust to stand the sight of the atrocities he witnessed in the East. But there is not a word about any inner protest, on grounds of conscience, against the extermination of the Jews. True, when pressed by the Attorney General, who asks him,

And you did not mind being the great dispatcher of death?
he replies:

I did mind, I minded very much—more than anyone would suspect. It was not for nothing that I submitted this to my superior many times, asking him to give me another assignment (Session 94, pp. 11-12).

But this version, that he asked to be relieved of his functions for reasons of conscience, is contradicted by the defendant himself. When his counsel asks him,

> It seems from the remarks in the Memoirs taken down by Sassen that you yourself were quite satisfied with the [Wannsee] Conference. Would you like to explain that? (Session 79, p. 2).

his answer was:

> Yes, but the origin of my satisfaction is to be sought in another direction, not in that of Heydrich's satisfaction . . . When I thus could confront my own efforts to solve the Jewish question with the result of the Wannsee Conference, at that moment I had a feeling of satisfaction, such as Pontius Pilate felt, for I felt free of any guilt. Here, at the Wannsee Conference, the most prominent people of the Reich at that time, the bigwigs, gave the orders; I had to obey . . .

Let us remember that before the Wannsee Conference he had already seen what he had seen in the East, and had begun shipping German Jews to the slaughter. Yet, in spite of this, he feels—so he testifies here—like Pontius Pilate; that is, like a man who has found a way to silence his conscience. And this is in fact his basic contention: that the order releases him from all struggles with his conscience; that blind obedience in conformance with the oath of loyalty comes before all and stands above all, and that in its presence there is no place to hear the voice of conscience. Dr. Grüber, the German pastor, one of the righteous Gentiles of the world, who because of his activities on behalf of the persecuted Jews was himself thrown into a concentration camp, gave us the following description of this type of German mercenary, the *Landsknecht*:

> A German *Landsknecht*, the minute he dons his uniform, puts his mind and his conscience temporarily aside. We say, "he deposits them in the supply room" (Session 41, p. 76).

And here, in the evidence of the defendant, is the argument in all its nakedness:

> The responsibility, however, and the matters of conscience must lie with the leadership of the State (Session 88, p. 9).

Later, under cross-examination by the Attorney General, he retreats a little from this extreme position, and grasps at the most wretched of excuses (Session 95, pp. 33-34):

> To my mind, breaking an oath of loyalty is by far the worst crime and offense that a man can commit.

Q. A crime greater than the murder of six million Jews, one and a half million of them children? Is that correct?

A. Not that, of course. But then, I was not involved in the extermina-

tion. Had I been engaged in the extermination, I probably would
have shot myself.

This answer calls to our minds some remarks, in the same spirit, that
he noted down in his comments on the article in *Life* Magazine—comments that had to do with the work of Department IVB4:

> We had nothing to do with atrocities, but went about our business
> in a decent way (T/51, second paragraph).

Which is to say, had he been ordered to throw the gas container into the
midst of the victims, then his conscience would have been stirred, but
since it was his duty to hunt down the victims in the various countries
of Europe and convey them to the gas chambers, his conscience remained
at peace, and he obeyed the orders without hesitation.

The Attorney General contended that if the defendant had truly and
sincerely wanted to be released from his murderous task, he would have
found ways of attaining his object. He could have asked to be transferred
to the front; he could have evaded his duty under various pretexts, as
others did; or he could have announced openly that his heart was not in
the work assigned to him. In the evidence before us, there is some ground
for these contentions. For instance, Justice Musmanno speaks of his conversations with Schellenberg, who told that men were released from the
Special Operations Units when it became clear that they were unable
to take part in the murders (Session 39, pp. 77-80). Such a case (concerning a man named Jost) is also mentioned in the declaration of Best,
which was submitted in the *Einsatzgruppen* trial (T/687), and in an
affidavit of Burmeister concerning the release of the defense witness, Six,
from the Special Operations Units (T/688, pp. 24-26; see also the evidence by Six himself in the present case, p. 8). In addition, Himmler's
speech at Poznań implies that anyone who showed signs of recoiling
from the occupation of murder could obtain a release from that assignment (T/1288, p. 151). But we do not intend to investigate this problem
in depth, because we believe that the whole discussion is not to the
point, since such a question never troubled the defendant. He never
thought of foregoing his important role, carried out from behind the desk
at the RSHA headquarters, a role to which he had been elevated because
he was an expert in the problem that kept the Third Reich and its leaders
so busy. It is quite probable that he was not at ease when witnessing
bloody scenes with his own eyes. Perhaps he even spoke about this to
Müller, although it is difficult to accept this as a fact, because such a
display of weakness would not be fitting for an SS man like him, for
whom one of the main virtues was toughness. As we have shown, the
version given by the defendant himself is far from clear on this subject;
and insofar as he did speak about qualms of conscience, his words are
not credible, since they are altogether contrary to his real attitude toward
his work on the front against the Jews during all phases of the campaign.

With this we reach the heart of the discussion concerning the inner feelings that motivated the defendant in his activities. That he was merciless in everything he did—this can hardly be disputed. One example will suffice: In connection with the transaction concerning "blood for goods" in Hungary, he was asked what moved him to favor this transaction. He explained that he became involved with this matter because Becher had been competing with him and poaching on his preserves in questions of Jewish emigration. Then he was asked by his counsel:

In discussions with your superiors, did you point out to them that you felt pity for the Jews and that one ought to help them?

And the defendant replied:

I am giving evidence under oath and I must tell the truth. I did not approach the matter out of pity. Moreover, I would have been fired, if I had even broached the subject (Session 86, p. 16).

And replying to the Attorney General on the same subject:

Q. . . . You will perhaps admit that your heart was not in this affair?
A. I never claimed that it was. I have already said that this was done for reasons of utility. I did not say that this was a rescue operation (Session 103, pp. 18-19).

That is to say, the possibility that human beings would be able to save their lives in this way never entered into his considerations. These things reveal to us that same block of ice or marble that Dr. Grüber saw before him when he used to go to the defendant on the humanitarian missions he had taken upon himself.

But the defendant tried to convince us that it was obedience to orders, and this alone, that motivated and guided him in all his activities, and that only blind obedience, "corpse-like" obedience (*Kadavergehorsam*), silenced his conscience. To substantiate this contention, he represented himself as a minor official, having no opinion of his own concerning the matters with which he had to deal, and lacking all initiative in his work.

We have already dealt with this contention in a different context, when we examined it in the light of the actual deeds done by the defendant. We now repeat that, from the point of view of his inner approach toward his work as well, the picture that the defendant has tried to draw before us appears to us to be a complete distortion. It is true that the defendant was obedient as required of a good National Socialist, and as an SS man in whom blind discipline to the farthest extreme had been inculcated. But that does not mean that he did his work only because compelled by an order. Quite the contrary. At every stage he did his work because of inner conviction as well, wholeheartedly and willingly. We shall review briefly the evidence that has led us to this conclusion.

The defendant admits that he was a zealous National Socialist, devoted to his *Führer* (T/37, p. 325), but he contends that he was no anti-Semite. The answer to this contention is found in the words of the witness Dr. Grüber (Session 42):

Q. Did you find in the defendant a personal hatred of the Jews, anti-Semitism, or was it National Socialist fanaticism that you saw in him?

A. It is difficult to separate the two. National Socialist fanaticism was organically connected with anti-Semitism. As far as I know, these two elements went hand in hand.

Indeed this is common knowledge: In Hitler's bogus ideology, the elevation of the German people to the position of the "master race" is bound together with hatred of the Jews and their degradation to the rank of "subhumans."

It is likely that the defendant did not believe in Streicher's crude methods of incitement, for he considered himself an expert in the fight against Jewry—one who had studied the problem through and through—and he was so regarded by his superiors. As an expert, he understood that crude methods are not necessarily efficient. However, his attempt to argue that he, the expert on Jewish affairs in the RSHA, that precisely *he* of all people was a "white raven," a National Socialist who did not hate Jews, is without foundation. Had a man like this, who stood at the center of the fight against the Jews—first in the propaganda stage of the fight and later in the implementation—shown the slightest deviation from the anti-Semitic orthodoxy demanded even of ordinary members of the party, he could not have remained where he was for a single day. The heads of the SD and the Gestapo under whose jurisdiction he worked would certainly have soon detected any such deviation. But let us quote the words of the defense witness Six, who knew the defendant at close quarters from the time he worked in the SD Head Office, when Six was head of the branch in which the defendant worked. In his evidence submitted in Germany, he says: "Eichmann believed wholeheartedly in National Socialism. . . . I believe that when in doubt, Eichmann invariably acted according to the Party doctrine in its most extreme interpretation" (p. 6).

The evidence before us fully confirms these words. Even today, writing his comments on the article in *Life*, the defendant explains his words to Sassen as to why he became disenchanted with Hitler (T/48, p. 8): "I said that the real war agitators were the infernal high finance (*die infernalische Hochfinanz*) circles of the Western Hemisphere, whose lackeys are Churchill and Roosevelt, and whose puppets, whose pawns in this game of theirs, are Hitler, Mussolini, Daladier, and Chamberlain." The "infernal high-finance circles" are, of course, the Jews, according to the concepts of the "Protocols of the Elders of Zion," that same "International Finance Jewry" about whom Hitler spoke in his speech in January 1939, when he threatened to exterminate the Jews. The defendant used the same language as late as 1957, according to his own words. So deep was his conviction from past days that the Jews are the enemies of humanity, that he reached a new peak in the development of the Nazi mythology: Hitler himself was merely a plaything in the hands of the Jews. In the same way the defendant unhesitatingly adopted the official Nazi doctrine that the Jews, having declared war upon the German Reich, must be exterminated as enemies. As Himmler said in his speech in Poznań on October 4, 1943: "We had the moral right on behalf of our people—the duty to exterminate this people which wanted to exterminate ours" (T/1288, p. 2). This philosophy of hatred echoes through the defendant's words in the Sassen Papers in the part (file 17) written in his own handwriting, the authenticity of which he admitted (*ibid.*, p. 735): "The slogan on both sides was: The enemy must be exterminated! And world Jewry . . . obviously had declared war upon the German Reich."

A few lines earlier, he explains that the Jews had always been the enemies of the German people, not only since the outbreak of the war, and that Hitler had already declared war upon them many years before (*ibid.*, p. 734).

And again he has an explanation ready: The intention was not actual extermination, for after all the British people, or the French people, were not exterminated during the war (Session 96)—an obviously invalid explanation.[108]

Miss Arendt tries to explain away Eichmann's party membership. She knows for certain that "he did not enter the Party out of conviction, nor was he ever convinced by it—whenever he was asked to give his reasons, he repeated the same embarrassed clichés about the Treaty of Versailles and unemployment. . . . He had no time and less desire to be properly informed, he did not even know the Party program, he never read *Mein Kampf*" (p. 29). Later she states that "when he told the Jerusalem court that he had not known Hitler's program he very likely spoke the truth: 'The Party program did not matter, you knew what you were joining'" (p. 39). But a circumstance during his stay in Argentina, where he lived from 1950 to 1960, throws a different light on his faith in National Socialism and his loyalty to Hitler. In the course of the pretrial interrogation he was asked about an article that had appeared in the Hamburg (Germany) weekly *Der Stern*.[109] According to this article Eichmann, while in Argentina, had read Gerhard Boldt's *The Last Days of the Reich Chancellery*,[110] which was critical of Hitler's conduct of the war, and had written scathing comments in the margins of the book. For instance: that the author should be flayed for criticizing Hitler and that "with such riffraff we had to lose the war."[111] He made no denial of the accuracy of the report in *Der Stern* but considered his comments to be his private affair.

If all this, together with his crimes, does not add up to the words and deeds of a fanatical anti-Semite and National Socialist, there is more. Rudolf Höss, the notorious commandant of the Auschwitz concentration camp, wrote his autobiography in Cracow, Poland, while awaiting execution.[112] He devoted a whole chapter to Eichmann. In the Sassen Papers, Eichmann considered Höss to be a "comrade and friend worthy of love,"[113] and in court he admitted that he had been on good terms with Höss.[114] According to Höss, "Eichmann was completely obsessed with his mission and also convinced that this extermination action was necessary in order to preserve the German people in the future from the destructive intentions of the Jews." He also states that Eichmann was strongly opposed to temporary reprieve of those Jews who were "selected" as capable for slave labor in German factories, for he was afraid that this might jeopardize the Final Solution; and that Eichmann labored hard to speed up the extermination process, "since it was impossible to anticipate the final result of the war."[115] Höss also writes:

He [Eichmann] was completely obsessed with the idea of destroying every single Jew that he could lay his hands on. Without pity and in cold blood we must complete this extermination as rapidly as possible. Any compromise, even the slightest, would have to be paid for bitterly at a later date. In the face of such grim determination I was forced to bury all my human considerations as deeply as possible. Indeed, I must freely confess that after these conversations with Eichmann I almost came to regard such emotions as a betrayal of the Führer.[116]

There are numerous cases known to us of *individual Jews* hunted down by Eichmann.[117] In no instance did he grant a reprieve. Two examples will be recounted here—one in which Eichmann held his ground in face of demands emanating from an Axis government and a fraternal party, the other in which he withstood the energetic appeal of one of the highest officials of the German Government.

Jenny Cozzi, living in Riga (part of the Occupied Eastern Territories, in which Eichmann, according to Miss Arendt, had no authority), was the widow of a high-ranking, non-Jewish Italian army officer. The Italian Government wanted her to return to Italy. Though certain interested Nazi agencies objected to the release of Mrs. Cozzi on a variety of grounds,[118] Eichmann in his correspondence treated this case as one of a Jewish person wanting to escape her prescribed fate, and he advised his Foreign Office on March 15, 1943, as follows: ". . . now as before, I consider it irresponsible (*nicht für vertretbar*) to release the Jewess Cozzi for return to Italy from the ghetto in Riga. I therefore request once again that the Italian Embassy in Berlin be made to abstain from further interceding in behalf of the Cozzi woman."[119] The Foreign Office answered that the Italians were insistent and urged him to reconsider his position in the light of the fact that Italy was an ally. After this, the Italian Fascist Party intervened, requesting the woman's release. Eichmann's final reply came on September 25, 1943: "In view of the changes which in the meantime have taken place in the political situation in Italy [the reference is to Badoglio's capitulation to the Allies], I refrain from going any further in the matter. I have given instructions that the Jewess Cozzi be housed, for the time being, in the Riga concentration camp."[120]

The second example involved Jochen Klepper, a Protestant "Aryan" writer and poet of renown. He was a protégé of Wilhelm Frick, Reich Minister of the Interior, one of the top government officials in Nazi Germany, who served during the war as Plenipotentiary General for Civil Administration. Klepper was married to a Jewess, Hanni, who had two daughters, Brigitte and Renate Stein, from her first marriage (to a Jew). Though Brigitte had been able to leave the country, Renate stayed with her mother and stepfather, doing compulsory labor in a Berlin factory.

The only thing Frick was able to promise Klepper was assistance in obtaining exit visas for Hanni and Renate; protecting them inside Germany was out of the question. Frick, who among other things had under him all the local police in Germany, assigned a Police Major and a Ministerial Councillor (*Ministerialrat*) named Draeger to arrange the exit visas with the Gestapo. On December 9, 1942, following Draeger's intervention, Klepper went to the RSHA. There, however, he was told by Eichmann (who had jurisdiction over exit visas for Jews) that Renate might have a chance of obtaining an exit visa, but that Hanni would not be allowed to leave with her daughter. The thought of the fate awaiting his wife—compulsory divorce from her "Aryan" husband and eventual deportation to the East—was unbearable to Klepper. But appeals were of no avail. On December 10 Eichmann informed Klepper that the decision was final. Upon returning from the Gestapo offices, Klepper wrote in his diary: "In the afternoon I was at the Security Office. We shall die now. This, too, is up to God. Tonight we shall go to our death together." The next day Jochen Klepper and his family committed suicide.[121]

According to Miss Arendt, Eichmann had not been indoctrinated by National Socialism, Mein Kampf, or the Nazi Party program, but had been indoctrinated by Zionism. Thus she writes that the reading of Theodor Herzl's Der Judenstaat "converted Adolf Eichmann promptly and forever to Zionism" (p. 36). It was Eichmann, however, who, together with Herbert Hagen, presented the vicious anti-Zionist report of 1937 (it was not "duly published," as Miss Arendt claims on page 57), which stated that the plan for emigration of Jews to Palestine "was out of the question." Miss Arendt, without indicating her source, says that the two "were ordered" to write the "thoroughly negative report" (p. 57). Though Eichmann busied himself with preventing emigration to Palestine of Jews who "are biologically valuable material . . . many of them veteran Zionists,"[122] and though his purpose was the destruction of the Jewish people, especially of these "biologically valuable" Jews, she can speak of him as "forever" converted to Zionism.

On page 191 she states that "according to his own, emphatically repeated testimony, [Eichmann] had learned all he knew about the Jewish question from Jewish-Zionist authors, from the 'basic books' of Theodor Herzl and Adolf Böhm." Aside from the question of what "emphatically repeated testimony" she is referring to, one wonders about her astounding conclusions: (1) That Dr. Servatius' objections to trial by Jewish judges might be countered by the argument that inasmuch as Eichmann too was a Zionist, he was being tried by his peers. (2) That Eichmann's attitude toward Jews was based on Zionist authors, not on Nazi literature concerning the Jewish question, not on the documentation of the Gestapo, not on the reports of the Einsatzgruppen, or the Wannsee Minutes, not even on Nazi journals, such as the Völkischer Beobachter, which he used to swallow daily with enthusiasm—according to his own admission.[123] Indeed, Eichmann's own writings on the "Jewish question" are as far removed as possible from all traces of Zionist thought.[124]

Miss Arendt herself writes that in 1939 "Eichmann's solution was a police state" (p. 73), which is hardly compatible with Zionist ideals. She alleges that Eichmann had Zionist "relapses" (p. 59): In March 1945 he "again showed himself to be very interested in Zionist matters" in an interview with one of the inmates of Theresienstadt. Note the date and her use of the plural "relapses." She reproaches the counsel for the defense for not having mentioned this in his *plaidoyer.*

Eichmann's Conscience and the "New Type of Criminal"

Eichmann at the Jerusalem court is described by Miss Arendt as an almost inanimate figure: "And the more 'the calamity of the Jewish people in this generation' [Hausner's words] unfolded . . . the paler and more ghost-like became the figure in the glass booth, and no finger-wagging . . . could shout him back to life" (p. 6). (Few found him lacking "life" during the twenty-six sessions of cross-examination.[125]) His feelings are also described: "During the trial, he showed unmistakable signs of sincere outrage when witnesses told of cruelties and atrocities committed by S.S. men— though the court and much of the audience failed to see these signs . . . and it was not the accusation of having sent millions of people to their death that ever caused him real agitation but only the accusation . . . of one witness that he had once beaten a Jewish boy to death" (p. 96). This appears on the same page as "he had also sent people into the area of the *Einsatzgruppen,* who . . . killed by shooting" and "he was probably relieved when . . . this [the shooting] became unnecessary because of the ever-growing capacity of the gas chambers."

Miss Arendt claims that it "had been said at Nuremberg over and over again by the defendants and their counsels" that a "new type of criminal" came into being who "commits his crimes under circumstances that make it well-nigh impossible for him to know or to feel that he is doing wrong," and she puts Eichmann into this category (p. 253).[126] However, the final pleas of the defense counsels on behalf of the individual defendants and Professor Jahrreiss's speech on the legal aspects of breach of peace, as well as the final statements of the defendants themselves, contain no such statement or plea.[127] With certain variations, the defendants and their counsels argued the noncriminality of the acts charged to them and, subsidiarily, the implacable consequences of the *Führerprinzip*. There is nothing concerning the "new type of criminal." Moreover, some defendants admitted the criminality of their acts.[128]

Somewhat inconsistently Miss Arendt quotes with approval Eichmann's statement that he "never thought of . . . a solution through violence" (p. 27, also on p. 79), and writes that he never "suspected the existence of such sinister plans" (p. 72). Two questions arise in regard to these statements: (1) Did Eichmann really never suspect the existence of such sinister plans? (2) When was he formally advised of the decision on the Final Solution?

As to the first question, an unequivocal answer was given by Eichmann in the following circumstance: On September 21, 1939, a meeting was held of top SS men concerned with the Jewish question, with Eichmann in attendance. A record of this meeting was discovered by the Israel police and submitted to the court.[129] In the record the expression *Endziel* (final aim) is used with reference to the Jews. Asked by Superintendent Less in the pretrial interrogation how he interpreted the expression *Endziel*, Eichmann replied without a moment's hesitation, "It means physical extermination," and added that "this basic idea was already rooted in the minds of the higher leaders, or the men at the very top . . ." (quoted by Miss Arendt on p. 72). From this it becomes clear that at least as early as September 1939 he was aware of what was in store for the Jews. Miss Arendt herself adds a second case that proves his knowledge of "a solution through violence" before he was officially advised of this solution by Heydrich in 1941: "Moreover . . . a few weeks before he was called to Heydrich, he had received a memorandum from an S.S. man . . . submitting for his consideration a proposal as to 'whether it would not be the most humane solution to kill those Jews who were incapable of work through some quicker means' . . . Eichmann . . . probably had not been in the least shocked by it" (pp. 89-90).[130]

As to the second question, the court painstakingly investigated it and came to the conclusion that Eichmann had already been formally notified of the Final Solution as early as the summer of 1941.[131]

Although Miss Arendt insists that Eichmann had no inkling of the Final Solution before the late spring of 1941, she writes that the Madagascar plan, conceived by Eichmann one year earlier, "in the summer of 1940 . . . was always meant to serve as a cloak

under which the preparations for the physical extermination of all
the Jews of Western Europe could be carried forward" (p. 71). She
makes several comments concerning this project (pp. 70 ff.), but
she does not relate many details of the plan, which included the
deportation of four million Jews within four years; their complete
isolation from the outer world; a provision that Madagascar would
be a "police state" supervised by the RSHA (not an independent
"Jewish State," for the plan explicitly stated that no independent
state was envisaged); employment of the Jews in forced labor under
the supervision of German masters; financing of the project out of
the property of expelled Jews and by a special tax to be paid by
the Jewish citizens in vanquished Western countries as "reparations
for damage caused to the German nation by the Jews economically
and otherwise as a result of the Versailles Treaty."[132]

In discussing the Madagascar plan, Miss Arendt speaks of
Eichmann's "dream once dreamed by the Jewish protagonist of the
Jewish State idea, Theodor Herzl," but she is not bothered by
Eichmann's linking himself with Herzl. The court, however, expressed its indignation that Eichmann "dared mention in one and
the same breath his plan with the name of Herzl from whom, so
he says, he drew inspiration."[133]

Miss Arendt states that "the Madagascar project was top secret"
(p. 42) and that it was supposed to have been implemented "in the
midst of war" (p. 71), except that lack of time "brought the . . . enterprise to naught" (p. 72). It is difficult to see how one top secret
plan could serve as a "cloak" for another, the Final Solution. The
plan was actually intended for the period after ultimate victory over
France, when France had ceded Madagascar to Germany, and when
the seaways to Africa would be open.[134] The plan was shelved
because the Vichy regime was unable either to conclude a peace
treaty with Germany or to cede Madagascar to her.

With reference to the Wannsee Conference—a meeting held in
January 1942, at which were present some top civil servants in
Ministries, whose cooperation was sought by the RSHA for the
implementation of the Final Solution—Miss Arendt stresses that
what was being accomplished at the Wannsee Conference was
being done by an elite.[135] "His conscience was indeed set at rest
when he saw the zeal and eagerness with which 'good society'
everywhere reacted as he did" (p. 111). Why did Eichmann have
to wait to be impressed at Wannsee? Had he been unimpressed by

Hitler, Himmler, and Heydrich, from whom he knew (much earlier) about the Final Solution? Miss Arendt accepts Eichmann's excuse "that there were no voices from the outside to arouse his conscience" (p. 112) and his statement that "he could see no one, no one at all, who actually was against the Final Solution" (p. 103). And she considers "pertinent" Eichmann's words: "Nobody came to me and reproached me for anything in the performance of my duties" (p. 116). "No one at all" against the Final Solution! What of the officials of such occupied countries as France, Italy, Denmark, and others with whom Eichmann had to fight because of their opposition to the Final Solution;[136] the Allies' protests and warnings, which were well known to Eichmann;[137] and the victims and their representatives, such as Kasztner,[138] who requested "to stop the death-mills" at Auschwitz? Indeed, "no one at all" is far from the truth. We find Eichmann resorting to a system of deception even in regard to Reich offices.[139]

According to Miss Arendt, stopping "the death mills at Auschwitz" was "outside his [Eichmann's] competence and outside the competence of his superiors" (p. 103). How then did it happen that they were stopped after all? Was it not because Eichmann's "superior," Himmler, so ordered?[140] Did not Hitler himself consent to exclude from the Final Solution some 40,000 Hungarian-Jewish men, women, and children?[141] In arguing that no one opposed the Final Solution she states that the top men in the Civil Service in Nazi Germany, "the under-secretaries [among whom were the active participants at Wannsee] . . . were frequently not even Party members" (pp. 99-100). This is not true. All the participants at Wannsee were party members, and more than half of them were even members of the SS.[142] On the other hand, there is no evidence that "the élite of the good old Civil Service were vying and fighting with each other for the honor of taking the lead in these 'bloody' matters" (p. 101).

Miss Arendt can write: "So Eichmann's opportunities for feeling like Pontius Pilate were many" (p. 120). And she can consider him sincere when he declared in Jerusalem that the annihilation of the Jews was "one of the greatest crimes in the history of Humanity" (p. 19). Yet this same man, as late as 1957, declared before Sassen[143] that he was sorry only that he had not succeeded in exterminating all the eleven million European Jews (the figure appearing in the Wannsee minutes).

The question asked by the judges "whether the accused had a conscience" (p. 89) is criticized by Miss Arendt for introducing a moral issue that "may not have been legally relevant" (p. 85). She herself deals with the problem of Adolf Eichmann's conscience at length (e.g., pp. 120 ff.). She writes that his conscience functioned "within rather odd limits" (p. 89). What does she mean? In the period during which the *Einsatzgruppen* were active in the East, Eichmann was charged with transporting Jews into the area in which these killing units operated. Regarding this, he said—and Miss Arendt quotes him—"I never denied that I knew that the *Einsatzgruppen* had orders to kill" (p. 90). Yet he denied knowing that Jews from the Reich whom he had transported to the East were also being killed. Surely, if he knew what the *Einsatzgruppen* were doing in the East and persisted in shipping German Jews into their area of operations, his statement cannot possibly be truthful. But Miss Arendt accepts his denial when she observes, "his conscience rebelled not at the idea of murder but at the idea of German Jews being murdered." In line with this, she devotes much space (pp. 88-89) to Eichmann's allegation that he tried to ship German Jews to Lodz, where presumably they were safe, instead of to Riga, where they would have been exterminated. While claiming on behalf of Eichmann (who "had forgotten all about it") that here "he actually had tried to save Jews," Miss Arendt admits that even those Jews were after all shipped to Riga. In fact, not Eichmann but Himmler had decided to ship the German Jews to Lodz.[144]

It should be noted that Miss Arendt was not unaware of the deportation of thirteen hundred German Jews from Stettin to the Lublin area in February 1940 (p. 139). What happened to these men of "German culture" is told in the judgment:

The expulsion from Stettin was carried out in a single night, that of February 13, 1940. The Jews were forced out of their apartments. They were allowed to take one suitcase with them. The head of each family had to sign a waiver declaration with respect to all his property. They were not allowed to take any food for the way. Thirteen hundred persons were removed, among them infants and aged people. Those who could not walk were carried to the railway station on stretchers. After only twenty-four hours the first corpses were taken off the train. The deportees were transported to Lublin and from there, all of them—men, women, and children—were conducted on foot to villages 26-30 kilometers away from the city, with the temperature 22 degrees [centigrade] below zero and the snow deep. During this march, which lasted 14 hours, 72 persons fell by the wayside, most of whom froze to death. One of the reports from which these details are taken (T/666; T/669) tells of a woman who was found frozen along the way, holding in her arms a child of three whom she had tried to shield from the cold with her clothes. Most of those who reached the three villages were billeted in stables and barns, under terrible unhygienic conditions. By March 12, 1940, 230 people of this transport had died. When questioned on the reports of this deportation, the defendant replied: "Yes. There is indeed a grain of truth in these reports. The reason is the excessive speed with which this deportation was ordered to be carried out: the total time from the moment the order was given to its execution was 15 days." (Session 76, pp. 116-120.)[145]

In order to support her point about Eichmann's conscience, Miss Arendt refers to a letter[146] in which Wilhelm Kube, *General-kommissar in Weissruthenien* (part of former Eastern Poland and of Soviet Byelorussia) had complained to his superior, *Reichs-kommissar* Lohse, that German Jews, "people from our own cultural milieu," were treated in the same manner as were the *Ostjuden*.[147] Quoting from this letter, she concludes that Kube's "words may give us an idea of what went on in Eichmann's head" (p. 90), thus implying that Eichmann, like Kube, had felt a measure of sympathy for the German Jews. The most that Eichmann had claimed—and she quotes him—was that he "did not know that Jews from the Reich evacuated to the East" (p. 90) were killed there. Kube is used here as the mirror of Eichmann's thought, though there is considerable documentary evidence that Kube was, for a Nazi, exceptionally humane (and not only in his attitude toward German Jews)[148] and that, had he not been murdered in September 1943 by a woman employed in his household, he would have landed in a concentration camp. According to Himmler, Kube's Jewish policy had "bordered on treason";[149] one would hardly expect Kube's thinking and Eichmann's to have much in common.

The treatment of Eichmann's conscience by Miss Arendt is contradictory. On the one hand, she pictures Eichmann as a "law-abiding citizen" who followed "the law of Hitler's land [which] demanded that the voice of conscience tell everybody: 'Thou shalt kill'" (p. 134); on the other hand, she proceeds on the assumption that his conscience was not at peace with his work and that it was "silenced" (p. 122). Following the report of an alleged "good" deed performed by Eichmann, we are told: "Yes, he had a conscience, and his conscience functioned in the expected way for about four weeks [II, 94: "three weeks"], whereupon it began to function the other way around" (p. 89). But she adds that during the time the Jews were shipped into the area of *Einsatzgruppen* operations "his conscience functioned normally." Further on she says "the sad and very uncomfortable truth of the matter probably was that it was not his fanaticism but his very conscience that prompted Eichmann to adopt his uncompromising attitude" (p. 131). She is undecided whether his conscience was awake and directing his attitudes or had been put to sleep by those attitudes.

She suggests that in both his silenced conscience and in his uncompromising attitude he was guided by Kant's categorical imperative. Yet she admits that the equation of Eichmann's behavior with that demanded by Kant's categorical imperative is "outrageous, on the face of it" (p. 120), in view of the fact that "Kant's moral philosophy is so closely bound up with man's faculty of judgment, which rules out blind obedience" (p. 121). Still, she maintains that criminals of Eichmann's sort "in one respect" indeed followed Kant's precept: "a law was a law, there could be no exceptions" (p. 122). This is in contradiction to what she says on the previous page—namely, that the Kantian philosophy demands "that a man do more than obey the law," and that this demand in Eichmann's "household use" of Kant meant that one must "identify his own will with . . . the will of the Führer" (pp. 121-122). To be sure, she reports that "He then proceeded to explain that from the moment he was charged with carrying out the Final Solution he had *ceased to live* according to Kantian principles . . ." (p. 121). But she explains what went on in Eichmann's mind: "he had not simply dismissed the Kantian formula as no longer applicable, he had distorted it to read: Act as if the principle of your actions were the same as that of the legislator or of the law of the land—or, in Hans Frank's formulation of 'the categorical imperative in the Third Reich,' which Eichmann might have known: 'Act in such a way that the Führer, if he knew your action, would approve it'" (p. 121). This is incredible. In the first place, Hans Frank's speech, made at the Munich Technological Institute at the annual academic celebration,[150] was delivered in such complex legal German (*Juristendeutsch*) that it could hardly have been read—or understood—by the nonexpert. Moreover, Miss Arendt's application of the

Frank formula to Eichmann is a classic case of *petitio principii*: it assumes that Eichmann knew how Hitler would react to Eichmann's deeds, whereas Miss Arendt protests that Eichmann never read *Mein Kampf*, that he was unaware of the Nazi Party program, that his "loyalty" to Hitler was due not to his ideas but to the fact that Hitler was a self-made man (twice repeated, on p. 111 and p. 133). Finally, the whole argument collapses when we recall that when Eichmann's hunt after Jews collided with Hitler's direct orders, the first triumphed over the second.[151]

The District Court approached the problem of Eichmann's conscience in the only logical way—namely, by analyzing the motives for his actions. The court rejected his excuse of "corpse-like obedience" as well as his version of his inner attitude toward his own work, and concluded that "at every stage he did his work because of inner conviction as well, wholeheartedly and willingly."[152]

In the course of a theoretical discussion on the class of criminals to which Eichmann belongs, Miss Arendt says: "Dostoevski once mentions in his diaries that in Siberia, among scores of murderers, rapists, and burglars, he never met a single man who would admit that he had done wrong" (p. 47). Dostoevski, however, said exactly the opposite:

I was in penal servitude, and I saw "desperate" criminals . . . Not one of them ceased to consider himself a criminal. . . . Mostly, they were gloomy, pensive people . . . It was a rule not to speak about this. Nevertheless, I believe, probably not one among them evaded long psychic suffering . . . I remember their faces—and believe me, not one of them, in his innermost, considered himself right![153]

How might Eichmann properly be characterized? Miss Arendt does not visualize him as a calculating and deliberately evil man. But she pictures him as undeniably ludicrous (p. 49). She points out examples of "macabre humor" which "easily surpasses that of any Surrealist invention"—for example, the fate of Bertold Storfer, whom Eichmann appointed to be a "Jewish official," and who in his naïveté believed that Eichmann would get him out of Auschwitz (pp. 45 f.).[154] Of the taped police examination she writes that it "constitutes a veritable gold mine for a psychologist—provided he is wise enough to understand that the horrible can be not only ludicrous but outright funny" (p. 43). The Eichmann-Brand episode,[155] too, is "horrible comedy" (p. 180). She says of Eichmann: "It was difficult indeed not to suspect that he was a clown" (p. 49), but in the same breath she counsels to take him seriously (p. 49). She is proud to have been the only reporter to have noticed his "clowneries": "His worst clowneries were hardly noticed and almost never reported" (p. 49). The only examples she offers of his "clowneries" are that he changed his mind in regard to testifying in his own case, having originally resolved against testifying under oath; and that he asked for mercy, having originally been opposed to the idea (pp. 49-50). What is there clownish about this? Are not these the normal reactions of a man on trial for his life?

Miss Arendt objects to calling Eichmann a "monster." She tells us that the Attorney General charged, "And there sits the monster responsible for all this" (p. 6). In fact, he did not use the expression "monster," nor did Mr. Hausner ever characterize Eichmann as "the most abnormal monster the world had ever seen" (p. 253). The Attorney General's phrase ("a cruel and fanatical man, implacable in his enmity, this evil Eichmann")[156] was a paraphrase from the Book of Esther: "An adversary, an inimical man, this wicked Haman."[157] But even assuming the word "monster" had been used, it is difficult to accept Miss Arendt's repudiation of the word as applied to Eichmann, and to believe with her that "Everybody could see that this man was not a 'monster'" (p. 49). How should we describe a man who, with fanatical zeal, tried to catch every last Jewish woman and every single Jewish child so that they might be butchered? The picture is even more horrifying if we accept Miss Arendt's statement that Eichmann "had been shocked out of his wits" when he actually had to watch the executions in 1941 (p. 85). To have been present at such horrors and then to have seen to it that not a single family should escape the same fate—what word should we use to describe such a man?

We have before us Eichmann's statements as well as deeds. In his conversation with Sassen in 1957 he described in detail how he conducted his own private war against the Jews. He told of trains which rolled at first from Holland, filled with Jewish deportees— "it was simply magnificent" ("*es war eine Pracht*")—and how, later, difficulties arose which forced him to fight, often against German officials and generals, until he managed to "pry loose" (*loszueisen*) another 5,000 or another 2,000 Jews.[158] If this, when added to the catalogue of crimes already listed, is not "monstrous," what is?

Using Eichmann as an example, Miss Arendt advances the criminological theory of the "banality of evil," an expression that appears in the subtitle of her book. According to her view, the most decent person can become, under certain circumstances, a criminal. Proceeding from the assumption that Eichmann was an average person with an "innate repugnance toward crime" (p. 88), she concludes that any compatriot of Eichmann could have become an Eichmann; there is nothing specific in him, his character, or his activities. She even characterizes Eichmann as "the truth-revealer for generations to come" (p. 72), meaning that he revealed the "truth" of the "banality of evil"—an explanation, incidentally, provided not in her book but in a subsequently published open letter.[159]

Whether or not Miss Arendt's theory has merit as a generalization, it clearly is neither substantiated by, nor relevant to, Adolf Eichmann's "unprecedented" (p. 250) case. For he was no average man and possessed no ordinary criminal skills, nor did he ever show in his actions a repugnance for what he was doing. It is hardly legitimate for a historian to generalize from a single, uncommon case.

According to Miss Arendt, the burden on Eichmann's conscience was not "The Murdered Jewish People"—the title of a poem by Yitzhak Katznelson,[160] the martyred poet of the Catastrophe—"but, as it turned out, that he had once slapped the face of Dr. Josef Löwenherz" (p. 42). It is true that in court Eichmann made this claim, and the fact that at least one person is prepared to believe him shows that this hypocritical play for sympathy was not made wholly in vain.

Concluding Remarks

One stands baffled before Hannah Arendt's image of Eichmann: a trustworthy man, who often lied; a man without education, who learned Hebrew, could read ("haltingly") a Yiddish newspaper, read Adolf Böhm's *The Zionist Movement* and even such difficult works as Kant's *Critique of Practical Reason* or Hans Frank's *The Technique of Government*; a man without intelligence, who was expert in negotiation, in organization, and in reading documents; a receiver of orders, who defied Himmler (in fact, also Hitler); a man without initiative, who made the first experiment in forcible removal of Jews from one country to another (Nisko) without any authorization from above, and who concluded his career in this respect by forcing 50,000 Hungarian Jews to march in the November cold to the Austrian frontier, and "hoped" to send 50,000 more by the same way; a man of conscience, whose conscience prompted him to send to their extermination more and more of his victims.

Even more enigmatic is Miss Arendt's image of Eichmann's relation to Nazism. The man she holds to have been without convictions, to have been a party member who had never read the party program or Hitler's *Mein Kampf*—this is the man who regretted that along with the Jews 100,000 German non-Jews, "enemies" of the Nazi regime, had not also been exterminated, and who, in his Argentine hideout, wanted to flay an author of a book critical of Hitler.

No less bizarre is her image of Eichmann's attitude toward the Jews. The man whom she takes to have been free of "fanatical anti-Semitism" is the same man who told Sassen, "To be frank with you, had we killed all of them, the 10,300,000, I would be happy and say: all right, we have destroyed an enemy."[161]

From the historical documents available to us, the real Eichmann emerges: a man of extraordinary driving power, master in the arts of cunning and deception, intelligent and competent in his field, single-minded in his mission to make Europe "free of Jews" (*judenrein*)—in short, a man uniquely suited to be the overseer of most of the Nazi program to exterminate the Jews.

2

War Crimes Trials
and International Law

The basic history of the war crimes trials following World War II is sufficiently simple to be understood by anyone who makes a serious study of it.[1] But Miss Arendt has not mastered this history.

To begin with, she creates confusion by her indiscriminate use of singular or plural in connection with the Nuremberg trial (trials), failing to indicate which Tribunal or Tribunals any particular remark refers to. Thus, she cites "the judgment of the Nuremberg Trials" (*sic*, V, 131) and a number of references to "Nuremberg Trials" (pp. 4, 200, 201, 251) with unexplained use of the plural. Similarly, references to the "Nuremberg Tribunal" (p. 251) or to "Nuremberg" (pp. 233, 236, 251, 252) appear without any modifier. In connection with Globke's testimony (p. 100), she makes a simple reference to "Nuremberg."[2] "Nuremberg judges" (p. 236) is as vague as "Nuremberg Trials"; the specific references to Donnedieu de Vabres (pp. 236, 251) are to a judge of the International Military Tribunal. On page 235 she mentions the "International Military Tribunals," although there was only one such Tribunal for the major war criminals of the European theater. While it might be legitimate to use "Nuremberg" for the total complex of trials of major war criminals in Nuremberg both under the International Military Tribunal (IMT) and under the Nuremberg Military Tribunals (NMT), it is always necessary to differentiate between the former and the latter. The former was international (inter-Allied) by its constitution and by its composition; the latter by its constitution. The panel of judges in the NMT was, however, exclusively American, although it was independent of the American judicial system.[3]

Miss Arendt does not have a firm grasp of the details of the individual trials. For example, she says on page 114 that the "Nuremberg court" was not in possession of the minutes of the

Wannsee Conference. This time the reference is obviously to Case XI (the Ministries Case) of the Trials of War Criminals before the Nuremberg Military Tribunals. She writes that because the Tribunal was not in possession of the minutes of the Wannsee Conference, it believed Wilhelm Stuckart's testimony that he had known nothing of the extermination program, and therefore sentenced him only to time served. This is incorrect. The prosecutor, Robert M. W. Kempner, had discovered the minutes in the files of the German Foreign Office, and introduced them as key evidence.[4] It is precisely for this reason that the Tribunal did *not* believe Stuckart. Stuckart was sentenced to "time served" and released from prison solely because of medical evidence that he was mortally ill, and not because the Tribunal placed credence in his testimony.[5]

All this could have been found in Kempner's *Eichmann und Komplizen*,[6] listed in Miss Arendt's Bibliography. In his book, Kempner reports in full his examination of the following participants in the conference: Wilhelm Stuckart, Gerhard Klopfer, Georg Leibbrandt, Friedrich Wilhelm Kritzinger, and Erich Neumann. A photostatic reproduction of the copy of the minutes used by Kempner in the Ministries case was submitted in evidence to the Jerusalem court[7] and distributed to the reporters.

Even the International Military Tribunal is terra incognita to Miss Arendt. She confounds the "act of state" objection (immunity from prosecution for certain acts committed on behalf of the state) with the *par in parem* principle (immunity of the State itself and of special categories of persons from foreign jurisdiction) (p. 18). In tracing the background of Dr. Servatius' defense of Eichmann, she writes that his plea at Nuremberg in the defense of Fritz Sauckel was "acts of state" (p. 87). In fact, Dr. Servatius based his defense in that case on more orthodox lines without recourse to "act of state."[8]

She offers the following statement on the behavior of the defendants before the International Military Tribunal: ". . . at Nuremberg . . . the various accused presented a nauseating spectacle by accusing each other—though none of them blamed Hitler!" (p. 66). She returns to the subject in a different context (pp. 157-158), repeating that "at the Nuremberg Trials . . . the defendants accused and betrayed each other." These statements are incorrect. Out of twenty-two defendants, all but three (Göring, Funk, and Baldur von Schirach) attacked Hitler.[9] Typical of such attacks are the following two statements, made by Alfred Rosenberg and Hans Frank, respectively: "To an ever-increasing degree Adolf Hitler drew persons to himself who were not my comrades, but my opponents. With reference to their pernicious deeds I must state that they were not practising the National Socialism for which millions of believing men and women had fought, but rather, shamefully misusing it. It was a degeneration which I, too, very strongly condemned."[10] And "Adolf Hitler, the chief defendant, left no final statement to the German people and the world. Amid the deepest distress of his people he found no comforting word. He became silent and did not discharge his office as a leader, but went down into darkness, a suicide."[11] In the case of Hermann Göring, though he personally did not attack Hitler, his counsel did.[12] There were no mutual recriminations during any public session.

Concerning the judges at Nuremberg, Miss Arendt writes that "their most severe punishment, the death penalty," was meted out "only to those who had been found guilty of . . . a 'crime against humanity' . . . The notion that aggression is 'the supreme international crime' was silently abandoned when a number of men were sentenced to death who had never been convicted of a 'conspiracy' against peace" (p. 236). Again, this is incorrect. In fact, Göring, Ribbentrop, Keitel, Rosenberg, and Jodl were sentenced for all four crimes attributed to them by the indictment, including crimes against peace and "common plan and conspiracy to wage aggressive war." Only Streicher was condemned to death for crimes against humanity alone; Kaltenbrunner, Frank, Sauckel, and Bormann (*in absentia*) were condemned for war crimes and crimes against humanity; Seyss-Inquart and Frick for crimes against peace, war crimes, and crimes against humanity.[13]

Miss Arendt frequently refers to "Successor trials," though no such term exists in international law. The "so-called [V, 58] successor trials" are mentioned first on page 200. The meaning of the term is indicated later (pp. 238, 242, 248), when the numerous "Successor trials" are identified as those that followed what she calls the "Nuremberg trials." Once (p. 237) she seems to define these to have been trials in formerly Nazi-occupied territories.[14] Elsewhere (pp. 242, 249), when discussing the place of the Jerusalem trial in the system of postwar trials, she identifies the Jerusalem trial as the "last of the Successor trials." In reality, the

Nuremberg trial of major war criminals conducted before the International Military Tribunal was followed by (1) the Subsequent Trials before the NMT in Nuremberg, (2) trials conducted in Germany by each of the occupying powers, and (3) national trials.

Miss Arendt belittles the claim of the Jerusalem court that in the Eichmann trial, and in it alone, the Jewish Catastrophe "occupied the central place in the court's proceedings, and [that] it was this fact which distinguished this trial from those which preceded it," and she characterizes the court's statement as "at best, a half-truth" (pp. 236-237). Later she makes an exactly opposite statement: "What had been mentioned at Nuremberg only occasionally, and, as it were, marginally—that 'the evidence shows that . . . the mass murders . . . were . . . part of a plan to get rid of whole native populations'—was in the center of the Jerusalem proceedings, for the obvious reason that Eichmann stood accused of a crime against the Jewish people" (p. 252). In the judgment of the International Military Tribunal, as published in the January 1947 issue of the *American Journal of International Law*, references to crimes against humanity in regard to Jews are scattered throughout and cover the equivalent of fourteeen pages out of a total of 160. The International Military Tribunal never made a claim that the Jewish question was central to its proceedings. In fact, the Jerusalem trial differed from other trials of Nazi war criminals and their accomplices in the following two ways: (1) Insofar as the trials of the Nuremberg Military Tribunals, military tribunals of occupying powers, and tribunals in formerly occupied countries dealt with Jewish questions, they were limited to crimes committed in particular areas, ghettos, camps, institutions, etc., and to the war period only. The Jerusalem trial was concerned with crimes committed without territorial limitations, and throughout the whole Nazi period. (2) The Jerusalem court dealt not with crimes against citizens (or residents) of any one country, but with crimes against the Jewish people, whatever their country of citizenship.

Miss Arendt's knowledge of other international instruments is equally unreliable. The European Convention for the Protection of Human Rights and Fundamental Freedoms was not "established . . . under the auspices of the Council of Europe's Commission of Human Rights" (p. 228), which did not exist at that time, but under the auspices of the Council of Europe.[15] The Commission on Human Rights is one of the organs created by the Convention.[16]

As for the Hague Conventions, it should be noted that in 1907 not one Convention was adopted, as erroneously assumed by Miss Arendt (p. 234), but thirteen separate Conventions and the additional "Declaration relating to the launching of projectiles or explosives from balloons and other kinds of aircraft."[17] Her statement (p. 234) that Russia had never signed the 1907 Hague Convention is also inaccurate. The Czar's regime, on whose initiative the two Hague Conferences were called, did ratify all the Conventions,[18] but the Soviet Government did not consider itself bound by this ratification.[19] An any rate, Miss Arendt's statement is irrelevant even if it is taken to apply to the U.S.S.R. The judgment of the International Military Tribunal reinterpreted the "general participation clause" of the Fourth Convention (which states that the Convention shall be binding only if *all* the belligerents are parties to it) in the light of subsequent developments, and *unanimously* held that the clause no longer applied. Noting that "several of the belligerents in the recent war were not parties to the Convention" the Tribunal went on to say:

> In the opinion of the Tribunal it is not necessary to decide this question. The rules of land warfare expressed in the [Fourth] convention undoubtedly represented an advance over existing international law at the time of their adoption. But the convention expressly stated that it was an attempt "to revise the general laws and customs of war," which it thus recognized to be then existing, but by 1939 these rules laid down in the convention were recognized by all civilized nations, and were regarded as being declaratory of the laws and customs of war which are referred to in Article 6(b) of the Charter [of this Tribunal].[20]

Equally incorrect is her claim that Italy did not ratify the Hague Conventions of 1907 (p. 234). Italy ratified Convention X.[21]

She implies, in her serial version (V, 103), that the International Military Tribunal relied on the Geneva Red Cross Convention of 1906. In fact, that Convention was replaced by the Convention for the Amelioration of the Conditions of the Wounded and Sick in Armies in the Field, of July 27, 1929, and the International Military Tribunal relied on this agreement instead.[22] (In her book (p. 234) she leaves out the date of the "Geneva Convention.")

Argentina, she says, "had signed an international Convention declaring that the perpetrators of crimes against humanity 'will not be deemed to be political criminals'" (p. 219). First, it must be pointed out that international conventions are not generally identified by indefinite articles. It is also difficult to understand why her reference to the more specific, though no more relevant, Genocide Convention in V, 80, was replaced by the vague reference to *an* international convention. Second, her reference to the *signing* of this Convention, demonstrates her unfamiliarity with the procedure that was followed. The "Genocide Convention" (officially, "Convention on the Prevention and Punishment of the Crime of Genocide") was unanimously adopted by the General Assembly of the United Nations on December 9, 1948, Argentina being among those to vote for it.[23] Miss Arendt reports the adoption (pp. 240-241) but seems unaware that such adoption merely opened the Convention for ratification or accession, and that the Convention did not come into force until January 12, 1951, after the twentieth ratification had been deposited. Immediately after the vote in the General Assembly, and for about a year thereafter, a number of states *signed* the Convention, Argentina *not* being among them. However, signature of an international convention by a plenipotentiary is usually subject to ratification by the competent organ of government; and ratification can also be carried out without prior signature. Argentina deposited her instrument of accession (subject to reservations regarding Articles IX and XII) on June 15, 1956.[24]

In the third place, the Genocide Convention does not contain the provision referred to by Miss Arendt. Article VII of the Convention states that "Genocide and other acts enumerated in Article III [all directly related to genocide] shall not be considered as political crimes *for the purpose of extradition.*"[25] Thus, the Article refers specifically to genocide, and not, as Miss Arendt thinks, to crimes against humanity in general; in addition, it does not declare that the perpetrators of these crimes "will not be deemed to be political criminals," as Miss Arendt misquotes its provision (p. 219), but deals exclusively with the problem of extradition.[26]

She asserts that " '. . . the Law for the Prevention and Punishment of Genocide' . . . was discussed but not passed" by the Knesset, and therefore "genocide, not being covered by an Israeli law, could not properly enter into its [the Jerusalem court's] considerations" (p. 247). Actually, the law was adopted by the Knesset on March 29, 1950.[27] But Eichmann was not prosecuted under this law.[28]

Law in Theory and Practice

Miss Arendt admits to being a layman in matters of law (p. 242), but she nevertheless sets out to attack international criminal law, the war crimes trials, and in general the prevailing theories of criminal law.

No discussion of international criminal law can be confidently undertaken without a study of the leading treatises of this branch of law by Antonio Quintano Ripollés,[29] Hans-Heinrich Jescheck,[30] Jean Graven,[31] and Stefan Glaser,[32] not to speak of dozens of monographs.[33] Acquaintance with this literature is not discernible in Miss Arendt's text or Bibliography. Nor does she realize to what extent international criminal law has progressed since World War II. Yet she undertakes to deliver lectures on their specialized subjects to Justice Robert H. Jackson, who has been called by an eminent jurist the "initiator of international criminal law"[34] and Sir Hersch Lauterpacht, the author of Article 6 (the Article defining War Crimes) of the Nuremberg Charter. Justice Jackson is taken to task (p. 251) for listing only agreements and accepted customs as sources of international law[35] and for failing to request the trial judge to render justice according to his own intuition "without the help of . . . positive, posited laws." An example of what could emerge from such a method of administering justice is supplied by Miss Arendt (pp. 254-256) when she advises the judges in the Eichmann trial what they should have said to the defendant. Sir Hersch Lauterpacht is reprimanded (pp. 132-133) for "deliberate refusal to take notice of the central moral, legal, and political phenomena of our century." This reproach is made against a universally recognized international lawyer and philosopher.[36]

The layman who contrives his own theory of law, and on the basis of it proceeds to criticize panels of experienced jurists, runs great risks. Miss Arendt's theory concerning the emergence and development of new law can be formulated in her own words in the following two propositions:

1. "If a crime unknown before, such as genocide, suddenly makes its appearance, justice itself demands a judgment according to a new law" (p. 233).

2. "In consequence of this yet unfinished nature of international law, it has become the task of ordinary trial judges to render

justice without the help of, or beyond the limitation set upon them through, positive, posited laws" (p. 251).

Her theory ignores the real sequence of events in the case of "appearance" of a new crime. The order is as follows: (1) Acts of a nature not foreseen in the existing criminal codes occur—for example, the theft of electrical power rather than movable property, the traditional object of theft. (2) The legal community, alerted to such deeds, passes on their criminality on the basis of existing laws—by way of interpretation, analogy being excluded. (3) Failing that, and in view of the principle (in which all mankind has a stake) that no act is a crime without a law forbidding it (*nullum crimen sine lege*),[37] the legislature—national or international—intervenes, defines in exact terms the elements of the crime, and provides for punishment. Then, and only then, can courts act in applying such punishment in concrete cases. This is true not only for the Continental but also for the Anglo-Saxon system of law. To deposit, as Miss Arendt suggests, any unsolved problem resulting from lacunae in laws into the lap of a trial judge is universally considered to be an unsuitable method of filling gaps in law.

It is certainly inappropriate to demand of a court that it pass judgment without any assistance from existing law. A court does not consider cases on its own initiative. Cases reach it only in accordance with the existing rules of procedure, following action by police and the public prosecutor. In practice, therefore, Miss Arendt's theory of spontaneous growth of law would not extend the function of the courts; instead, her theory would require the prosecutor or the police to define deeds to be criminal where there is no existing law. This would invite anarchy.

To all appearances, Miss Arendt never saw a criminal code. She writes: "For just as a murderer is prosecuted because he has violated the law of the community, and not because he has deprived the Smith family of its husband, father, and breadwinner, so these modern, state-employed mass murderers must be prosecuted because they violated the order of mankind, and not because they killed millions of people" (p. 249). But what is "the law of the community" if not, in this case, the particular prohibition to deprive "the Smith family of its husband, father, and breadwinner"? What is it that violates the "order of mankind" if not the killing of millions of people? Miss Arendt is apparently unaware that criminal codes do not define common law crimes as violation of the law of the national community, but more exactly as separate punishable acts. The elimination of the element of individuality in criminal law would result in the dehumanization of criminal law.

As an illustration of the operation of criminal law, let us take a simple example: theft. The act of stealing violates a right that every person possesses; a court will judge and sentence a thief for the particular criminal deed which, first and foremost, deprives the victim of his movable property. This is the immediate purpose of any particular trial. But in a developed national legal order, the particular law (in our example, the law protecting property) constitutes part of a branch of law—criminal law—whose *ultimate* objectives are the protection of the order itself in all its manifestations. In a highly developed legal system, there exist in the criminal codes—in addition to laws governing such particular crimes as theft—special laws governing crimes against the existing national order.

The status of international criminal law cannot be measured by standards borrowed from national legal systems. In international criminal law we have not yet gone beyond laws defining individual crimes, to laws defining crimes against the world order. This fact does not exclude the interpretation of crimes such as genocide, crimes against humanity, crimes against peace, and war crimes as being directed *ultimately* against the world order. The interpretation of crimes such as these as affecting mankind as a whole is not unreasonable, but it has no direct bearing on the legal status of the individual crimes themselves.

A milestone in the development of international criminal law appears in the Sixth Report of the International Law Commission, published in 1954, in which a chapter is devoted to the Draft Code of Offenses Against the Peace and Security of Mankind.[38] The definitions of individual crimes are listed in Article 2 (altogether, thirteen punishable acts, including genocide and "inhuman acts"). In view of the developing nature of international law, it was not found possible to include a special punishable act against the international order analogous to the usually accepted—in national laws—acts against national order. Instead, the Draft Code opens with this clause: "Offenses against the peace and security of mankind, as defined in this code, are crimes under international law, for which the responsible individual shall be punished."

Miss Arendt's statement that, of the crimes that came under

the jurisdiction of the Tribunal at Nuremberg, "only . . . the crime against humanity was new and unprecedented" (p. 234) leaves unexplained the key fact that what was new was the extension of war crimes to any civilian population, *including* the population of the occupying country itself. She quotes approvingly Julius Stone to the effect that "the mass murder of the Jews, if they were Germany's own nationals, could only be reached by the humanity count" (p. 237), but she did not grasp its meaning.[39] What Professor Stone meant was that insofar as the crimes against the Jews were committed in occupied territories, they fell under the traditional concept of war crimes; but insofar as they were committed against Germany's own citizens, they fell only under the provisions of Article 6(c) of the Charter of the International Military Tribunal, which reads in full:

CRIMES AGAINST HUMANITY: namely, murder, extermination, enslavement, deportation, and other inhumane acts committed against any civilian population, before or during the war, or persecutions on political, racial or religious grounds in execution of or in connection with any crime within the jurisdiction of the Tribunal, *whether or not in violation of domestic law of the country where perpetrated.*[40]

Furthermore, this innovation could hardly be called "unprecedented." Such an extension of the traditional definition of war crimes was already foreshadowed in the so-called Martens clause of the Fourth Hague Convention of 1907:

Until a more complete code of the laws of war has been issued, the High Contracting Parties deem it expedient to declare that in cases not included in the regulations adopted by them, the inhabitants and the belligerents remain under the protection and the rule of principles of the law of nations, as they result from the usages established among the civilized peoples, from the law of humanity, and from the dictates of the public conscience.[41]

Miss Arendt believes that "what had prevented the Nuremberg Tribunal from doing full justice to this crime [crime against humanity] was . . . that the Charter demanded that this crime . . . was to be tied up with the other crimes [crimes against peace and war crimes]" (p. 237).[42] While it is true that in the Charter crimes against humanity were subject to connection with crimes against peace and war crimes, it is equally true that the Nazi mass crimes were perpetrated during the war. Furthermore, there has been a process of gradual emancipation of the concept "crimes against humanity" from connection with these two crimes. In the Control Council Law No. 10, no mention was made of crimes against peace and war crimes in the definition of crimes against humanity.[43] (However, the case law under this new version of the definition is not uniform.[44]) The same is true in regard to the practice of German courts under British occupation.[45] The connection with these two other crimes is still present in the Nuremberg Principles,[46] but does not appear in the Code of Offenses against Peace and Security of Mankind,[47] nor does it appear in the Israel law.[48]

In addition, Miss Arendt asserts that there is a "basic misunderstanding" in defining " 'crimes against humanity' as 'inhuman acts' " (p. 252). She apparently prefers to interpret "crimes against humanity" as crimes against "mankind in its entirety". This is in direct contradiction to accepted usage in international law as reflected, for example, in the official Russian text of the Nuremberg Charter, where the word corresponding to "humanity" is *chelovechnost* (humaneness), not *chelovechestvo* (mankind);[49] and in the translation used in official German-language documents, where the word is *Menschlichkeit* ("humaneness"), not *Menschheit* ("mankind").[50]

Miss Arendt also does not realize that a distinction exists between the legal definition of "crimes against humanity" and of "genocide." Thus she can write: "It is essentially for this reason: that the unprecedented, once it has appeared, may become a precedent for the future, that all trials touching upon 'crimes against humanity' must be judged according to a standard that is today still an 'ideal.' If genocide is an actual possibility of the future, then no people on earth—least of all, of course, the Jewish people in Israel or elsewhere—can feel reasonably sure of its continued existence without the help and the protection of international law" (p. 250). Here, as elsewhere (pp. 247 ff., 253 ff.), she erroneously considers the two terms ("crimes against humanity" and "genocide") interchangeable.[51]

As for arriving at "a valid definition of the 'crime against humanity' " (p. 251), it was clearly not the function of the Jerusalem court to *establish* such a definition, as Miss Arendt would like it to have done; rather, it was its duty to apply the existing one found in the Israel law of 1950 under which the court operated. The charge she brings that no mention was made in the judgment that the extermination of a people is more than a crime against that people—that it is also a crime against "international order" (p. 252)—is a result of careless reading of the judgment. The court expressly stated in its judgment that the crimes against the Jewish people were crimes under the law of nations.[52] The implication is clear: they are also crimes against the world order for whose protection the law of nations exists.

Genocide—a term coined in 1944 by the Polish-Jewish legal scholar Raphael Lemkin[53]—cannot be treated as an abstraction unrelated to existing international and national law. We must always be careful to differentiate between genocide as a purely conversational concept, as a common law concept as stated in the "Reservations" case of the International Court of Justice,[54] and as a strictly statutory concept under the Genocide Convention and the laws enacted in its implementation. Is the statutory concept of genocide, then, equivalent to murder? Not quite. Under the Genocide Convention, not only "killing members of the group," but also "causing serious bodily or mental harm to members of the group; . . . deliberately inflicting on the group conditions of life calculated to bring about its physical destruction in whole or in part; . . . imposing measures intended to prevent births within the group; . . . forcibly transferring children of the group to another group" may qualify as acts of genocide—provided, however, that they are "committed with the intent to destroy, in whole or in part, a national, ethnic, racial or religious group, as such." Other factors, such as the number of persons affected, are not decisive in the definition. The allegedly "pernicious" identification (p. 249) of murder and genocide, attributed to the court, would have been a valid objection had the court failed to distinguish between the two, and in particular to emphasize Eichmann's intent to destroy Jewry as a whole; but this is precisely what the court did *not* fail to do.[55]

Miss Arendt says more than once that genocide (as fact and legal concept) is unprecedented (pp. 233, 250). Certainly the destruction of European Jewry was unique in its continental scope, in its psychological pressures, in its technical methods, in its masses of active perpetrators (members of one of the most educated peoples of the world), in its involvement of the three pillars of the Nazi regime (State, Army, Party), in its connection with pseudo-scientific racial theories in general and Judaistic pseudoscience in particular, and in its absolute (six millions) and relative (the high percentage of the victims in relation to European Jewry—namely, two-thirds—and to world Jewry—namely, one-third) figures of victims. It was also unique in the revulsion of the non-Nazi world, in the universal realization of its inherent criminal character under existing law and of the responsibility of individuals for these crimes, and in the determination of the world community to take measures for the prevention of its repetition by affirmation of the Nuremberg Principles, by adoption of the Genocide Convention, and by outlawing war in the United Nations Charter. But could it be really claimed—as Miss Arendt does—that history knows of no previous cases at all of genocide, and genocide of the Jews in particular?[56] Similarly, is it reasonable to maintain that legally genocide is an altogether unprecedented crime? In its advisory opinion of May 28, 1951 (Reservations to the Genocide Convention), the International Court of Justice unanimously expressed the opinion that "the principles underlying the Convention are principles which are recognized by the civilized nations as binding on States, even without any conventional obligations."[57] What the Convention and the laws issued under the Convention have actually done is to spell out customary legal principles in a precise and specific text.

In the midst of her discussion on genocide, Miss Arendt turns to the question of what properly constitutes an international concern, and what constitutes a national crime. "The crime of the Nuremberg Laws [anti-Jewish laws passed in Germany in 1935] was a national crime," she maintains; "it violated national, constitutional rights and liberties, but it was of no concern to the comity of nations" (p. 246).[58] This is inaccurate. Even the earlier Nazi anti-Jewish legislation of 1933 was a matter of international concern insofar as the area of Upper Silesia in Germany was concerned. This area was under a special regime established under the Polish-German Geneva Convention of May 15, 1922, which, inter alia, outlawed any discrimination on the basis of race, religion, or language. An appeal against the discriminatory 1933 Nazi legislation was filed with the League of Nations in the so-called Bernheim case, with the result that Germany suspended the application of anti-Jewish legislation to the 10,000 Jews in Upper Silesia for the period of the validity of the Convention (i.e., till July 15, 1937) and undertook not to apply its subsequent legislation (including the Nuremberg Laws) to this area. This action, based on international law, but affecting an internal region of Germany, provided a breathing spell for Upper Silesian Jewry.[59] While everywhere in

Germany Jews were being reduced to the state of pariahs, those living in Upper Silesia continued to enjoy equal rights, to practice medicine and law, and to hold office.[60]

The Nuremberg Laws were also a violation of the unanimous *voeu*[61] of the Assembly of the League of Nations on September 21, 1922, which declared that "the States not bound by international obligations should, nonetheless, observe in the treatment of their racial, religious or linguistic minorities at least as high a standard of justice and tolerance as was required by the Minorities Treaty and the decisions of the Council."[62]

Miss Arendt's views on what is of international concern do not conform with the ruling of the Permanent Court of International Justice in the case of the Nationality Decrees issued in Tunis and Morocco, which declared: "The question whether a certain matter is or is not solely within the jurisdiction of a State is an essentially relative question; it depends upon the development of international relations."[63]

Her argument is based on a legal misconception. She writes: "According to international law, it was the privilege of the sovereign German nation to declare to be a national minority whatever part of its population it saw fit, as long as its minority laws conformed to the rights and guaranteees established by internationally recognized minorities treaties and agreements" (p. 246). She nowhere indicates her source for any such international law. There are no cases or procedures in the practice of international law for declaring a group to be a national minority. *A la rigueur*, it can be claimed that there is no prohibition or restriction in international law to declare part of a population a national minority. Moreover, in the positive law of the then valid European regional system for protection of minorities, the object and beneficiary of international protection was an individual citizen (not a group of citizens) of a country whose race, language, or religion differed from that of the majority.[64] Finally, there is no evidence that Nazi Germany declared or intended to declare German Jewry to be a national minority. The exact opposite is true. When the first anti-Jewish measures appeared in Nazi Germany, they caused a commotion among German minorities in the rest of Europe who had co-operated for years with the Jewish minorities, particularly in the so-called Nationalities Congresses. The leaders of these German minority groups realized that their position as spokesmen for minorities was being undermined, and they went to Berlin in order to persuade the German Government to cease and desist from these measures, which also served to endanger the position of the German minorities.[65] While we are not in possession of the full record of this fateful discussion, it is known on the authority of Dr. Ewald Amende, the Secretary-General of the Nationalities Congresses, that *the Nazis took the view that the Jews in Germany were not a national minority group,* and that therefore the German minorities should not worry about their position. There is not a single official statement of the Nazi regime in which Jews anywhere in Europe are referred to as a national minority; the term was apparently reserved for the German and Hungarian minorities. As for the legality of the laws themselves, the anti-Jewish policies were carried out with the aid of measures whose "legality" was never seriously considered even by the Nazis. Hitler himself expressly stated this on April 23, 1933, in the debate on the *Ermächtigungs-gesetz* (the "legalization" of the Nazi dictatorship, under which all anti-Jewish legislation was passed), when he said that the purpose of introducing the bill in the Reichstag was "to permit us to take what we can take anyway."[66]

Miss Arendt continues: "'Enforced Emigration' . . . or expulsion, which became official [German] policy after 1938, did concern the international community, for the simple reason that those who were expelled appeared at the frontiers of other countries, which were forced either to accept the uninvited guests or to smuggle them into another country . . ." (p. 246). The position in international law is contrary to her stand. Though concern with human rights and fundamental freedoms, however inadequate, is among the elements of the Charter of the United Nations, provisions for cases involving refugee movements are at present fragmentary and far from generally accepted.

There are no permanent limits to domestic jurisdiction or to matters of international concern. They depend on the changing patterns of relations between the internal and the international order.

The Legal Basis for War Crimes Trials

This section can best be started by indicating the legal basis for the war crimes trials during the years following World War II. The trials were based on the following sources:[67]

1. The Interallied Declarations on the Punishment of War Criminals (of January 13, 1942; of December 17, 1942, condemning the German policy of extermination of the Jewish people; of January 5, 1943; of November 1, 1943, known as the Moscow Declaration).[68]

2. The Four Power Agreement of August 8, 1945, and the Charter of the International Military Tribunal.[69]

3. Control Council Law No. 10, enacted by the four occupying powers—France, the U.S.S.R., the United Kingdom, and the United States—by virtue of Germany's unconditional surrender, and applied by the Nuremberg Military Tribunals and some German courts during the occupation.[70]

4. National legislation of formerly occupied or satellite countries: the Soviet Union, Austria, Poland, Bulgaria, Greece, Czechoslovakia, Hungary, France, Belgium, Luxembourg, Denmark, Italy, The Netherlands, Norway, Romania, Yugoslavia (almost all special legislation enacted during or after the war to punish war criminals).[71]

5. The regular criminal code of Germany, as applied to trials of war criminals by German courts.[72]

It might also be noted that the Nuremberg Principles were twice unanimously adopted by the General Assembly of the United Nations, the most representative organ of organized mankind, and that they constitute at present part of the law of the United Nations.[73] Neutral states (like Switzerland and the Vatican) and former enemy states (Federal Republic of Germany) have accepted these principles, at least partly.[74] The same principles form the basis of the Draft Code of Offenses Against the Peace and Security of Mankind adopted by the International Law Commission, one of the two leading legal organs of the United Nations.[75]

As a prelude to questioning the legality of the Eichmann trial, for which "the Nuremberg Trials were cited in Jerusalem as valid precedent" (p. 233), Miss Arendt denies the validity of the Charter and of the judgment of the International Military Tribunal on three grounds, drawn from (1) the nature of the International Military Tribunal as a "court of victors"; (2) a theory of "precedent"; and (3) the *tu quoque* principle. A refutation of these objections is in order.

Apparently as the result of reading some German critics,[76] Miss Arendt repeats the assertion made by these critics that "the International Military Tribunals were international in name only, that

they were in fact the courts of the victors,[77] and the authority of
their judgment [was] doubtful in any case" (p. 235). These are
unfounded charges. To be sure, the International Military Tribunal
was composed of representatives of the victorious powers, but these
powers constituted the overwhelming majority of mankind.[78] The
only significant groups not represented were Germany, who, after
her unconditional surrender, lost her status as a subject of international law and became instead an object of international action;[79]
Germany's European satellites, who underwent a change in their
regimes and returned, as far as international law was concerned, to
their status *quo ante*; and the neutrals, who, by standing aside while
the other nations were engaged in a life-and-death struggle against
an enemy of all mankind (including the neutrals themselves), forfeited the right to sit in judgment.[80] Understandably, they never
even asked to participate in war crimes trials.

Miss Arendt advances a theory of precedents, and claims that
retroactive laws are justified as long as "they applied only to crimes
previously unknown" (p. 233).[81] Under this reservation, only
"crimes against humanity," according to her, were "new and unprecedented," and hence subject to retroactive legislation; not so
was the crime of aggressive warfare, which "is at least as old as
recorded history" (p. 234). Contrary to Miss Arendt (p. 233),
neither the International Military Tribunal nor the Jerusalem court
acted under premise of the retroactivity of their laws, inasmuch as
both courts considered these laws to have been established international law long before the crimes were committed. In addition,
the Germans had been duly and repeatedly warned since January
1942.[82] Miss Arendt's theory breaks down entirely when account is
taken of the difference between "new and unprecedented" acts and
"new and unprecedented" crimes. Historical acts (of a communal
or individual nature) may or may not be "new and unprecedented";
it is the historian's task to decide. But in criminal law the question
is not whether a particular kind of act is unprecedented. The
relevant question is whether the kind of act being considered has
been declared criminal by competent authority or by uniform usage.
Thus, "aggressive warfare" as well as "defensive wars" are as old
as recorded history, but not so the legally discriminating concept of
"aggressive war." For centuries war, the "ultimate recourse of kings"
(*ultima ratio regum*), was considered an unprohibited exercise of
sovereignty. But in the period between the two World Wars some-

thing happened: The concept of two types of wars (aggressive and defensive) entered the science and practice of international law. Miss Arendt claims that though "aggressive warfare . . . had been denounced as 'criminal' many times before, it had never been recognized as such in any formal sense" (p. 234). But the judgment of the International Military Tribunal expressly held that "the criminality of war of aggression" was part of universal international law even before the Briand-Kellogg Pact of 1928 and surely under it.[83]

On the one hand, she writes (p. 234) that the violations of the Hague and Geneva Conventions were "war crimes" (although there is no formal statement to this effect in the Conventions), but on the other hand she does not interpret as crimes violations of the Briand-Kellogg Pact, which is still in force.[84] The International Military Tribunal had this to say on the subject:

But it is argued that the pact [Briand-Kellogg Pact] does not expressly enact that such wars are crimes, or set up courts to try those who make such wars. To that extent the same is true with regard to the laws of war contained in the Hague Convention. The [Fourth] Hague Convention of 1907 prohibited resort to certain methods of waging war. These included the inhuman treatment of prisoners, the employment of poisoned weapons, the improper use of flags of truce, and similar matters. Many of these prohibitions had been enforced long before the date of the Convention; but since 1907 they have certainly been crimes, punishable as offenses against the laws of war; yet the Hague Convention nowhere designates such practices as criminal, nor is any sentence prescribed, nor any mention made of a court to try and punish offenders. For many years past, however, military tribunals have tried and punished individuals guilty of violating the rules of land warfare laid down by this Convention. . . .[85]

The third argument advanced by Miss Arendt against the Nuremberg judgment is drawn from the "you too" (*tu quoque*) principle. However, she does not explain the meaning of this principle and its role in the system of the Nuremberg trials. In the Nuremberg trials, the principle of *tu quoque* was invoked by the defense in two slightly different versions: (1) The plea was offered that "the act is not criminal because you have done the same." (2) The plea was offered that "since you and others have done the same, it is to be assumed that this general practice constitutes—by way of uniform usage—an authorization to act this way."

The International Military Tribunal released Admiral Dönitz

from responsibility for unrestricted submarine warfare on the strength of British and United States practice, accepting in his case the second of the foregoing versions. The Tribunal said:

> Shortly after the outbreak of war, the British Admiralty, in accordance with its *Handbook of Instructions* of 1938 to the merchant navy, armed its merchant vessels, in many cases convoyed them with armed escort, gave orders to send position reports upon sighting submarines, thus integrating merchant vessels into the warning network of naval intelligence. On October 1, 1939, the British Admiralty announced British merchant ships had been ordered to ram U-Boats if possible.

> In the actual circumstances of this case, the Tribunal is not prepared to hold Dönitz guilty for his conduct of submarine warfare against British armed merchant ships. . . .[86]

> In view of all the facts proved, and in particular of an order of the British Admiralty announced on 8 May 1940, according to which all vessels should be sunk at sight in the Skagerrak, and the answer to interrogatories by Admiral Nimitz that unrestricted submarine warfare was carried on in the Pacific Ocean by the United States from the first day that nation entered the war, the sentence of Dönitz is not assessed on the grounds of his breaches of the international law of submarine warfare.[87]

The International Military Tribunal also released Admiral Raeder from responsibility for the same reason.[88]

The Nuremberg Military Tribunals discussed the problems arising from the first version of the *tu quoque* principle with great frankness and fairness and came to the following conclusions:

> It must be admitted that Germans were not the only ones who were guilty of committing war crimes; other violators of international law could, no doubt, be tried and punished by the state of which they were nationals, by the offended state if it can secure jurisdiction of the person, or by an international tribunal of competent authorized jurisdiction. . . .[89]

> These Tribunals were not organized and do not sit for the purpose of wreaking vengeance upon the conquered. Was such the purpose, the power existed to use the firing squad, the scaffold, or the prison camp without taking the time and putting forth labor which have been so freely expended on them, and the Allied Powers would have copied the methods which were too often used during the Third Reich. We may not, in justice, apply to these defendants because they are Germans standards of duty and responsibility which are not equally applicable to the officials of the Allied Powers and to those of all nations. Nor should Germans be convicted for acts or conducts which, if committed

by Americans, British, French, or Russians would not subject them to
legal trial and conviction. Both care and caution must be exercised not
to prescribe or apply a yardstick to these defendants which cannot and
should not be applied to others, irrespective of whether they are nationals
of the victor or of the vanquished.[90]

On the legal value of this type of plea the Nuremberg Military
Tribunals made the following findings:

The further objection was made that one of the nations, namely, the
U.S.S.R., cooperated in the promulgation of Control Council Law No.
10 after it had engaged in a war of aggression which is made criminal
under the law; this objection also is without merit. The London Agreement and Charter from which Control Council Law No. 10 stems has
been approved by 19 nations other than the four signatories thereto. We
need not and do not determine whether the charge that one of the
signatories of the London Agreement and Charter and Control Council
Law No. 10 is guilty of aggressive war, for such determination could
avail the defendants nothing. Under general principles of law, an
accused does not exculpate himself from a crime by showing that another
committed a similar crime, either before or after the alleged commission
of the crime by the accused. . . .[91]

It is no defense in the view of this Tribunal to assert that international crimes were committed by an adversary. . . .[92]

The defendants have offered testimony and supported it by official
documents which tend to establish that the Union of Soviet Socialist
Republics entered into a treaty with Germany in August 1939, which
contains secret clauses whereby not only did Russia consent to Hitler's
invasion of Poland, but at least tacitly agreed to send its own armed
forces against that nation, and by it could demand and obtain its share
of the loot, and was given a free hand to swallow the little Baltic states
with whom it had then existing nonaggression treaties. The defense
asserts that Russia, being itself an aggressor and an accomplice to
Hitler's aggression, was a party and an accomplice to at least one of the
aggressions charged in this indictment, namely, that against Poland, and
therefore was legally inhibited from signing the London Charter and
enacting Control Council Law No. 10, and consequently both the
Charter and Law are invalid, and no prosecution can be maintained
under them.

The justifications, if any, which the Soviet Union may claim to have
had for its actions in this respect were not represented to this Tribunal.
But if we assume, arguendo, that Russia's action was wholly untenable
and its guilt as deep as that of the Third Reich, nevertheless, this cannot
in law avail the defendants or lessen the guilt of those of the Third

Reich who were themselves responsible. Neither the London Charter nor Control Council Law No. 10 did more than declare existing international law regarding aggressive wars and invasions. The Charter and Control Council Law No. 10 merely defined what offenses against international law should be the subject of judicial inquiry, formed the International Military Tribunal, and authorized the signatory powers to set up additional tribunals to try those charged with committing crimes against peace, war crimes, and crimes against humanity.

But even if it were true that the London Charter and Control Council Law No. 10 are legislative acts, making that a crime which before was not so recognized, would the defense argument be valid? It has never been suggested that a law duly passed becomes ineffective when it transpires that one of the legislators whose vote enacted it was himself guilty of the same practice or that he himself intended, in the future, to violate the law. . . .[93]

While the Tribunal placed no limitations on the scope of defense counsel's representations, as in justice it should not, it does not follow that everything was relevant to the issue in the case. It is only by hearing an argument that one can conclusively determine its materiality or lack of materiality. However, the Tribunal now decides, after hearing and analyzing all the evidence, that discussions in this case on the antewar relationship between Germany and Russia are immaterial. It further decides that representations on the postwar relationship between Russia and the rest of the world are equally irrelevant.

Although advancing the proposition that Russia signed a secret treaty with Germany prior to the Polish war, the defense said or presented nothing in the way of evidence to overcome the well considered conclusion of the International Military Tribunal that Germany started an aggressive war against Russia. On the basis of this finding alone, Russia's participation in the Allied Council which formulated Law No. 10 was legal and correct and in entire accordance with international law.[94]

In regard to the crime of indiscriminate bombing, where again the *tu quoque* "defense" was advanced, the Nuremberg Military Tribunal said:

Then it was submitted that the defendants must be exonerated from the charge of killing civilian populations since every Allied nation brought about the death of noncombatants through the instrumentality of bombing. Any person, who, without cause, strikes another may not later complain if the other in repelling the attack uses sufficient force to overcome the original adversary. That is fundamental law between nations as well.

It has already been adjudicated by a competent tribunal that Germany under its Nazi rulers started an aggressive war. The bombing of Berlin, Dresden, Hamburg, Cologne, and other German cities followed the bombing of London, Coventry, Rotterdam, Warsaw, and other Allied cities; the bombing of German cities succeeded in point of time, the acts discussed here. But even if it were assumed for the purpose of illustration that the Allies bombed German cities without Germans having bombed Allied cities, there still is no parallelism between an act of legitimate warfare, namely the bombing of a city, with a concomitant loss of civilian life, and the premeditated killing of all members of certain categories of the civilian population in occupied territory. . . .[95]

It is argued that the atom bombings of Hiroshima and Nagasaki in Japan and the aerial raids upon Dresden, Germany, in the final stages of the conflict afford a pattern for the conduct of modern war and a possible justification for the criminal acts of these defendants. We do not think the argument is sound. The unfortunate pattern adopted in the Second World War was set by Germany and its allies when hostilities were commenced. The methods of warfare employed at Rotterdam, Warsaw, Belgrade, Coventry, and Pearl Harbor can aptly be said to provide the sources of the alleged modern theory of total war. It is not our purpose to discuss the lawfulness of any of these events. We content ourselves with the statement that they can give no comfort to these defendants as recriminatory evidence.[96]

Finally, in regard to the treatment of prisoners of war, the Nuremberg Military Tribunals took the following view:

The fact that the enemy was using prisoners of war for unlawful work as the defendant testified does not make their use by the defendant lawful but may be considered in mitigation of punishment. . . .[97]

It is the opinion of this Tribunal . . . that the use of prisoners of war by regiments and forward units of command in a combat area constituted a use in a position of danger . . . The fact that similar use was made of German prisoners by the enemy is only a factor in mitigation and not in defense.[98]

Miss Arendt is confused not only about the legality of the Nuremberg trials but also about the legal basis of the Eichmann trial in Jerusalem. To the extent that she views the Eichmann trial as merely another "successor trial," she admits that Israel's jurisdiction was justified: "Once the Jews had a territory of their own, the State in [sic] Israel (in V, 108: 'the State of Israel'), they obviously had as much right to sit in judgment on the crimes committed against their people as the Poles had to judge crimes committed in Poland" (pp. 237-238). But she declares that because Israel was a signatory to the Genocide Convention, the court needed either "to establish an international tribunal or . . . to reformulate the territorial principle in such a way that it applied to Israel" (p. 241), basing her argument on Article VI of the Convention, which states: "Persons charged with genocide . . . shall be tried by a competent tribunal of the State in the territory of which the act was committed, or by such international penal tribunal as may have jurisdiction with respect to those Contracting Parties which shall have accepted its jurisdiction."[99] Straddling the issue, she writes: "Insofar as the victims were Jews, it was right and proper that a Jewish court should sit in judgment; but insofar as the crime was a crime against humanity, it needed an international tribunal to do justice to it" (p. 247).

The simple fact is that the Genocide Convention is not applicable to acts committed before its effective date. The purpose of the Convention was to create a solid legal basis for future application and thus to put an end to the recurring criticism of the Nuremberg Charter as *ex post facto* law. Not only was the Convention itself supposed to be applied to cases tried *in futuro* only, but it was supposed to operate only on incriminating acts that have taken place after the entry of the Convention into force. These facts are clearly stated in the judgment.[100]

The suggestions made by Miss Arendt on what the Jerusalem court should have done can only amuse the jurist. Since when are national courts entitled to "establish an international tribunal"? The national court, faced with an objection to its jurisdiction, has only two choices: either to reject such an objection and go on with the trial or to accept the objection and declare itself incompetent. There is no third choice. No less gratuitous is her suggestion that the court should have interpreted the territoriality principle as referring not to a territory but to the "space between individuals in a group whose members are bound to, and at the same time separated and protected from, each other by all kinds of relationships, based on a common language, religion, a common history, customs, and laws" (p. 241). By such a criterion, for example, Italy could claim jurisdiction over Italian emigrants with respect to crimes committed by them anywhere in the world. It is not difficult to see what a chaos of jurisdictions this would produce.

Miss Arendt's belief that international crimes belong to an international court[101]—i.e., that "the only proper court to try these crimes was an international tribunal" (p. 233)—is based on the mistaken assumption that international crimes come under international jurisdiction by their very nature. The Jerusalem court, well aware of the demands of international law, summarized the situation as follows:

. . . not only is it true that international law does not deny or limit the jurisdiction of individual States with respect to such crimes, but in fact quite the opposite is the case: in the absence of an International [Criminal] Court, international law depends on the legislative and judicial organs of each and every State. . . .[102]

The question of the criminal jurisdiction of States had already been dealt with in 1927 by the Permanent Court of International Justice in the Lotus case. In its judgment this court wrote:

Now one first and foremost restriction imposed by international law upon a State is that—failing the existence of a permissive rule to the contrary— it may not exercise its power in any form in the territory of another State. In this sense, jurisdiction is certainly territorial; it cannot be exercised by a State outside its territory except by virtue of a permissive rule derived from international custom or from a convention. It does not, however, follow that international law prohibits a State from exercising jurisdiction in its own territory, in respect of any case which relates to acts which have taken place abroad, and in which it cannot rely on some permissive rule of international law. Such a view would only be tenable if international law contained a general prohibition to States to extend the application of their laws and the jurisdiction of their courts to persons, property and acts outside their territory, and if, as an exception to this general prohibition, it allowed States to do so in certain specific cases. But this is certainly not the case under international law as it stands at present. Far from laying down a general prohibition to the effect that States may not extend the application of their laws and the jurisdiction of their courts to persons, property and acts outside their territory, it leaves them in this respect a wide measure of discretion which is only limited in certain cases by prohibitive rules; as regards other cases, every State remains free to adopt the principles which it regards as best and most suitable.

This discretion left to States by international law explains the great variety of rules which they have been able to adopt without objections or complaints on the part of other States; it is in order to remedy the difficulties resulting from such variety that efforts have been made for many years past, both in Europe and America, to prepare conventions, the effect of which would be precisely to limit the discretion at present left to States in this respect by international law, thus making good the existing lacunae in respect of jurisdiction or removing the conflicting jurisdictions arising from the diversity of the principles adopted by the various States. . . .[103]

Though it is true that in all systems of law the principle of the territorial character of criminal law is fundamental, it is equally true that all or nearly all these systems of law extend their action to offences committed outside the territory of the State which adopts them, and they do so in a way which may vary from State to State. *The territoriality of criminal law therefore, is not an absolute principle of international law and by no means coincides with territorial sovereignty.* . . .[104]

. . . it is certain that the courts of many countries, even of countries which have given their criminal legislation a strictly territorial character, interpret criminal law in the sense that offences, the authors of which at the moment of commission are in the territory of another State, are nevertheless to be regarded as having been committed in the national territory, if one of the constituent elements of the offence, and more especially *its effects,* have taken place there.[105]

The authority of this judgment is sometimes questioned on the ground that—the members of the court being equally divided—the decision was adopted by the casting vote of the President. However, a careful study of the dissenting opinions, especially when considered retroactively and in the light of the particular background created by World War II and its aftermath, is more likely to strengthen the authority of the judgment than to weaken it, particularly in view of the admission by the dissenting judges of the legitimacy of exceptions. A few examples may illustrate this statement. Judge Loder of The Netherlands based his dissenting opinion on the position that—

The criminal law of a State . . . *cannot* [underlined by the Judge] extend to offences committed by a foreigner in foreign territory, without infringing upon the sovereign rights of the foreign State concerned.[106]

Does this hold good also for crimes committed in an "area of lawlessness" characterized by territorial, political, and ideological discontinuity? Judge Nyholm of Denmark wrote:

It will, however, be well to remember that international law is liable to continual variations and that there would seem to be a tendency towards a relaxation in the strict application of this principle [*scil.,* the principle of territoriality].[107]

Judge Nyholm's contention is borne out by changes in the treatment of this problem in different editions of Oppenheim's authoritative treatise, *International Law*. The third edition of 1920,[108] quoted in Lord Finlay's dissenting opinion,[109] and the eighth edition of 1955 (edited by H. Lauterpacht),[110] show identical wording in posing the question—

. . . whether States have a right to exercise jurisdiction over acts of foreigners committed in foreign countries, and whether the home State of such an alien has a duty to acquiesce in the latter's punishment in case he comes into the power of these States.

But how different the answers! While the third edition, admitting that the question is "controversial," flatly stated that it "ought to be answered in the negative," the eighth edition states: "Some answer this question in the negative," and then observes:

This is probably the accurate view with regard to some cases. But it is not a view which, consistently with the practice of States and with common sense, can be rigidly adopted in all cases.

None of the dissenting judges could have foreseen the Nazi regime and its implications.[111]

Miss Arendt compounds confusion by adding still another, different, conclusion: "it was Eichmann's de facto statelessness, *and nothing else*, that enabled the Jerusalem court to sit in judgment on him" (p. 219). In fact, Eichmann's claim to German nationality was stated by the defense counsel, Dr. Servatius, in the fifth session. The Attorney General took no exception to this claim, and neither did the authorities of the Federal Republic of Germany. But it was not this imaginary "de facto statelessness" that enabled the court to try him; it was, rather, the factual presence of Eichmann in Israel. On the one hand, Miss Arendt expresses dissatisfaction with Germany's refusal to grant Eichmann "the customary protection *due its citizens abroad*" (p. 219), and on the other hand proclaims Eichmann to be a *de facto* stateless person (as if there were two categories, *de jure* and *de facto* statelessness) having no claim to such "protection."

Here is what really happened: Subsequent to Eichmann's transfer to Israel, the Eichmann case (*der Fall Eichmann*) was discussed by the German Bundestag in a number of sessions,[112] although the subject of the debates was not so much Eichmann himself but rather the general policy of obtaining extradition to Germany of German war criminals who had fled abroad. These debates, and the statements made at these occasions by the Federal Minister of

Justice, Dr. Fritz Schäffer, reveal (1) that Germany was interested in obtaining from Israel for utilization in future German war crimes trials any relevant information that might come to light in the course of the trial of Eichmann in Israel, and (2) that Germany was prepared to try Eichmann in case Israel would not do so. Nowhere in the debates is there any reference to Eichmann's "German nationality" or to "statelessness."[113]

It might be added that no reference to Eichmann's alleged statelessness can be found in the judgment of the Administrative Court in Cologne, delivered on April 4, 1961, in the case of Dr. Servatius *vs.* the Federal Republic of Germany.[114] The matter under consideration by the court was whether or not the Federal Republic of Germany was under legal obligation to pay the fees for Eichmann's defense. It is significant that while the Administrative Court expressed its doubts regarding Eichmann's German citizenship and was rather inclined to consider him an Austrian citizen, it reached its decision without ruling on the validity of his claim to German citizenship.

Concerning the question of jurisdiction, the eminent jurist Julius Stone, Challis Professor of International Law and Jurisprudence at the University of Sydney, had the following to say in his report to the Australian Section of the International Commission of Jurists:

While in a fuller account I would embrace two or three minor criticisms of the organization and procedure of the trial, my general conclusion obviously was that the trial has been a fair one based on lawful jurisdiction. And because I myself entertained criticisms before I attended the Court, which I now think groundless, I have wondered since my return from Jerusalem why all of us, Jew or Gentile, have tended at moments to be rather carping in a technical way about the whole business. My analysis of myself, which I put forward tentatively as a rational if somewhat Freudian explanation of a phenomenon not easily explicable in other ways, is that we all knew of the nature of the horrors which the evidence would thrust before our eyes for weeks and months in the press, on the radio and on television, and that subconsciously we resisted it. Yet all of us also felt a certain guilt or at least obligation towards the victims of these crimes, if only in terms—"There, but for the grace of God . . ." And we felt, therefore, a duty at least to be willing to learn about their sufferings.

From the struggle that went on between these two motives, of duty to learn and resistance to the duty to learn, we subconsciously try to escape by finding reasons why the Israeli Court ought not to try Eich-mann. If, as it were, the Israel Court were not entitled to try, then we were not obliged to listen and learn. I suspect that many of the more baseless technical objections to the trial are merely rationalizations of our natural resistance to apprehending the details of these years of inhumanity.[115]

The Jerusalem court based its jurisdiction on the Israel law of 1950, which, contrary to Miss Arendt's contention (p. 233), is not a juridically retroactive law, being based on generally accepted principles of international law. In the judgment the court wrote:

Our jurisdiction in this case is based on the Nazis and Nazi Collaborators (Punishment) law, a statute the provisions of which are unequivocal. The court has to give effect to the law of the Knesset, and we cannot entertain the contention that this law conflicts with the principles of international law. . . .

But we have also carefully studied the sources of international law, including the numerous authorities cited by learned counsel for the defense in the thorough written brief upon which he based his oral pleadings, and by the learned Attorney General in his comprehensive oral pleadings, and we have failed to find any foundation for the contention that the Israel law is in conflict with the principles of international law. On the contrary, we have reached the conclusion that the law in question conforms to the best traditions of the law of nations. . . .[116]

We have said that the crimes dealt with in this case are not crimes under Israel law alone, but are in substance offenses against the law of nations. . . . The crimes in question were not freely created by the legislature which enacted the [Israel] Nazis and Nazi Collaborators (Punishment) law, 5710/1950. Rather, the crimes defined in the law were in accordance with the precise pattern of international regulations and conventions that have served to define crimes under international law.[117]

In its concurring opinion, the Israel Supreme Court wrote:

(1) The crimes of which the Appellant was convicted, which were defined by the [Israel] law [of 1950], can be seen to have always been considered crimes under international law—actions forbidden under the law of nations, and entailing individual liability;

(2) The uniquely universal character of these crimes vests in each and every State the right to try and punish anyone who had a hand in them.[118]

Concerning the Israel law, Miss Arendt writes: "the Nazis and Nazi Collaborators (Punishment) Law of 1950 is wrong, it is in contradiction to what actually happened, it does not cover the facts" (p. 249). This statement is absurd. First, she does not explain what she means by "wrong." A law may not be characterized as "right" or "wrong," with the possible exception of laws inspired by immoral objectives, which Miss Arendt never claims this law to be. Second, how can a law be "in contradiction to what actually happened"? Laws are not narratives of past history; they simply prescribe the rules according to which the court measures the facts. Nowhere does Miss Arendt claim that the facts considered by the Jerusalem court were not measurable by the law. Third, she does not explain how the main purpose of the trial could have been achieved (as she expressly says it was on p. 250) with a deficient law.

She discusses (p. 85) the application of Section 10 of the Israel law to Eichmann, although this Section in no way applies to him, as can be seen from its text, which reads in full:

If *a persecuted person* has done or omitted to do any act, such act or omission constituting an offense under this Law, the court shall release him from criminal responsibility—

(*a*) if he did or omitted to do the act in order to save himself from the danger of immediate death threatening him and the Court is satisfied that he did his best to avert the consequences of the act or omission; or

(*b*) if he did or omitted to do the act with intent to avert consequences more serious than those which resulted from the act or omission, and actually averted them;

these provisions shall not, however, apply to an act or omission constituting an offence under Section 1 or 2(f).

Section 2(f) refers to murder, while Section 1 reads:

1. (*a*) A person who has committed one of the following offences—
    (1) done, during the period of the Nazi regime, in an enemy territory, an act constituting a crime against the Jewish people;
    (2) done, during the period of the Nazi regime, in an enemy country, an act constituting a crime against humanity;
    (3) done, during the period of the Second World War, in an enemy country, an act constituting a war crime,
    is liable to the death penalty.
    (*b*) In this section—
    "crime against the Jewish people" means any of the following

acts, committed with intent to destroy the Jewish people in whole or in part:

(1) killing Jews;

(2) causing serious bodily or mental harm to Jews;

(3) placing Jews in living conditions calculated to bring about their physical destruction;

(4) imposing measures intended to prevent births among Jews;

(5) forcibly transferring Jewish children to another national or religious group;

(6) destroying or desecrating Jewish religious or cultural assets or values;

(7) inciting to hatred of Jews;

"crime against humanity" means any of the following acts: murder, extermination, enslavement, starvation or deportation and other inhumane acts committed against any civilian population, and persecution on national, racial, religious or political grounds:

"war crime" means any of the following acts: murder, ill-treatment or deportation to forced labor or for any other purpose, of civilian population of or in occupied territory; murder or ill-treatment of prisoners of war or persons on the seas; killing of hostages; plunder of public or private property; wanton destruction of cities, towns or villages, and devastation not justified by military necessity.[119]

Eichmann was prosecuted under Section 1 of the law, and hence Section 10 did not apply.

Miss Arendt expresses surprise (p. 87) that the defense counsel, Dr. Servatius, did not "fall back on the argument of superior orders." (She admits that application of the "superior orders" plea in Eichmann's case "was a very remote possibility in view of the enormity of the crime.") But Section 8 of the Israel law, referring to Article 19 of the 1936 Palestine Criminal Code Ordinance, expressly excluded this plea in connection with crimes of the type imputed to Eichmann. Dr. Servatius did not use the "superior orders" argument because he knew the law.

In the Sassen Papers,[120] Eichmann expressly repudiated the invocation of the superior orders plea: "I thought it over," he told Sassen, "and when I realized the necessity for it, I carried it through with all the fanaticism that an old National Socialist would expect from himself and which my superiors, no doubt, expected of me. They found me, according to their experience, to be the right man

in the right place. . . . This I say today, in 1957, to my own disadvantage. I could make it easy for myself. I could now claim it
was an order I had to carry out because of my oath of allegiance,
but this would be a cheap excuse, not compatible with my code of
ethics."

Another error regarding the Israel law is Miss Arendt's statement
that the death penalty was mandatory in Eichmann's case (p. 225).
The District Court found that the mandatory nature of the death
penalty provided in the 1950 law had been invalidated by the 1954
amendment of the Criminal Code.[121] Under this interpretation the
judges imposed the death sentence not because of its mandatory
nature in the law but as a just punishment.

Miss Arendt's confusion concerning the legal background of the
trial is further exemplified in her statement (p. 22) that the "indict-
ment implied" that Eichmann had acted out of "base motives."
Leaving aside the question of Eichmann's motives (discussed in
Chapter 1), it is to be noted that "base motives" are nowhere
referred to or implied in Israel's Criminal Code Ordinance. It is
interesting that a "base motives" clause does appear in the German
Criminal Code,[122] but the West German Supreme Court
(*Bundesgerichtshof*) held that in cases involving the destruction of
European Jewry *there is no need to require evidence that the in-
criminated persons acted on base motives (niedrige Beweggründe).*
Thus, for example, in the Georg Schlosser case, the court held:

The argumentation (*Ausführungen*) of the lower court (*Landgericht*)
denying the presence of base motives ignores the fact that the act of
killing was carried out as part of the National Socialist extermination
measures against the Jews. This extermination action was in its entirety
determined by the base motivation that every Jew is because of his race
an *Untermensch* who has no right whatsoever to exist. The contempt
of man characterizing this motivation is so clearly shown by the way in
which the action (*Vorgehen*) against the Jews was implemented that it
can be considered all but impossible that a reasonably sane person, even
if he was merely superficially acquainted with the National Socialist
incitement against the Jews (*die nationalsozialistische Judenhetze*) and
with its ever increasing repressive measures, did not comprehend it. He
who with this knowledge participated personally (*selbst*) in this extermination action did, as perpetrator, as a rule endorse (*machte sich . . .
zu eigen*) these base motives or, as accomplice, promote an act which
he recognized as killing out of base motives.[123]

Crimes Against Humanity and Crimes Against the Jewish People

The substitution of "crimes against humanity" for "crimes against the Jewish people," advocated by Miss Arendt (p. 240), would hardly do justice to the special place of the "Jewish question" in the totality of Nazi doctrine and practice, and to the particular methods employed by the Nazis for dealing with Jews as compared with other racial, national, or political groups. It may therefore be useful to give a partial answer to two questions: (1) What place did the Jews occupy in Nazi ideology? (2) To what extent can the treatment of Jews be compared to that of other groups?

The prominent place of the "Jewish question" in Nazi doctrine in the "years of struggle" (*Kampfjahre*) has been highlighted by one of Hitler's district party leaders, Albert Krebs, in a book written fourteen years after the end of World War II:

In spite of enormous (*grösster*) soldierly achievements and a succession of splendid victories, Germany lost the war in 1918 because the "German" parties, led and misguided (*verführten*) by Jews and other supra-national powers, had stabbed the fighting front in the back. Subsequently, in Versailles, the same supra-national powers transformed Wilson's peace of conciliation (*Verständigungsfriede*) into a peace of *Diktat* which through annexations and demands for reparations had the purpose of slowly strangling the still strong German people. At the same time, in order to ensure this destruction, the leadership of world Jewry utilized as the shock troops of chaos the Communist Party, which had come out of a Russia subjugated in the October Bolshevist Revolution, while inside Germany the parties of compliance[124] (*Erfüllungsparteien*), because of their weakness or because they, too, followed instructions from above, brought about the pauperization (*Verelendung*) of the masses, thus playing into the hands of our enemies in the East and West. For this reason, no matter whom, or what, the National Socialist fought—Versailles, capitalism, the Red Front Fighters, the department stores, the democratic politicians of compliance—he always fought the same enemy. To destroy this enemy meant to end German misery with a single blow. It was, therefore, wrong to become involved too deeply with one individual problem—socialism, for instance. This only diverted attention from the real objective [*Kampfziel*]. "What is socialism?" Hitler roared at me in 1930. "A Jewish invention devised to set the German people against each other."[125]

In the years following the *Machtergreifung* (seizure of power),
the Nazis had successfully acted in accordance with the letter and
spirit of this doctrine.

As for other "races" (that is, nationalities and peoples), particular targets of Nazi wrath were the Poles, among the Western Slavs;
and the Russians, among the Eastern Slavs. Among the Southern
Slavs, the Serbs, particularly those living in Croatia, were subjected
to the cruel wrath of the local Fascists.[126]

What was the Nazi policy in regard to the Poles?[127] There were,
to be sure, numerous individual and wholesale executions of Poles:
"actions" of physical destruction against the intelligentsia, the
Catholic clergy, and the national leadership in general.[128] But,
fortunately, there was no extermination campaign against the Polish
people as a whole. This notwithstanding, the total civilian dead in
Poland during the war and occupation was estimated by Polish
authorities immediately after the war at 5,384,000 Polish citizens, of
whom 3,200,000 were Jews.[129] Those Poles who were considered
wholly or partly of German stock were assimilated by way of the
Deutsche Volksliste (German Ethnic Register); others, not of German stock but considered "racially desirable," were condemned to
compulsory "re-Germanization" (*Wiedereindeutschung*). The great
majority of the Poles were to be enslaved in the service of the
"master race." The Government-General was, at least temporarily,
destined to serve as a reservoir of slave laborers, deprived of a
leadership of their own and kept culturally on an elementary school
level. Such was the program for the Government-General outlined
by Hitler on October 2, 1940, as recorded by one of his top aides,
Martin Bormann:

They [the Poles] would have to export their own labor (*Arbeitskraft*),
i.e., themselves, as it were, in order to subsist. . . . We must keep in
mind, under all circumstances, that there must be no Polish masters
(*keine polnischen Herren*); where there are Polish masters, they would
have to be killed off (*umgebracht*), however cruel that may sound. . . .
The Government-General is a Polish reservation, a huge Polish labor
camp. . . . The Government [General] is the pool of unskilled labor
(*Ausleih-Zentrale für ungelernte Arbeiter*), particularly of agricultural
laborers.[130]

A German historian makes the following comment in connection
with this quotation: "What emerges from [Hitler's] pronouncements

is a concept of colonial exploitation by a master-race presented in the most primitive terms, such as has probably never existed in history, at least not on a conscious level."[131]

Even exploitation might not have been the last word of Nazi anti-Polish fury. In a speech made by Himmler on March 15, 1940, to the commandants of the camps in occupied Poland, he foresaw "the disappearance of the Poles from the world" (*Dann verschwinden alle Polen aus der Welt*) and "the extirpation (*Ausrottung*) of the *Polentum*," and he expressly formulated the mission of the German people as "the destruction of all Poles" (*alle Polen zu vernichten*).[132] Happily, these sinister plans did not come to fruition.

There were other, slightly less cruel, voices. Thus, Dr. Erhard Wetzel, a high official in the Ministry of Occupied Eastern Territories, wrote:

It goes without saying, that one cannot resolve the Polish problem by liquidating the Poles as is being done with the Jews. Such a solution would brand the German people into the far future and would cost us sympathy on all sides, especially since other peoples might envisage that they would be similarly treated at a future time.[133]

The Draft Memorandum of March 1943, drawn up (after German reverses on the Eastern front) by Dr. Gollert for the Göbbels Ministry,[134] throws additional light on German intentions in regard to the Poles. In substance, it says that the Government-General is eventually to be incorporated into the Reich. It suggests three possible solutions as to what to do with the Polish population of fifteen million: (1) Germanization of the Poles; (2) their evacuation; (3) their extermination: "Certainly it can be justified before history to resort to such extreme measures for biological reasons, as, for instance, was necessary in the case of the Jews. But to eliminate an alien people of fifteen million simply in this way is not worthy of a cultured nation." All three possibilities are, however, rejected by Gollert, for various reasons. Instead, he proposes to solve the problem by dividing the Polish population into three categories, each of which should be treated in a different way: (1) those who should be Germanized eventually; (2) those who are important as workers, who should be allowed to stay in the Government-General; (3) those in whom the Germans are not interested at all. "In this third category of about two to three million belong all those who have no value for us Germans. These are not only the Polish fanatics, who, of course, will have to be extirpated completely, but all asocial elements, all the sick and other persons. . . . It will be impossible to avoid extreme measures in regard to this third category. . . ." Gollert goes on to state that if these steps are approved, the Polish population should be familiarized with them immediately by means of appropriate propaganda.

Miss Arendt speculates that "had the Germans won the war, the Poles would have suffered the same fate as the Jews—genocide" (pp. 198 f.). While this is arguable, her "proof" is unfounded. She says: "This is no mere conjecture; the Poles in Germany were already being forced to wear a distinguishing badge in which the 'P' replaced the Jewish star, which as we have seen was always the first measure to be taken by the police in instituting the process of destruction." (See also the paperback edition, p. 216.) Two comments suffice: First, the process of destruction was not "always" preceded by the badge. Thus, for example, the victims of the first wave of *Einsatzgruppen* in the Soviet Union wore no Star of David, and the execution of Poles in Poland was carried out without preceding stigmatization. Second, the "P" badge for Polish forced laborers and the *Ostabzeichen* (an embroidered square bearing the inscription "OST") for Soviet citizens were not the first step in the physical destruction of these peoples, the great majority of whom remained in their own countries and did not wear humiliating badges. Instead, the badges were introduced as a means of preventing any social intercourse between the German "*Übermenschen*" and the Slavic "*Untermenschen*" in Germany.[135]

Miss Arendt states that "the Nazis had exterminated a large proportion of the Jewish intelligentsia at the same time that they killed Polish intellectuals and members of the professions—in marked contrast, incidentally, to their policy in Western Europe, where they tended to save prominent Jews in order to exchange them for German civilian internees or prisoners of war. . . ." (p. 109). Neither her facts nor her interpretations have any basis. There was in Poland a savage "action" against non-Jewish intellectuals, without whom the Poles might forever be rendered "inferior."[136] The Jews, however, were *all* destined for destruction, though at an early stage of this process some individual Nazi "actions" took place on the initiative of the local *Führers* against special groups (e.g., children, elderly people, sick people) or—much rarer—against members of certain professions.[137] *All* Jews, including converted Jews, irrespective of profession and education, were herded into the ghettos and eventually destined for extermination qua Jews. The concerted action against the Polish intelligentsia and the individual actions in some places against Jewish professionals did not take place "at the same time." In addition, there is no record of an exchange of "prominent Jews" for Germans, in Western Europe or anywhere else, although there were instances of exchange of individual Jews (of no particular standing) for individual Germans.[138]

As regards the treatment of the Russian population, the most important regulation was the Commissar Order (*Kommissarbefehl*), distributed in the early part of June 1941, shortly before the invasion of the U.S.S.R.[139] This order was meant to apply to Soviet territory occupied by the Nazis. Whatever the status of the Final Solution was at that time,[140] for the next six months—between the invasion of the U.S.S.R. and the Wannsee Conference—the extermination of Jews in these territories was carried out under the authority of this order. While it is true that the victims of the *Kommissarbefehl* were "by no means only Jews" (p. 94), the difference, in its application to Jews and non-Jews, is a radical one.

The Commissar Order was implemented under a number of Operational Orders, the first and most important of which was Operational Order No. 8 of July 17, 1941.[141] "All Jews" is the formula used in this Operational Order, whereas nine specific categories are listed for the non-Jewish population—for example, "all important officials of the State and the Party," and "agitators and fanatical Communists."[142] On September 12, 1941, Heydrich issued a supplementary directive to Operational Order No. 8, in which he urged the screening teams to be more discriminating.[143] In this directive he told his men that an engineer was not necessarily a Bolshevik, and that intellectuals, in terms of the order, were "primarily professional revolutionaries, writers, newspaper men, and employees of the Comintern." In regard to non-Russian nationalities, he wrote: "Ukrainians, Byelorussians, Azerbaijanians, Armenians, Northern Caucasians, Georgians, members of the Turkic nations (*Turkvölker*) are to be designated simply (*schlechthin*) as suspect and thereupon treated according to instructions only if they actually are fanatical Bolsheviks, political commissars, or otherwise dangerous elements." Heydrich's concern that his killing commandos might confuse non-Jews with Jews and by mistake kill the wrong people is demonstrated by a passage from the same document in which he says: "It should be noted that the Turkic people in particular frequently look Jewish and that circumcision alone does not necessarily constitute proof of Jewish descent (for instance, Muslims)."

The subsequent treatment by Nazi Germany of Soviet prisoners of war and civilians was appalling. They were pitilessly exploited as slave laborers. Of some 5,754,000 Soviet prisoners of war, barely one million survived the camps in Germany.[144] There are no official statistics concerning the fate of another 2,792,669 *Ostarbeiter* in Germany, but it is safe to guess that not all of them returned home.[145] Nazi plans concerning the future, as outlined in the *Generalplan Ost*,[146] foresaw mass population transfers and perpetual enslavement of Russian populations. The anti-Soviet policy was complicated and partly neutralized by power politics, the Communist issue, and the "nationalities policies," which were intended to favor other nationalities at the expense of the Russians. There is no published evidence of any Nazi plans for wholesale extermination of Russians.

Equally significant were the differences between the Nazi treatment of Jews and of Communists outside the Soviet Union. Anticommunism was the foremost *political* tenet in Nazi philosophy, and Communists were persecuted in Germany from the very start of the Nazi regime. Communists were the first inmates in German concentration camps; for a time they were the largest single group in those camps.[147] But, to the Nazis, "Aryan" Communists remained racially acceptable individuals and were looked upon as at least potential converts to National Socialism.[148] The Jewish concentration camp prisoners, on the other hand, were "on the lowest level of the camp's social order, subject to the contempt and brutality not only of the SS but also of their fellow prisoners, who sometimes shamelessly exploited their utter powerlessness."[149]

An illustration of the differences in Nazi policy toward Jews and Communists is furnished by no less an authority than Himmler. In his speech before the SS generals on October 4, 1943, at Poznań, in which he so candidly discussed the extermination of the Jews as a vital necessity, he also talked about the Communists, no doubt just as candidly.[150] The Communists in the Reich, he boasted, have been successfully dealt with, their leaders, "like most of the criminals," having been put into concentration camps. There is no mention of extermination in regard to them; Himmler was satisfied with their imprisonment. It is true that many Communists, caught as resistance fighters in occupied countries, were shot or otherwise murdered. But there was no order, published or secret, calling for the extermination of non-Soviet Communists as a group.

In her testimony before the Jerusalem court, Raya Kagan, who worked in the Auschwitz Office of Vital Statistics, where the deaths of prisoners were recorded, stated that in the files of murdered "Aryan" prisoners a cause of death, albeit fictitious, always had to be entered. But in the files of Jews who had been gassed, only the stereotyped expression "SB" (*Sonderbehandelt*—"given special treatment") was entered, and these files were subsequently destroyed. And notwithstanding the passion of the Nazis for sticking punctiliously to the rules of bureaucratic procedure, those Jews who were taken to the gas chambers right from the train were not even entered in the camp registry. Thus Communists, though enemies of the Nazi State, were still considered human beings whose deaths had to be recorded, while the Jewish "subhumans" were allowed to disappear without leaving a trace. It is a supreme irony that those Jews who had committed a crime or an offense—i.e., Jews who were not mere Jews but also criminal offenders—were treated as something better than the other Jews. "They were not included in the transports and deportations. They were not treated as *Transport-juden* [transport-Jews], and therefore during selections the cards of these Jews would be removed from the selection lot."[151]

There were also profound differences between Nazi treatment of Jews and of Gypsies,[152] though the fate of the latter has often been compared to that of the Jews. The Nazi attitude toward the Gypsies vacillated between two extremes. At one extreme was a certain fascination with the supposed Aryan racial purity of Gypsies; no less a racist than the Nazi ideologist Alfred Rosenberg expressed such fascination.[153] An opposite point of view held that the Gypsies were subhuman and ought to be done away with. As early as 1935, members of the SS office on racial policies discussed a plan to exterminate the Gypsies by herding them on board ships and drowning them.[154] In the case of the Jews, there was never vacillation and never an alternative extreme.

Nazi activities vis-à-vis the Gypsies were directed at all times at those in Germany or in German-controlled territory (in particular, in Poland). No attempts were made to carry out anti-Gypsy policies on an all-European basis. Even Germany's satellites, Romania and Hungary, which contained large Gypsy populations, were not asked to take any measures against these populations. There were, however, sporadic actions of considerable violence against Gypsies in other parts of Europe. Thus, Mobile Killing Unit (*Einsatzgruppe*) D, responsible for the physical destruction of the Jews in the Crimea, included among its victims Gypsies as well.

At least three factors motivated the Nazis to persecute the Gypsies: (1) "crime prevention"; (2) the "asocial behavior" of the victims; (3) the "racial inferiority" of the victims. The racial factor was the only one officially referred to in the Nazi persecution of the Jews.

Neither the 1920 Nazi Party program nor the Nuremberg Laws of 1935 foreshadowed discrimination against the Gypsies. Discriminatory treatment by the Nazi regime started not with its seizure of power but at the end of the sixth year of the regime, in December 1938, with the ordinance *Zur Bekämpfung der Zigeunerplage* ("To Counter the Gypsy Pestilence"). Subsequently, in October 1939, the "cleansing" of "Greater Germany" of all Gypsies was planned; it was partially carried out a year later.

Mass deportation of German Gypsies to Auschwitz took place in the early part of 1943. At the Auschwitz train depot, they were not subjected to selections of fit and unfit for work, with the result that no one was gassed immediately on arrival. The gassing of Gypsy children and adults unfit for work started some two years after the gassing of Jews, and lasted one month.[155]

While exact statistics are still not available,[156] it is estimated that from 20 to 45 per cent of the European Gypsy population perished. In Poland, there are now approximately as many Gypsies as Jews,[157] whereas before the war the size of the Gypsy population was known to be a small fraction of the size of the Jewish population.

There is another unique aspect to the Nazi treatment of Jews. Throughout the war the Nazis carried out a systematic campaign of destruction against Jewish children, gassing them in the extermination camps and carrying out "actions" against them in the ghettos. Although the German wrath also extended at times to children of other peoples—notably to Gypsy children during one month of gassing in Auschwitz, and to Czech children deported from the unhappy village of Lidice[158]—the sustained fury of Nazi brutality was reserved for Jewish children alone. The following three brief accounts give an idea of what a *Kinderaktion* in a ghetto was like.[159]

Ilya Ehrenburg, writing during the war, described what took place in Stavropol in August 1942:

At first, they [the Gestapo] said that children over eight years old were to report. Then they told the assembled women to bring all children "for registration"; and they murdered the children . . . [160]

In Kovno, an "action" took place in the ghetto at the end of March 1944:

As soon as the Gestapo men and their helpers, the Vlasov men,[161] had broken in upon the ghetto, they went about their work with enthusiasm. From every corner they dragged children, and old and sick people, out of the houses and loaded them into buses with covered windows. The buses then were driven out of the ghetto. The wailing and screaming penetrated to the very midst of the heavens.

Trying to drown out the cries of the children and of the mothers who had been forced to drag their little ones with their own hands up to the buses, the Gestapo blared record music in the cruising buses.

If mothers would refuse near the buses to give up their children, they were set upon by specially trained dogs, which would attack them wildly and bite them until they would lose consciousness and let their children fall out of their hands. The Gestapo men would then murderously throw the children into the buses.

Mothers who stubbornly held on to their children were shot on the spot or thrown into the cars along with the children.[162]

In Vilna, an "action" against approximately 200 children took place in the military labor blocks *Heereskraftpark* (H.K.P.) and *Kailis* on the eve of Passover, March 27, 1944. According to Dworzecki, the children "were transported to a German hospital in Cracow. Some of the children had their blood removed to provide transfusions for Germans."[163]

The Jewish situation during the war, even when compared with the treatment of Poles and Russians, Communists and Gypsies, was unique for these reasons: (1) The destructive will of the Nazis was aimed at the totality of Jews, while it was directed at only a part of other groups. (2) The Final Solution for the Jews was to be achieved immediately, during the war, whereas decisions on the ultimate fate of the others were postponed till after victory. (3)

Hitler's war against the Jews had priority over his war against all other groups. (4) In the Jewish case alone, there was an absence of inhibitions, conflicting purposes, and compromises, and a complete disregard for rational considerations, which did have a part in Nazi persecution of non-Jews.

Concluding Remarks

In all discussions that touch on legal problems, Miss Arendt displays unfamiliarity with her subject. She knows neither the present status of international criminal law nor its history and development. She is unaware of the criteria for jurisdiction and for solving conflicts of jurisdiction. She has no clear idea of the way in which new law emerges, or of the function of law in national and international society. She misreads and misinterprets the Israel law under which Eichmann was tried, and she fails to comprehend the basis for, and factual history of, the war crimes trials in general.

In view of her own admission to being a layman in the field, one can only wonder why she took it upon herself to attack the work and thought of competent jurists who distinguished themselves in advancing the rule of law and the principles of justice in the international community.

3

The Eichmann Trial

Purpose of the Trial

After stating that "the purpose of a trial is to render justice, and nothing else" (p. 232), Miss Arendt concedes that the "main purpose—to prosecute and to defend, to judge and to punish Adolf Eichmann—was achieved" (p. 250). She is quick, however, to condemn the trial for "failures and shortcomings" (p. 246), and to reproach the court for, among other things, never "rising to the challenge of the unprecedented" (p. 241), for "the extreme reluctance . . . to break fresh ground" (p. 241), and for not "coming to grips" with "fundamental issues" (p. 251)—namely, with political, moral, and legal issues of the broadest nature. This she says despite her own earlier statement concerning the procedure of the court: "Justice demands . . . that all other questions of seemingly greater import . . . be left in abeyance" (p. 3).

The Israel court conducted itself properly; it obeyed the demands of justice. The court did not assume the role of creator: it did not create procedure; it did not create legal terminology; and it did not seek to devise its own system of justice, as Miss Arendt would like it to have done. Nor did it allow itself to undertake excursions into areas of speculative thought, into the broader reaches of history, politics, and morality, beyond the sphere of proper judicial activity. The judgment of the District Court defined the scope of the trial with great care, and the opening sections of this judgment could serve as a model statement of the limitations of the judicial process. The rest of the judgment provides an excellent illustration of the principles embodied in the introduction. The court wrote:

Adolf Eichmann was arraigned before this court on charges of unsurpassed gravity relating to crimes against the Jewish people, crimes against humanity, and war crimes. The period of Hitler's rule in Germany and in Europe serves as the historical background for the crimes attributed to him, and the different counts of the indictment encompass within them the Catastrophe that befell the Jewish people during that time— a historical event saturated with blood and anguish, which will live in memory to the end of time. This is not the first occasion on which the Catastrophe has been made the subject of proceedings in a court of law. It was dealt with extensively before the International Military Tribunal in Nuremberg, at the trial of the foremost among the major war criminals, and also in several of the Subsequent Trials. However, this time the Catastrophe has been placed at the center of the proceedings, and it is this feature that sets apart this trial from all those which have preceded it. Hence the inclination, evident both in and out of court, to broaden the scope: there could be sensed a desire, easily understandable in itself, to present within the framework of this trial a comprehensive and exhaustive historical account of the Catastrophe, and in the course of this to emphasize also the outstanding manifestations of heroism displayed by the ghetto fighters, the insurgents in the death camps, and the Jewish partisans. There were those too who sought to conceive of this trial as a platform for the investigation of searching questions— questions newly raised by the Catastrophe and others long since raised that have now reappeared and been reawakened with increased intensity in the wake of the unprecedented cataclysm which overtook with fury the Jewish people and the entire world midway through the twentieth century. How could it happen in the full light of day? Why did this great evil come from the Germans? Could the Nazis have achieved their evil design were it not for the help given by other peoples among whom the Jews lived? Could the Catastrophe have been averted even in part had the Allies displayed greater willingness to help the persecuted Jews? Did the Jewish people in the free world do everything in its power to be aroused and arouse others to the aid of its brethren? What are the psychological and social origins of the mass hate called "anti-Semitism"? Can this long-standing disease be cured, and by what means? What must the Jews and the other peoples learn from all these things, and what must every human being learn in his relations to his fellow man? And more questions of various sorts, that cannot even all be listed.

The path of the court in the midst of this storm of bewildering questions has been and remains clear: It may not be enticed by the temptation to be carried into provinces where it does not belong. The judicial process has methods of its own, fixed by law, and these are immutable, whatever the subject of the trial may be; otherwise, we would impair the course of justice and judicial deliberation—which must be carefully watched over, being in its own right an important social and educational value—and the trial would resemble a rudderless ship tossed about by the waves.

The purpose of every criminal trial is to investigate the truth of the charges brought by the prosecution against the defendant and, if the defendant is convicted, to sentence him justly. Whatever has to be examined to attain these aims must be examined in the trial, and whatever is foreign to these aims must be excluded from the deliberations; a court of law is prohibited from venturing to exceed these limits, and such a venture, if made, is bound to end in dismal failure. A court is not equipped to examine questions of a general nature such as those we have mentioned. For example, in order to describe the historical background of the Catastrophe, a great mass of documents and testimonies was submitted to us—material which was collected with great devotion and doubtless with a genuine desire to present as complete a picture as possible. But all this is hardly more than a minute portion of the existing source material on the subject. Under our legal system the court is by its very nature "passive," for it does not introduce evidence on its own initiative, as would a Board of Inquiry. The ability of the court to describe broad historical events is therefore limited in any case.

And as far as fundamental questions of nonlegal nature are concerned, no one has vested in us the authority to pass judgment in such matters, and our opinions carry no greater weight than those of anyone else who has devoted himself to the study and contemplation of such questions.[1]

Jurisdiction of the Court

Miss Arendt implies that the fact that Eichmann was "kidnaped" from Argentina invalidates Israel's claim to jurisdiction (pp. 240, 242).[2]

Faced with a case of a defendant brought to the court by irregular means, a case pregnant with international implications, the court had to examine all aspects of the law applying to such a contingency.[3] The court found no provision in national (Israel) law restricting its jurisdiction in the case. Since Israel is a member of the international community and of the United Nations, it was only natural that the court turned its attention to international law as well. No prohibition of jurisdiction over Eichmann could be found in any international convention binding on Israel, or in the customary international law. To see whether there was a violation of the "general principles of law recognized by civilized nations,"[4] the court examined the case law of the United States and of Great Britain, and satisfied itself that these two nations, bearers of recognized high standards in their legal tradition, did not consider abduction a defect which deprives a court of its jurisdiction. On the basis of these considerations the court held itself competent to try the defendant.

Miss Arendt demonstrates a lack of care in reading the precedents cited by the court by claiming (p. 242) that "None of the . . . precedents applied, because they invariably concerned a fugitive from justice who was brought back not only to the place of his crimes but to a court that had issued, or could have issued, a valid warrant of arrest—conditions that Israel could not have fulfilled." As can be seen from the judgment, the *forum deprehensionis* has not always and everywhere been subject to the two conditions which Miss Arendt believes govern the application of this rule. In spite of this criticism, she finally states, "those who are convinced that justice, and nothing else, is the end of law will be inclined to condone the kidnaping act" (p. 243).

Miss Arendt reproaches the court (p. 242) for not mentioning the "relevant" Berthold Jacob case in connection with the Eichmann abduction. Jacob was a German political émigré who was very active in exposing Nazi Germany's massive rearmament. He was lured by Nazi agents to Basel, on the frontier of Germany and Switzerland, and abducted in March 1935 to Nazi Germany under conditions which caused the Federal Government of Switzerland to take a grave view of the incident. Public opinion in Switzerland and France was outraged. Under the threat of the arbitration and conciliation treaty between the two States being invoked, and fearful of public revelation of his secret rearmaments, Hitler ordered Jacob's return.[5] Unlike Eichmann, however, Berthold Jacob was no fugitive from justice, there were no proceedings against him anywhere, and the Jerusalem court had no reason to discuss his case.

Another irrelevant digression is Miss Arendt's account of the assassinations of Talaat Bey (Talāt Paṣa) and Simon Petlyura. She devotes two pages to these two acts of individual terror (pp. 243-245). Talāt Paṣa was Grand Vizier of Turkey during World War I. He was assassinated on March 15, 1921, in Berlin-Charlottenburg (Germany), where he lived in exile, by an Armenian student named Sogomon Teileryan, in revenge for the Turkish massacre of the Armenians during World War I.[6] Simon Petlyura, a Ukrainian leader, who lived in exile in Paris, was assassinated on May 25, 1926, by Sholom Schwartzbard in revenge for the pogroms against Jews of the Ukraine during the civil war following the October Revolution in Russia.[7] Miss Arendt states (p. 244) that similarities exist between these cases and the Eichmann case. In fact, there are none.

In her attempt to discredit Israel's search for Eichmann, Miss Arendt goes so far as to express doubts about the Israel Government's account of the abduction. She proceeds on the unproved assumption that "Eichmann had made many efforts to break out of his anonymity," which in her view is "the truth of the matter" (p. 217). She finds it "rather strange that it took the Israeli Secret Services several years . . . to learn that Adolf Eichmann was living in Argentina under the name of Ricardo Klement" and expresses doubt "that the Israelis had indeed pursued this search through the years. Which, in view of the facts, seems doubtful" (p. 217). She further claims that the process of testing the information available to the Secret Service "was not done very expertly" (p. 218). One page later, speaking for Adolf Eichmann as if she had consulted him privately—for there is no recorded statement on the subject— she says that "Eichmann immediately recognized that this was professional work."

In connection with the abduction, Miss Arendt reports on the first encounter of the Israel public with the presence of Eichmann in Israel. She states that Prime Minister Ben-Gurion "announced to Israel's *wildly cheering* Knesset that Eichmann had been 'found by the Israeli Secret Service'" (p. 217). The official record of the Israel Knesset reports the following statement made by Prime Minister David Ben-Gurion at the meeting of May 23, 1960:

I have to inform the Knesset that a short time ago one of the greatest Nazi war criminals, Adolf Eichmann, who was responsible together with the Nazi leaders for what they called "The Final Solution of the Jewish Question," that is, the extermination of six million of the Jews of Europe, was discovered by the Israel Security Services. Adolf Eichmann is already under arrest in Israel and will shortly be placed on trial in Israel under the terms of the law for the trial of Nazis and their helpers 5710-1950.[8]

There is not a word about cheers. The correspondent of the *New York Times* noted that the announcement of Ben-Gurion was made "with dramatic understatement" and continued: "Members were startled by the news."[9] The *Herald Tribune* wrote: "The news hit Israel . . . like a thunderbolt. The Knesset was too surprised to react."[10] *Haaretz* (Tel-Aviv) carried the following report:

The first moment everybody remained frozen to his chair. No one believed his ears. When they had recovered from the staggering blow, a wave of agitation engulfed the hearers—agitation so deep, that its likes had never before been known in the Knesset. Their faces pale, people jumped from their places and asked each other whether they had really heard what they did. The parliamentary reporters rushed in from their booths in order to obtain details or exchange information and opinion. The members of the Knesset also left their places, in order to "digest" the government's statement. In this electrified atmosphere the subsequent survey by the Minister of Foreign Affairs found no listeners in the Knesset.[11]

Nor are cheers to be heard on the tape recording of this session of the Knesset.[12]

Israel never tried to deny that Eichmann's abduction was in violation of Argentine law. Miss Arendt omits mention of the diplomatic negotiations with Argentina and of the most significant aspect of the Israel-Argentine conflict—the debate and resolution in the Security Council.[13] It is well worth noting that the Israel-Argentine conflict is one of the few in the long history of conflicts between States caused by irregular seizures for purpose of trial that have ended in a formal agreement between the parties. The moment the "inexigibility"—a term introduced by Helen Silving in her remarkable article in the *American Journal of International Law*[14]—of his return became clear to Argentina, the case was settled. In Felix Luna's published conversations with Arturo Frondizi, President of Argentina at the time of Eichmann's abduction, the following dialogue occurs on the Eichmann case:

Felix Luna: "The abduction of the Nazi official [*jerarca*] Adolf Eichmann, had—you surely remember it—international repercussions, because of the event itself, as well as for the Argentine protest to Israel. However, this protest got diluted, without obtaining, apparently, the demanded satisfaction. Was that so?"

Mr. Frondizi: "The abduction of the Nazi Eichmann was a clear violation of international norms on the part of Israel. That is the way Argentina stated it. My Government did its duty, but had to face two kinds of [local] pressures: the one of those who considered that no claim was to be formulated because such a claim would mean that we protect a criminal like Eichmann, and the pressure of those who wanted to transform the problem into a matter of persecution against the Jews."[15]

The fact is that Eichmann's was one of the few cases of abduction where there was no real conflict of jurisdiction. Not a single state, not even Germany or Argentina, asked for the extradition of Adolf Eichmann.[16]

In another attack on Israel's competence to try Eichmann, Miss Arendt asserts that the absence of German and Austrian defense witnesses "served to refute Israel's claim that an Israeli court was, at least technically, the 'most suitable for a trial against the implementers of the Final Solution,' because documents and witnesses were 'more abundant than in any other country'" (p. 201). She continues: "the claim with respect to documents was doubtful in any event, since the Israeli archive Yad Vashem was founded at a comparatively late date and is in no way superior to other archives" (p. 201).

A discussion of defense witnesses and their function at the trial follows later in this chapter. First let us examine Miss Arendt's claim regarding the archives of *Yad Washem Martyrs' and Heroes' Memorial Authority* in Jerusalem. Though it is true that *Yad Washem* was officially incorporated only in 1953, important archival collections destined for the institution were brought to Israel years before. Among them are such valuable collections as those of Upper Bavaria, Munich, Slovakia, Austria, and Poland, of the Displaced Persons Camps (*Sheerit Hapleita*), and many others. Moreover, *Yad Washem* is foremost among the extant archives which concentrate on material of Jewish origin regarding the Catastrophe, without limiting themselves to particular areas of persecution and extermination. *Yad Washem* possesses at present the most complete and most extensively catalogued collection available anywhere of documents relevant to the internal history of European Jewry under Nazi impact.[17]

The overwhelming majority of captured documents of Jewish interest—e.g., the exhibits of the various Nuremberg Trials, the Foreign Office Archives in Bonn, the German *Bundesarchiv* in Koblenz, and the records of the *Institut für Zeitgeschichte* in Munich—are available, in photocopies or on microfilm, in Jerusalem. Moreover, the collection of German documents in *Yad Washem* is actually superior to that contained in other archives. For example, unpublished material of Jewish interest from the German Foreign Office (*Auswärtiges Amt*), kept originally in Whaddon Hall, England, was available in photocopy in *Yad Washem* even before it was returned to Bonn, and it played an important part in the Eichmann Trial.

In addition, *Yad Washem* has a rich collection of material from archives in Eastern Europe, unavailable elsewhere. Finally, there is the fact that documents discovered in the 1950's were not yet available to the Subsequent Trials, but were collected by *Yad Washem* and made available to the Eichmann trial.

Conduct of the Trial

According to Miss Arendt, the Prime Minister of Israel, David Ben-Gurion, "had in mind" a "show trial" in Jerusalem (p. 2). She also says that he was the "invisible stage manager of the proceedings" (p. 3). She offers no support for these serious accusations, beyond the descriptive statement that the proceedings took place "on a stage before an audience" (p. 2), that the auditorium was planned with "a theater in mind" (p. 2), and that the judges were "seated at the top of the raised platform, facing the audience as from the stage in a play" (p. 4). Actually, the arrangement in Israel was standard. Nowhere are the judges seated below the level of the public; nowhere does the public face the judges from a raised platform.

Continuing her attack on Ben-Gurion, she imputes to him, without evidence, a desire for a trial "with its stress on general issues to the detriment of legal niceties" (p. 15), as if such a desire would have been binding on the judges. Ben-Gurion, however, at no time voiced anything like this sentiment. She disparages (p. 249) his well-reasoned objections to demands for international jurisdiction.[18] In another place, she states that Ben-Gurion and the prosecutor "probably" expected the witnesses of the resistance to testify that only Zionists resisted the Nazis (p. 108), implying that they were disappointed when it appeared from the testimony that *all* groups participated in the resistance. The accusation is absurd. The Attorney General did not hesitate to call to the witness stand a Communist leader in Israel, Dr. Adolf Berman (a former resident of Warsaw).[19] On the other hand, Professor David Wdowinski, of the New School for Social Research (New York), was called to testify on the activities of the Revisionists.[20] Incidentally, a large part of the testimony of Abba Kovner dealt with the tragic fate of the Jewish Communist resistance leader Izhak Witenberg.[21] Under the rules of procedure, the prosecutor was obliged to interrogate his witnesses *before* they took the stand. He knew beforehand what information they had to offer, and it was precisely for this reason that he called them; their testimony could hardly have been unexpected.

In her paradoxical style, Miss Arendt also writes that "the trial never became a play" (p. 7); nor does she deny the "scrupulous fairness of all technical arrangements" (p. 1). But the very first paragraph of her book characterizes the German translation of the proceedings in the Jerusalem court as "sheer comedy, frequently incomprehensible," and leaves the reader with the impression that this characteristic is applicable to the trial as a whole. She suggests that the selection of the German-Hebrew translators from the "high percentage of German-born people" was made according to the principle of "the . . . very powerful 'Vitamin P,' as the Israelis call protection [i.e., pull] in government circles and the bureaucracy" (p. 1). No proof is offered. The fact is that there was more than one German translator, and what fault she may have found in one of them does not necessarily apply to all of them. Moreover, a translation of the Attorney General's opening statement was available to the defendant in writing; the overwhelming majority of the documents were in German; the judges, all of whom were raised and educated in the German language, themselves translated their questions to the defendant into German; the defense counsel conducted the examination of Eichmann in German; and the cross-examination by the Attorney General was translated for the most part not simultaneously but consecutively, to insure the greatest accuracy possible.

A special target for Miss Arendt's censure is Gideon Hausner, who, as Attorney General of the State of Israel, led the prosecution. Consider her charges against him:

1. Mr. Hausner is charged with having held press conferences during the trial (p. 3). The fact is that he neither called nor participated in any formal press conference during the period of the trial. Of course, informal contact with the press was maintained throughout the trial by both prosecution and defense.

2. Miss Arendt implies (p. 3) that there was a conflict between the concept of justice as held by the presiding judge, on the one hand, and the State of Israel, represented by Gideon Hausner, on the other. She forgets that in a court of law the judges and the prosecution perform different tasks. The basic function of the Attorney General in a criminal case is to study the material and to

present all relevant credible information to the court. He does not decide whether the available information is sufficient for conviction; this is the function of the judge. Into the same category of mis-understanding of judicial processes belongs her statement that "the . . . judges . . . were put in the position of having to defend" Eichmann (p. 193). They made no attempt to "defend" him; they acquitted him of insufficiently substantiated allegations and con-victed him on proved charges. Determining that a particular allega-tion is not sufficiently founded and defending a man charged are two widely different functions. She reveals ignorance of the respec-tive functions of the prosecution and the court when she finds fault with Mr. Hausner because of the court's alleged "rewriting of the prosecution's case" with a "fundamentally different approach" (p. 193). The function of the court is to pass judgment on the basis of the facts revealed in the trial, with due regard to their interpreta-tions by prosecution and defense. A careful comparison of the judgment with the opening and closing statements of the prosecu-tion reveals that there is a difference between them, but also that they share a great deal in common.

3. In answer to Defense Attorney Servatius' objections to the ninth point of the indictment (Eichmann's part in the deportation of Polish citizens, including non-Jews, from the annexed territories), the tenth (crimes against humanity perpetrated on the Slovenians), the eleventh (deportation and murder of gypsies) and the twelfth (deportation of the children of Lidice)—all on the ground that the victims were non-Jews—the Attorney General responded that he included these counts "because we make no ethnic distinctions."[22] Miss Arendt proposes that Mr. Hausner should have said that he included the four counts objected to by Servatius "because he [Eichmann] committed them" (p. 4). Now, it is hardly necessary for a prosecutor to reiterate, in explaining his charge sheet, that he believes the defendant to have committed the acts with which he is charged. Such a reply might even have been considered im-proper. The filing of the charge itself indicates that the prosecution believes it has at least *prima facie* proof to substantiate its charges. The rest is up to the trial court. What the prosecutor was called on to explain was why he, as the representative of the Jewish State, included in the indictment charges concerned with non-Jews as well as with Jews. Mr. Hausner's answer was entirely correct and within the scope of the law. The intent of his statement was clearly

understood by everyone except Miss Arendt, who finds this "a remarkable sentence for a prosecutor to utter in his opening speech," adding that "it proved to be the key sentence in the case for the prosecution" (p. 4). The reader will look in vain in her book for an explanation of this remark.

4. The Attorney General is charged with failure to expose "the complicity of all German offices and authorities in the Final Solution" (p. 15). There is no indication by Miss Arendt of any specific "authority" or "office" left out by Mr. Hausner. His opening statement contained a lengthy, exhaustive discussion of the "offices" and "authorities" involved in the Final Solution,[23] not to mention the numerous references to such "offices" and "authorities" sprinkled throughout the address.

5. Mr. Hausner is charged with not having kept his promise to the court that his evidence would "encounter . . . doctors and lawyers, scholars, bankers, and economists—in those councils that resolved to exterminate the Jews" (p. 15). She is mistaken. He and those attending the trial "encountered," at a meeting with Heydrich, on September 21, 1939, Professor Ohlendorf and Professor Six, and Dr. Best and Dr. Meier.[24] At the meeting of January 30, 1940, concerning deportation from the annexed territories, they "encountered," among others, Dr. Lasch, Dr. Tröger, and Dr. Rasch.[25] They found among the participants at Wannsee Dr. Stuckart, Dr. Freisler, Dr. Buehler, Dr. Schöngarth, and Dr. Lange.[26] At the meeting on the spoliation of Jewish property they found as participants Dr. Globke, Dr. Essen, Dr. Siedler, Dr. Habermann, Dr. Kraeuter, Dr. Rajakovic, Dr. Schwandt, Dr. Feldscher, and Dr. von Coelin.[27] Among the defendants in the *Einsatzgruppen* trial (evidence in this case constitutes part of the documentation of the Eichmann trial[28]) they found the professors Ohlendorf and Six, the lawyer Dr. Walter Blume, the former judge Martin Sandberger, the economist Willy Seibert, the philologist and historian Eugen Steimle, the former Protestant minister Ernst Biberstein, Dr. Werner Braune, Dr. Walter Haensch, the lawyer and economist Gustav Nosske, and the musician Waldemar Klingelhöfer.[29]

6. Parts of Hausner's opening statement are characterized by Miss Arendt as "bad history and cheap rhetoric" (p. 16). A fair reading of it makes the opposite impression. The statement is logical and systematic. It examines the SS and SD; the Gestapo; the defendant; the Final Solution of the Jewish problem; the

extermination in Poland, in the U.S.S.R., in the annexed territories, in Northern, Western, and Southern Europe, and in Hungary; and the concentration camps. It presents the charges and then the evidence. In its own judgment, the court did not essentially change the organization of the material, except by departing somewhat from the geographic order. Miss Arendt does not disclose how she would have framed the opening statement, except to indicate that she would have omitted all reference to the historical background and to Jewish suffering (pp. 3, 4). It is worth noting that the Nuremberg indictments and especially the German indictments (*Anklageschriften*) for crimes connected with the Final Solution,[30] despite their narrower framework, include considerable background material, among which is contained material on Jewish suffering.

It is of some interest to read what other observers had to say of the opening statement made by the prosecutor. Patrick O'Donovan, reporting for the London *Observer*, wrote on April 23, 1961:

So the trial has become a classic confrontation of opposites. The future is judging the past. It is justice at its most satisfying. The meek have reversed their role and they have their oppressor. This is what one felt—and it sent a sigh round the court—when the prosecutor began his speech with "O Judges of Israel."

It is perhaps the reason why this trial has attracted so many reporters, more than have attended a summit meeting, more than went to Nuremberg.

Of course, there is, too, the endless interest in any extreme aberration of human conduct. And the Eichmann story coming out of a past that is already barely credible has a bizarre compulsive quality that orders up one's interest. But the marvel remains that it is the Jews trying without anger or gloating or cynicism the chief survivor of their enemies.

In the *Saturday Evening Post* of June 10, 1961, T. S. Matthews said:

When Gideon Hausner, Israel's Attorney-General, rose to deliver his indictment of Eichmann, the great speech of his career, his voice was firm, but at first the papers shook in his hands. Not for long, however. I think it likely that this speech will take its place among the great orations of mankind. From its opening phrases, "When I stand before you, judges of Israel, to accuse Adolf Eichmann, I do not stand alone . . ." to the final sentence—"And the judges of Israel will pronounce true and righteous judgment"—it was as eloquent and grim as a Hebrew Prophet's denouncing the wickedness of an apostate ruler.

In *The Carolina Israelite* (Charlotte, N.C.) of May-June, 1961, Harry Golden commented:

In Jerusalem I sought out two famous journalists who had been critical of the Eichmann arrest and the trial in Jerusalem and found they had changed their minds after the first week of testimony. So did many of the leading lawyers and editors around the world who had previously voiced skepticism and doubt.

The dignity of the trial communicated its purpose at once. By the first of June there were few journalists and lawyers in the Western world who were not satisfied that this story not only had to be recorded for history but that it was being told at the right time and in the right place, and under the correct conditions.

One man brought about this change in attitude of world opinion and that man is Gideon Hausner, Israeli Attorney-General, the prosecutor.

Hausner put the trial in proper perspective by a superbly-worded indictment during the first four sessions.

When he began, "I stand before you judges of Israel," I felt a sudden chill. A quick glance around the court-room convinced me that most of the five hundred journalists and writers shared my experience.

Hugh Trevor-Roper, Regius Professor of Modern History at Oxford, an observer at the Nuremberg and the Jerusalem trials, wrote in the *Sunday Times* of April 23, 1961:

It was a wonderful performance; nine hours of expositions and oratory, a great physical and greater emotional strain. For who could recount without emotion all the infamous acts set in motion by this "murderer at the telephone" who himself (he assured us) is so squeamish that he could not have been a doctor and was liable, like Himmler, to faint at the sight of death?

I don't think the speech added greatly to our historical knowledge, apart from a few details which will have to be documented anyway; but Dr. Hausner struck the right note; he held the court from beginning to end. Moreover, from his speech there emerged a picture of Eichmann which contrasts dramatically with the spectacle of the grey, lipless robot behind the glass.

7. Mr. Hausner, discussing Eichmann's mental state in an article in the *Saturday Evening Post*,[31] quoted Professor Lipot Szondi, a psychiatrist famous for his tests of the mentally disturbed.[32] On the basis of this article, Miss Arendt writes that "the psychiatrists" held Eichmann to be "a man obsessed with a dangerous and insatiable urge to kill, arising out of a desire for power" and "a perverted, sadistic personality" (pp. 22-23).[33] She concludes: "In

which case he would have belonged in an insane asylum." What she failed to quote from the Hausner article was this crucial sentence: "However, they [the tests] also confirmed he was legally sane and responsible for his actions." The Israel Ministry of Health also made extensive psychological tests—characterized by Miss Arendt as "the comedy of the soul experts" (p. 22)—which established, as did Szondi's tests, that Eichmann was legally sane. Miss Arendt seems not to know that normality is not a necessary condition for legal sanity.[34]

8. Miss Arendt implies that the prosecution deliberately withheld Adler's *Theresienstadt*[35] from the court because, on the strength of the evidence contained in that book, "the picture [presented by the prosecution] would indeed have been greatly damaged" (p. 106). The Adler book was not submitted to the court for the simple reason that in criminal cases books can be submitted (in the absence of an agreement between the parties) only where there are no living witnesses. Since there were living witnesses to testify on Theresienstadt, there was no need to submit a book, though Adler's book was praised by Bar-Or of the prosecution and placed at the disposal of the court.[36] The book was given to Eichmann three months before the opening of the trial, and he read it.[37]

9. Innuendo reflecting on the integrity of the Attorney General is apparent in Miss Arendt's comment on the following facts: The prosecution submitted to the court, without elaboration, the statement Eichmann made in May 1960 following his seizure in Argentina.[38] This statement did not have on it an exact date. Neither the prosecution nor the defense raised any doubts as to the place where the declaration was written, nor did Eichmann raise any questions. There was therefore no need to examine Eichmann on this score. But Miss Arendt finds that the lack of an exact date on the statement raises the suspicion that it was written in Jerusalem and concludes: "The prosecutor, who may have known better, did not cross-examine him [Eichmann] on this point; clearly, the less said about this matter the better" (p. 220). The implication is that Hausner was in collusion with the authorities to misrepresent the declaration.

10. Miss Arendt states that the prosecution exaggerated Eichmann's role, making him appear "the superior of Himmler and the inspirer of Hitler" (p. 193; see also p. 52). There is no evidence that Hausner or any other member of the prosecution ever stated or implied this.

11. Miss Arendt implies (p. 4) that Mr. Hausner's visit to the United States, made while the decision of the Israel Supreme Court was still pending, was well publicized. Actually he was in the United States incognito. Only when he made a surprise appearance at a B'nai B'rith gathering in Washington did his presence in the United States become known, and this occurred after the conclusion of the proceedings in the Supreme Court.

12. Finally, Miss Arendt accuses Mr. Hausner of displaying "love of showmanship" (p. 2), "theatrics characteristic of a more than ordinary vanity" (p. 3), and "grandiose" rhetoric (p. 6). By contrast, Professor Julius Stone had this to say about the way the prosecution was conducted:

. . . The other pointer to the mood and spirit of the trial came when I happened to meet Prosecutor Gideon Hausner after he had offered this document [the Sassen Papers], but before the court had ruled on it. I asked him bluntly why, if the document was so important to the Prosecution, he had tried to put it in as of right, instead of asking the Court under Section 15 to admit it under its discretional power.[39] His answer both astounded me and filled me with admiration. He said he agreed that it would have been *within the letter* of Section 15 to ask the Court to use its discretion to admit it. But he and his colleagues for the prosecution felt, he said, that though within the letter of Section 15, it would not have been *within the spirit*. For Section 15 was in his opinion designed rather to cover relevant but not vital facts, whereas the Sassen document was an admission by the accused of an essential part of the facts in issue implicating him. He felt, therefore, that it ought to go in as of right and that he should not rely on the court's discretion.[40]

Lord Birkenhead wrote in the *Daily Telegraph* (London) of April 19, 1961:

Many of us who have attended the early sessions of the trial have been surprised by the widespread belief that Eichmann could not be impartially tried by a Jewish court, and that the proceedings must therefore be unfair.

How could this be when every word, every gesture in court is being scrutinized by 500 trained and suspicious men, while the attention of this whole world is focused upon it as through a burning-glass?

Indeed, far from being unfair, it is already evident that the Israeli Attorney General, Mr. Hausner, is leaning over backwards in his determination to ensure that scrupulous justice is observed and the defense given every conceivable latitude.

This gifted and attractive man who was born in Poland and speaks with reverence of Blackstone and Grotius, . . . has so set the tone of the proceedings that a decorum is observed in this court which is equal to any in England, and might be imitated with advantage by some of the nations who have disputed its legality.

The following comment concerning the Attorney General was made by the court in its judgment:

The Attorney General himself emerged honorably from the dilemma to which we have alluded above [the problem of the scope of the trial], the burden of which he too must have felt to its fullest extent. In spite of some slight deviations now and then from the narrow path which the court found itself obliged to designate, Mr. Hausner conducted all stages of the prosecution with the skill of a jurist practicing on the highest professional level. In the brilliant opening statement, bold in expression and broad in scope, and again when summing up, he was able to provide an outlet for the deep emotions that stir the hearts of the entire people.[41]

When it comes to an evaluation of the evidence presented in the trial, Miss Arendt's account is again unreliable. She states that "the facts for which Eichmann was to hang had been established 'beyond reasonable doubt' long before the trial started, and they were generally known to all students of the Nazi regime" (p. 51). She also states repeatedly that the facts of the case were not in dispute (pp. 85, 130, 142, 190, 194, 243). To be sure, the judgment of the International Military Tribunal, delivered in 1946, had discussed Eichmann's assignment to direct the Final Solution, saying:

In the summer of 1941 . . . plans were made for the "final solution" of the Jewish question in all of Europe. This "final solution" meant the extermination of the Jews, which early in 1939 Hitler had threatened would be one of the consequences of an outbreak of war, and a special section in the Gestapo under Adolf Eichmann, as head of Section B4 of the Gestapo, was formed to carry out the policy. . . . Adolf Eichmann . . . has estimated that the policy pursued resulted in the killing of 6,000,000 Jews, of which 4,000,000 were killed in the extermination institutions. . . .[42]

And the criminal nature of Eichmann's organization had been recognized by the Tribunal when it said:

. . . A special section of the Gestapo office of the RSHA under *Standartenführer*[43] Eichmann was set up with responsibility for Jewish matters, which employed its own agents to investigate the Jewish problem in occupied territory. Local offices of the Gestapo were used first to supervise the emigration of Jews and later to deport them to the East both from Germany and from the territories occupied during the war. *Einsatzgruppen* of the Security Police and SD operating behind the lines of the Eastern front engaged in the wholesale massacre of Jews. A special detachment from Gestapo headquarters in the RSHA was used to arrange for the deportation of Jews from Axis satellites to Germany for the "final solution."[44]

But the fact that Eichmann's role had been recognized earlier does not contradict the fact that vast amounts of new evidence concerning his activities and authority were revealed in the trial. Indeed, new elements were revealed in abundance in Eichmann's extensive pretrial interrogation by the Israel police;[45] in the cross-examination of Eichmann at the trial (of which Miss Arendt says, on p. 202, that his "testimony in court turned out to be the most important evidence in the case");[46] in the documents of the German Foreign Office, screened with great care by the Israel police, which established Eichmann's connection with various events and actions through letters of transmittal containing direct references to him;[47] in the minutes of the meeting of the RSHA of September 21, 1939 (mentioned by Miss Arendt on p. 69), discovered by the Israel Police Office 06 (in charge of pretrial investigation);[48] in the Düsseldorf Gestapo files;[49] in a series of documents from Josef Löwenherz's private archives;[50] in the previously unknown Wisliceny surveys;[51] and in the testimonies given by Jews who were in Eichmann's power and by other witnesses.

New evidence was also supplied by the Sassen Papers.[52] The defense fight against their admissibility as evidence was largely successful. These Papers originally constituted a draft of a book which was presumably to explain the Nazi destruction of European Jewry. In Miss Arendt's book, on page 19, the Sassen documents are defined as "the interview that he [Eichmann] had given in 1955 in Argentina to the Dutch journalist Sassen"; on page 49 they are described as "disorganized, rambling notes he [Eichmann] made in Argentina in preparation for the interview with Sassen"; and on pages 216-217 she asserts that "Eichmann made copious notes for the interview, which was tape-recorded and then rewritten by Sassen, with considerable embellishments." Nothing of the sort happened. Eichmann told his story to Sassen, a Dutch Nazi who, unconvinced of the need for the extermination of the Jews, proved to be a rather severe interrogator. The conversations were all recorded on tape and then typed out. The typescript was submitted to Eichmann for corrections. Only one of seventeen folders and some of the pages—those containing corrections and marginal notes written in Eichmann's hand—were admitted as evidence by the District Court.[53] The parts admitted as evidence proved to be very damaging to Eichmann.[54]

Miss Arendt does not pretend to have read the original Sassen Papers, except for the parts admitted in evidence before the court (p. 260), but she does not hesitate to say that "every line of these scribblings shows his [Eichmann's] utter ignorance of everything that was not directly, technically and bureaucratically, connected with his job, and also shows an extraordinarily faulty memory" (p. 49). This statement is inaccurate, as any reader of the papers could verify. It is interesting to note, however, that Miss Arendt does not deny that the papers reveal Eichmann to have been very knowledgeable in all areas that were "directly, technically and bureaucratically, connected with his job," even though this fact alone contradicts the picture of Eichmann as an ignorant, passive robot in the Nazi regime.

In order to cast further doubt on the status of the evidence against Eichmann, Miss Arendt states that "the additional facts . . . would never have appeared to be 'beyond reasonable doubt' if the defense had brought its own evidence to bear upon the proceedings," including his "ideology with respect to 'the Jewish question'" (p. 51; see also p. 53). Of course, his real "ideology" was well known to the defense counsel and was aptly summarized in the judgment.[55] Miss Arendt, criticizing the defense counsel, Dr. Servatius, says that he failed to mention testimony favorable to the defendant (p. 59); that he "could have quoted in support of Eichmann's thesis" the writing of Maunz (p. 21),[56] but he did not; that he could have called as witnesses "the former agents of Aliyah Beth,"[57] but he did not (p. 56); that he "could have pointed to the fact that Eichmann . . . appointed his old Jewish associates [sic] in the emigration business" (p. 106),[58] but he did not; that he could have made use of the contacts between Jewish partisans and Polish and Russian resistance (p. 108),[59] but he did not.

She deplores the fact that the defense counsel had no research staff (p. 201). Dr. Servatius, who was active as counsel for defense in the trial of the major war criminals (for Fritz Sauckel and the Leadership Corps)[60] and in the Subsequent Trials (Karl Brandt, Franz Eirenschmalz, Paul Pleiger, and Wilhelm Stuckart),[61] was obviously well aware of the status of the documentation, and expressed no need for a staff to search after new documents. Miss Arendt admits that "there were more than enough documents left to tell the story of the Final Solution" (p. 200). Indeed, such a search for new material would have been a hopeless undertaking in view of the fact, known to Miss Arendt, that "Eichmann's department . . . had burned its files" (p. 200). Miss Arendt minimizes the importance of this, since "all its [Eichmann's department's] correspondence had been addressed to other State and Party offices, whose files fell into the hands of the Allies." This is an erroneous statement. In the first place, the files of Section IVB4 did not consist of correspondence alone. They consisted also of drafts of documents and records of meetings; and of statistics of the extermination program, as we know on the authority of Höss himself.[62] Secondly, as for the correspondence, the fact is that out of the archives of the fifteen regional Gestapo offices (*Stapostellen* and *Stapoleitstellen*)—the most important correspondents of Section IVB4—only one, that of Düsseldorf, was found. This file, to which researchers had previously paid scanty attention, was submitted to the Jerusalem court in its entirety at the request of the defense, but it could offer no comfort to Eichmann. The files of two local offices of the Gestapo, in Würzburg and in Neustadt an der Weinstrasse, were also found. None of the records of the other Gestapo offices containing material relevant to the Eichmann case fell into the hands of the Western Allies. A survey by Gerhard L. Weinberg, *Guide to Captured German Documents* and *Supplement*,[63] and the *Guides to German Records Microfilmed at Alexandria*,[64] reveal no substantial Gestapo (central or local) files.[65]

There is no basis for Miss Arendt's complaint that Dr. Servatius "had received the crumbs from the rich man's table" (p. 201). In fact, Dr. Servatius received from the Attorney General, even before the trial started, all the documents that were known to the prosecutor, including the pretrial testimonies of potential witnesses. The overwhelming majority of these documents were later submitted during the court proceedings, among them such as provoked Dr. Servatius' comment "I agree to their submission, since they are in favor of the defendant."[66] Many documents which the Attorney General found impossible to submit (e.g., affidavits of living persons who could not be subjected to cross-examination) were submitted on Dr. Servatius' initiative. In these cases, no objection was raised by the prosecution to his request for admission of the documents. The fact is that there were no other documents available that were relevant to Eichmann.

Miss Arendt's attitude toward the use of Nuremberg documents is ambivalent, depending on whether she finds them helpful or harmful to Eichmann's cause. She deplores (p. 67) the use of statements of former high-ranking Nazis by the prosecution; at the same time she attacks the prosecution (p. 136) for ignoring Mildner's (also a "high-ranking Nazi") testimony submitted by the defense.[67] Mildner's testimony on the responsibility for the actual killing was based on what he had learned from his comrades concerning the Security Police; his second-hand testimony contradicts the findings of the Nuremberg Tribunal in the Pohl case, insofar as the physical destruction of Jews is concerned.[68]

When it comes to discussing testimony given before the court, Miss Arendt mentions only twelve Jewish witnesses; the rest are treated with total silence. There were altogether twenty-eight Jewish witnesses from the countries under Eichmann's exclusive jurisdiction, in addition to witnesses from Germany, Austria, and the "Protectorate," who had direct contact with Eichmann. It is true that there were among them persons "of some prominence," (p. 204), but most of the witnesses were ordinary people. The former were for the most part those with whom Eichmann had dealt, since, insofar as he dealt directly with Jews, it was usually with "leaders." The latter generally concerned themselves with testimony about the actual destruction of Jewish communities. The court, during the examination of these witnesses, is characterized as a "mass meeting" (p. 107). In connection with the Kistarcsa episode,[69] Miss Arendt endorses (p. 183) Eichmann's declaration that he did not remember the episode. She ignores the contrary testimony given by Jewish witnesses.

A climax is reached in her description (pp. 203-204) of the evidence of Mr. Yehiel "Dinoor" (correctly spelled Dinur), one of the survivors of Auschwitz, who has written a number of books on the subject under the pen name "Ka-tzetnik."[70] The witness, who was clearly laboring under an extreme state of strain and excitement, fainted after having been in the witness-box for about a minute.[71] Miss Arendt calls one of his statements "a little excursion into astrology" (p. 204). The name Dinur, which the witness had given as his real name, she characterizes as an "unlikely" name. To her it may have been, but it is not "unlikely" to the many Jews who bear it, or to those familiar with one of the leading Jewish historians of our time, who bears the same name.[72] She finds it necessary to write that Dinur, after having "fainted . . . answered no more questions" (p. 204). She disparages his writings without giving evidence of having read them. She attributes his fainting to his "disappointment." She represents the judges and the Attorney General as being impatient with him. The judgment, referring to the magnitude of the sufferings of the Jewish people, does in fact mention the incident, but in the following terms: "Perhaps it is symbolic that even a writer, who himself went through the inferno called Auschwitz, could not muster strength when called to testify and collapsed in the witness-box."[73]

Reporting on the testimony of Zindel Grynszpan, Miss Arendt, for some reason, devotes a page (pp. 206-207) to his son Herszl Grynszpan, who in 1938 assassinated the German Embassy Counselor in Paris, vom Rath. Challenging the generally accepted view that the assassination was an act of revenge for the expulsion of Polish Jews from Germany, she declares that "it is generally known that this explanation is unlikely" (p. 206). But what explanation does she offer for the assassination? She rejects homosexuality as the reason, saying: "The story of his [vom Rath's] homosexuality was probably fabricated by the Gestapo." In fact, the Nazi authorities (in their secret indictment) attributed the story to Herszl Grynszpan himself, and branded it "brazen and false."[74] Miss Arendt speculates: "Grynszpan might have acted as an unwitting tool of Gestapo agents in Paris" (p. 207). But this too she is not prepared to endorse. There remains, in fact, the only explanation—namely, the generally accepted view, implied by the court as well.[75] What Miss Arendt omits to mention in connection with this story is the one and only fact that was relevant to the Eichmann trial: As revealed in the Sassen Papers,[76] and in Eichmann's pretrial interrogation,[77] Eichmann was sent to investigate the case and to interrogate Herszl Grynszpan at least twice, which shows to what extent he was considered the important figure in Jewish matters in the Nazi regime.[78]

The language Miss Arendt uses in describing witnesses who told of Jewish suffering during the Nazi terror reveals her strange animosity toward the victims: "the trial began to degenerate into a bloody show" (p. 7); an "endless procession of witnesses" (p. 189); potential witnesses "flocked spontaneously to the trial authorities and also to Yad Vashem . . . to offer themselves as witnesses" (p. 189). The truth is not as simple as that. Some witnesses were willing and even eager to testify, but others refused to do so. Some volunteered their service, while others were sought out by the authorities. Miss Arendt considers their evidence (the "general picture") to be "confused and confusing" (p. 163). She states that "the presiding judge did not like the term ["general picture"] and he did not like the picture" (p. 107). There is no evidence for this assertion.

Miss Arendt found only a "few" great moments in the trial (p. 64). She records two: Dr. Servatius' insistence on all "killing," including "killing by gas," being a "medical matter" (p. 64), and Abba Kovner's story of the German *Feldwebel* (Sergeant-Major) Anton Schmidt (pp. 209-212), who was heroic in his help to the Jewish underground. (Concerning the equally heroic wife of Kovner and Lisa Magun's self-sacrifice, not a word.[79]) To other observers there were many great moments in the trial, of which the following may serve as examples: (1) Dr. Leon Weliczker Wells, of Lwów, related how, being then sixteen years of age, and a member of the grave-digging squad, he could only long "to be shot so that [his] blood would spurt out and he could drink it to quench [his] raging thirst, made unbearable by pneumonia and typhus."[80] Wells, now a brilliant physicist, told in detail of his miraculous survival; his presence on the witness stand could hardly fail to call to mind the countless other Jewish talents that were lost to the world in the Final Solution. (2) Rivka Joselewska, who witnessed the shooting of all her family in a pit, recounted how she was herself shot there, but was not killed, and became the only one of her village to survive.[81] (3) Dr. Aaron Peretz of the Kovno ghetto told of the children's games there. He described the impact of the Nazi behavior on their young souls:

The children in the ghetto would play and laugh, and in their games the entire tragedy was reflected. They would play grave-digging; they would dig a pit and would put a child inside and call him Hitler. And they would play at being gatekeepers of the ghetto. Some of the children played the parts of Germans, some of Jews, and the Germans were angry and would beat the other children who were Jews. And they used to play funerals . . .

The Jewish child was prematurely grown up. We were amazed to observe how children three or four years old understood the tragedy of the situation: how they clammed up when it was necessary, how they knew when to hide. We ourselves could not trust our ears when we heard small children, offered a sedative, say: "Doctor, this is not necessary, I shall be quiet, I shall not scream."[82]

(4) Michael Podkhlebnik recounted to a hushed courtroom how, while digging pits under the watchful eyes of German and Ukrainian guards, he suddenly noticed among the gassed Jews his wife and two children.[83]

According to Miss Arendt, Eichmann "must suffer for what he has done, not for what he has caused others to suffer" (p. 6)—a hairsplitting distinction. In fact, the sufferings and injuries caused to the victim are the real reason for incrimination; where there is no injury there is no crime. Miss Arendt attacks the prosecution for being "interested primarily in the suffering of the Jewish people" (p. 188). She claims that the "case was built on what the Jews had suffered, not on what Eichmann had done" (p. 4). In fact, the documentary material was oriented exclusively toward the immediate purpose of the trial. The same is true in regard to Eichmann's pretrial interrogation and the cross-examination; the witnesses, too, testified on the immediate issue of Eichmann's activities and responsibility.

Miss Arendt is apparently unaware that it was the duty of the prosecution to prove the results of the crime, and that this was done in Jerusalem for the first time. The trials conducted by the International Military Tribunal and the Nuremberg Military Tribunals, insofar as they dealt with the Jewish Catastrophe, dealt only with abstractions, such as disfranchisement, spoliation, forced emigration, deportation, stigmatization, ghettoization, forced labor, and extermination. What lay behind these words for millions of men, women, and children remained largely unexplored, and had never been examined by a court of law. A careful study from this viewpoint of the International Military Tribunal, the Pohl, Ohlendorf, and Ministries cases, as well as the I. G. Farben and Krupp cases, indicates only a small amount of testimony relating personal experiences of the victims.[84] The explanation of the judgment that the testimony was necessary because "the accused denied all the counts in the indictment" is found by Miss Arendt to be "curiously inconsistent," since "the accused . . . had never denied these facts in the indictment, he had only denied that he was responsible for them 'in the sense of the indictment'" (p. 190). This is an incorrect interpretation of Eichmann's answers and of the law. In the first place, what was asked from Eichmann was not acceptance or denial of facts but an answer of "guilty" or "not guilty" to the individual counts of the indictment, which refer both to the facts and their legal evaluation. Eichmann answered in the negative. Miss Arendt criticizes both the prosecution and the defense for not asking Eichmann what he meant when he pleaded "not guilty in the sense of the indictment" (p. 18). The phrase, however, is not a recondite one; it had been used earlier by some of the Nuremberg defendants.[85] Its practical effect was to saddle the prosecution with the full burden of proof. This is because Israel law admits only two pleas—"guilty" or "not guilty." Faced with Eichmann's formulation of his plea, the court, proceeding on the presumption of innocence, interpreted it as a plea of "not guilty," thus forcing the prosecution to prove guilt on every count.

Eichmann was charged with having, together with others, murdered millions of people by knowingly collecting and transporting them to places where they were to be killed. In order to prove the crime of murder, the prosecution had to adduce proof that these people were in fact killed, and in what circumstances. All such evidence was strictly relevant. That certain facts were not in dispute has no legal significance. In felonies there exists at present no procedure under which the defendant can admit certain facts and thus absolve the prosecution from its burden of proof in relation to them. The District Court was therefore acting in full accord with legal principle when it held that because the defendant had pleaded in substance "not guilty" to all counts, the evidence referred to could not have been dismissed as irrelevant.[86]

Miss Arendt does not like the testimony of Pastor Grüber, who "had belonged to the numerically small and politically irrelevant group of persons who were opposed to Hitler on principle . . . and whose stand on the Jewish question had been without equivocation" (pp. 114-115). He had intervened in favor of Jews at the risk of his own life. She says that "his testimony was vague; he did not remember, after so many years, when he had spoken with Eich-

mann, or . . . on what subjects" (p. 115); that his testimony that
Eichmann behaved like "a block of ice," like "marble," during their
conversations was inadmissible as evidence (p. 116); and that his
characterization of Eichmann as a "bicycle rider" was contradicted
by other evidence (p. 116).

None of these assertions is true. In his evidence Grüber said
quite clearly that he came to deal with Eichmann regarding "professional questions, questions relating to emigration, or any questions with regard to Jews, . . . not only individual cases but also
more general cases."[87] His reply that Eichmann reacted to all his
entreaties like a piece of ice or marble was perfectly admissible and
to the point. As for Eichmann's being the "bicycle rider" whose
head is bent low before his superiors, while he treads on his subordinates, there was no evidence to the contrary, and ample sup-
porting evidence.[88]

Miss Arendt's allegation that Grüber never tried to influence
Adolf Eichmann (p. 116) is contradicted by Grüber's own testimony:

> Preachings must not be heard always in the imperative. A preacher
> is not good if he always uses the imperative mood. And I want to tell
> the court: I once arrived tired at the office in *Kurfürstenstrasse* and had
> the impression that the accused had a good day—a day of goodwill
> perhaps. Maybe he sympathized with me, for he said, "Why all this
> activity on your part? No one will thank you for your doings, for your
> activities for the benefit of the Jews. There will be no thanks coming
> from them." I answered him, because I believed that this was a man
> who once belonged to the Templars' Order, and as such knew Palestine.
> I said, "Do you know the road leading from Jerusalem to Jericho?" and
> he nodded. I said, "On this road there was once a Jew brought down by
> robbers, and he who had helped that Jew was a man who was not a
> Jew. The God whom I worship, He told me, 'Go and do as he did.'"
> This is what I told the accused.[89]

Dissatisfaction with Pastor Grüber leads Miss Arendt to say (p.
116) that his "interpretations and conclusions" should have been
stricken from the record. She is obviously unaware of the fact that
in trials before panels of professional judges (as opposed to trials
before juries) evidence presented by either side cannot be stricken
from the record; the court is considered able to distinguish relevant
from irrelevant evidence. She also comes out with the fanciful suggestion that the pastor's testimony "could have strengthened the case

for the defense, for Eichmann had never given Grüber a direct answer, he had always told him to come back, as he had to ask for further instructions" (p. 116). Here is what Grüber actually said with regard to Eichmann's need to consult with his superiors:

> As far as my recollection goes I would always leave his office with a definite "no" on his part, or sometimes he would put me off saying that I should wait for a decision. . . . Never did I leave his office with a positive answer whatsoever. It was either a "no" or some sort of non-committal answer. . . . But I do not recall that he would ever say that "I have to speak with my superiors." . . . I was always under the impression that the man did not have to consult his superiors.[90]

But Miss Arendt has little use for this man who could rightly be called the conscience of German Protestantism.

She supplies misinformation regarding another witness, Michael Musmanno. In her serial version she wrote: "Though Judge Musmanno had sat on the trials of the administrators of the concentration camps [Pohl case] and the members of the mobile killing units in the East [Ohlendorf case], he had not once mentioned Eichmann's name in his judgments" (IV, 122). The fact is that both in the judgment of the Pohl case[91] and in the Ohlendorf case,[92] references to Adolf Eichmann did occur. On March 16, 1963, Justice Musmanno wrote a letter to *The New Yorker,* which printed a summary of it.[93] Notwithstanding these facts, Miss Arendt, in her book, reformulated her charge without changing its substance: "Mr. Musmanno had sat on the trials of the administrators of the concentration camps, and of the members of the mobile killing units in the East; and while Eichmann's name had come up in the proceedings, he had mentioned it only once in his judgments" (p. 192). Her original charge in *The New Yorker* also included the following statement (later omitted in the book): "After he [Musmanno] had finished his job as judge, however, he had set out, on his own initiative and knowing hardly a word of German, to interview the Nuremberg defendants in their prison" (IV, 122). There are two errors in this brief sentence: (1) Justice Musmanno's job at Nuremberg was finished on April 11, 1948.[94] By that time the Nuremberg defendants whom he had interviewed had been dead for almost two years (the major war criminals under the International Military Tribunal were executed on October 16, 1946). The interviews were held *before* he became a judge at Nuremberg. (2) The interviews were held not on his own initiative but under military assignment. These details are established in the records of the Eichmann trial.[95] Though Justice Musmanno did not know German, he could speak English with Ribbentrop, Dönitz, Raeder, von Schirach, and von Papen, and Italian with Frank. With the rest he spoke through interpreters, one of whom was Dr. Gilbert, also a witness in the Eichmann trial.

Miss Arendt also states, wrongly, that "German witnesses for the defense were excluded from the outset, since they would have exposed themselves to arrest and prosecution in Israel under the same law as that under which Eichmann was tried" (p. 114). Indeed, in listing three "failures" of the court, she makes the claim that "the court did not admit witnesses for the defense" (p. 251), and she accuses the Attorney General of breaking his promise not to "block the way" for defense witnesses (p. 200). She writes "that Israel was the only country in the world where defense witnesses could not be heard, and where certain witnesses for the prosecution, those who had given affidavits in previous trials, could not be cross-examined by the defense" (p. 201). Suppose the trial had been held in one of the formerly occupied countries—e.g., Czechoslovakia. Would the witnesses for the defense have been keen to go to Prague? There is not a single known case of a former Nazi willing to testify abroad in war crimes trials. The facts are these:

1. The court expressed a preference for all witnesses to give evidence in person before it, but considered the procedure described here in Item 3 as "sufficiently effectual."[96]

2. Among the witnesses for the defense from abroad some were in detention;[97] others were free but would indeed have exposed themselves to arrest and prosecution in Israel;[98] still others, for whose presence the defense pressed most, were granted immunity, but refused nevertheless to come to Jerusalem.[99] They simply did not wish to come.

3. All sixteen defense witnesses from outside Israel were interrogated by courts of law in Germany, Austria, and Italy. Detailed questionnaires were approved by the prosecution, the defense, and the Jerusalem court, in accordance with normal practice. All the witnesses (except Wilhelm Höttl in Austria) were heard in the presence of representatives of both the defense and the prosecution, and additional questions suggested by the replies to the questionnaire were also answered. The Jerusalem court used this testimony with the requisite caution.[100]

Miss Arendt herself was not averse to using the testimony of one of the witnesses (Grell, on p. 42) when it suited her purposes.

Her indictment of the conduct of the trial is summarized in her statement that "the irregularities and abnormalities of the trial in Jerusalem were so many, so varied, and of such legal complexity that they overshadowed during the trial . . . the central moral, political, and even legal problems that the trial inevitably posed" (p. 232).

Since Miss Arendt is not an expert in the law of criminal procedure, as she herself admits (p. 242), it is hardly her privilege to berate the prosecution and the court for their conduct of the case. Compare her statement with the following evaluation of the trial, given by the eminent jurist Professor Peter Papadatos of the University of Athens, who served as the official observer for the International Commission of Jurists. In his report he wrote:

Speaking quite objectively, though in no way putting ourselves in the place of the judge, we must admit that the evidence submitted on this count, documents as well as the evidence of witnesses, was quite conclusive and clearly revealed the important role of "co-ordinator" which Eichmann played in the carrying out on a gigantic scale of this genocide.

The procedure followed before the District Court and the Supreme Court for the judgment of Eichmann was, generally speaking, the normal procedure laid down by Israeli law for penal cases. It should be said that this procedure, which is identical to that under Anglo-Saxon law, guarantees all the fundamental rights of the defense and, as a rule, provides conditions for a fair trial.

It is true that, for prosecutions arising under Law 1950/5710, the court may under the provisions of this law depart from rules of evidence, if it has good ground for believing that this will allow the truth to be established and ensure a fair trial. However, every time the court decides on a departure of this kind, it must set out the reasons for its decision in writing. This right is a dangerous one although, if one thinks of the special circumstances in which the criminal activities of the Nazis took place, necessary. The District Court did not abuse this rule and gave clear and precise reasons each time it had to depart from the normal rules of evidence.

. . . The Eichmann Trial will undoubtedly occupy a leading place amongst the great trials of our century concerned with international penal law. Its proceedings need careful study. This is not only for the legal questions which it raises or which it resolves but mainly because it reveals to us certain aspects of the extreme in crime today. For it is essential to understand the causes and results of such crime in order to be in a better position to fight against it.[101]

The Judgment and Its Execution

Miss Arendt shows a reluctant—and qualified—admiration for the judges of the District Court. She admits their many good qualities, but stops short of praise. She tells of their correction of "a great number of errors [these "errors" are not specified] . . . though probably not all" (p. 151); their "firm grasp on the intricate bureaucratic setup of the Nazi machinery of destruction, so that the position of the accused could be understood" (p. 193),[102] though not so firm that they wouldn't benefit from reading Hilberg (p. 66); their "attitude to the defense," though it is "perhaps a shade over-polite" (p. 2). She is impressed with their "high degree of independence and fairness" (p. 196), but she calls the judgment a "failure" (p. 251) and asserts that "the court . . . never rose to the challenge of the unprecedented" (p. 241).

She further claims that the court failed "even in regard to the unprecedented nature of the origins of the Israel state" (p. 241). But the judgment contained the following:

> The connection between the State of Israel and the Jewish people needs no explanation. The State of Israel was established and recognized as the Jewish State. The Declaration of Independence of 5 Iyar, 5708— May 14, 1948—(Official Gazette No. 1) opens with the words: "It was in the land of Israel that the Jewish people was born." It goes on to survey the history of the Jewish people from ancient times through the Second World War; mentions the Resolution of the United Nations General Assembly of November 29, 1947, requiring the establishment of a Jewish State in Palestine; declares that it is the "natural right of the Jewish people to be, like every other people, self-governing in its sovereign State"; and proclaims "the establishment of a Jewish State in Palestine—the State of Israel." It would seem that there is no need for any further proof of the obvious connection between the Jewish people and the State of Israel: this is the sovereign State of the Jewish people.[103]

Another shortcoming according to Miss Arendt is "that the line sharply distinguishing the Nazi-controlled territories to the east and southeast from the system of nation-states in Central and Western Europe was never mentioned" (p. 163). From the viewpoint of the prosecution and the judgment it should not have been. The fate of the Jewish population in the nation-states on the one hand, and in the "belt of mixed populations" on the other, was not determined by artificial lines on a map but depended on numerous factors. Geographically speaking, the basic criterion for categorization of territories in the judgment was the degree of Eichmann's responsibility in the territories concerned. In this respect the judgment made it clear that while in the Government-General there were "channels of command wherein the accused had no part"[104] and while in the East he again was not alone, in the rest of occupied Europe and in "Greater Germany" he was the chief implementer of the Final Solution.[105] This covers nation-states (France, The Netherlands, Norway, and Italy), the binational and bilingual state of Belgium, and countries in the "belt of mixed populations" (Hungary, Romania, Bulgaria, Greece, Serbia, Croatia, and Slovakia).

Moreover, the court found "that in the RSHA, which was the central authority dealing with the Final Solution of the Jewish question, the defendant was at the head of those engaged in implementing the Final Solution."[106] The court further held:

. . . that all the acts perpetrated in implementation of the Final Solution of the Jewish question are to be regarded as one single whole, and that the criminal responsibility of the defendant is to be decided upon accordingly.[107]

And the court concluded:

There is, of course, no better example of [the comprehensive nature of the crime against the Jewish people] than the "Final Solution" itself. The crime in this case originated with Hitler's extermination order, to destroy physically the Jewish people. It was not an order to exterminate the Jews of Germany, or of France, or of Hungary, or of Poland, or of the Soviet Union—each Jewish community separately. It was not an order to exterminate first one million Jews, then another million, and so on. Rather, it was a single, all-embracing order, and the intention of the chief planners and implementers was the same as the intention of the initiator: single and all-embracing. Their criminal intent was not renewed at various times; it was not limited, for example, to the first deportations to Lodz, Minsk, and Riga, so that it could be fulfilled with the conclusion of these deportations, later to be revived with the following deportation; rather, the criminal intent continued in full force, going on to encompass all activities that were undertaken, as long as the overall operation was not completed.

So too the objective aspect—the "actus reus": When the order was given to exterminate the Jews, it was clear that this is an operation of utmost complexity. It was not easy to kill millions of people scattered throughout the population at large. One has to find the victims and isolate them. Not every place is convenient for killing. Not everywhere is the population likely to tolerate the killing of their neighbors. The victims must therefore be transferred to suitable places. The time is a time of war. All hands are needed for work. Working strength should not simply be wasted, and for this reason one should take advantage of the working strength of the victims, as long as their muscles are able to function. It is therefore clear at the outset that a complex bureaucratic machine is required to carry out the operation. Every member of the extermination team above a certain rank knew that such a machine was required, and that it was in existence and was functioning, although not everyone knew how each particular part of the machine functioned, with what means, at what pace, or even where. Hence, the extermination enterprise was a single all-embracing act, and should not be split up into distinct acts or campaigns carried out by different people at different times and in different places. Throughout the whole time, in every place, a single crew of men cooperated in carrying it out.

It follows that everyone who took part in the extermination of the Jews, having knowledge of the plan for the Final Solution and intending to further this plan, is to be considered an accomplice to the extermination of the millions who were exterminated during the years 1941-1945; and it makes no difference whether his activities ranged over the entire extermination front, or only over one or more sectors of that front. His responsibility is that of a "principal offender" who committed the entire crime together with other accomplices. With due apology, we shall cite an example that appears trivial by comparison to the case we are discussing, but can serve to clarify what we have said: Two persons may join hands to forge a document, in such a manner that each forges only a part of it. In this case, they are both responsible as principal offenders, for in the words of our Criminal Code (Section 23(1)(a)), each one of them "committed one of the acts which constitute the crime," and it is not necessary that both should be present at the time each of them carries out his part of the crime.

This is also the rule prevailing in the English common law (Macklin, 168 E.R. 1136; Glanville Williams, Criminal Law, p. 177) and also in United States law. We quote from Wharton's Criminal Law, 12th ed., Vol. 1, p. 340, par. 255:

> "If part of a crime also be committed in one place and part in another, each person concerned in the commission of either part is liable as principal."[108]

In the paperback edition (p. 244), Miss Arendt asserts that the court, in writing the judgment, dropped "the prosecution's charge of 'conspiracy,' which would have made him [Eichmann] a 'chief war criminal,' automatically responsible for everything which had to do with the Final Solution." The court did not drop this charge, for the simple reason that the prosecution did not make such a charge in the indictment (or in any statement before the court).

Another misreading of the judgment is revealed in Miss Arendt's statement that "Eichmann . . . had steadfastly insisted that he was guilty only of 'aiding and abetting' in the commission of the crimes with which he was charged, that he himself had never committed an overt act" (p. 224). This was not Eichmann's defense at all, and Miss Arendt herself seems to have realized it on p. 21, where she asks whether he might not "have pleaded guilty . . . as an accessory to murder." Her "great relief" that "the judgment . . . in a way recognized that the prosecution had not succeeded in proving him wrong on this point [viz., that he was guilty only of "aiding and abetting"]" (p. 224) is premature. In fact, the court explicitly singled out this concept as inapplicable to the Eichmann case. She herself quotes with approval (p. 225) the court's dictum that "in such an enormous and complicated crime . . . wherein many people participated . . . there is not much point in using the ordinary concepts of counseling and soliciting to commit a crime."[109] Miss Arendt is on both sides of the fence at the same time.

The judgment of the Israel Supreme Court is criticized by Miss Arendt because it supposedly stated the following "dangerous nonsense": "It was a fact that the appellant had received no 'superior orders' at all. He was his own superior, and he gave all orders in matters that concerned Jewish affairs" (p. 192). This is not what the court said. Section 17 of Part III of the Supreme Court judgment, after referring to the facts mentioned in Section 16, which "also constitutes . . . a decisive rebuttal of learned counsel's . . . contention, . . . that the appellant was acting on orders from above," continued as follows:

In fact, the Appellant did not at all receive "superior" orders; he was the superior, he was the giver of orders in all that pertained to Jewish affairs; he gave orders and commands not only in the absence of explicit orders from those who were set above him in the line of command, but also occasionally even in direct contravention to orders from above.

This formulation was *not* intended to replace the finding of the District Court in Section 232 of its judgment to the effect that Eichmann was both receiver *and* giver of orders. (Indeed, the

Supreme Court accepted the judgment of the District Court in its entirety, without reservations.[110]) The sentence just quoted from the Supreme Court's judgment must be read in context, in conjunction with the previous section, where numerous particular actions of Eichmann are listed.

Miss Arendt ascribes the origin of what she calls "dangerous nonsense" to the prosecution, and especially to the evidence given by Justice Musmanno. Musmanno, however, gave testimony to the effect that Eichmann was not under *binding* superior orders, and that he could have avoided killing innocent Jewish populations if he had really wanted to. Musmanno gave specific instances taken from the *Einsatzgruppen* case, which revealed that those who really rebelled at killing unarmed innocent civilians had no great difficulty in being excused from the ghastly assignment.[111]

Discussing the Israel Supreme Court's judgment, Miss Arendt writes: "and to make this confirmation the judges would not have needed two months and fifty-one pages" (p. 227)—as if the process of confirming a decision of a lower court requires less time than the process of "revision" (p. 202) or "review" (p. 226) of such a decision. Had she read the decision carefully, she would have found that the Supreme Court reformulated the part of the judgment dealing with the "preliminary objections" raised by Servatius and succinctly summarized Eichmann's activities. The reasons that prompted the Supreme Court to do this are stated as follows:

Let it be said at once that we fully concur, without any hesitations or reservations, in all its [the judgment of the lower court] conclusions and reasoning, because they are firmly based on a great mass of legal opinion cited in the judgment and on abundant evidence drawn and sifted from the monumental amount of evidence submitted in the trial. Furthermore, it is our obligation to point out that were it not for the grave outcome that resulted from the decision of the District Court and that constitutes the subject of this appeal, we would have seen no need whatever to present arguments separately and in our own words—as we are about to do—since the conclusions of the District Court rest on solid foundations.[112]

Miss Arendt asserts that "a group of professors from the Hebrew University in Jerusalem [actually, not only university professors but also others, altogether fifteen persons in public life], headed by Martin Buber," pleaded "for clemency" for Eichmann (pp. 227-228). The truth is that Buber refused to plead for clemency because, in his own words, the "unmerciful subhuman was not worthy of mercy" (*der gnadenlose Untermensch keiner Gnade wert war*). His main reason for cosponsoring a petition against carrying out Eichmann's death penalty was his view that it would be contrary to the "meaning" (*Sinn*) and the dignity of the Jewish people to put an end, in a sense, to its case against National Socialism by executing this "henchman" (*Handlanger*).[113] Miss Arendt, however, is disappointed with Buber for having dodged, "on the highest possible level, the very problem Eichmann and his deeds had posed" (p. 230).

While no adverse comment is made by Miss Arendt in regard to the punishment itself, she condemns the speed with which it was carried out (p. 228). She is apparently unacquainted with the rule of "Inui Hadin" in Jewish law, a rule that does not permit unnecessary postponement of the execution of a sentence.[114] She claims that the protests against Eichmann's execution "were widespread and they were voiced by people of influence and prestige" (p. 228). No names are given. If one judges public opinion by the press, then the exact opposite is true.[115]

Miss Arendt makes the claim (p. 254) that "the justice of what was done in Jerusalem would have emerged to be seen by all if the judges had dared to address their defendant in something like the following terms," and she proceeds to give her own formulation of what the court should properly have said (pp. 254-256). The only true reason Eichmann had to die, she writes, was that "no member of the human race can be expected to want to share the earth with you" (p. 256), since "neither these 'races' [those that were to have been eliminated from the surface of the earth] nor mankind as a whole could permit him to stay among the living" (V, 133; not repeated in the book). This has the same ring as the "sound instinct of the people" (*gesundes Volksempfinden*) guiding the notorious Nazi People's Courts (*Volksgerichte*) that tried enemies of the regime.[116] Who is there to rule whether or not members of the human race can or cannot "be expected to want to share the earth" with people like Eichmann? Shall it be part of the findings of the court? By what methods could the court reach such a conclusion?

The judgments of the District Court and the Supreme Court were commented on by many experts. Three samples serve as a contrast to Miss Arendt's comments. The distinguished British military jurist, Mr. G. I. A. D. Draper, wrote:

In conclusion, it may be said that the legal reasoning upon which the decision of the two courts is based presents a coherent and convincing whole. Attempts to destroy this framework of legal reasoning will undoubtedly be made, but it is open to considerable doubt whether such attempts will command much weight with jurists of repute. The two courts skilfully avoided the enunciation of new principles of law but, it is suggested, honestly and effectively applied existing principles of international and municipal law to a set of facts as novel as they were atrocious. This feat the judges of Israel have performed with outstanding legal skill and erudition. In so doing they showed the world a pronounced example of high judicial integrity. Rarely have judges been required so to discipline their private emotions and revulsion. They abided by that duty fully and faithfully. Out of the great Catastrophe in the history of the Jewish race a judicial precedent has been forged that can stand without fear as a lasting tribute to Jewish justice, and as an event of which the State of Israel may justifiably be proud.[117]

Telford Taylor, United States Chief of Counsel at the Subsequent Trials, while maintaining his reservations in regard to jurisdiction, the concept of crime against the Jewish people, and the death penalty, considers the judgment as

noteworthy for its lucidity and dignity . . . The most impressive feature of the Tribunal's Judgment is its meticulous and dispassionate assessment of the evidence . . . Its [the trial's] conduct by the Judges has been generally and deservedly praised . . . In all these respects [evidence and its evaluation] therefore, the Eichmann Trial is to be accounted a success . . . The corpus of international penal law is a small one and in many respects the Eichmann Judgment is an important increment.[118]

Professor Georg Schwarzenberger of the University of London commented:

Thus, all that it is possible to say on the level of international law is that, either because of the acquiescence of the Federal Republic of Germany (as in relation to the exercise of war crimes jurisdiction in a state of peace) or because of the absence of prohibitory rules (as in relation to crimes against humanity and against the Jewish people) the Nazis Punishment Law of 1950 and its application by the Court are not in conflict with international law. In an ethical perspective, that is to say, viewing the law from the point of view of the standard of civilization, it is possible to be more forthcoming and to acclaim the three substantive provisions of the Nazis Punishment Law as much as its jurisdictional sections, and for the same reasons: as a revindication of the standard of civilization against a totalitarian relapse into barbarism of diabolical dimensions. . . . Thus, both the Eichmann Trial and the Judgment pass the tests of international law and the standard of civilization with flying colours.[119]

By-products of the Trial

The ultimate purpose of the administration of criminal justice is metajuridical: deterrence, sanction, reform, and restraint. The metajuridical purpose does not, however, contradict the immediate purpose of doing justice, nor can the court be responsible for the public or press, which, neither trained in nor bound by professional legal ethics, may seek to make out of the trial something that it should not be. Furthermore, it is inevitable that certain trials, especially trials such as those conducted at Nuremberg and Jerusalem, generate side effects not directly related to their judgments.

In the introductory portion of its judgment, the District Court wrote:

. . . we are not disregarding the many educational benefits latent in the very holding of this trial, both for those who live in Israel and for those who are beyond its borders. To the extent that such benefits have attended these proceedings, they are to be welcomed. Similarly, the testimony given at this trial by survivors of the Catastrophe, who on the witness stand unveiled what had been locked in their hearts, will doubtless provide valuable material for students and historians. But as regards this court, all these things are no more than by-products of the trial.[120]

One of the by-products of the trial was the mass education of the citizens of the State of Israel in the history of the dreadful catastrophe which befell the Jewish people. The real problem was this: Israeli youth had grown up with the impression that the Jews in the Diaspora did not and could not defend themselves. To the Israeli youth—according to their own ways of living, thinking, and reacting—this behavior was incomprehensible. Furthermore, the Diaspora as a whole, with its history of survival and its present-day complicated problems, was something strange, something the young Israelis did not feel at ease with.

It was by no means clear at the outset what the impact of the trial would be. Many were afraid that it would needlessly stir up what should stay buried and unrecalled. As it turned out, the trial on the whole worked in the opposite direction: It was a kind of catharsis to the adults, and a revelation to the young, who, for the first time, became aware of what had happened. There were, as Miss Arendt says (p. 6), people "like myself, who knew by heart all there was to know" and did not want to attend the trial or even listen to broadcasts of it. But the bulk of the population behaved otherwise.[121] One met people listening attentively to the proceedings (parts were broadcast over the radio), their ears glued to transistor radios in the street and at places of work—so much so, that the government had to issue a circular that civil servants were not to listen during office hours. People arranged their schedules according to the broadcasting, and particularly followed the daily summary after the seven o'clock evening news. At crucial moments of the trial, which were transmitted in full, one might walk along any street and listen to the proceedings pouring out of the open windows of every flat. In the course of 121 sessions of the court, 83,500 people visited the courtroom. About 350 yards from it, the proceedings were shown by closed-circuit television in a hall containing more than 500 seats, which was filled almost to capacity all the time. The spectators were by no means mainly "middle-aged and elderly people, immigrants from Europe" (p. 6). This is not true. To Jews of Oriental origin, and to young Israelis (at the beginning of the trial secondary schools were closed because of a prolonged teachers' strike), this was the first real contact with the mysterious calamity they had been told somehow concerned them.

A reporter from the *Jerusalem Post* was in the annex to the courtroom on the opening day, and there interviewed two elderly people from Central Europe, two men in their twenties from Iraq, a sixteen-year-old son of Hungarian parents, a Jerusalem workman in his thirties, and a twenty-year-old soldier from a northern kibbutz who chose to spend his leave listening to the proceedings. Why did the people listen, why did they attend, if they felt it to be superfluous, as Miss Arendt claims? Why did they queue up at the police station, where tickets of admission were issued, and return repeatedly after having been turned away because no more tickets were available? Why did they come to Jerusalem from all over the country to see the trial? Nobody compelled them, nobody urged them, nobody even asked them to. According to Miss Arendt, those who knew the history of the period did not need to be reminded. But people did continue to come and to listen.

Equally without foundation is her statement that the young

generation in Israel did not care about the trial (p. 6). Surveys conducted and reported by Dr. Aryeh Bauminger and Mr. Shimeon Redlich present a different picture.[122] The Attorney General received hundreds of letters from youngsters, some of which were published. The general tenor of their feelings was: "Thank you for opening our eyes to learn what really happened there."

The impact on Israeli writers was profound. In a discussion printed in *Maariv*, the popular Israel evening newspaper, Miss Geula Cohen approached four authors of different generations— among them two born in Israel (*sabras*), Moshe Shamir, novelist and dramatist, and Dalia Ravikovitz, poet. Among the questions put to them was, Why is it that the Israeli writers of today have not given adequate literary expression to the great catastrophe of our generation, the extermination of European Jewry? The discussion was analyzed in an article by Moshe Bar-Natan.[123] The following excerpt is his report on Shamir's reply, with some direct quotes from this novelist:

As for the catastrophe of European Jewry, it is not quite true to say that our literature has failed to reflect the tragedy, but we are troubled by the feeling that it has not yet found adequate expression. The difficulty is that "just as the catastrophe was something hellish and inconceivable, so we are waiting for a work that will express something of our inability to grasp the catastrophe, the fact that we confront it with empty hands. If we have no literature about the catastrophe, that is first and foremost because we have no literature about *ourselves*." What is required is . . . not an adequate perspective, but just the contrary. Until Hebrew authors feel the catastrophe as a personal tragedy, they will not be able to write about it. The trouble is that from the cold biographical point of view, the Yiddish writers were "*inside* the burning house," while the Hebrew writers saw it from the outside.

If some of the younger authors, like Aharon Appelfeld, Yehuda Amihai, Ben-Zion Tomer and Natan Shaham, have begun to write on these subjects, it is first of all because they experienced those horrors in their childhood and are trying to purge themselves of the burden of that experience. And there is a second reason, a recent event which has brought the subject home to the younger generation "as a personal, moral problem." That is the Eichmann Trial, not only in itself but against the background of the affluent society—Israeli version, in the sixties of this century: the dramatic and shattering contrast between the world that the trial presented with such terrific force, and the life that surrounded the courthouse, with people going to listen to the proceedings in their private Volkswagens, with German gasoline in their tanks. "The force of testimonies of death at the trial, against the background of our *dolce vita*, have caused me, more than anything else, to feel the catastrophe for the first time as a personal problem of my own." . . . The real subjects that await expression . . . are not the catastrophe and its resurgence in themselves, but "the catastrophe and ourselves today," or "the significance of the resurgence in our own lives."

Dalia Ravikovitz was reported to have felt

that the tragedy of European Jewry lies like a heavy shadow over her own generation, especially after the Eichmann Trial. "Even I," she says, "who am the third generation in this country, felt during the trial as if I were experiencing these things for the second time . . . The Holocaust is like an exploding hand grenade; each of us has been struck by his own private splinter, which he carries in his body. Even if we do not know it, therefore, the Holocaust is the central theme in our literature, until even love songs become songs of nightmare and children's songs cannot distract our attention from the miseries of maturity."

Mr. Bar-Natan added the following observation:

It seems to me that this sensitivity to the oppressive burden of the slaughter, this feeling of guilt that weighs on Shamir when the Eichmann Trial brings home the contrast between the sufferings of European Jewry and the carefree life of the average Israeli, shows that the gulf between the younger generation in Israel and the Diaspora Jew is not so deep, or so unbridgeable, as appears at first sight.

Concerning the impact of the Eichmann trial on the Federal Republic of Germany, Miss Arendt states (p. 10): "In one respect Mr. Ben-Gurion's expectations for the trial were not altogether disappointed; it did indeed become an important instrument for ferreting out other Nazis and criminals." On the next page she says that "he [Ben-Gurion] had *not* foreseen . . . that Eichmann's capture would trigger the first serious effort made by Germany to bring to trial at least those who were directly implicated in murder." However, her facts are wrong, and her notions about what went on in Germany are confused.

In the German Federal Republic, efforts to bring war criminals to trial were intensified following the creation of the *Zentrale Stelle der Landesjustizverwaltungen* (Central Agency of the Ministries of Justice in the States) at Ludwigsburg.[124] Under Erwin Schüle, this agency began its efforts on December 1, 1958, and there is no evidence that the Eichmann trial had a direct influence on the course of proceedings against persons charged before German judicial bodies with perpetrating "crimes of Nazi violence" (*nationalsozialistische Gewaltverbrechen*). What happened during and after the Eichmann trial was that greater interest in the problem was generated, owing to the publicity given the proceedings.

There is also no basis for Miss Arendt's statement that local German courts before the Eichmann trial had been unwilling "to prosecute on the basis of the material sent them from the Central Agency" (p. 11). Her statement that Eichmann's "sensational capture" and the prospect of his trial had an impact strong enough "to persuade the local courts to use Mr. Schüle's findings" (p. 11) is based on her misunderstanding of the function of the Central Agency in a country where criminal jurisdiction is given over exclusively to the States. The procedure is not as simple as Miss Arendt seems to think. The Central Agency, after completion of its preliminary investigation, transmits the results to the competent state prosecutor's office (*Staatsanwaltschaft*) for further investigation (including a judicial one), which may result in an indictment (*Anklageschrift*). Only after this entire procedure has been completed does a trial take place in the competent court.

Miss Arendt contends that "the results were amazing" (p. 11). While it is true that the investigation of Eichmann and the simultaneous investigations in Germany of other cases had their impact in Germany, Miss Arendt's details are far from accurate. She declares that the "native reluctance to do anything about 'murderers in our midst'" was "overcome" by "the time-honored means of posting rewards for the capture of well-known criminals" (p. 11). However, this method was used only in one State (*Land*)—namely, Hesse. Miss Arendt further contends that Hermann Krumey, one of Eichmann's associates, was arrested only after the capture of Eichmann. In fact, he had already been arrested in 1957, was freed, was rearrested in 1960, and tried in 1964. She also says that Gustav Richter, former "Jewish adviser" in Romania, was arrested at the same time. Not only is he still free; he has even been invited, despite his wartime activities, to testify in compensation cases as an expert on Jewish questions in Romania. And she reports Wilhelm Zöpf (paperback edition, page 14) to have been arrested following Eichmann's capture. Actually, he was arrested in 1959, released in 1960, and is still free. She errs also in her description of the

Martin Fellenz case (p. 13) when she says that this "former Higher S.S. and Police Leader" was sentenced to four years in prison for participation in the murder of 40,000 Polish Jews. Actually Fellenz was the chief-of-staff (*Stabsleiter*) of Julian Scherner, who was the SS and Police Leader in Cracow, with the rank of SS-*Sturmbann-führer*. The judgment against him has not yet become effective; the German Supreme Court (*Bundesgerichtshof*) threw out the decision of the lower court on appeal of the Attorney General, and a new trial will take place.[125]

Miss Arendt errs also in regard to the criminal law of Germany. She says that "after May, 1960 . . . only *first degree murder* could be prosecuted" (p. 12). This is a term borrowed from Anglo-Saxon law. The statute of limitations of twenty years under German law refers to the two types of murder defined in the German Criminal Code (*Totschlag*, manslaughter; and *Mord*, murder) and both to the main culprit and to those charged with complicity. Moreover, the statute of limitations is suspended with respect to any particular party for the duration of a judicial action involving that party.[126]

Miss Arendt expresses surprise at the "small amount of post-trial literature" (p. 232). This is a severe accusation against historians, jurists, and observers who might have been expected to write and comment on the trial. The fact is that there is an extensive post-trial literature. A partial list is offered in Part I of the Bibliography.

Concluding Remarks

The conduct of the Eichmann trial was entirely correct. The proceedings took place in full accordance with the rules and practices of national and international law, and with the principles of justice as interpreted by the most advanced legal systems.

4

Jewish Behavior
in the Face of Disaster

The Charge of Jewish Cooperation

In the opening pages of her book, Miss Arendt declares specifically that it was inadmissible for the court to consider the question "How could the Jews through their own leaders cooperate in their own destruction?" (p. 3). Yet she later charges that "the gravest omission from the 'general picture' was that of a witness to testify to the cooperation between the Nazi rulers and the Jewish authorities, and hence of an opportunity to raise the question: 'Why did you cooperate in the destruction of your own people and, eventually, in your own ruin?'" (p. 110). She devotes considerable attention to this question.

Miss Arendt justifies her digression from the strict limits of the trial on two grounds: (1) She feels it necessary to fill in the "inexplicable lacunae" (p. 106) in the judgment, for the sake of revealing to all eyes the "whole truth," the story "in its true dimensions" (p. 111). (2) She claims that the subject is relevant to the trial proceedings since "the prosecution's case would have been weakened if it had been forced to admit that the naming of individuals who were sent to their doom had been, with few exceptions, the job of the Jewish administration" (p. 106). Actually, in moral and statutory law the enforced cooperation of a helpless victim is usually considered a factor *aggravating* the responsibility of the criminal. Such cooperation, even if it had occurred as stated by Miss Arendt, could have provided no comfort to the defense.

The charges Miss Arendt levels against the Jews are serious. They deserve to be listed here, even partially. Some of her charges:

1. ". . . the whole truth [*sic*] was that there existed Jewish community organizations and Jewish party and welfare organiza-

tions . . . on . . . the local . . . level. Wherever Jews lived, there were recognized Jewish leaders, and this leadership, almost without exception, cooperated in one way or another, for one reason or another, with the Nazis. The whole truth was that if the Jewish people had really been unorganized and leaderless, there would have been chaos and plenty of misery but the total number of victims would hardly have been between four and a half and six million people" (p. 111).

2. "Jewish officials" became "instruments of murder" (p. 105), and "could be trusted" to carry out orders connected with deportation (p. 104). (This is said as if the relationship between the Nazis and the "Jewish officials" was based on "trust" and not on terror, a word practically missing in her book.)

3. "The Nazis gave enormous powers" to people who were "as a rule the locally recognized Jewish leaders" (p. 104), whose cooperation was "one of the most important prerequisites for their [the Jews] seizure" (p. 150).

4. Jewish cooperation "was 'of course the very cornerstone' of everything he [Eichmann] did" (p. 104, repeated on p. 110).[1] (Everything? fixing the quotas? securing transportation? selecting victims for deportation? rounding them up? policing them en route?)

5. Eichmann received the "cooperation" of the Jewish Councils "to a truly extraordinary degree" (p. 104). (What is ordinary in such cases?)

6. Jewish "cooperation" was "universal" (p. 109).

7. "To a Jew this role of the Jewish leaders in the destruction of their own people is undoubtedly the darkest chapter of the whole dark story" (p. 104).

Speaking for Eichmann, Miss Arendt declares (pp. 103-104) that "of course he did not expect the Jews to share the general enthusiasm over their destruction"—an interesting example of misplaced whimsicality—"but he did expect more than compliance." (There is nothing in the record to indicate Eichmann's expectations.)

And more. Miss Arendt finds that Jewish "cooperation" put an end to the "clear-cut division between persecutors and victims" (p. 106). It is difficult to conceive a statement more offensive in respect to the dead, and more ignorant of the moral and legal basis for responsibility.

The view widely held by students of the Second World War is that the murder of six million Jews was the direct responsibility of Nazi Germany which carried it out, and that it was indirectly aided by the almost universal passivity of the non-Jewish conquered populations, the neutrals, and the Allies, who by action or inaction did next to nothing to prevent it. The destruction of six million Jews—and not the "role of the Jewish leaders"—is the "darkest chapter" of Jewish history during the Nazi period, and indeed during all time.

Apparently believing that detection of Jewish origins in non-Jewish persons (the top Nazis were not above making use of innuendos of Jewish origin as means of intimidation or controlling each other[2]) is relevant to the history of the Jewish Catastrophe, Miss Arendt adds the charge (pp. 118-119) that "it was generally known" (but on pp. 160-161 she says that it "was a highly confidential matter") that two of the most notorious mass murderers of Jews, Reinhardt Heydrich and Hans Frank, were themselves Jews: Heydrich a half-Jew, and Frank "probably . . . even a full Jew." (There are significant differences between the various versions of the book. In the serial version, III, 64, Frank is depicted as "at least a half-Jew and probably even a full Jew"; and the reference to Frank on pp. 160-161 has no parallel in IV, 78. In the paperback edition all references to Frank's Jewishness are omitted.) She even suggests a connection between their "Jewishness" and their alleged repentance before death: "it is difficult not to suspect that what they repented of was not murder but that they had betrayed their own people" (p. 119). This conclusion follows her statement that "among the major war criminals, only two repented in the face of death" (p. 118)—namely, Frank and Heydrich. In fact, we know that Baldur von Schirach,[3] Field Marshal Keitel,[4] and Albert Speer[5] repented—all three of them major war criminals. Miss Arendt says that Heydrich was reported to have repented "during the nine days it took him to die from the wounds inflicted by Czech patriots" (p. 118). The source of this information is not given. Heydrich's biographer, Charles Wighton, makes no mention of such repentance.[6] Gerald Reitlinger writes that "for six days Heydrich endured the agony of a severed spine, expressing, it is said, deep contrition for his actions."[7] Reitlinger's source was a book that did not give an original source and did not tell whether the alleged contrition was for anti-Czech or for anti-Jewish actions. As for Hans Frank, it is true that in his conversations with Dr. G. M. Gilbert, the International Military Tribunal's psychologist, he admitted his guilt, but not without hedging.[8] The same thing happened in the April 18, 1946, session of the Tribunal. Replying to the question of his defense counsel, "Did you ever participate in the annihilation of the Jews," Hans Frank told the Tribunal: "It is no more than my duty to answer your question in this connection with 'yes.' A thousand years will pass and still this guilt of Germany will not have been erased."[9] But in the session of August 31, 1946, in his final plea, Frank recanted his repentance:

There is still one statement of mine which I must rectify. On the witness stand I said that a thousand years would not suffice to erase the guilt brought upon our people because of Hitler's conduct in this war. Every possible guilt incurred by our nation has already been completely wiped out today, not only by the conduct of our wartime enemies towards our nation and its soldiers, which has been carefully kept out of this Trial, but also by the tremendous mass crimes of the most frightful sort which—as I have now learned—have been and still are being committed against Germans by Russians, Poles, and Czechs, especially in East Prussia, Silesia, Pomerania, and Sudetenland. Who shall ever judge these crimes against the German people?[10]

So much, then, for Miss Arendt's claim that Heydrich and Frank, and they alone, repented, which is without foundation. Her tale that they were Jews—so pregnant with the implication that Jews were directly responsible for the mass murder of their own people—turns out also to be false. A search in the personal dossiers of these two men, both available in the Berlin Document Center (the custodian of the Central Archives of the Nazi Party) reveals the following: The detailed genealogy (*Ahnenliste*) of Reinhardt Tristan Eugen Heydrich, which goes back four generations, does not contain any trace of Jewish "blood" or religion in the family.[11] The problem of his pure Aryan origin was raised by Rudolf Jordan, Party District Leader (*Gauleiter*) of Halle-Merseburg, in a letter addressed to Gregor Strasser in Munich, dated June 6, 1932 (before the Nazis came to power). The reason for raising the problem was that in Hugo Riemann's *Musik-Lexikon*[12] the name of Reinhardt's father, Bruno (director of the Conservatory of Music in Halle), was accompanied by the words *"eigentlich Süss"* in parentheses, meaning "real name Süss." Since Süss was a name widely used by German Jews (though not exclusively a Jewish name), the apparatus of investigation was set in motion. Sixteen days later, a report prepared by Dr. Gercke of the Nazi Information Service (*N. S. Auskunft*) in Munich stated categorically that Reinhardt Heydrich was "of German origin and had no colored or Jewish blood" (*deutscher Herkunft . . . und frei von farbigem und jüdischem Bluteinschlag*). The reason for the mixup was that Reinhardt Heydrich's grandmother, née Ernestine Wilhelmine Lindner, had been married a second time, to one Gustav Robert Süss. By her first marriage, with Reinhold Karl Julius Heydrich, she had been the mother of numerous children (among them Reinhardt's father, Bruno) and was frequently referred to as Süss-Heydrich. Neither her first husband, Reinhold Heydrich, nor her second husband, Gustav Robert Süss, were of Jewish origin. The *Musik-Lexikon* in the post-1916 editions did not carry the compromising "*eigentlich Süss*" parentheses.[13]

The *Ahnenliste* of Hans Frank, which goes back to 1750, shows no trace of Jewish blood or religion.[14] It should be borne in mind that Hans Frank was one of the first disciples of Hitler. He early became the legal adviser of the Nazi Party and was very active in party affairs. It is inconceivable that Hitler would have selected Frank for such an important function had Frank had any Jewish ancestors. Hitler would hardly have exposed himself to the charge of employing a person of Jewish origin, particularly in such sensitive positions as Minister of Justice of Bavaria or Governor General of the Government-General.

Only Eichmann was directly involved in the Jerusalem trial. The problem of the responsibility for the enormous Jewish losses during the Nazi period was not part of the proceedings. In particular, Jewish "cooperation" with Nazis was not a subject of the trial. We are forced, however, to enter into a consideration of these matters for the simple reason that Miss Arendt has chosen them as the basis for some of her most exceptionable remarks. Indeed, her question "How could the Jews through their own leaders cooperate in their own destruction?" (p. 3) is a heavily loaded question. First, it assumes that they did "cooperate," and simply asks how they could have done it. Second, it implies that Jewish communities were everywhere under the guidance and direction of "their own leaders," which means persons with previous standing, present authority, and a certain degree of independence—leaders presumably chosen in some way or other voluntarily by the communities. Third, it implies, in the phrase "cooperate in their own destruction," that the leaders knew all along the fate in store for their charges and for themselves. Fourth, it explicitly states that not only the "leaders" but also "the Jews through their own leaders" were responsible, in a grand suicidal manner, for their own annihilation.

One stands aghast at this distortion of the historical facts. Many of Miss Arendt's charges contradict even the data she herself brings out in her book; all of her charges stand in contradiction to the actual history of the Catastrophe. I shall here attempt to set aright some of her charges.

The Administration of Hitler's Europe

Throughout Nazi-occupied Europe the Germans used the native administrative organs. Generally, these were not avowedly collaborationist. In certain countries the Germans devised some form of German supervisory machinery which could control the native civil service from the top and thus keep a watch over the agencies of government operating at the lower levels. In The Netherlands they set up four German "General Commissariats" to direct the work of the Dutch Secretaries-General, and these four commissariats were in turn responsible to the Reich Commissioner in The Netherlands, Arthur Seyss-Inquart, for the orderly conduct of their departments within the domain of their activity. The Dutch provincial and municipal administrations were supervised by a German *Beauftragter*, a person having political rather than administrative experience.[15] Essentially the same policy was followed in Belgium[16] and in Norway prior to the formation on February 1, 1942, of a collaborationist National Norwegian Government, with Vidkun Quisling as Prime Minister.[17] In the occupied zone of France, the Germans only supervised the French administrative system, which was run from Vichy by French administrators.[18] In the Government-General (in Poland), the villages, towns, and town districts (*Stadtkreise*) remained in the hands of Polish officials. These administrative units were brought together in communal associations (*Gemeindeverbände*) and were placed under the supervision of German district chiefs.[19] A similar administrative structure was set up in the *Reich Commissariat* of Ukraine.[20] As for Ostland the situation was as follows: In the General District (*Generalbezirk*) of Byelorussia there was no central Byelorussian administration. Not so in the General Districts of Lithuania, Latvia, and Esthonia, where along with indigenous local administrations there were also local central bodies appointed by the respective General Commissioners with the approval of the Reich Commissioner Lohse.[21] Needless to say, in German satellites and countries allied with the Axis powers (Croatia, Slovakia, Romania, and Hungary), the administration remained in local hands, with the Germans exercising their influence through diplomatic channels.

We have it on the authority of one of the top Nazi leaders, Alfred Rosenberg, that the reason for using local administrations was that the Germans suffered from a shortage of administrative personnel and had therefore to exercise great economy in the use of manpower.[22] For example, in the whole of Belgium, according to the *Frankfurter Zeitung* of May 18, 1942, "only about 475 German officers, officials and specialists"—together with all assistants, a total of 830 persons—"suffice to run the whole country, or more accurately, to govern and guide it." This estimate excludes the military personnel, and presumably also the police personnel and the SS men.[23]

Thus, although some countries had Nazi collaborators in their native governments, particularly in the top echelons, the administrative apparatus, consisting of tens of thousands of officials, contained people who in their hearts hated the invader. It was, however, the "cooperation" of these reluctant officials that made continued Nazi occupation possible. Serving the Germans, the local administrators had to implement Nazi orders, even those directed against their own compatriots; with few exceptions, they complied. Under conditions of sustained Nazi terror, little else could have been expected. After the war, no one summarily condemned the entire local administration, or population, for having contributed to the misery of the country and to sufferings of individuals. Only those who acted out of identification with the Nazi objectives or for their own benefit were prosecuted and duly punished.

The following figures serve to indicate the extent of the postwar judicial activity involving allegedly genuine collaborators in former occupied or Nazi-allied Europe.[24] In France during 1945-1952, 10,519 Frenchmen were executed for wartime collaboration, and 2,400 collaborators were still in prison in 1952. In Norway, 46,085 people were found guilty of treason and collaboration during the war. In Czechoslovakia, as of November 1, 1946, 18,496 had been charged as war criminals or collaborators, the overwhelming majority of them as collaborators. In Denmark, 13,600 people were tried as collaborators, but the punishments were mild. In Belgium, a total of 180,000 people were accused of pro-Nazi activities and sympathies. In Hungary, the People's Tribunals instituted proceedings against 29,917 persons before June 31, 1948, prepared indictments against 20,778, and delivered judgments in 10,613 cases, nearly all of them involving collaborators. Romania conducted trials against collaborators—generals, officials, and politicians—but the number of people prosecuted was small.

A few words about the "cooperation" of the general populations of occupied Europe:[25] Due to the requirements of the armed forces, the German civilian labor force was reduced from 39,415,000 on May 31, 1939, to 35,920,000 on September 30, 1944, while the number of foreign laborers in Germany grew from 301,000 to 7,487,000 during the same period; none of them rebelled. These colossal numbers of non-German laborers in Germany were only part of the European labor force exploited by the Nazis. Local employment in one's own country did not mean that a worker was producing goods for distribution within its borders or, indeed, that his labor was in any way benefiting his native land. The *Organisation Todt* (named after Todt, German Minister of Public Works), responsible for the building of roads, railways, bridges, and pillboxes, for the digging of trenches, and for the construction of such large-scale works as the Atlantic Wall, which stretched from the north of Norway to the Spanish border, employed hundreds of thousands of foreign workers in their own countries. Large-scale industrial production (including armaments) in occupied or German-allied Europe also involved hundreds of thousands of foreign laborers. No over-all estimate has been made of the number of persons who were engaged in work beneficial to the German war effort, other than those employed in the Reich. Some idea of the scale of German employment of foreign workers may be gathered from official French statistics: The Germans gained 15,053,989,000 man-hours from French workers in France as compared with 7,748,568,000 man-hours from Frenchmen working in Germany.

Needless to say, industry and raw materials, food and agriculture, transport and finance were all strictly controlled by the occupying power. The population as a whole (with the exception of the resistance fighters) submitted to this order of things. It is clear that noncooperation and nonacquiescence on the part of the non-Jewish population would have been a strong weapon against the invader, in view of the dependence of the German war effort on foreign labor. Except for occasional strikes or acts of sabotage, no concerted action was ever undertaken. This is not surprising, of course, in light of the conditions under Nazi terror. The most drastic measures were taken by the Nazis against Soviet prisoners of war. Though these prisoners were military men, brought up in Soviet and Russian patriotism, and trained in the use of weapons, they too are not known to have offered any resistance—except for one group in Southern Germany.[26]

Such were the conditions in Hitler's Europe.

Some Preliminary Observations on the Study of the Catastrophe

It is a fact that most students of the Jewish aspects of the Nazi period have drawn almost exclusively on source material of German origin, from among the vast quantities of German material captured at the end of the war. For example, two major studies of the Catastrophe (listed by Miss Arendt in her Bibliography, and ostensibly relied upon by her) are Gerald Reitlinger's *The Final Solution*[27] and Raul Hilberg's *The Destruction of the European Jews*.[28] A careful review of the source material referred to in these volumes reveals it to be almost entirely of German origin, and to be almost totally lacking in documents of Jewish origin. The results of research based on such one-sided source material should not be difficult to foresee.[29]

The obstacles confronting a scholar who wishes to obtain a balanced view of the period are formidable. The material emanating from Jewish sources is written in a variety of languages, chiefly Hebrew, Yiddish, Polish, and Hungarian. Scholars of this period of Jewish history must have at least some of these languages at their command; otherwise, the main sources are a closed book to them. In addition, the organization and analysis of the large amounts of source material available has hardly begun, and the collection of data on internal Jewish relations is still being actively pursued. At present the main sources are two series of town histories, written in

Hebrew;[30] a few hundred Memorial (*Yizkor*) Books on individual Jewish communities destroyed during the period of the Final Solution;[31] monographs on major ghettos, such as those of Warsaw,[32] Vilna,[33] Kovno,[34] Białystok,[35] Lodz,[36] Cracow,[37] Šiauliai (Shavli),[38] Częstochowa,[39] and Lwów,[40] located in the area of Poland and the Soviet Union; and a rich collection of autobiographies, personal memoirs, and eyewitness testimonies, published and unpublished.[41] The Bibliography of the present volume, in Parts II and III, lists some key guides to the growing literature.

The methodological problems connected with this source material have been explored only in a preliminary way. Articles on these problems have been published in Warsaw,[42] London,[43] and Jerusalem.[44] An ongoing discussion is being centered on them in the major institutions of research into the Catastrophe, located in Jerusalem, New York, London, Warsaw, and Paris (see the Bibliography, Part II, on these institutions). Here, too, the major task is yet to be done.

The problems facing the researcher in the internal Jewish aspect of the history of the Catastrophe are varied and enormous. Among the subjects that require study are the territorial limits of jurisdiction of the various Jewish Councils; fields of competence of the Jewish Councils, in particular in connection with the supply of labor and "participation" in the deportations; the polyarchy (municipal administration, Nazi *Ghettoverwaltung*, SD and SS, *Judenrat*, Jewish police and its multiple subordination, and the like); the fluctuation in composition of the *Judenräte* and the continuity or discontinuity of their membership with traditional communal leadership; selection, nomination, election (genuine and fictitious), resignation, dismissal, and filling vacancies; personal motivations; internal conflicts within Jewish groups concerning strategies and tactics vis-à-vis the *Judenräte*; the opposition to the *Judenräte*; the moral problems facing the *Judenräte*; *Judenräte* and the rabbinate; *Judenräte* and the Jewish police; differences in relations between the *Judenräte* and the Nazi-tolerated Jewish organizations on the one hand and the underground on the other; the status and functions of employees of the *Judenräte*; the forms and methods of Nazi deception, terror, and direct interference; Nazi appointments; the suicides; and the repressions against members of the *Judenräte*. Attention must also be paid to particular types of *Judenräte* in various regions: the German *Reichsvertretung* (later, *Reichsver-*

einigung), the Vienna *Kultusgemeinde, Zentrale der Ältestenräte der jüdischen Kultusgemeinden Ost-Oberschlesiens* in Sosnowiec, the Jewish *Ältestenrat* in Prague, the *Union Générale des Israélites de France* (UGIF), the *Joodse Raad voor Amsterdam*, the *Association des Juifs en Belgique*, the *Ústredňa Židov* in Slovakia, the *Magyar Zsidók Központi Tanácsa* in Hungary, the *Centrala Evreilor din România*, and the Nazi-appointed Chief of the Jewish community in Saloniki.

Generally speaking, the entire study of this aspect of the Catastrophe is still in its formative stage. While some of our present findings may be considered final, the great majority of the questions can be given only tentative answers. With this understanding, an attempt is made in the following pages to limit the discussion to the presentation of well-established conclusions. Care is taken to indicate where the results are only tentative and to provide always the sources for statements.

Origins of the Jewish Councils

The idea of recruiting Jews to assume responsibility for the administration of the segregated Jewish communities originated with the Germans, and had been tried out by Eichmann—before the outbreak of the war—in Berlin, Vienna, and Prague.[45] It received official sanction on September 21, 1939, in the notorious meeting of SS leaders (including Eichmann).[46] As a result a large number of Jewish Councils were set up, even before Hitler had decided on the nature of the Final Solution. The Jews were in no position to oppose this move, especially since it was impossible in the very nature of things for millions of people to be without some organized administration. (Consequences of the chaos ensuing upon a breakdown of communal organization are discussed later.) For example, the Warsaw *Ältestenrat* (Council of Elders) was established on October 23, 1939, by order of the Nazi chief of police (*Polizeipräsident*).[47] The proclamation (*Aufruf*) establishing this Council was issued in three languages—Yiddish, Polish, and German—and began with the following preamble:

A census of all Jews in Warsaw is required for the purpose of regulating the economic conditions in Warsaw. For this purpose a Council of Elders of the Jewish Community has been established under former Senator Adam Czerniakow. It will operate in the building of the Jewish Religious Community, Warsaw, Grzybowska 26/28.[48]

Even this brief account serves to illustrate the main features of the beginnings of the Jewish Councils: The Councils were established by order of the conqueror, for stated purposes whose legitimacy could hardly have been called in question, and whose execution could no more (and indeed, far less) be resisted by the Jews than it could be by other elements of the population.

When the Nazi Special Operations Units (*Einsatzgruppen*) were given their final instructions for their operations in conquered Poland, specific orders concerning the establishment of Jewish Councils were included. The instructions were formulated at the meeting of SS leaders in September 1939, in which Eichmann participated, and were issued in a top secret letter from the Chief of the German Security Police to all commanders of the *Einsatzgruppen*.[49] After indicating that "the chief prerequisite to attaining the ultimate goal (*Endziel*)[50] is the concentration of the Jews from the countryside into the large cities," the letter devotes the following special section to Councils of Jewish Elders:

(1) In each Jewish community, a Council of Jewish Elders is to be set up which, as far as possible, is to be composed of the remaining influential personalities and rabbis. The Council is to be composed of [up to] 24 male Jews (depending on the size of the Jewish community). It is to be made *fully responsible* (in the literal sense of the word) for the exact execution according to terms of all instructions released or yet to be released.

(2) In case of sabotage of such instructions, the Councils are to be warned of severest measures.

(3) The Jewish Councils are to take an improvised census of the Jews of their area, possibly divided into generations (according to age)

    a. up to 16 years of age,

    b. from 16 to 20 years of age,

    c. and those above,

and also according to the principal vocations, and they are to report the results in the shortest possible time.

(4) The Councils of Elders are to be made acquainted with the time and date of the evacuation, the evacuation possibilities, and finally the evacuation routes. They are, then, to be made personally responsible for the evacuation of the Jews from the country.

The reason to be given for the concentration of the Jews to the cities is that Jews have most decidedly participated in sniper attacks and plundering.

(5) The Councils of Elders of the concentration centers are to be made

responsible for the proper housing of the Jews to be brought in from the country. The concentration of Jews in the cities for general reasons of security will probably bring about orders to forbid Jews to enter certain wards of the city altogether, and to forbid them, for reasons of economic necessity, for instance, to leave the ghetto, to go out after a designated evening hour, etc.

(6) The Council of Elders is also to be made responsible for the provision of adequate supplies to the Jews on the transport to the cities.

No scruples are to be voiced, if the migrating Jews take with them all their movable possessions, as far as that is at all possible technically.

(7) Jews who do not comply with the order to move into cities are to be given a short additional period of grace when there is good reason. They are to be warned of strictest penalty if they should not comply by the appointed time.

Gradually, these provisions became much more severe, but the basic idea of making the Jewish Council an instrument imposed by the Nazis on the Jews to control them remained intact.

The texts of the official orders have little in common with the way Jewish Councils originated and functioned in practice. The following is a report by Shmuel (Artur) Zygelboim on the beginning of the Jewish Council in Warsaw. (Zygelboim was a member of the Council in Warsaw. He later became a member of the Polish National Council, the parliamentary arm of the government-in-exile in London, and committed suicide in protest against the indifference of the world to the Jewish Catastrophe.) His report:

The first meeting of the *Judenrat* took place in the middle of October. A Gestapo officer by the name of Mende came to the meeting and delivered a speech as if he were speaking to criminals. He ordered the *Judenrat* to stand while listening. He said that the fate of the Jews and of the *Judenrat* was in the hands of the Gestapo. The *Judenrat* is not to approach any other Nazi offices. No discussions. "The *Führer* law reigns here." What the Gestapo orders, has to be executed promptly and meticulously, "not in the Jewish manner." He, Mende, will see to it that the Jews do as ordered, or else. . . .[51]

Three weeks after the appointment of the *Judenrat* in Warsaw, its members were suddenly called to an urgent meeting. It was on a Sabbath. At 12 o'clock Gestapo men came to the chairman and ordered him to call a meeting for 4 o'clock the same day. Out of the 24 members of the *Judenrat* only 16 could be located. With heavy hearts and grave thoughts we waited in the conference room of the Jewish community building. It was not the first time that the Gestapo had suddenly summoned us. Each time we had been faced with some new persecution order or with some obnoxious assignment which we refused to carry out. We knew that we were playing with fire, that sooner or later we would refuse once too often and the Gestapo would submit us to torture or shoot us and take vengeance on all Warsaw Jews . . . At quarter past four the doors were abruptly forced open. Gestapo men entered, rifles, pistols, and whips in their hands. They took up places in half-circle around us and looked at us with angry, evil eyes without saying a word. They appeared so unexpectedly, with such force and in such a terrifying manner that all sixteen people seated around the table jumped up. For a long time there was an agonizing, stifling stillness in the room. The Gestapo men, standing around, saying nothing, looked at each one of us, some artfully smiling, until one of them barked out in barracks-like tone: "All present?"

The chairman handed him the attendance list and the Gestapo man called out each member . . . The roll call finished, the Gestapo men, taking along the chairman, went into the latter's office. After 15 minutes, a Gestapo officer came out and said: "You, listen and be careful! The *Judenrat* consists of 24 members and 24 alternates. Only 16 are present. I give you half an hour to fetch all the others. Forty-eight Jews must be present. No discussion! An order is an order." The officer left; the chairman came back and we tried to consider what to do. After some deliberation it was decided that in order to produce the full contingent of the membership, we will enlist Jews from outside the *Judenrat* wherever we may find them. We called in all clerks of the *Judenrat* who were present in the building at the time, and a few Jews who happened to pass by the building and a few Jews from the Jewish funeral parlors which were located close by. A list of all those present, of whom more than half were included by sheer accident, was then submitted to the Gestapo officer. He ordered that all assemble in the meeting hall and form two lines—one of the members of the *Judenrat* and the other of the alternates.

Thus we stood for a long time, waiting until the door was thrust open once again and about 50 Gestapo men under the command of an officer entered the hall. All carried pistols or whips. Quietly we stood facing each other—the two rows of Jews, and the Gestapo men in between the rows. The beasts and we, their prey, looked at each other in silence; upon all of us looked down from the walls the portraits of generations of rabbis. Some of the Gestapo men took pictures; we kept standing and waiting.

Finally, in a threatening, harsh voice the officer uttered: "Jews, you listen to me, and listen carefully! The commandant has ordered that all Jews of Warsaw must leave their present homes and move to the streets that have been designated for the ghetto, not later than Tuesday. To assure that the order is strictly carried out, all 24 alternates will be taken hostages. With their heads they are responsible for the exact execution of the order. You, the members of the *Judenrat*, are also responsible with your heads. We are not taking you away now simply because somebody must remain here to take care of the execution of the order." The 24 Jews, present only by accident, were then surrounded by the Gestapo men. Orders were shouted: "About Face, Forward March!" and they marched out. Outside, in the street, trucks were waiting and the Jews were carried away.[52]

Miss Arendt has very little to say concerning these origins of the Jewish Councils. She is not unaware of the fact that the Jewish leaders were in the power of the Nazis. In fact, she states that "the only Jews Eichmann remembered were those who had been completely in his power" (p. 58), i.e., the Jewish officials. But she later asserts that ". . . the establishing of Quisling governments in occupied territories was always accompanied by the organization of a central Jewish office, and . . . where the Nazis did not succeed in setting up a puppet government, they also failed to enlist the cooperation of the Jews" (p. 104). Even aside from the implication that members of the "central Jewish office" were all Quisling-like traitors, this statement is false. There was no connection at all between the establishment of collaborationist local governments in conquered territories and the organization of a "central Jewish office." There was no "central Jewish office," even in Quisling's own country, Norway. Nor were there Jewish Councils in such satellite countries as Croatia and Bulgaria. On the other hand, while there were no Quisling governments in The Netherlands or in Poland, there *were* Jewish Councils in these countries.

Who were the members of the Jewish Councils appointed by the Nazis? They were *not* "as a rule the locally recognized Jewish leaders" (p. 104). There could indeed have been no such continuity, even in a loose sense, in the occupied territories of the Soviet Union, where for two decades no communal Jewish organizations had existed, or in Theresienstadt, a Nazi-built Jewish settlement. The fact is that no uniform pattern can be found regarding the presence or absence of continuity between the prewar Jewish organizations and the Jewish Councils. The situation differed radically from place to place, and from year to year in the same place. Even where there was originally a measure of continuity, the Germans usually acted according to the principle of negative selection, replacing people of standing with newcomers.[53] Conditions in the ghettos were often intentionally complicated; and conflicts were created by shipping both baptized Jews and Gypsies into the ghettos and by appointing converts to high administrative posts, as in the case of Józef Szeryński, chief of the Warsaw Ghetto police.[54] Frequently there were many organizations in the same community at the same time, with varying degrees of authority, prestige, and communal support. For example: in Warsaw the Jewish Council and the Jewish Social Self-Help organization (both under some form of Nazi control), the American-financed Joint Distribution Committee office, and the popularly elected Tenants' Committees existed for a long time side by side, with overlapping membership and activities.[55] In Slovakia the official Jewish Council (Ústredňa Židov) cooperated with the illegal "Working Group" under Rabbi Michael Dov Ber Weissmandel and Gisi Fleischmann.[56] In Romania the traditional Jewish leadership under Dr. Wilhelm Filderman (even after his removal from office), the chief rabbi Alexander Shafran, and the Zionist leaders Abraham Leib Zissu and Mischu Benvenisti, together made strenuous and partly successful efforts to stop the deportations to Transnistria and to return the deported Jews to their homes.[57] In Hungary there was the Jewish Council responsible to Eichmann and the Zionist Refugee and Rescue Committee, which helped refugees from neighboring countries and organized underground escape from Hungary to other countries.[58]

The variety in the degree of continuity of Jewish leadership under Nazi domination was so great that generalizations simply cannot be made concerning their nature. This diversity can be illustrated clearly by the following four examples: Warsaw, the largest Jewish community in Europe; Lodz, the second largest; Saloniki, an ancient 50,000-strong Sephardic community; and Transnistria. In Warsaw the original Ältestenrat (of October 1939) was made up of personalities mostly identified as members of the prewar Advisory Council (under the Commissioner of the Jewish Community) appointed by the Polish Government. While none of these had been elected, they were persons of standing in the Jewish community.[59] The Commissioner himself, Maurycy Majzel, disappeared at the outbreak of the war. The Mayor of Warsaw appointed Adam Czerniakow[60] as his successor. During the first six months of the existence of the Ältestenrat, a considerable number of its members dropped out and were replaced by persons selected by Czerniakow (he had become chairman of the *Ältestenrat*) on approval by the German authorities. The process of replacement was a continuous one. In this connection it should be noted that no clear-cut line separated the traditional Jewish political parties in their attitudes toward participation in the Jewish Councils, and that the majority of the party leaders in Poland considered participation in the Jewish Councils as the lesser evil.[61]

In Lodz the situation was different. There were two experiments with collective leadership, the second less continuous with the past than the first. The first group, the Council of Elders chosen by Mordecai Chaim Rumkowski, the Jewish Elder, was dissolved by the Nazi authorities, and twenty of its members were sent to *Straflager* (penal labor camp) Radogoszcz, where the majority perished.[62] Rumkowski then appointed an entirely new Council of Elders, which soon lost its more independent members, who had been men of high standing in prewar Lodz.[63] Thus the discontinuity early became complete in Lodz.

Even more striking was the discontinuity with the past in historic Saloniki, which has been called "a veritable small-scale democratic republic."[64] One of the first acts of the German authorities (April 15, 1941) was the detention of members and officials of the Jewish community organization and the sealing off of buildings owned by the community. The Nazis appointed Saby Saltiel "President of all Jews of Greece."[65] Saltiel acted without any contact with the duly elected Jewish Community Council and under the vigilant eyes of the SS and SD. He was later replaced by Dr. Zevi Koretz, the rabbi of the community, who had been arrested on May 17, 1941, and shipped to Vienna, where he was held until his return to Saloniki. Koretz accepted the nomination (December 1942) against the advice of the then inactive Community Council and created an advisory council, with the approval of Dr. Kalmes of the Gestapo. Not all those who were invited to join did so.[66] Dr. Koretz was dismissed and arrested on April 10, 1943, following his participation in an audience with the Greek Prime Minister Rhallis for the purpose of preventing the planned deportations.[67] He was shipped to Bergen-Belsen and there died of typhoid.[68]

A fourth example, Transnistria (occupied Soviet territories under German and Romanian control), can serve to illustrate the rare occasions when Jews spontaneously created their own organization under the most trying circumstances.[69] Here is what the Romanian-

Jewish historian, Matatias Carp, wrote about the situation in this area:

Among the elements which combined to contribute to the physical and spiritual annihilation of the Jews deported to Transnistria, those enumerated above—sickness, hunger, torture, expulsions, or their specter— were the most important ones. If these did not succeed in accomplishing total extermination, this was due to a "miracle"—the tremendous Jewish vitality and inexhaustible Jewish energy. Only a handful of people—often even one single man—endowed with initiative, courage, a strong will, working power, and authority, and impelled at times by the instinct of self-preservation, or out of human or Jewish solidarity, was able to organize a community for these uprooted, destitute, desperate, and persecuted masses.

The leaders installed themselves without being elected, often without being appointed or confirmed by anybody.

Institutions arose spontaneously, in a natural way, according to need and misery.

Thus, slowly and gradually, with human sacrifices, primitive means and experience, out of dust, blood and ashes, in the midst of sickness, hunger, and misery, there developed the Transnistrian social phenomenon, which in less than six months transformed a crowd of lost and stupefied people into an organized community. Jewish self-administration in Transnistria attained the dimensions of the administration of a State which not only evoked the admiration of the persecutors but also succeeded sometimes in changing their attitude and even in having a government official removed.

Thus, due to Jewish energy, the "miracle" of Transnistria was brought about, namely, that about 60,000 Jewish lives were rescued from sickness, from hunger, and from the brutality of man—among these over 15,000 local Jews.[70]

Legally and morally, the members of the Jewish Councils can no more be judged accomplices of their Nazi rulers than can a store owner be judged accomplice of an armed robber to whom he surrenders his store at gunpoint. Even so, people appointed to the *Judenräte* were faced from the very start with the question of whether or not they should accept the appointment. It is the consensus of the literature that in the earlier periods this question was answered in the affirmative, in the hope of deceiving the Germans, or of bribing them, or of winning them over.

The situation changed when the Germans invaded the U.S.S.R. People in newly occupied areas became reluctant to accept membership in the Councils, having heard something of the tribulations of the Jewish Councils in German-occupied parts of Poland. Thus, in Eyszyszki, in July 1941, the rabbi had to draw lots to choose members of the Council from among the reluctant community because of the lack of volunteers.[71] But even during this period, membership in such Councils was generally considered to be a communal duty.

On the basis of the vast documentation at our disposal, we can say with some confidence that the basic strategy of the overwhelming majority of the Jewish Councils during the period of the Final Solution was based on two assumptions: (1) that Nazi Germany would ultimately be defeated; (2) that not all inmates of the ghettos would survive. (The latter assumption had begun to gain currency even before the Nazi program of extermination had been launched.) The first assumption underlay the Councils' universal policy of procrastination. The second assumption meant that—since *all* Jews probably could not be saved—ways and means had to be found to rescue as many Jews as possible.

The strategic and tactical consequences of these assumptions can be grouped under three general statements:

1. The Councils took pains to offer no open defiance to the Nazi masters, deeply convinced that this approach protected the community from greater misfortune than they were faced with at the time.[72] This policy was reenforced by the permanent terror maintained by the Nazis, who threatened—and carried out—reprisals and collective punishments for violations of their orders. There were many variations in the application of this policy, ranging from perfunctory to genuine compliance with Nazi orders, and from support to condemnation of clandestine Jewish resistance.

2. The Councils almost everywhere adhered to the philosophy of "rescue through work," believing that Jewish labor would thus come to be considered important to the Nazi war effort.[73] It was not imagined that the Nazi commitment to racism would be so irrational as to permit systematic weakening and destruction of a sorely needed labor force.

3. Gradually the Councils came to recognize bribery as an aid to survival, and they sought out corrupt Nazi officials on all levels. But corruption is not a one-sided affair. It also corrupts the corruptor. To do this sort of "dirty work," the traditional Jewish leadership, insofar as it was represented in the Jewish Councils, had

to have recourse to people of dubious character over whom they gradually lost control.

One thing is clear. No blanket statements can be made concerning the nature, previous status, or character of the members of the various *Judenräte*. They differed in their political affiliations, their education, their occupations, their origins (some being indigenous, others being refugees), their degree of courage in confrontations with the Nazis, their intelligence, and their cleverness. All these elements are relevant to a fair evaluation of individual members as well as of the collective leadership. For example, the differences were great between the numerous *Judenräte* in various areas of Nazi control; between those in established Jewish communities and those in communities constituted *ad hoc* (like Theresienstadt) or reconstituted for a short while (as in Soviet Byelorussia and the Ukraine, following the stabilization of the Russo-German front in 1942). Only one statement can be made with the assurance of finality: Jews were not forming queues at the Gestapo offices to offer their services to the Nazis. The idea of the *Judenrat* was initiated by the Nazi *Judenwissenschaft* ("Judaistic science," in this case a pseudoscience),[74] given concrete form by the Nazi political and bureaucratic machinery, and implemented by the Gestapo and SS in the territories under their control.

Authority, Influence, and Activities of the Jewish Councils: Tragic Choices

The Jewish Councils, according to Miss Arendt, received from the Nazis "enormous powers" (p. 104). Their powers are listed by her as follows: compilation of the lists of persons and their property; securing money from the deportees to defray the expenses of their deportation and extermination; keeping track of vacated apartments; supplying police forces to help seize Jews and get them on trains; and handing over the assets of the Jewish community in good order for final confiscation. She gives the following particulars on the Jewish Councils' role in the deportation: "The Jewish Councils of Elders were informed by Eichmann or his men of how many Jews were needed to fill each train, and they made out the list of deportees. The Jews registered, filled out innumerable forms, answered pages and pages of questionnaires regarding their property so that it could be seized the more easily; they then assembled at the collection points and boarded the trains. The few who tried to hide or to escape were rounded up by a special Jewish police force" (p. 102). Note that in this passage Miss Arendt pictures the Jewish Councils as receiving "information" from "Eichmann or his men." This is in direct contradiction to her contention (pp. 197-198) that the Eastern territories (including Poland), where the majority of Jewish Councils were situated, were not within the domain of Eichmann's office. In fact they were, although not exclusively.

The impression given by Miss Arendt is that the only functions of the Jewish Councils were those connected with the final stage of the Nazi anti-Jewish policies; she ignores the vast welfare functions performed by the Councils from the earliest stages. The main activities of the Jewish Councils, however, before and even after the Final Solution had been initiated, were the positive attempts to preserve the physical and moral existence of the communities in all circumstances, and by all means and above all to preserve "God's image" in the trying conditions of life under Nazi-induced terror.

A typical Jewish Council maintained the following offices: ghetto police, ghetto court, fire brigade, labor, economic affairs, food, housing, health, social affairs, statistics, and education.[75]

Speaking of the "enormous powers" of the Jewish Councils, Miss Arendt neglects to mention that these Councils were under strict and constant supervision of the Nazis in and outside the ghettos.[76] The length to which this supervision went can be seen from the case of Lodz, where, side by side with the Jewish Elder inside the ghetto, there was a purely Nazi ghetto administration outside the ghetto. This administration kept a watchful eye on what was going on in the ghetto. For example, the telephones of the Elder, Mordecai Chaim Rumkowski, were tapped. The voluminous transcription of the tapes of these conversations was preserved and has been found.

There is no evidence that a "special Jewish police force" (p. 102) existed anywhere for the specific purpose of rounding up those who tried to hide or to escape. (The role of the regular Jewish police force in the deportations is discussed later in this chapter.) In addition, the overwhelming majority of the Jewish Councils had no authority over property which had been left in the "Aryan" sections before ghettoization. The only recorded case[77] of a Jewish

Council having authority over private property of Jews is in the "Protectorate" (the Czech-populated area of Bohemia-Moravia). A careful reading of the documentation reveals that even there the Jewish community organization had no authority over Jewish property which had in the period of emigration belonged to Eichmann's *Zentralstelle für jüdische Auswanderung*. The administrative apparatus of the Jewish community was used simply for collecting and sorting out the property of the deportees. Jewish property taken over by the *Zentralstelle* was transferred to Germany or distributed to the local Nazis. It is superfluous to say that no such authority was given to the Jewish Council in the Nazi-built community of Theresienstadt; the Council certainly did not "defray the expenses of their [the Jews'] transportation and extermination" (p. 104). Furthermore, keeping track of vacated apartments (p. 104) was rarely a function of the Councils. And, while in some cases (Warsaw and Lodz[78]) the Jewish Councils were given the exact numbers of deportees required and the timetable of their departure, this was hardly the rule.

Generalizing the case of Theresienstadt, Miss Arendt claims that the deportations of Jews from the ghettos to the extermination camps were carried out on the basis of lists drawn up by the Jewish Councils. In fact, there were different methods of selecting ghetto Jews for deportation, subject to the arbitrary will of the Nazi authorities, who always had the last word. In some places—Warsaw, Lwów, Lublin, Częstochowa, and Cracow, for example—selection was made by streets or neighborhoods;[79] in many towns, by assembly in the market place.[80] Where deportation was done by lists, upon the demand by the German authorities to supply a specified *number* of persons, the lists were as a rule drawn up by the Jewish Councils, and then sent to the local Gestapo. These lists were by no means the last word. On the one hand, certain sectors of German industry sometimes succeeded in having people they needed stricken from the lists; on the other hand, the Gestapo did not always remain satisfied with the total number of deportees and in such cases used to hunt for unlisted Jews and catch whomever they could. For example, in Włocławek, a list of deportees destined for Lodz (in October 1941) was not submitted to the Gestapo by the required deadline. The Germans themselves then drew up the lists and, as a sanction, added another 182 persons to the originally requested number—without enlarging the transportation space allotted to the shipment.[81] Nor did the Jewish Councils always accept the responsibility, when it was assigned to them, for listing people as "fit" (*einsatzfähig*) or "unfit" (*einsatzunfähig*). In one of the few lists available,[82] dated February 10, 1942, referring to the town of Krosno in Eastern Galicia, 531 persons are listed as fit, 42 as unfit, and 1,499 (almost 75 per cent) are listed without classification. We do not know what happened to those who were unclassified, or to the Council that had the courage to present such a list.

The Jews selected for deportation were rounded up for the most part by the SS, the Gestapo, the Kripo (Criminal Police), or the Regular Police, at times with the assistance of the Jewish police (*Ordnungsdienst*). In matters of deportation, the Jewish Councils often had no authority over the Jewish police. Frequently the Jewish police was not involved. Thus, in the September 1942 "action" in Lodz, the Jewish police was active only the first two days. The results were not considered satisfactory by the Nazis, and the next day Günther Fuchs, chief of the Jewish Section in the Criminal Police and Specialist (*Sachbearbeiter*) for Jewish Affairs in the city, took over and it was he who directed the transports to Chełmno.[83] In particular, Fuchs used to make the selection and arrange for transportation of the required numbers of Jews each time, often by cordoning off blocks of houses and searching the dwellings.

In her discussion of the Jewish leadership, Miss Arendt quotes out of context. She declares that "in the Nazi-inspired, but not Nazi-dictated, manifestos they [the Jewish leaders] issued, we still can sense how they enjoyed their new power" (pp. 104-105). The only manifesto mentioned by her is that of the Central Jewish Council in Hungary, and she quotes one sentence out of nine: "The Central Jewish Council has been granted the right of absolute disposal over all [communal] Jewish spiritual and material wealth and over all Jewish manpower" (p. 105). She returns to this on page 178: "On the very evening of their arrival,[84] Eichmann and his men invited the Jewish leaders to a conference, to persuade them to form a Jewish Council, through which they could issue their orders and to which they would give, in return, absolute jurisdiction over all Jews in Hungary." (The reader can judge for himself the appropriateness of the verbs "invite" and "persuade.") Miss Arendt has missed the implied meaning of this declaration, clear to the Budapest Jews, that pursuant to the German occupation all Jewish organizations—communal, welfare, charitable, and others—

were immediately dissolved and the Jewish Council was to fill in the vacuum thus created. She finds the "enjoyment of power" in the tone of the manifesto. It is difficult to follow this line of thinking, the more so if one reads the full text of the manifesto:

Brothers! The Hungarian authorities negotiate exclusively with the Central Council, which is the only body informed of instructions affecting the lives of the entire Jewish population. The individual members of the Council and all persons failing to carry out to the full instructions received from the Council are answerable with their lives. Brothers! The organisation of Hungarian Jews is under an obligation to execute official instructions: this means that the Central Council is not an authority, but simply an executive body carrying out the orders of the authorities.

The Central Council cannot permit orders to be disregarded on account of lack of discipline. The Jewish Council cannot tolerate the non-observance of instructions by individuals, as this would lead to a disaster of unprecedented magnitude for the whole of the Jewish population. On receiving orders from the Central Council it is the duty of every person to report at the place and time indicated. The Central Jewish Council has been granted the right of absolute disposal over all [communal] Jewish spiritual and material wealth and over all Jewish man-power. You, women and girls, men and boys, are all the executors of the instructions issued by the Central Council. You must realise that every decision, however momentous it may be, is the outcome of official intervention and that the life of every individual and the existence of the community as a whole depend on such instructions being fully observed. May God guide you and give you strength to attend faithfully to your duty![85]

An indicator of the degree of influence possessed by the Councils would appear to be the relative survival rate of Council members, as compared with the population at large. Miss Arendt explicitly states that among the "privileged categories" who survived were "as usual, the personnel of the *Judenrat*" (p. 170). Somewhat later, she admits that in the East (where most of the losses took place) "even the members of the Jewish Councils were invariably exterminated" (p. 199). As a matter of fact, even outside the East not all members of the Jewish Councils survived. The survival of the members of Jewish Councils, wherever it happened, was not due to their being a "privileged" category but to the fact that the liberation (or the "stop deportation" order) occurred in some places before the end of the extermination of the Jews at a time when the Council members still had to carry out functions imposed on them

by the Nazis. Where the Nazi extermination program was concluded, the members of the Councils were "invariably exterminated."
Where it had not yet come to an end, there were survivors among
members of Jewish Councils. For example, as far as Germany was
concerned, Eichmann himself saw to it that the Jewish administrators be done away with. In a telegram dispatched April 22, 1942, to
15 local branches of the Gestapo, Eichmann ordered them to use
the Jewish functionaries throughout the process of deportation, to
ship them out gradually, and to deport the remaining ones along
with the last transport.[86]

The major implication of Miss Arendt's charge that "Jewish
cooperation" was an important, even crucial, element in the mass
murder of Europe's Jews is that the Jewish Councils were in a
position somehow to influence the course of Nazi policy. This point
is basic to her argument, and it alone makes it possible for her to
hold the Councils accountable for a large part of the fate of their
brethren. It is therefore essential to examine in detail the facts and
figures of the situation, despite a reluctance to discuss the Catastrophe in terms of statistics and calculations. Throughout this discussion I use the figures reported by Hilberg,[87] on whom Miss
Arendt relies heavily. I adhere to these figures not because I
subscribe to them in every detail, but only to illustrate how even
the data available to (and supposedly used by) Miss Arendt contradict her words.

Hilberg estimates the total number of Jewish losses at 5,100,000,
a number that becomes for Miss Arendt "between four and a half
and six million" (p. 111; "between five and six million people" in
III, 50). For the purposes of the present discussion, it is necessary
to subtract from this total figure the number of victims from areas
in which either there was no Jewish "cooperation" at all or Jewish
"cooperation" had no influence on the final outcome. To these areas
belong the occupied territories of the U.S.S.R., with 900,000 victims;
and Poland, with 3,000,000 victims. This is what Miss Arendt has
to say on these areas: "The East was the central scene of Jewish
suffering, the gruesome terminal of all deportations, the place from
which there was hardly ever any escape" (p. 188); "the fate of the
Jews there [in the Eastern occupied territories] had never been in
the balance" (p. 198; in IV, 130 "in question"); "it was a foregone
conclusion that they [Jews of the East] would all have to die"

(IV, 131; left out on p. 199). And elsewhere, referring to the Madagascar plan as a "cloak under which the preparations for the physical extermination of all the Jews of Western Europe could be carried forward," Miss Arendt observes: "No such cloak was needed for the extermination of Polish Jews" (p. 71). Moreover, she states explicitly that in the East, "the Jewish bureaucracy . . . played no part in the seizure and the concentration of the Jews" (paperback edition, p. 218).

Thus it becomes necessary to subtract from the total figure (which is here taken, with Hilberg, to be 5,100,000) 3,900,000 victims whose ultimate fate was certainly not influenced by the existence of *Judenräte*. There remain 1,200,000 instances where the influence of Jewish Councils and of Jewish police might have had a part in the final outcome of the extermination.

The following is a compilation of Jewish losses in places where Miss Arendt herself does not find Jewish participation to have been a factor:

1. *Union Générale des Israélites de France* (UGIF) was not appointed by the Germans but by the French Commissariat of Jewish Affairs, and had no part in the deportations. No Jewish Council was in existence in Italy. This accounts for 70,000 victims.

2. The 60,000 Jews of Yugoslavia (including those of territories, which had been attached by the Germans to Bulgaria) were destroyed without "help" of Jewish Councils.

3. No Jewish Councils with competence in matters of deportation existed in Romania, which accounted for 270,000 casualties.

4. The last deportation of 12,000 Slovakian Jews was carried out exclusively by the Germans and without any Jewish "cooperation."

5. The Jewish Council in Hungary had no part in the process of deportation of 300,000 Jews of Hungary and Subcarpathian Russia to Auschwitz.

6. While Rabbi Koretz of Saloniki at first obeyed the Nazi authorities, there is no evidence that he had a direct part in the deportations of 60,000 Jews from Greece and Rhodes, including those from Athens, where there was no *Judenrat*.

7. In Belgium, 25,000 Jews were deported. According to Miss Arendt, there was no *Judenrat* in Belgium, and hence the Jews were not "responsible" for the deportation process. Actually, there was a Jewish Council, called *Association des Juifs en Belgique*. According to the official report of the Belgian Government (mentioned by

Miss Arendt, but apparently not familiar to her), the *Association* only sent out summonses. (For details see Chapter 5, under Belgium.)

Altogether 797,000 Jews were annihilated without any Jewish "help." Deducting this figure from 1,200,000, there remain 403,000 casualties from the following countries, where there were Jewish Councils that had some role in the compilation of lists:

1. Greater Germany (including the Protectorate), 250,000.[88]
2. The Netherlands, 105,000.
3. Slovakia, 48,000.[89]

The fact is, then, that 403,000—and not "between four and a half and six million"—is the number of Jews who were killed in areas where existing Jewish Councils (in some areas also Jewish police) might conceivably have had influence on the outcome of the deportations to extermination camps. Did the Jewish Councils have any responsibility even for the fate of these 403,000 victims? In the light of the evidence, one can only conclude that the role played by Jews was negligible, that it could not have been decisive in the final outcome. Miss Arendt herself admits that the machinery of the all-powerful Nazi State—its political, civil, economic, police, and SS administration, and, not infrequently, the German Army—worked to annihilate the Jews (pp. 135-136). She is also aware that anti-Jewish actions were a matter of such high priority that railroad cars were provided for deportation even during the times of greatest danger on the war fronts (p. 195).

To implement their anti-Jewish schemes, the Nazis assigned three large groups to this purpose:[90]

1. The State and party apparatus—namely, the SS (including the Waffen-SS); the various branches of the RSHA (especially the Gestapo) and its subordinate agencies; the Regular Police; the officials of the Jewish Affairs sections in the Foreign Office and in the Ministries of Interior, Economics, Justice, Propaganda, and Finance; and parts of the Army, which cooperated in the murder of Jews.

2. Volunteer units of Russians, Ukrainians, Byelorussians, Lithuanians, Latvians, and *Volksdeutsche* (persons of German origin living outside Germany).

3. Local government forces, such as the police in localities of "Greater Germany" and police units and local officials in countries under German control (occupied countries and satellites).

These groups comprised tens upon tens of thousands of persons. The *Einsatzgruppen* numbered about 3,000 to 4,000. The SS-*Wirtschafts und Verwaltungshauptamt* (WVHA), which administered the concentration camps, had (including staff and guards) about 48,000 members. It employed at the end of 1944 more than 24,000 persons merely to supervise slave laborers and to administer their "assets." The number of men who served as guards in the concentration camps was estimated by August Harbaum (chief of Section A/V4 of the WVHA) at 45,000 for the period March 1942 to April 1945; and the number of women at about 5,000. The total number of concentration camp guards during the years 1934-1945 is estimated at 70,000.[91] The SS as a whole numbered about 950,000 in 1944, of whom at least 100,000 served in implementing Nazi terror.

The entire Security Police and Security Service contained somewhat less than 70,000 men. Section IV of the RSHA, the Gestapo, numbered between 30,000 and 40,000; the SD between 3,000 and 4,000.

The Regular Police was used sometimes in whole regiments. In the Government-General alone it is estimated to have been nearly 30,000 strong in 1943.[92]

No estimates are available on the number of people employed in the other categories of the three large groups used by the Nazis to exterminate the Jews.

With these armies of men actively participating in the Final Solution, and with the high priority assigned to this work, the Nazis were capable of accomplishing their aims without resorting to the assistance of "Jewish leaders."

There is no evidence that the motivation in accepting and maintaining membership in the *Judenräte* was not generally honorable. There is much evidence to the contrary.[93] As soon as members became aware of the destination of the deportees, moral crises arose to which reactions were varied. Most members of the Councils chose to stay with their communities: "Let us perish along with all the other Jews" was the reaction of the Jewish Council at Baranów when they were offered an opportunity to run away.[94] For the average leaders, the terror inspired by the Nazis, the feeling of responsibility toward the Jewish community, and sometimes human frailty had a part in the fateful decisions that ensued. There were also members of the *Judenräte* who cooperated clandestinely with the resistance movements, or who dared to defy orders of the Gestapo. To cite a few examples: The chairman of the *Judenrat* of Baranowicze, Owsiej Izikson, and his secretary, Jenny Men, were shot for refusing to deliver children and sick and aged people. When the murderers confronted Izikson during the first "action" and requested the delivery of the old and sick Jews, he replied: "I gave you everything you asked from me, but I am not going to give you Jews. I am no master (*balabos*) over human life." The chronicler who recorded this adds: "With this reply he forfeited this world, but gained his place in the world to come."[95] A similar answer was given to the Gestapo by the chairman of the Jewish Council in Ratno, David Aharon Szapiro. Following an alleged act of sabotage in that town on November 4, 1941, the SS requested twelve hostages to atone for this "crime" by their death—four Gentiles and eight Jews. The Gentiles supplied their quota, but the chairman of the *Judenrat*, Szapiro, refused to do so: "You may take *me* away, but I am not going to deliver to death innocent people." He, his colleague from the *Judenrat*, Isaac Grabow, and six more Jews seized by the Nazis were shipped to the prison of Kowel. Through strenuous efforts, his community and neighboring communities succeeded in having him released from prison, unfortunately only for a short time. His fate was sealed in a subsequent "action."[96] Dr. Joseph Parnas, first chairman of the Jewish Council in Lwów, was shot for refusing to supply the required quota of slave labor.[97] The chairman of the Złoczów Council, Dr. Majblum, was shot for refusing to sign a paper acknowledging that the reason for deportation of Jews was an outbreak of typhus in the ghetto.[98] The "commissar" (chairman) of the Jewish Council in Mława, Eliezer Perelmuter, the benefactor of the ghetto and a most dedicated communal leader, was arrested on January 23, 1942, by German police and shot the next day.[99] In the summer of 1942 the Gestapo called in five members of the Stanisławów *Judenrat*, including the chairman, Mordecai Goldstein. First four members were shot; a few days later Goldstein was hanged.[100] Dr. Scharf, chairman of the *Judenrat* in Delatyn, was murdered by a Gestapo man with an ax.[101] Also hanged, with twelve policemen and Council members, was the third chairman of the Jewish Council in Lwów, Dr. Henryk Landsberg (the second, Dr. Rotfeld, died a "natural death"), in September 1942, apparently for his contacts with the

Polish underground.[102] All seven members of the Jewish Council in Nowogródek, with the chairman, Herz Ciechanowski, were shot as soon as the Germans learned that they knew the truth of the Nazi policies.[103] Repressions were also exercised against the first two chairmen of the Cracow *Judenrat*. The first chairman, Dr. Mark Biberstein, was dismissed, convicted of some unspecified crime, jailed, freed, and shipped to the camp at Płaszów, where he died of starvation.[104] His successor, Dr. Artur Rosenzweig, was charged with laxity in the organization of the first "resettlement" of May 31, 1942, and was deported with his family. He was succeeded by a commissar, David Guter.[105] All members of the Częstochowa Jewish Council were shot by the Gestapo on March 20, 1943, on the pretext that they exploited the Jews.[106] The executive chairman of the German-Jewish *Reichsvertretung* (and later of the *Reichsvereinigung*), Otto Hirsch, whose activities won widespread praise in the community, was arrested and had to undergo Gestapo tortures on several occasions. The last arrest was made by Eichmann in his office on February 26, 1941; from there Hirsch was brought to Mauthausen, where he was murdered on June 19, 1941.[107]

When, in postwar proceedings, Waldemar Machol, the German former Chief of the Security Police in Białystok, was on trial for his life in Poland, he admitted that Ephraim Barash, member of the *Judenrat*, and Izhak Marcus, the chief of the Jewish police (*Ordnungsdienst*), had, as far as he knew, protected the Jewish community in various difficult situations.[108]

The Jewish police were as varied as the communities in which they served or from which they came. At times they were the object of severe criticism by Jews for their activities. On the other hand, they were also often the object of drastic action on the part of the Nazis. Thus, in Mława, the Nazis arrested twelve Jewish policemen on the charge of negligence in carrying out the German orders and hanged them publicly.[109] In Rohatyn (Eastern Galicia) the Germans, on June 6, 1943, shot the whole Jewish police detachment and hanged them publicly.[110] In the Kovno Ghetto the chief of the Jewish police, his assistants, and some forty policemen were shot on charges of helping the partisan movement, building bunkers, and the like.[111]

There is evidence that some Jewish lives were rescued through the work of certain Jewish police detachments. In Kovno, the Jewish Council and the Jewish police helped youths escape from the ghetto and join the partisans.[112] In Riga, the Jewish police in the ghetto for Eastern European Jews was helpful and lived in harmony with the ghetto community.[113] In Baranowicze, the chief and the overwhelming majority of the Jewish police were active in the resistance movement.[114] When the ghetto police was ordered by the Nazi police to invite Jews in hiding to come into the open and to assure them there was no danger, they did so, but added: "Lo, Yehudim." ("Don't, Jews!").[115]

In 1947-1948, in The Netherlands, a Jewish Court of Honor tried members of the Jewish Council, including the two cochairmen, Asscher and Cohen, and condemned their policy on several counts.[116] In the DP camps, Jewish survivors conducted their own trials against former members of the Jewish Councils and police. The *Documentary Projects* at the YIVO Institute of Jewish Research in New York have compiled a comprehensive inventory of the material in the YIVO collection relating to the DP's. Another important depository of pertinent material is *Yad Washem*, in Jerusalem, and its Tel-Aviv branch. Some 2,500 new accounts given by survivors, containing abundant information on ghettos, Jewish Councils, and Jewish police, have been collected by *Yad Washem*, in addition to the thousands of testimonies turned over to it by now defunct Jewish historical commissions—altogether some 25,000 personal accounts. They relate to various areas of persecution and extermination, including Poland, the U.S.S.R., Lithuania, Latvia, Transnistria, and Transylvania. The YIVO collection also contains files of proceedings of special DP courts set up to try former members of Jewish Councils, ghetto and camp policemen. These courts did not remain in existence for long. Though they might have had a certain moral authority, they lacked official legal status, and not all their judgments were implemented. In due course the occupation authorities prohibited the continuation of these courts. In their place, a Rehabilitation Commission was established by the Central Committee of Jewish DP's in the American Occupation Zone in Munich. This commission continued the activities of the DP courts, pronouncing only such sentences as could be implemented—for example, prohibiting the condemned to participate in communal activities for a certain period (or permanently). The commission could also declare the condemned man a traitor to the Jewish people and deliver him to the military authorities; but it is not known whether such a sentence was ever pronounced.[117] Similar activities were undertaken also in other zones of concentration of DP's.

All these quasi-legal and legal proceedings were carried on with two aims in view: (1) To punish former inmates of the ghettos and concentration camps whose behavior was disgraceful. (2) To rehabilitate persons unjustifiably maligned. The trials went on even after the dissolution of the DP camps, in the countries where former inmates had settled; they were conducted mainly before communal and informal courts, in some places also before State courts.

The first legislation ever passed by a State to cope with such cases in a comprehensive manner was Israel's Nazis and Nazi Collaborators (Punishment) Law 5710/1950.[118] It was designed as a remedy for complaints received against persons accused of aiding the Nazis. It is significant that this carefully conceived law does not consider membership in a Jewish Council or a Jewish police force to be in itself evidence of any criminal act whatsoever. Nor does this law take any attitude, positive or negative, vis-à-vis the activities of the Jewish Councils in general.

In addition to her indictment of the members of the Jewish Councils—an indictment which does not stand up under an examination of the complicated facts—Miss Arendt claims that she knows "the physiognomies of the Jewish leaders during the Nazi period very well" (p. 105) and makes serious accusations against certain individual leaders, only one of whom is still living.[119] For example, she draws a caricature of Rabbi Leo Baeck, a noted German Jewish leader, and she distorts his role in Germany and in Theresienstadt. She presents Baeck as "former Chief Rabbi of Berlin," a person "who in the eyes of both Jews and Gentiles was the 'Jewish Führer' " (p. 105; omitted in the paperback edition, p. 119). As one of many "voluntary 'bearers of secrets,' " officials whom "no one bothered to swear to secrecy," Baeck is charged with concealing the truth from the inmates of Theresienstadt "out of 'humane' considerations, such as that 'living in the expectation of death by gassing would only be the harder' " (p. 105).

To call Leo Baeck (who, incidentally, was not Chief Rabbi of Berlin; such an office or title did not exist) a "Jewish Führer" in the known connotation of the term *Führer* is offensive. The source for this statement is probably Hilberg,[120] who was careful to note that the expression "Jewish Führer" applied to Baeck was a casual remark by Eichmann's assistant, Dieter Wisliceny; it was left to Miss Arendt to ascribe the use of the epithet to "Jews and Gentiles" in general. Her misrepresentation of Leo Baeck has been dealt with by Juda Cahn[121] and, in a thoroughly documented article, by Adolf Leschnitzer.[122]

An indication of the true stature of Dr. Baeck emerges from the following prayer composed by him on the eve of the High Holidays 5795 (1935), upon passage of the Nuremberg Laws by the Nazi regime, and read from the pulpit in Germany:

At this hour, all Israel stands before its God, Who judges and forgives. We shall examine our ways before Him, examine what we have done and what we have not done, examine where we have gone, and where we have kept away. Wherever we have failed, we shall say openly, "we have sinned," and with a firm will to mend our ways we shall pray before God, "please, forgive us."

We stand before our God. With the same courage with which we confess our sins, individual and collective, we shall declare with deep aversion that the lies against us, and the defamation of our religion and its teachings, are far beneath our dignity. We stand by our faith and our fate. Who was it that revealed to the world the secret of the One Eternal God? Who introduced to the world the idea of a pure way of life, and of the sanctity of the family? Who gave the world a sense of respect for human beings, cast in the image of God? Who set forth before the world the commandment of social justice? The spirit of Israel's prophets and the revelations of God to the Jewish people have played a role in all these ideas. In our faith, in Judaism, they have developed and continue to develop. In the face of these facts all attacks must fail.

We stand before our God; in Him we trust. In Him has our history, our steadfastness throughout all change, and our perseverance in all oppression found true meaning and dignity. Our history is a history of spiritual greatness and spiritual worth, to which we turn when attack and injury are directed against us, when distress and sorrow threaten to submerge us. God has guided our fathers from generation to generation. He will continue to guide us and our children through the tribulations of our own days.

We stand before our God. His commandments, that we obey, give us strength. Before Him we bow, but we stand upright before men. Him we serve, but we stand fast through the change of events. With humility we trust in Him; our road lies clear before us, and we see what lies ahead.

All Israel stands before its God at this hour. Our prayer, our faith, our creed is the same as that of all the other Jews in the world. We look at each other, and we know what we are; we look up to our God, and we know what will remain.

"Behold, He who watches over Israel does not sleep or slumber."
"He who brings peace in Heaven will bring peace to us and to all of
Israel."

Sadness and pain fill us. In silence, in a moment of silence before
our God, we will express what is in our hearts. And this silent meditation
will speak more strongly than any words can speak.[123]

Miss Arendt also criticizes Pinhas Freudiger, a member of the
Hungarian Jewish Council, "an Orthodox Jew of considerable dignity" (p. 110) who testified at the Eichmann trial.[124] He left
Hungary for Romania, and this earns him a reprimand from Miss
Arendt (p. 110): Why did he not tell the other people to escape?
The reason is very simple: Mr. Freudiger left Budapest on August 10, 1944. By that time all the Jews in Hungary outside Budapest
had already been deported to Auschwitz, and the Budapest Jews
had been reassured by the Hungarian ruler Horthy (and they believed in the firmness of his decision) that no more deportations
would take place, as indeed they did not before Szálasi came to
power. Freudiger himself left at the suggestion of Wisliceny, who
warned him that Eichmann intended to deport him and his family
(despite the general suspension of deportations). We know this
from Wisliceny's testimony, which was not contradicted by Eichmann.[125]

Miss Arendt ridicules Freudiger and the Hungarian Jewish
Council (p. 178). She tells of "one of the most remarkable non-
sequiturs uttered on the witness stand: the future members of the
Central Jewish Committee (as the Jewish Council was called in
Hungary) had heard from neighboring Slovakia that Wisliceny,
who was now negotiating with them, accepted money readily, and
they also knew that despite all bribes he 'had deported all the Jews
in Slovakia. . . .' From which Mr. Freudiger concluded: 'I understood that it was necessary to find ways and means to establish
relationships with Wisliceny.'"

This statement is devoid of foundation. Here are the relevant
passages of Freudiger's testimony at the Eichmann Trial:

Q. When did you first learn about Wisliceny?
A. In September 1942.
Q. Who informed you about him?
A. Rabbi Weissmandel [head of the "Working Group" in Slovakia]
   asked for money from us for Wisliceny, which Weissmandel said

had been promised to him. I don't remember the amount requested—
about $40,000.

Q. What for?

A. For the stoppage of the deportations. At that time 58,000 Jews had
already been deported but 2,000 to 3,000 were waiting for their
turn. A deal was made with Wisliceny that for $40,000 to $50,000
he would stop the deportations . . .

A. . . . as soon as I heard the name Wisliceny, I had an entirely different approach to the matter [the Hungarian Jews' situation].

Q. What was your approach?

A. My approach was, that after what had happened in Slovakia—
Wisliceny was the one who deported the Slovak Jews[126]—that now
he had come to Hungary, and they certainly did not send him for
a vacation. On the one hand, I knew that he had finally received the
funds I had sent to Slovakia. I knew, then, that it was necessary to
find a way to establish contact with Wisliceny. . . .

Referring to his session with Wisliceny in the Rabbinical Semi-
nary, Freudiger gave the following account:

A. . . . He [Wisliceny] just said a few words to Dr. Nisson Kahan
[a Zionist leader, one of the three persons to whom Bratislava Jewish
leaders had directed Wisliceny, the others being Freudiger and
Baroness Edith Weiss, leader of the Reform Jewish group] and then
sent him to another room and we remained alone. He closed the
door and told me to sit down. Usually, we did not sit [in the presence
of the Nazis], but remained standing. He told me: "I have a letter
for you, read it."

Q. From whom was it?

A. I read the letter. It was a letter from Rabbi Weissmandel of blessed
memory. It was written in Hebrew, and was a short letter. He wrote
me that "finally fate has caught up with Hungarian Jewry" and
suggested that I continue to deal with the "Europa-Plan" that they
had started with Wisliceny and that was known to me. In general,
this was a letter expressing confidence in Wisliceny, that we could
negotiate with him. I read the letter. Wisliceny asked me: "Did you
read it?" I answered: "Yes." "Did you understand?" "Yes." "Return
the letter to me," he said. I returned the letter to him. He tore it into
small pieces and threw it into the stove. After this he asked me:
"What do you have to say to this letter?" I answered: "I am at your
disposal." He told me: "From now on, we need all the money
arriving from abroad." I asked him: "Do you mean 'we need' or
'I need'?" I wanted to know whether the deal was an official or a

private one. He told me: "This is none of your business." I had no reply to this. Thereafter he told me: "You will hear from me again." That was all, and I left.

Freudiger thus knew that a number of Slovak Jews had been rescued through the Weissmandel-Wisliceny deal. He was aware that it was Wisliceny who had been in charge of the deportations and that Wisliceny apparently could also stop them. The expression of confidence in Wisliceny by Rabbi Weissmandel gave him further impetus to negotiate. For Freudiger, the decisive point about the Wisliceny-Weissmandel deal was that it had worked. Under the agreement between Wisliceny and the Slovak Government the latter had to deliver 60,000 of the 80,000 Slovak Jews to the Germans. The Jewish deal with Wisliceny was arranged when some 2,000 to 3,000 Jews of this quota were still in Slovakia. Wisliceny succeeded in delaying their deportation, and in addition resisted Slovak pressure for the deportation of the remaining 20,000 so-called "economically necessary" Jews. The Jews left in Slovakia were subsequently deported by the Nazi authorities in October 1944, following the suppression of the Slovak national uprising; but this occurred after Wisliceny had gone.

Another person attacked and misrepresented by Miss Arendt is Dr. Rezsö Kasztner, the chairman of the Zionist Council in Budapest. On pages 37-38 she represents the agreement between Kasztner and Eichmann for the emigration of Jews as permission for "the 'illegal' departure of a few thousand Jews . . . in exchange for 'quiet and order' in the camps." The agreement is characterized on page 105 as an "even more gruesome" truth: "Dr. Kasztner, in Hungary, for instance, saved exactly 1,684 people[127] with approximately 476,000 victims."[128] On page 128 the rescue of the Kasztner group is presented as a purely commercial operation in which a thousand dollars was paid "per Jew." But Miss Arendt herself admits that "with their [the Hungarian police and State Secretaries] help, Eichmann could be sure that everything, the issuance of the necessary decrees and the concentration of the Jews in the provinces, would proceed with 'lightning speed'" (pp. 181 f.). No part in this process was provided for the Jewish Councils or for Dr. Kasztner. No Jewish police was operating in Hungary.

Another example of Miss Arendt's denigration of individual leaders of the Jewish community, is the case of Mordechai Chaim Rumkowski, the Elder of the Lodz Ghetto (p. 105). Although Rumkowski was not a "recognized Jewish leader" and the methods of carrying out his policy of "rescue through work" are debatable, the fact that the Lodz Ghetto was maintained longer than any other at least partly vindicates his policy. By the end of July 1944 the Red Army had reached the Vistula and established a bridgehead on its western shore, south of Warsaw. At that time there were still tens of thousands of Jews in the Lodz Ghetto. The Red Army did not continue its advance, but stopped some 70 miles from Lodz. Less than a month later, in August 1944, the 68,000 Jews still alive in Lodz were "resettled," i.e., killed.[129]

Rumkowski's behavior is open to criticism, but it is not true, as Miss Arendt writes, that he was called "Chaim I," as if the head of a dynasty. According to Emmanuel Ringelblum[130] he was nick-named "King Chaim" (*Król Chaim*), one of the many instances of gallows humor among the Jews. Miss Arendt makes no mention of the last known act of his life: When one of the last transports to Auschwitz was ready for departure, Rumkowski voluntarily joined the deportees, among whom was his brother's family.[131]

Miss Arendt nowhere attempts to probe the terrible moral dilemma facing members of the Jewish Councils, nor does she discuss the tragic range of choices confronting these sorely pressed leaders. In order to give an idea of the horrible situation these men were in, several statements written by people who were either directly involved or were contemporary observers of the tragedy are offered here for their documentary value, even though I do not necessarily agree with their contents *in toto*. One statement, from Šiauliai, was written by a man of scholarship and reflection; one from Vilna, by a Jewish man married to a non-Jewess, who could have remained free but chose to share the fate of his fellow Jews; one by an inmate of Theresienstadt, an eminent social psychologist; one by a man who, though not having been a member of a *Judenrat* in Hungary, had firsthand information on the alternatives before it; one by the chief of police in the Lodz Ghetto as reported by a German anti-Nazi writer; one by a non-Jewish observer of the life in the Cracow Ghetto; and finally, one by a seven-year prisoner in concentration camps.

In November 1943 Dr. Eliezer Yerushalmi, an inmate and chronicler of the Šiauliai Ghetto wrote in his diary:

Maybe it is preferable that we too, the last remnants of Lithuanian

Jewry, should die in a way that will sanctify the name of the Lord, and not debase ourselves before our murderers. What sense will there be in our life even if we save it? Do we have the right to forgive the blood of our brothers and sisters for the grace of life extended to us? Or should we perhaps stick to life with all our powers and by all means, if only to be able to tell the world? But what world? The one which is directly responsible for our disaster? Maybe it is better to take with us to the grave our secret sorrow and pain and let the world choke with its murder.[132]

Jacob Gens (chief of police of Vilna Ghetto and later head of the ghetto), in a speech before Jewish writers and journalists in the ghetto, spoke openly about the dilemma facing him. Miss Arendt notes ironically that he felt like a savior who "with a hundred victims save[s] a thousand people, with a thousand ten thousand" (p. 105). (In her book the name of Gens does not appear, but the allusion is doubtless to him; see III, 42.) Here is his speech:

Many of you consider me a traitor, and many of you are astonished to find me at a literary meeting at the ghetto. Gens leads you to death, and the same Gens wishes to rescue Jews from death. Gens orders the demolition of hideouts, and the same Gens tries to provide the ghetto with papers, work, and useful activity. I make the account of Jewish blood, not of Jewish honor. If I am asked to supply a thousand Jews, I do it, because if we Jews will not supply them, the Germans will come and take with violence not a thousand but thousands and thousands— and the whole ghetto will become a free-for-all. With hundreds I rescue thousands, with a thousand which I supply I rescue ten thousand . . . I, Jacob Gens, if I survive, will go out from the ghetto dirty, blood on my hands, but I shall present myself to a Jewish court and tell them: I have done everything to rescue more and more Jews of the ghetto and lead them to freedom. In order to enable a remnant to survive, I had to lead Jews to death; in order to enable other people to leave the ghetto with a clear conscience, I had to plunge into dirt and act without conscience.[133]

Gens was shot by the Gestapo.[134]

Speaking as a Jew from Prague, H. G. Adler, himself a former inmate of Theresienstadt Ghetto, and a severe critic of the Theresienstadt *Judenrat*, argues:

From the beginning, there were only two possibilities. In March 1939 [when the Germans occupied Bohemia-Moravia], one could have made the decision, even at the price of one's own life, to disband the Jewish communities and institutions and to destroy all registers and documents; or one could have followed a policy whose objective was to delay the worst, negotiate cleverly, and alleviate the situation. The latter road was followed to the bitter end; it led to terrible entanglement and, ultimately, to ruin. The men responsible must not be condemned blindly. Some of them demonstrated the virtues of good will and self-sacrifice; yet nearly all had many weaknesses, as a result of which they were defeated by the SS even in circumstances where a correct appraisal of the enemy, skill, more circumspection and foresight, and, sometimes, also greater courage could have achieved more, at least for the moment.[135]

Rezsö Kasztner, a leader in the Hungarian Jewish rescue operations, wrote the following:

If it [the *Judenrat*] functions [as intended], if it is docile, it may accelerate the process of liquidation. If it refuses to obey, it brings about sanctions against the community without being certain of delaying the process of liquidation. Between those extreme poles, there are a number of intermediate possibilities depending on the flexibility of the persons involved and on the strength of the temptation to which they are exposed. Nearly everywhere in Europe, the *Judenrat* followed the same road. Step by step, they were made tractable. In the beginning, relatively unimportant things were asked of them, replaceable things of value like personal possessions, money, and apartments. Later, however, the personal freedom of human beings was demanded. Finally, the Nazis asked for life itself. For this, it was the task of the *Judenrat* to decide who would go first, who later. In sacrificing to Moloch, cruel criteria came into being, including age, merit, and achievements. Personal considerations pressed to the foreground: degree of kinship, personal sympathies, even self-interest. The road the *Judenrat* took was tortuous, and led nearly always to the abyss. Everywhere the Jew was confronted with the same problem: Shall I—whoever I am—be the traitor in order to help or even to rescue others now and then, or shall I forsake the community, surrender my dreaded responsibility to others? Is not flight from responsibility also something like betrayal? If I accept the burden, where must I draw the line that will release me from the unbearable responsibility for national suicide, for the execution of my people? How can one draw the boundary between self-sacrifice and betrayal? It is small wonder that wherever a Jewish *yishuv* was left, these questions came up again and again. That demagoguery played its part in this is almost a natural phenomenon. To judge the *Judenräte* in retrospect, on the evidence of testimony of witnesses, files, and documents, exceeds in difficulty nearly everything earthly justice has ever had to deal with.

In a larger sense the complex question of the *Judenrat* by no means concerns a typically Jewish phenomenon. During the war and occupation years, the European peoples provided some far worse examples of moral disintegration. Only few remained firm when the psychological pressure exceeded the limits which humans are normally capable of bearing. Moreover, it would be entirely out of place to compare the *Judenrat* with the ordinary Quislings and collaborationists, because only the Jews were haunted by the nightmare of total physical destruction: every other nation had at its disposal some means of self-preservation, self-defense, and self-assertion. If anything could be called specifically Jewish, it was the sense of duty which the Jewish community believed it could expect from all of its people even in moments of the greatest danger and the most desperate decisions.[136]

An anti-Nazi German writer who twice visited the Lodz Ghetto, under fantastic circumstances,[137] attributed to Leo Rosenblatt, the chief of the Jewish police, the following answer to the moral problem involved in the selection of victims for deportation:

And I must select the people for it [deportation for gassing]. If I refuse, I'll be shot. This would be the simplest solution for me. But what happens then? The SS already said it: then they'll make the selections. That would mean that those with unbroken spirits, the pregnant, the rabbis, the torah scholars, the professors, the poets would go into the oven first. But if I stay, I can take the volunteers. Often they urge to be taken. And sometimes I have as many as I have to report. Sometimes though, there are less. Then I can take the dying, indicated to me by the Jewish doctors, and if there are not enough of them, the mortally ill. But if there are still not enough, what then? Then I can take the criminals; but, God protect us, who does not become criminal here? In our ghetto money, which we have to print on the basis of our account of German money, a loaf of bread costs 300 to 500 marks. I know mothers who denounce their neighbors for a slice of bread, so their children won't starve to death. Who wants to sit in judgment here? And yet: if I can't reach the full amount in any other way? Often it works without the criminals. But not always. And at times, not even they will be enough. Then one can take the very old. But what kind of yardstick is that? Mr. Hielscher, I am a poor Jew from Lemberg. I have learned my business, and I also was able to lead my battery. But what one is to do here, that I haven't learned. I have asked the leaders of the community, the rabbis, the torah scholars; they all have told me "you are doing the right thing; stay and make the selections the way you have thought it out." I have asked the congregations into which we have divided the ghetto; I have asked the old people, the condemned, the mortally ill: they have all agreed with me, Mr. Hielscher, and yet I no longer enjoy being alive. I implore you by the God in whom you believe: if you know a better way than the one I have found, show it to me, and I shall bless you day and night. And if you don't know a better one, tell me: shall I stay or shall I have myself shot?[138]

Tadeusz Pankiewicz, a Polish pharmacist in the Cracow Ghetto, of whom more will be heard later, gives his evaluation of the moral choices before the Jewish Councils:

For honest people the work in the *Judenrat* was a very unpleasant duty. It was not easy to execute orders against one's will, to circumvent the law, to try to delay things, to find a way to convince thousands of people that it was not the *Judenrat* who gave the orders but that the *Judenrat* was forced to execute the orders of the Germans. Many people in the ghetto maintained an unfriendly attitude toward the *Judenrat*, though with the exception of a few cases nobody could find concrete reasons to blame them. After the war I used to hear many people express their opinion time and time again that those who, if I may say so, held leading positions during the occupation should have relinquished their offices. However, they forgot that to resign was equivalent to signing one's own death sentence, and someone would have to take over anyway. Wasn't it therefore better to have in the *Judenrat* people the majority of whom were upright men, rather than that their places be taken by individuals in the service of the Germans, as presumably happened in some places? Naturally, to be a hero, to sacrifice oneself for the public sounds nice, but one has to be born that way. Just as not every one is born a genius, so not everybody is capable of sacrificing his life. This is a fact of life and it will always remain so. What is most striking to me is that these reproaches were brought up only *after* the war, when, after regaining their freedom, people quickly started to forget the conditions of life during the SS and Gestapo terror. But, I better leave the judgment to the historians, they surely will do a better job than I.

The German authorities' attitude toward the *Judenrat* was doubtless much worse than toward the Jewish police [*Ordnungsdienst*]. Compared to the *Ordnungsdienst*, the *Judenrat* was less useful to the individual German, and this was what counted most to the Nazis. There can be no talk therefore of any confidence in the *Judenrat* on the part of the Gestapo.[139]

Discussing the situation in the Buchenwald camp on the eve of its liquidation, Benedikt Kautsky, himself an inmate of concentration camps for seven years, tells about the alternatives facing the administration, which was in the hands of the inmates themselves, in April 1945:

. . . Word was passed [by the Camp Elder] not to comply with the order [of the commandant to assemble for evacuation]. The commandant waited for a while; then he summoned the Camp Elder and explained to him that he would assemble the next transport with all means of force [at his disposal] unless the camp itself saw to it that within half an hour 3,000 men assembled on the roll-call square, ready to march. This risk the camp could not take—6,000 to 8,000 heavily armed SS men against perhaps 35,000 prisoners, a large number of whom were not fit to fight. This would have led to the very bloodbath which the responsible prisoners had always wanted to avoid. From this moment on the administration of the camp, in all essentials, was placed in the hands of the prisoner functionaries . . .

. . . There [the SS's] only task was to evacuate from the camp as many prisoners as possible and, if possible, not to leave there any people "in the know" . . . but they no longer had enough authority to be really effective.

Nevertheless, if we did not want to endanger everything, we could not risk a serious clash. Thus the last days were filled with a nerve-racking tug of war between the SS and the prisoners' camp administration. The latter used techniques of obstruction wherever possible, put up passive resistance up to the point where violence by the SS was imminent, but above all tried very deliberately to protect the bona fide political prisoners of all nationalities from being evacuated. This was probably the most difficult part of the task that lay on the shoulders of these prisoners: they had to assume responsibility for the death of thousands in order to save thousands of others. For the last time, the [prisoners'] law of the camp was in effect; for the transports the undesirable elements were deliberately selected . . . but, since there were not enough of them, the weakest too were chosen, among them most of the people who were dying anyway. As much as I had been questioning this law of the camp in the past, this time I could not deny that there was justification for applying it, since now this criterion for selection was the only fair one. It was a horrible sight and a bitter task, especially for the political prisoners, to collaborate, first on that seventh of April and then on the days thereafter, in the ever repeated evacuation of the Little Camp, which always filled up again with the new admissions from the sub-camps. When the prisoners from S-3 arrived, we had literally the impression of walking dead going to their own funeral; but for the very reason that the majority of these unfortunate beings could be expected to die anyway, it was justifiable to save with their lives thousands of healthy people.[140]

These examples were all taken from the period of the mass deportations. It would, however, be a mistake to believe that Jewish leaders or observers were not tormented by the same moral dilem-

mas even earlier. From the outset of the war there was the problem
of providing for the basic needs of all inhabitants of the ghetto.
Emanuel Ringelblum, writing in his diary on May 26, 1942, discusses (without reaching any conclusion) the limitations on the
help given by the organization called Jewish Social Self-Help:

Welfare work does not solve the problem, even though it helps people
for a short time. People must die anyway. Organized community efforts
only prolong their suffering, but do not offer survival. For this purpose
millions of zlotys a month are necessary, and they are not available. It
is a fact that those who eat at the public kitchens die if kitchen soup and
dry bread is their only food. The question therefore arises: Would it not
be more practical to appropriate the amount of money at our disposal
for the benefit of a selected group of public leaders, for the spiritual
élite, etc.? But even these selected persons constitute too large a group
for our means to be sufficient. And why should we condemn to death
artisans, laborers, and other valuable people who were productive in
their home towns, whom war and the ghetto have reduced to a subhuman status—to waste and rubbish and to candidates for mass graves?
The tragic problem is, therefore, still with us: what are we to do? Give
a spoonful to everyone or give enough for survival to a small group?[141]

The moral problem involved for those who were called upon to
prepare lists of deportees tormented the minds and hearts of the
members of the Judenräte and precipitated a hot debate, with the
rabbinate participating. This was known as the "Maimonides debate," because an important source in the Jewish religious law for
such contingencies was Maimonides' law code.[142] Not everywhere
were the decisions the same.[143]

The way such decisions were made, the anxiety accompanying
them, and the all too human tendency to blame one's own people
is vividly described in the following text, reflecting conditions
typical in the smaller Jewish communities:

The colony Heidemülle was located near the township Kowale-
Pańskie, in the district of Turek, Poznań province. It consisted of sixteen
villages, and the Germans herded there, on Yom-Kippur 1941, the Jews
of Turek, Dobra, Uniejów, Tuliszków, Brudzew, Władysławów, and
similar small places. For a short time, we were left in peace.

At the end of October 1941, all of us suddenly became restive.
People whispered that the Judenratältester, Hershel Zimnawoda, had
come back from Turek terribly excited. Everybody expected something
had to happen. On November 4, Hershel called in the rabbis and told

them: "The *Landrat* [district chief] demands that I hand over a list of all Jews of the colony and write alongside each one's name either the letter 'F' or 'U': 'F' for *Fähig* [fit] and 'U' for *Unfähig* [unfit]. As a rule, children up to 12 years of age and people over 65 years of age are to be marked with the letter 'U'. You are the rabbis, you must give me your opinion as to what, according to the traditional law, I am supposed to do. If I do not deliver the list, the Germans themselves will do as they please." The following rabbis were present: Rabbi Isachar Dov Ber, of the town Dobra; Rabbi Pinhas Weiss of Turek; Rabbi Lewenthal of Uniejów; and the Rabbi of Władysławów, whose name escapes me. Rabbi Ber was the son of the Rabbi of Sompolno, author of the volume *Imrei Zvi* (*The Sayings of Zvi*) and teacher of Nahum Sokolow. He was known for his deep piety; the other rabbis were also great sages.

The rabbis began their deliberations on Wednesday, November 5, at ten in the morning, at the home of Rabbi Weiss in the village of Młyny. People said that they saw Rabbi Ber at dawn that day going to the river for ritual ablutions. All the rabbis fasted that day. A *minyan* [ritually prescribed quorum of Jews, consisting of ten adult males] assembled in the house of Elyokim Rosenzweig to say prayers. The rabbis meditated until evening but they were unable to agree on the ruling. Though at the time none of us knew that the letter "U" actually meant deportation to the extermination camp at Chełmno, people instinctively felt that those marked "unfit" could expect nothing good. For this reason the rabbis deliberated so long and it took them so much time to determine whether, according to traditional law, a Jew may jeopardize the life of another Jew. The deliberations continued all through the next day. We were extremely tense concerning the decision. All of us felt that our fate depended not on the Germans but rather on what the rabbis might decree. Their judgment was delivered in the afternoon of Thursday, November 6. The judgment of the rabbis was that, according to the religious law, a decree of the government is obligatory and must be obeyed. Therefore, Hershel must deliver the list. Everyone, however, has to be given the chance to check the list to see how he has been marked. The chairmen of the Jewish communities of Dobra, Uniejów, Tuliszków, Władysławów, and Brudzew should themselves deliver the lists of the Jews of their places.

The forms which were to be filled out contained the following columns: running number; last name; first name; age; "F"; "U".[144]

On a similar occasion in Kovno, Rabbi Abraham Duber Cahana Shapiro delivered the following opinion to the Jewish Council:

If a Jewish community (may God help it) has been condemned to physical destruction, and there are means of rescuing part of it, the leaders of the community should have courage and assume the responsibility to act and to rescue what is possible.[145]

A different view was taken by the Vilna rabbinate following the first delivery of Jews by Jacob Gens, the head of the ghetto.

After this action the religious circles held a conference and sent a delegation consisting of four rabbis to Jacob Gens. . . . They told him that according to religious law a Jew may be delivered to the authorities if charged with common law crimes, but not simply as a Jew. The rabbis advised Jacob Gens that he had no right to select Jews and deliver them to the Germans. Jacob Gens replied that by participating in the selections and delivering a small number of Jews, he is rescuing all the rest from death. The rabbis answered with the following quotation from Maimonides: ". . . if pagans should tell them [the Jews] 'give us one of yours and we shall kill him, otherwise we shall kill all of you,' they should all be killed and not a single Jewish soul should be delivered."[146]

The alternative of suicide was often considered. Dr. Philip Friedman has recorded ten cases of suicides of members of the *Judenräte*.[147] Research going on in the Documentary Projects has revealed many severe acts of repression on the part of the Nazi authorities against members of the *Judenräte*, and at least forty acts of suicide. For example: Dr. Joseph Hepner, a member of the Łomża Jewish Council, put an end to his life in view of the hopelessness of the Jewish situation.[148] Markus Horowitz, "the protector of Kołomyja Ghetto," chairman of the Jewish Council, refused to intervene against the deportation of his own wife on the ground that if he cannot liberate all other Jews he has no moral right to do it for his wife. In November 1942 he committed suicide with his sister after losing hope of rescuing the remnants of Jewish Kołomyja.[149] The chairman of the Jewish Council of Bereza Kartuska, Jacob Schlossberg, and some of its members hanged themselves, refusing to participate in the final action against the Jews of that community.[150]

The case most widely known is that of Adam Czerniakow, chairman of the Warsaw Ghetto *Judenrat*, who committed suicide. According to a memoir by Adolf and Barbara Berman, written in Warsaw in October 1942 and published in 1963, the immediate reason for Czerniakow's suicide was the Gestapo plan to start the deportation of children.[151]

This problem of suicide can be regarded from two points of

view: (1) In considering this act of a man who possessed a deep sense of personal and communal responsibility, we can only bow our heads before the man and his self-sacrifice. (2) In approaching the same problem from the overall viewpoint of Jewish survival in the conditions of Nazi terror, we are left with the unanswerable question, Would not the Jewish community in Warsaw have fared better with a person like Czerniakow at its head than with his less influential successor, Marek Lichtenbaum?[152]

Behavior of the Victims

Miss Arendt writes of "the submissive meekness with which Jews went to their death—arriving on time at the transportation points, walking on their own feet to the places of execution, digging their own graves, undressing and making neat piles of their clothing, and lying down side by side to be shot" (p. 9). Elsewhere she refers to the "moral collapse . . . among the victims" (p. 111).

This picture contrasts radically with reality. Consider the following extract from a Lodz Gestapo report of June 9, 1942, dealing with the situation in Pabianice:

Since the Jews in the [Lodz] district had, of course, learned about the evacuation, they tried to throw the evacuation out of gear by smuggling out property, fleeing to the Government-General, and defying to the greatest extent the instructions of the authorities. Therefore this agency [the Lodz Gestapo] asked the RSHA for the severest measures against the Jews, and the *Reichsführer-SS* ordered the execution of Jews in several instances. As a result, to this date a total of 95 Jews have been hanged in public. Pursuant to these measures, the Jews acknowledged the energetic action taken here, by submitting for the most part without opposition to all instructions.[153]

Of the many eyewitness accounts of the circumstances of such deportations, one is quoted here at length. It was written by Tadeusz Pankiewicz, the only known non-Jew who by accident (his pharmacy happened to lie within the perimeter of the ghetto in Cracow) witnessed life in a ghetto from the first to the last day. From his pharmacy he had a view of Harmony Square (*Plac Zgody*), the place where the deportees were assembled. He told his story in a remarkable book published in Cracow in 1947. Here is his full account of the first deportation, the least horrible of the five he witnessed and reported, and two other accounts:

... The commissions, consisting of members of the Gestapo and officials of the Labor Office, have been working in the building of the Jewish Social Self-Help on May 29, 30, and 31, 1942. Small tables have been put up in the large hall in the building of the former Savings Bank, each table for one Gestapo man and one official of the Labor Office. In front of each table long lines of people are waiting with trembling hearts to see what their fate will be. Crowds are standing in front of the building for long hours in lines that extend for hundreds of meters. The Gestapo men arbitrarily decide on the spot who is to remain and who is to leave the ghetto. Those who do not receive permission to remain in the ghetto are too frightened to ask: Where will we be deported? What will happen to us? Will we be permitted to take some of our belongings with us? They are trying to reassure each other. Nobody believes in total annihilation. Nobody thinks of crematoria, gas-poisoning, or death by burning. Rumors spread for the first time that the Germans had disclosed secretly that the deportees will be taken to the Ukraine, where they will work on farms.

German railroad workers tell about large barracks that are awaiting the deportees. People believe these rumors, but new worries arise: where to get food, and whether they will be allowed to take along large amounts of provisions. In the meantime, the struggle for life goes on with all vigor. People try with all the means at their command to get their identification cards stamped by the SS *und Polizeiführer*, since only these stamps give the right to remain. Nobody realized at the time that the stamps determined life and death, and that their dispensation depended entirely on the whims of the Germans—that neither the fact that one is working nor the kind of work one has been doing has any significance. Paradoxical events take place: One person is denied the stamp, but gets the stamp without difficulty at the same table an hour later. Another person is refused the stamp at one table, but gets it at another. Coincidence, luck, the mood of the Gestapo man, his caprice, the extent of one's connections, the amount of bribe money, the sparkle and the size of the diamond—these are the chance occurrences which decide whether one remains or has to leave. The two-day registration is finished. People without stamps await their fate.

On June 1, 1942, the Jewish police [*Ordnungsdienst*] is ordered to remove all persons without stamps from their homes to Harmony Square. At night the Jewish police inspect the apartment houses and check identification cards. Persons destined for deportation are seized. This procedure goes on all through the night. Like a nightmare, like a dark vision of ghosts, the column of people, men and women, march at the dawn of June 2nd. Like shadows they move at a slow pace, carrying on their shoulders all their possessions, which bear down on them as does the tragic destiny of their wandering. Harmony Square is slowly getting crowded with people and with heaps of bundles, personal belongings wrapped in sheets and sacks, suitcases and all other imaginable pieces of luggage. The sun burns mercilessly. It will be hot today. Thirst parches the throats. Peoples' nerves are strained to the extreme. Two cars enter the Square through the gate and stop about 50 meters from my pharmacy. From the first car two Gestapo men get out. One of them walks over to the second car and exchanges a few words with its occupants. The second car then starts in the direction of the Jewish police. My pharmacy is open as usual, as on any other day. I am looking out, watching what will happen. What is going on? After a short while I notice that the two Gestapo men who remained at the Square take their guns out of their holsters, release the safety catches, and walk slowly toward the pharmacy. I cannot comprehend their intention. I look at my assistants with questioning eyes, and we exchange a few words about what is happening outside. We cannot comprehend the intention of the Gestapo men, nor do we understand against whom their actions are directed. We go through weird moments of waiting until the door opens and both of them enter, tall, handsome-looking men in excellently tailored SD uniforms, with opaque skull emblems on their caps. Without a word of greeting they approach the counter. "*Wünschen?*" ["What would you like?"] I ask, but get no reply. Their steely, penetrating eyes wander over our faces, over the pharmaceutical equipment and the medicines; glide over each thing, move over the walls, contemplate for a second the lighted holy icon, and look back at me and my staff. It is as quiet as a grave. I cannot comprehend it all. Without even exchanging a word between themselves, they put their guns on the marble counter, take out the ammunition clips and load their guns. We hear the crackling noise of guns being loaded and once more they release the safety catches. A faint smile appears on their lips, and they leave the pharmacy without saying goodbye.

The streets leading to Harmony Square became deserted. People are hiding in the halls of the buildings. Spiro [the chief of the Jewish police], accompanied by his entire staff, runs around like mad. The Gestapo men have already left the pharmacy, closing the door behind them. We look out and see one of them aiming his gun in the direction of Józefińska street. The Jewish policemen shout at the people. Suddenly we hear a shot fired—one shot, a second, and a third, and we see the gun being slowly lowered in the hand of the shooter. No voices are heard anymore; only the quick steps of the running *Ordnungsdienst* men interrupt the deadly stillness. Whom did he aim at? Did he hit? Why did he shoot? Perhaps only to frighten people? Did he aim at anybody? These thoughts rush through our minds. It turns out, after all, that the shot found its mark. Fortunately, it was not fatal. The Gestapo man who was the first to fire a shot in the ghetto was the SS-*Oberscharführer und Kriminalsekretär* Wilhelm Kunde, the *Referent* for Jewish affairs in the *Sicherheitspolizei*; the first man wounded was Dr. Weichert, chairman of the Jewish Social Self-Help.

New cars arrive all the time and new Gestapo men appear in the ghetto. One sees all kinds of uniforms and all kinds of ranks. Members of various military and police organizations as well as officials of different departments of the *Stadthauptmann's* office arrive. They came to gloat over the unusual spectacle. New clusters of people approach the Square. The crowd becomes thick and fills every open space. At first, people stand, but after a while they find places to sit, either on the ground or on their bundles. The scorching sun is merciless, the heat makes for unbearable thirst, dries out the throats. People come to the pharmacy continually; physicians, hospital nurses, and *Ordnungsdienst* men come to get medicines for those destined for deportation—Valerian drops, bromides, sedatives, heart medicine are the last purchases for those who are leaving. The crowd is standing or sitting—all wait, frozen with fright and uncertainty. Vans and trucks appear. People run toward them. They push each other, anxious to find a seat or room for their bundles. First place goes to those able to push forward or to make room for themselves with their elbows, force, and youth. It takes only a few minutes for the vehicles to be overcrowded with people and bundles. The Gestapo men watch, malicious smiles on their faces. For the second time today the door of the pharmacy is opened by Gestapo men. Two young ones, about 26 years old, come in. This time they greet us *"Guten Tag"* and ask whose pharmacy this is and how to get to the balcony above. I give the directions, they thank me and leave. Above, on the balcony, they take pictures so as to be able to demonstrate to the world how humane the German people are during the deportation ("resettlement," as they call it, because it was forbidden to use the term "deportation," just as the term "Jewish quarters" was used for the forbidden word "ghetto").

The cameras click, the pictures are taken, the film is turned in the professional Leica cameras. The propaganda fake is finished. Now it can go out into the world and become a document to testify some day to the innocence of the Germans. And people are still waiting. The heat torments without mercy, people fall off their feet from fatigue. Suddenly, a short order is heard: *Alle heraus! Schnell raus!* [All out, hurry out.] It sounds repulsive. In a split second the vehicles are emptied. The Germans with the *Ordnungsdienst* men at their command throw the suitcases and the bundles out, yank out old people, shove the younger ones, hurry, hurry. Frightened, people look at each other, as if to ask: What does all this mean? Was the show with the trucks staged only to take propaganda pictures?

The crowd of sitting people rises when the Germans start shouting, moves closer to each other. At first slowly, then more and more quickly people leave the Square chased and shoved, punched and set upon by the howling Germans. Their luggage bearing them down, some throw away the heavier pieces, while the SS men grab the belongings of others. Pushed, pressed and beaten, the crowd of scampering deportees, like a big snake, moves on alongside the street-car tracks in the direction of Płaszów. Presently, the square becomes empty. However, trucks full of bread continue to arrive, the last gift for the deportees from the remaining population (the *Judenrat* gave the order to all bakeries to bake bread the night before). The Square is empty and quiet. It was teeming with people just a short while ago, but now there are only the bundles they left behind. Those who remain cannot believe that all that has happened only a moment ago really took place. The impact is devastating. Shock has made it impossible to comprehend the events.

The ghetto is deserted. Right after the departure of the deportees the high-ranking Germans, the SS and Gestapo men, left in their cars. Only the *Ordnungsdienst* and the Specialists for Jewish affairs remained. Two hours later, they too left the ghetto. The walls of the ghetto are still surrounded by closely spaced guards: a sign that the action is not finished for today.

A terrifying, agonizing night approaches, a night during which nobody would close an eye. Nobody thought of sleep that night. A feeling of insecurity about the future engulfed those left in the ghetto. Despair and the realization of powerlessness against brutal force breaks them psychologically.

People who were denied the stamps on their identification cards either gave up further endeavors, entrusting their fate to destiny and not reporting for the first deportation, or tried to reverse the negative decision by whatever means possible. The ghetto makes telephone calls in all directions. Conversations with the chiefs of the various places where Jews are employed are going on incessantly. In many cases these interventions were successful. Either the employers came over personally or they settled the matter by talking to the Labor Office in the ghetto or to the Gestapo people by phone.

The Germans, however, are not satisfied with the number of the deportees. According to their estimate, not all people without stamps have reported for deportation.

An order is given to check the documents of all inhabitants of the ghetto and seize everyone without a permit. During the night of June 3-4, the Gestapo, the German Special Service [*Sonderdienst*], and the Jewish police functionaries checked the documents of people in the streets, hospitals, homes for the aged, in the apartment houses and homes. Beating, kicking, humiliation took place all the time. It lasted until morning. Early in the morning strong detachments of the *Sonder-*

dienst enter the ghetto fully armed. Alongside the Germans appear for the first time detachments of Polish police, the "blue ones," and groups of the Polish boys forcibly recruited for the so-called *Baudienst* [Construction Service]. German police take up positions at the Square. They stack their rifles before them. In the back, right beneath the windows of the pharmacy, the *Baudienst* takes up its positions. Across from them is the "blue" police and next to it, in a small side street, there are assembled Jewish physicians, men and women, and hospital nurses and stretcher-bearers, altogether a small group of ten people. According to a German order, their alleged task is to assist people who may faint. The white uniforms and aprons of the hospital personnel look uncanny against the blue uniforms of the police and the green ones of the German Special Service.

The march of the deportees has started. The first rows appear at the Square; people are pushed, stamped on, hit; like ghosts, they keep moving on at a slow pace, quietly, gravely, but with dignity. A few run in clusters, some run singly, others look as if they had lost their minds. They are all surrounded by German police, each one with his rifle in his hands, the finger on the trigger ready to shoot. People pass in front of my windows. All this is taking place amid constant screaming of the Germans, merciless beating, kicking, and shooting. Many are killed, many wounded during these very first moments of the deportation.

Before my eyes, as in a fiendish kaleidoscope, pictures appear simply not of this world; sounds of firing are heard in the ghetto; the Germans shoot at random into the crowd, at the wounded carried on stretchers, even at the dead; smoke pours out of their rifles. German officers carry revolvers, pokers, heavy staffs, or walking sticks. The hospital attendants take care of the wounded and the dead, picking their way through the dense crowd under constant shooting. The Germans shoot like mad, aim at random, at whim and fancy. It seems that blood and the dead bodies entice their bestiality, and the urge to kill and to deliver blows makes their sadism more intense.

According to the official German order, it was still permitted during this first transport to take along luggage, and this was not searched at the Square. This time the Germans thoroughly search many people either in the open at the Square or in halls and stores. As a rule, they take away the luggage and hit and maim people regardless of age or sex.

Physicians, nurses, and Jewish policemen constantly rush into the pharmacy to get medicines and bandages for the beaten, wounded, and those who fainted. The seriously wounded are taken to the hospital at Józefińska street. New groups of people hauled out of their homes arrive at the Square. Old people, women, and children pass by the pharmacy windows like ghosts. I see an old woman of around seventy years, her hair loose, walking alone, a few steps away from a larger group of deportees. Her eyes have a glazed look; immobile, wide open, filled with horror, they stare straight ahead. She walks slowly, quietly, only in her dress and slippers, without even a bundle, or handbag. She holds in her hands something small, something black, which she caresses fondly and keeps close to her old breast. It is a small puppy—her most precious possession, all that she saved and would not leave behind.

Laughing, inarticulately gesturing with her hands, walks a young deranged girl of about fourteen, so familiar to all inhabitants of the ghetto. She walks barefoot, in a crumpled nightgown. One shuddered watching the girl laughing, having a good time, when people around her were breaking down, stunned by fear. Old and young pass by, some dressed, some only in their underwear, hauled out of their beds and driven out. People after major operations and people with chronic diseases went by. All were chased by fear, bleeding, manhandled, amidst the ridicule and laughter of the soldiery.

Across the street from the pharmacy, out of the building at No. 2, Harmony Square, walks a blind old man, well known to the inhabitants of the ghetto; he is about seventy years old, wears dark goggles over his blind eyes, which he lost in the battles on the Italian front in 1915 fighting side by side with the Germans. He wears a yellow armband with three black circles on his left arm to signify his blindness. His head high, he walks erect, guided by his son on one side, by his wife on the other. "He should be happy that he cannot see, it will be easier for him to die," says a hospital nurse to us. Pinned on his chest is the medal he won during the war. It may, perhaps, have some significance for the Germans. Such were the illusions in the beginning.

Immediately after him, another elderly person appears, a cripple with one leg, on crutches. The Germans close in on them; slowly, in dance step, one of them runs toward the blind man and yells with all his power: *"Schnell!"* [Hurry!] This encourages the other Germans to start a peculiar game. Two of the SS men approach the old man without the leg and shout the order for him to run. Another one comes from behind and with the butt of his rifle hits the crutch. The old man falls down. The German screams savagely, threatens to shoot. All this takes place right in the back of the blind man who is unable to see, but hears the beastly voices of the Germans, interspersed with cascades of their laughter. A German soldier approaches the cripple who is lying on the ground and helps him to rise. This help will show on the snapshot of a German officer who is eagerly taking pictures of all scenes that will prove "German help in the humane resettlement of the Jews." For a moment we think that perhaps there will be at least one human being among them unable to stand torturing people one hour before their death. Alas, there was no such person in the annals of the Cracow ghetto. No sooner were they saturated with torturing the cripple than they decided to try the same with the blind war invalid. They chased away his son and wife, tripped him, and rejoiced at his falling to the ground.

This time they even did not pretend to help him and he had to rise by himself, rushed on by the horrifying screaming of the SS men hovering over him. They repeated this game several times, a truly shattering experience of cruelty. One could not tell from what they derived more pleasure, the physical pain of the fallen invalid or the despair of his wife and son standing aside watching helplessly.

It is difficult to describe every single case, the diversity of the German crimes, which took place before my eyes. Described individually, the episodes would look very similar; in fact, however, each incident was completely different even though it always started with beating, trampling, and often ended with shooting the victim. Each incident had its individual tragic angle.

The shots are echoing all over the ghetto. There are dead bodies; wounded people are carried on stretchers; blood leaves marks of German crimes on the sidewalks and streets. More people assemble in the Square. As on preceding days, the heat is unusual. Fire literally pours down from the sky. It is impossible to get water. People faint from heat and thirst. A small military car is parked in front of the pharmacy. The SS men are continuously loading valises filled with valuables they took from the deportees during the searches. Everything they see is taken; rings, wedding bands, watches (gold or metal), cigarette cases, even cigarette lighters. Some deportees look at each other; others wait for their turn; indifference and apathy show on their faces.

We learn more details—who was killed and where, and where the wounded are. The hospital is in action, the physicians give first aid to the wounded, and try to save those who committed suicide by taking poison—of which there were many cases.

When will all this end? This disturbing question is on everybody's mind. I look out of the pharmacy window, standing far back so as not to be seen from the outside. The Germans don't like witnesses to their crimes. Each time during such actions the streetcar traffic was discontinued and even German cars were stopped.

I look out and see a group of high SS dignitaries approaching the pharmacy. They stop right at my door. I hear their voices, I can understand each word, particularly since, as is their custom, they don't talk, they yell. I walk over close to the door and hide in a nook in the wall. It appears that they find the number of deportees to be unsatisfactory and assistance of the *Judenrat* to be at fault. They blame the chairman, whose name they constantly mention. A moment later I hear one of them yelling and whistling in the direction of the Jewish policemen who are assembled in the Targowa street. I hear the running of the Jewish policemen and see among them Spiro who stops not far from the SS men. He stands at attention, salutes, gets a sharp order to immediately bring over the chairman of the *Judenrat*, Dr. [Artur] Rosenzweig.

A man of 40, slim, his long face haggard, with nervous gestures, approaches the Germans. He talks to them quite unafraid, he speaks excellent German; his name is David Guter. A few minutes later, Rosenzweig appears; he walks slowly, hatless, his gray hair is blown by the wind, a middle-aged gentleman. He stops in front of the Gestapo and SS men and bows his head slightly. A moment of stillness, and then the dreadful words are snapped out by one of the SS men, who is using the abusive second person singular form: "Rosenzweig, you are dismissed from your position as of this moment. The action has not produced the desired results: neither the number of people delivered to the Square nor the method of their delivery was satisfactory." Dr. Rosenzweig does not answer, again he bows slightly and departs. The Germans turn to Guter and tell him that as of now, he will be responsible for everything. "*Jawohl!*" ["Yes, Sir!"], Guter replies, jumping at attention.

The ghetto has a new *Kommissar*, this is Guter's title. Who is Guter? A former salesman of fashion magazines, an extremely nervous man, slick, energetic, and articulate, he knows how to obey and execute the orders of the Germans as well as Spiro, but is much more intelligent and more critical than he. He has his own opinions and knows how to smuggle into his slickly delivered speeches phrases that testify to his cool approach and that do not escape his listeners. The fact that the Germans singled him out for such a "high" position went to his head, and his inferiority complex carried him away as it did with Spiro. Right after his appointment, he applied all his energy to his job. During the actions he used to run like a madman from one group of Germans to the other, gesticulating and screaming. Watching him, I was impressed with his colossal physical stamina.

Immediately after his removal from the office of chairman, Dr. Rosenzweig was arrested with his entire family, and was included in a group destined for deportation on that very day. Undoubtedly, it was not convenient for the Germans to have him around. Dr. Rosenzweig was an extremely fine and intelligent person, whose hands were clean. He had a university education and knew how to think and to reason critically. He was not impressed by the honor the Germans bestowed on him; it undoubtedly was a burden to him, as every leading position was for an honorable person in those times and circumstances.

What was the prevailing opinion about Dr. Rosenzweig? He was reproached for accepting events too passively, when one might alleviate the situation in regard to execution or date, though it might have no influence on the final outcome. Thus, for instance, it was possible, according to some people, to save physicians from deportation by intervention and, even when a physician was already in the transport, it was possible to get him out.

Expressing these opinions about Dr. Rosenzweig, people would not consider whether such intervention would have been effective or serve the purpose. What counted was the fact itself. The chairman was reproached for not acting [against the Germans] though he was strict and unyielding with his closest co-workers when they were of different opinion. People used to explain it by his apathy, resignation, and helplessness in the face of force, attitudes that led him to disbelieve the success of any mollifying endeavors whatsoever. He was eager to get out of his position, but knew well what was in store for him if he tried to.

The deportation has started. The Square slowly becomes empty of people. Some are transported in cars, others walk on foot, rushed on by the shouting Germans, pushed around, trampled on, beaten. They run along the Lwowska-Wielicka streets in the direction of Płaszów. On the way, guards of the German Special Service fire at those who cannot catch up with the others. The road of the deportees is marked by dead bodies.

At the railroad station of Płaszów they were loaded into cattle cars with quicklime sprinkled over the floors and small grilled windows up on the ceilings. They packed 120 persons to a car. The doors tightly closed, a German guard was posted at each car. No water or bread was allowed, and the scorching heat was unbearable. Some people had brought along their locksmith tools and managed to escape by breaking loose the window grill and jumping out of the train. They endangered their lives by hitting themselves against the railroad poles or by falling under the wheels of the moving train; but mostly death awaited them from the bullets of the escorting policemen.

There were some who broke the boards of the car floors while the train was moving and escaped through the hole when the train stopped at a station. After the train started again and passed over the bodies of the escapees, their further fate depended entirely on individual luck. A youngster whom I knew told me later that he had jumped off the moving train but was seen by the German guards. They fired at him several times. While jumping out, he hit a signal pole and, in addition, was wounded by the Germans; he lost consciousness and rolled down the railroad bed. He did not know how long he had been lying there. When he woke up it was night and dark. He crawled for a few hours until he reached the first house. It was the house of a peasant. Later he continued crawling from house to house during daytime. Not always were doors opened to him, not always did he get a friendly word of sympathy, but neither did anybody betray him. For weeks he aimlessly kept on going. His wounds had healed by the time he returned to the ghetto and there he stayed until it was completely liquidated on March 13, 1943.

During this deportation, the Gestapo man Kunde again visited me and, using the counter, he stamped the identification cards of some people upon the intervention of Spiro and Förster.

I recall the following scene from this period that characterizes the psychology of the Germans, that was simply incomprehensible at times. The *Referent* for Jewish affairs, *SS-Oberscharführer* Kunde, was taking a walk in the ghetto. He was generally considered one of the most lenient [Germans] as was his colleague *SS-Oberscharführer* Heinrich, another *Referent* for Jewish affairs. It was known that they would not beat or shout, and that they were amenable to certain "persuasions." People saw Kunde, and soon he was surrounded and begged to stamp their identification cards; he stopped and talked with them for a while. The crowd became more and more dense. Kunde noticed an approaching German across the street and fearing to be suspected of talking to Jews, he took his gun out and threatened to shoot. He even fired a shot, the bullet ricocheted and wounded the lady physician, Dr. Silberger. The crowd dispersed in panic. Together with the crowd, a little girl of about twelve ran madly. Kunde ran after her, caught up with her and asked why she was running; a passer-by whom he had accosted was his translator. Stammering with fear, the little girl said that she was afraid he would shoot her. "And what would you like to get from me?" he asked. "A stamp for my daddy and mommy," she said. "And what is your parents' occupation?" "My father is a shoemaker," she answered. He ordered her to fetch the identification cards of the whole family and he put the stamp on all of them. In such hands were placed the fates of thousands of people. Such and similar caprices often decided human destiny.

The ghetto is still surrounded by the *Sonderdienst*. Patrols of German police walk in the streets in measured steps. From time to time one hears shots fired by the guards surrounding the ghetto, particularly from the direction of Krzemionka, from where the ghetto can be seen as clearly as the palm of one's hand.[154]

All people in the ghetto talk about the fate of the deportees. Members of families left behind are trying to get some concrete news by all possible means. All kinds of speculations come up, the most unthinkable rumors are spread, each of them from the "very best source." Germans were always the authors of all this news, the so-called honest ones, those who allegedly betrayed the secrets of the German authorities. Such was the method the Germans used: to reassure by all means, to deceive and give hope that those deported are alive, so that people won't despair, and the aim of it all was to avoid any attempt at revolt.

This is the reason why the Germans introduced collective responsibility—it was meant as a means of suppressing the slightest threat of individual resistance. How many times did it happen that for an alleged offense, even the slightest one, the entire family of the guilty person was punished with death.

Rumors are spread that the deportees were taken to the Ukraine, that they will work on the farms there. Certain German railroad workers tell that they have seen with their own eyes a great number of barracks in which dwell Jews from all over Europe. They have a good life, work hard, but have everything they need, food and clothes. Naturally, they are heavily guarded, barbed wire encircles the barracks, nobody is allowed to come near; they are not allowed to write letters and this is the reason why no news is forthcoming from them. These story-tellers are flooded with requests that they visit the deportees, take messages from their loved ones, bring back replies. At first, the Germans pretend to refuse, say that they cannot do it now, that perhaps they will accommodate at a later time. To increase the price of the favor they make it look very difficult. People don't think of money now, pay as much as is requested, eager to cling to the little spark of hope. No consolation, nothing definite comes into the ghetto. The German disappears into thin air as soon as he gets the money, and people wait and hope. . . .

When we try to think now how the June deportations were organized, we can clearly perceive the deliberate perfidy the Germans applied to deceive the people, in order to rob their valuables together with their lives. The Germans, to make their job easier, issued glibly worded ordinances. The first order about the resettlement sounded very innocent, saying that because the ghetto is overcrowded, and in order to improve the living conditions of the inhabitants and to avoid the danger of infectious diseases, the authorities will have to resettle part of the Jewish population. Everybody is, however, entitled to take along as much as one can carry. In fact, people took large amounts of luggage, primarily, of course, their most valuable possessions, assuming that their fate would be the same as that of their predecessors whom the Germans transported to the Lublin area, and set free there.[155] Others thought that they might perhaps be sent to another ghetto. The people of the first transport actually took along all the luggage they were able to carry, but on their arrival at the station of Płaszów, the things were taken from them, though nobody was searched. The search was probably made after they arrived at their destination. This tactic had the purpose of convincing the people in the next transport to take along only small things and refrain from the heavier luggage. The Germans knew well that everybody would be eager to take along small valuables, jewelry, money, gold. When the time came for the second deportation, the Germans applied another method: they searched all people on the spot, thoroughly robbing them of everything they could lay their hands on. What they could not find was left to their colleagues at the places of destination. Larger bundles and bulky luggage were, as a rule, robbed at Harmony Square. What was left in the homes, was taken by the laborers of the [Polish] Construction Service, who were specially brought in for this purpose.

At the time of the third deportation, people who could not show their blue cards [authority to work in town] were seized on the spot and were not allowed to take any of their belongings from their homes, which were sealed off by the Jewish police.

On June 10, 1942, the German guards left the ghetto. The Jews relaxed. After a week of fear and insecurity about the next day, mentally exhausted, they seemed to regain their balance, though nervous breakdowns occurred often. Many reached the stage of apathy and resignation. The three June deportations were accompanied by a great number of suicides. People took their lives by taking potassium cyanide.

At first, it was quite difficult to find poison. Later, a source was discovered. The lamp factory of Mr. Wachs at Lwowska street used this stuff for the production of his merchandise. It was mainly from there that people obtained the poison, which was preserved as the greatest treasure. Entire families secured for themselves carefully weighed doses of poison in small vials, carrying it always, for any event, as the saying went. Those who were less fortunate used luminal or simply gas.

In the weeks following the resettlement, many people tried to find a way out of the ghetto, and a sizable number actually succeeded in escaping. From the building where the pharmacy is located the family of Dr. Oberländer escaped. So did Mr. Jutkiewicz with his mother and sister, and the wife of Dr. Felix and her daughter. During this time women used to dye their gray hair into various shades in order to look younger, because in many cases age determined deportation. Alongside the extreme pessimists, there are however people who are uncritically watching the events, people who refuse to draw somber conclusions from what is happening around them, people who still believe the Germans. With the stubbornness of maniacs, some of the inhabitants of the ghetto keep repeating that "good" Germans have reassured them that these deportations are the last act of the Jewish tragedy. These were mainly people working in town for the Germans.[156]

I remember a scene which will remain in my memory for as long as I live. Thousands of people are standing or sitting in Harmony Square. A dozen steps away stands a group of high-ranking SS and Gestapo men in their smart uniforms and shiny boots, with whips, staffs, pokers in their hands. They laugh and scorn all the time and, coming close to the Jews, hit them and trample over them as if to find an outlet for their energy. Their faces are ruddy, as if they were on fire. I have observed one case when a woman with a small baby at her breast fell to the feet of an SS man, asking him—I assume—to spare her life. Guter [the commissar of the Jewish Council] was close by this SS man. The woman cried, shouted, begged Guter to help her, and kept mentioning her name and her husband's profession. Nothing helps, the SS man kicks her brutally and walks away. But she refuses to submit, runs after him; on her way, she grabs Guter's hand and goes on begging. The German turns around and hits her with his whip over her head several times; Guter gets excited and pushes her off, yelling without mercy. The woman faints and falls down to the ground. A German Special Service man comes up, grabs her hand and, together with the baby, yanks her back to the group [of deportees]. This was the one and only case which I have seen when a Jew publicly begged a German for mercy.[157]

Jewish Special Units

In addition to the *Judenräte* and the Jewish police, a third Jewish group is accused by Miss Arendt of being "responsible" for the murder of Jews: the Jewish Special Units (*Sonderkommandos*) in the extermination camps. These Special Units were usually employed for a short while, and then killed. As long as they were kept alive, they lived in unspeakable conditions. The approximately sixty Jews in the Special Unit at the death camp in Chełmno were housed in a cellar and wore iron chains on their legs at all times.[158]

Miss Arendt interrupts her discussion of the indictment drawn up against Eichmann to observe that "Jewish *Sonderkommandos* (special units) had everywhere been employed in the actual killing process, they had committed criminal acts 'in order to save themselves from the danger of immediate death'" (pp. 85-86),[159] and that the work for which Jews were selected was "often operating the extermination machinery" (p. 101). She adds: "The well-known fact that the actual work of killing in the extermination centers was usually in the hands of Jewish commandos had been fairly and squarely established by witnesses for the prosecution" (p. 109). She casts a barb at the Greek Jews: "In Auschwitz, many Greek Jews were employed in the so-called death commandos, which operated the gas chambers and the crematoria" (p. 171). She says that the judgment of the District Court "by implication . . . took cognizance of the weird fact that in the death camps it was usually the inmates and the victims who had actually wielded 'the fatal instrument with (their) own hands'" (p. 224). Her source is the court's statement (quoted by her on page 225) that "in such an enormous and complicated crime as the one we are now considering . . . the degree of responsibility increases as we draw further away from the man who uses the fatal instrument with his own hands"—a statement meant to counter Eichmann's excuse that he never committed an overtly criminal act. Neither this statement nor any other in the judgment says or implies that the *victims* wielded the fatal instruments. Nor did any witness testify to that effect.

It was the SS men or their Ukrainian accomplices who did the work of the actual killing. The Special Units worked on corpses only, but did not take part in the gassing.[160] Far from being participants in crime, these helpless wretches gathered enough strength to stage an armed revolt in Treblinka on August 2, 1943, in which 455 inmates and four SS men perished, only a few of the inmates managing to escape.[161] The newly discovered diary of the Auschwitz Special Unit shows that its members, in compiling secret lists of victims, daily risked their lives for the sake of preserving a record of what took place.[162] Contrary to Miss Arendt's statement, the revolt in Auschwitz was not "one of the very few revolts in any of the camps" (p. 171). The fact is that in three out of the six extermination camps—in Sobibór,[163] in Treblinka,[164] and in Auschwitz[165]—there were revolts of the Special Units. In a fourth camp, Chełmno, the surviving members of the Special Unit resisted the Nazi orders to come out and be killed, and only two of them escaped, injured.[166]

By contrast, the caliber of the SS men in the camps is clearly demonstrated in the diary of Dr. Johann-Hermann Kremer,[167] an Auschwitz camp physician. He wrote that they literally competed to participate in the gassing actions because of the special rations they received for this type of duty: 5 liters of hard liquor, 5 cigarettes, 100 grams of sausage and bread.

The poet Günther Anders gave eloquent expression to the plight of the Special Unit men in his poem "What Would You Have Done?" inspired by a news item that told how some of the inmates of the camps were forced, before they were themselves burned, to service the ovens and dispose of the ashes.

Did you busily scrape the dust of friends and relatives
out of the oven?
And did you cart the wagon through the snow
to the ash heap of those who were burned?
Was the word meant for you: "You will live as long

as the oven smokes,
For you are needed?"
Covered with such dust, did your mouth
give the report in barracks language?
That extra soup, was it for the work of your shovel?
And the double ration for the sweat you shed?
And was the word for you: "Only late, at some unknown time,
After the coal comes the collier, too?"
Not you, not I. We remain untested.
Thus you may scrape the ovens every night,
And, in your dreams, at his side, push the wagon.
But you cannot grasp a jot of what was in the man's mind,
only that now and then he looked up, as if he were
thinking,
"And what would you have done?"[168]

By Whom and By What Means Could Jews Have Been Rescued?

In her book Miss Arendt does not indicate what might have been an alternative course of action for the Jewish leaders. In an interview given after her book appeared,[169] she offered the following opinion: "The Jewish leaders could have said to their communities: 'A terrible disaster has happened. We can no longer help you. We can only share your fate.'" Asked if that would not have been an invitation to anarchy, Miss Arendt replied: "Yes! and that's better—the Nazis numbered hundreds of thousands while millions of Jews would have gone underground."

This assumes that in Hitler's Europe the Jews outnumbered the Nazis tenfold, and millions of Jews could have gone underground; that there was no qualitative difference between the Nazis with the most powerful war machine in the world and the "civilian" Jews; and that the Nazis would have remained helpless in the face of this underground. Miss Arendt does not tell where it was possible to find in Europe local populations willing to conceal millions of Jews at the risk of severe punishment—death in Eastern Europe,[170] and either arrest or fine or "security measures" (i.e., confinement in a concentration camp) in Western Europe.[171] Were there no informers in Europe? Did not the Danish Resistance consider hiding the Jews, only to reject this proposal as too perilous even among the traditionally philo-Semitic Danes, insisting instead on escape to Sweden?[172] Has history ever recorded a case of millions going underground? In The Netherlands—a country with a three-century record of Jewish-Christian harmony—only 20,000 Jews out of 140,000 went into hiding; of these, one half, or 10,000, were caught.[173] According to Dr. E. Ringelblum, who was hidden twice by Polish friends, some 30,000 out of about 3,000,000 Jews in Poland were in hiding.[174] No estimate of the number of survivors from among those in hiding is available.

A critical appraisal of Miss Arendt's views on what Jewish leaders might have done requires consideration of three factors: (1) The degree to which the ultimate fate of the Jewish populations was known to the Councils. Clearly, no warnings could be issued by leaders who were unaware of the immediate danger. (2) The physical factors on which escape depended. (3) The consequences of disbanding the traditional Jewish communal organizations.

Using her own account of the situation in Denmark as a basis, Miss Arendt condemns Jewish leadership for concealing the truth of Nazi deportations from their communities. "They [the heads of the Jewish community in Denmark], in marked contrast to Jewish leaders in other countries, had then communicated the news [of the forthcoming deportation] openly in the synagogues on the occasion of the New Year services" (p. 156). This statement is incorrect.[175] No New Year services were held in 1943. A warning of the forthcoming deportation was given not by the heads of the Jewish community in the synagogues but by one rabbi to a small part of his congregation attending services on the morning *preceding* the Jewish New Year. The general warning came not from the "heads of the Jewish community" (at that time the community organization had already broken down) but from the Danes. Without the effort of the Danes, most of the Jews would have been caught, as they were everywhere else. The rescue of the Jews of Denmark was actually a result of two factors: a sympathetic local population and another nearby State (Sweden) ready and willing to accept the refugees. The following additional facts should be noted: During the entire period they were protected by the Danish Government (from April 9, 1940, until August 29, 1943), the Jews not only abstained from all illegal activity and dissuaded people from flight to Sweden, but they also kept the community register in perfect order lest the Germans, in examining the register, accuse them of some illegal behavior. This policy, openly debated at meetings of the communal bodies, was pursued in line with the policy of the Danish authorities. The necessity of this policy is illustrated by the following incident: When, in the spring of 1943, a number of young Jewish "pioneers" (*halutzim*) from Germany, who had found refuge in Denmark before the war, stole a boat and fled to Sweden, the Danish State Advocate was summoned to the Gestapo, where it was made clear to him that action would be taken against the whole Jewish community if such activities were not stopped. In due course, the Danes forwarded the Nazi orders to the community, which did everything it could to implement them.

As late as the end of September 1943, when deportations were imminent, the top Danish governing authorities (the Cabinet had resigned at the end of August) were still being kept in the dark by the Germans. When the news finally was broken to them (by the Jews, who themselves had been warned by prominent Danish politicians not in the government), they did not know what to do. Luckily, there were other Danes—members of the Resistance—who did know, and who proceeded to give the general warning. Of the Jews captured by the Germans and deported from Denmark to Theresienstadt, some were caught while fleeing, but most were found by the German police because they were poor and had no means and no connections to arrange for their escape, or because they were inmates of the communal old-age home, whom no one helped. These two unfortunate groups were caught precisely because the organization of the community had broken down completely. The slogan was: "Everybody looks after himself." For those who could not, there was no organization left to lend a hand.

Miss Arendt's misrepresentation of the situation in Denmark makes her attempt to use Denmark as a model pointless. In Denmark the Jews—leaders and ordinary folk alike—were unaware of what was in store for them, up to the very last minute. Elsewhere the situation varied from place to place, though generally there was ignorance of the future among all groups. To the person interested in studying this period, it is important to establish separately in each case to what degree the members of the *Judenrat* could have known—in view of the Nazi policy of deception—the ultimate destination of those who were deported. During Eichmann's cross-examination he admitted that *he used every kind of deception he could think of to make the Jews believe that they were not being sent to their death*.[176] The judgment contains the following description of such deception as exemplified in the case of Hungary:

In implementing the Final Solution, the defendant proceeded in accordance with the principles of psychological warfare as applied to misleading and deceiving the enemy. Here too we shall give just one of many examples: At his first meeting with the leaders of Hungarian Jewry on March 31, 1944, he gives certain instructions concerning the operation of Jewish institutions, etc. Then he turns to the terrified Jews with the following deceitful words:

He emphasized that these instructions would be enforced only for the duration of the war. Later the Jews would be free and could do as they pleased. Everything happening in connection with Jewish matters was only for the duration of the war. Once the war would be over, the Germans would again be as pleasant (gemütlich) as before. He emphasized that he appreciated frankness and that we, too, must also be outspoken with him. He would also be frank with them.

This description, from the book of Ernő Munkácsi,[177] was confirmed by the affidavit of Dr. Ernő Boda (T/1156) and by the defendant himself (Session 103). See also the affidavit of Dr. Ernő Pető (T/1157).[178]

The fact that in the U.S.S.R., too, the Jewish Councils of Elders were unaware of the real purpose of the lists they were ordered to prepare is confirmed by Otto Ohlendorf, former commander of *Einsatzgruppe D* and chief defendant in the *Einsatzgruppen* case. During his cross-examination by the presiding judge, he testified that in the territory of his *Einsatzgruppe* the Jewish elders were in no position to find out what was in store for them and their community since "no executions took place until the council of Jewish elders had completed their work of making up the list." When the lists in a city had been completed by the unsuspecting Jewish Council, "the Jews were then assembled all at once, at one time, for example in barracks or in a large school or in a factory site," and from there taken to the place of execution.[179]

The SS judge Konrad Morgen (mentioned earlier[180]) called Eichmann's methods of extermination "this unique system of deceit" (*dieses einzigartige Täuschungssystem*).[181]

Despite this stratagem used by Eichmann in the implementation of the Final Solution, Miss Arendt maintains that the "Jewish officials" knew what the destination of the deportations was (pp. 105, 178). While not a word is said by her about the deception of both leaders and victims, she admits that "in the camps elaborate precautions were taken to fool the victims right up to the end"

(p. 84). She must realize that the deception could not just have started "in the camps," and that, indeed, it would have been quite ineffective had it started there. When the same question of prior knowledge of the final destination of deportees arises in regard to non-Jews, who had incomparably better lines of communication and were not subject to the full Nazi fury, Miss Arendt's tune is quite different. In relating the story of the four thousand Jewish children in France who were shipped by Eichmann's men to Auschwitz, Miss Arendt accuses the French Chief of State, Marshal Pétain, and the Chief of Government, Pierre Laval, of responsibility for the fate of these children—an accusation not borne out by the facts (see Chapter V, under France). However, even while making this accusation, she finds it necessary to add that "Laval and Pétain thought in terms of these Jews being resettled in the East; they did not yet know what 'resettlement' meant" (p. 147). Laval did know. In his conversation with Oberg on September 2, 1942, he told Oberg of rumors in diplomatic circles concerning the fate of Jewish deportees, and asked what answer he should give to inquiries concerning this matter. The two agreed that in the future Laval should say that Jews from the occupied zone of France who are delivered to the occupying power are being shipped to the Government-General as labor.[182] Concerning the Bulgarian army's deportation of 15,000 Jews to the East, Miss Arendt declares "but it is doubtful that they [the Bulgarians] knew what 'resettlement in the East' actually signified" (p. 167). In short, according to Miss Arendt, the Jews—immured and isolated in their ghettos, and deceived by the Nazis at every turn—were better informed on Nazi plans than the French and Bulgarian leaders, collaborators of the Nazis.

Only after it has been established that particular Jewish leaders knew of the ultimate destination of the deportees, can the question arise: Did they impart their knowledge to the Jewish deportees and, if not, what were their motives? Miss Arendt charges Leo Baeck in particular with the crime of concealing from the inmates of Theresienstadt that they, when deported, would be gassed. Eric H. Boehm's book *We Survived*,[183] indicates that Baeck's policy was based on the conviction that "death was not certain for all." As Leschnitzer rightly noted,[184] this attitude was not dissimilar to the attitude of a doctor who in certain cases decides after thorough reflection not to inform the patient of the gravity of his situation. Although such a policy is in general debatable, it cannot be condemned outright.

Miss Arendt implies that the Jewish Councils should have instructed the people to escape from the Nazi terror (p. 110). Research on the entire question of rescue through escape is only beginning. Escape and rescue was not a matter in which the Jewish factor had a decisive role, if any at all.

Once war had engulfed Europe, people could be rescued from the Nazi extermination machine en masse, by "stopping the death mills"; in organized groups, by concerted action; or individually, by freeing themselves from the clutches of the Nazi terror machine wherever the opportunity offered itself.[185]

The first of these methods was completely outside the realm of Jewish influence and became a factor of large-scale preservation of life only as a result of major changes in the progress of war. It is a fact beyond dispute that toward the end of the war a word from Himmler—the order to stop the extermination—"rescued" more Jews than all the combined efforts of Jews and non-Jews during the entire war period. This fact must always be kept in mind in assessing the degree to which various factors were involved in saving Jewish lives. Although one cannot use in this context the terms *rescue* or *preservation of Jewish lives* in their usual meaning, which implies a humane motive, it is nevertheless a sobering thought, not to be ignored, that those directly and primarily responsible for the destruction of Jewish lives were the only people who could stop the destruction.

The second method was critically dependent on accidental external factors. The relative success of the organized rescue operations carried out by Rabbi Weissmandel in Slovakia and by the Kasztner Committee in Hungary (discussed elsewhere in this chapter and in Chapter 5) was due to the presence of Nazi officials, especially Wisliceny, who were willing to cooperate with the Jews in exchange for bribes. The survival of certain organized partisan groups (discussed elsewhere in this chapter) was usually due to the presence of non-Jewish groups ready to allow them to undertake their activities unmolested.

As for the third method, individual survival or escape, the possibility of rescue varied widely from place to place and from time to time (though at no place and at no time was the possibility likely to lead to success). Many factors came into play. In the first place, there was an internal contradiction within the Nazis' own policy, between the intense desire to exterminate the Jews as soon as possible and the desire on the part of certain circles to exploit them first for the purposes of war industry. Another factor was the effectiveness of bribes;[186] yet another was the various whims and wishes of local Nazi officials.[187] Geography played an important role, since often the availability of an open frontier was crucial— that is, a frontier of a country that was not itself bent upon the physical extermination of the Jews, and was ready to admit, or tolerate, refugees fleeing from mortal danger.[188] Equally decisive was the attitude of the local population, especially whether it was ready despite possible sanctions to hide Jews, either out of compassion or for a price.[189]

Another rescue factor was the attitude of the Vatican, a matter of some controversy.[190]

Yet another factor was the position taken by the International Red Cross. Its basic attitude vis-à-vis the persecution and extermination of European Jewry was expressed in an official report of the International Committee of the Red Cross, from which the following is taken:

Under National Socialism, the Jews had become in truth outcasts, condemned by rigid racial legislation to suffer tyranny, persecution and systematic extermination. No kind of protection shielded them; being neither prisoners of war nor civilian internees, they formed a separate category, without the benefit of any Convention. The supervision which the International Committee of the Red Cross was empowered to exercise in favor of prisoners and internees did not apply to them. In most cases, they were, in fact, nationals of the State which held them in its power and which, secure in its supreme authority, allowed no intervention in their behalf. These unfortunate citizens shared the same fate as political deportees, were deprived of civil rights, were given less favored treatment than enemy nationals, who at least had the benefit of a statute. They were penned into concentration camps and ghettos, recruited for forced labor, subjected to grave brutalities and sent to death camps, without anyone being allowed to intervene in those matters which Germany and her allies considered to be exclusively within the bounds of their home policy. . . .

The Committee could not dissociate themselves from these victims, on whose behalf it received the most insistent appeals, but for whom the means of action seemed especially limited, since in the absence of any basis in law, its activities depended to a very great extent upon the good will of the belligerent States.

The Committee had in fact, through the intermediary of the German Red Cross, asked for information concerning civilian deportees "without distinction of race and religion," which was plainly refused in the following terms: "The responsible authorities decline to give any information concerning non-Aryan deportees." Thus enquiries as a matter of principle concerning the Jews led to no result, and continual protests would have been resented by the authorities concerned and might have been detrimental both to the Jews themselves and to the whole field of the Committee's activities. In consequence, the Committee, while avoiding useless protests, did its utmost to help the Jews by practical means, and its delegates abroad were instructed on these lines. This policy was proved by the results obtained.[191]

The overall progress of the war—over which the Jews had no influence—had the greatest impact on the chances of individual survival. For instance, the Jewish Community of Old Romania (Regat), whose total deportation was originally prevented by the activities of the Jewish leadership, remained practically intact as a result of the Soviet advances on the southern front.[192] But even liberation did not necessarily mean rescue: No less than 14,000 inmates died in the concentration camp Bergen-Belsen during the first few weeks *after* liberation.[193]

Among the external factors that influenced the possibility of escape was the attitude of the governments-in-exile, whose encouragement or discouragement (expressed in advice and instructions relayed back to the home country) was of great importance in shaping the behavior of the local population. Unfortunately, the archives of the British Section of the World Jewish Congress—the main Jewish contact with the governments-in-exile that resided in Great Britain—have not yet been published.[194] Also important was the attitude of the neutrals, which was subject to the changing fortunes of the war. Admission to neutral territory was by no means generally granted; on the other hand, it was never completely denied. (Before the war, both Sweden and Denmark had discriminated between racial persecutees and political refugees in favor of the former.[195]) Miss Arendt accepts (p. 140) Eichmann's testimony that nobody was ready to receive Jews, explaining that there was no reason to behave differently toward Jews than toward other groups of foreigners seeking permission to enter. Here again she glosses over the *sui generis* nature of the Jewish refugee, particularly during the war. In this respect she is *plus catholique que le Pape même*. An opposite point of view was shown by Sweden, which gave shelter to Scandinavian Jews fleeing for their lives.[196] After the war Swiss public opinion was uneasy about the policies of the Swiss Government in regard to refugeees from Nazi persecution. At the government's request, Professor Carl Ludwig submitted to the Swiss Federal Council a remarkable report sharply critical of Switzerland's hands-off refugee policy.[197] These same two countries contributed to the survival of many Hungarian Jews in 1944 by issuing to them "protective passports" (*Schutzpässe*).[198]

The most powerful external factor was the United Nations coalition fighting the Axis powers. Ironically, while a tremendous amount of Nazi material exists, the archives of the anti-Nazi coalition (and of neutral states, including the Vatican) remain to a large extent sealed. The official and unofficial publications of diplomatic correspondence from the war period are highly selective.[199] The unwillingness of the Allied countries to open their files from the Second World War is exemplified in an incident involving the British Government that occurred during the Eichmann trial. During the consideration of the "blood for goods" episode, the hitherto unknown documents from the Weizmann Archives on the United Kingdom's policy in this case were submitted to the court.[200] Two members of the House of Commons requested the British Government to publish the relevant British documentation, but no action was taken.[201] Another item revealed in the Eichmann trial was the fact that Gerstein's report on the gassing of Jews in extermination camps had been communicated to a Swedish diplomat, von Otter, as early as August 1942. It appears that the report of von Otter on his conversation with Gerstein was communicated to the British Government *three years* later, in August 1945.[202] Insofar as the policy of the Allies in general is concerned, an article by Henry Morgenthau, Jr., in the November 1947 issue of *Colliers Magazine* opened up a small crack in the wall of silence surrounding United States and British diplomacy. Although the gigantic war machine of the Allies was busy extinguishing the great conflagration, it is still unproved that no resources were available to fight the fire that engulfed the House of Israel.

All these factors are either ignored by Miss Arendt or treated in such a way that the responsible parties are absolved from blame. She makes no mention of the many attempts of Jewish organizations outside the Nazi sphere of influence during the war to inform the world, to stir up the conscience of non-Jews, and to promote a Jewish war effort.[203] The reader of her book is left with the impression of total passivity and indifference on the part of the Jews.[204]

In listing the tragic choices open to the Jewish Councils, Dr. Adler (in the passage quoted earlier in the present chapter) mentioned the self-dissolution of Jewish communal organizations and the destruction of Jewish records. Such action might have been taken in the "Protectorate" on March 15, 1939, the date of the German invasion of Czechoslovakia. A suggestion to dissolve the Zionist organization there was considered by its leadership on that very day, and was rejected.[205] Such self-dissolution of the Jewish communal organization, however, would have been of no advantage at all; on the contrary, it would have made conditions worse.

In March 1939 the situation in Bohemia-Moravia was as follows:[206] The Supreme Council of the Unions of Jewish Communities, the Prague Jewish Community, and the Joint Social Commission of sixteen Jewish organizations, which was established after Munich, took care, *inter alia*, of thousands of refugees from Germany, Austria, and the *Sudetengebiet*. Their right to remain and work in Bohemia-Moravia was the responsibility of the local Jewish organizations, which also helped immigrants in danger of expulsion for political reasons or because they were "undesirable" aliens to emigrate. Moreover, these organizations played an essential role in the emigration of the indigenous Jewish population from Bohemia-Moravia. For example, there was an agreement between the Jewish organizations and the British Government under which funds from the loan granted to Czechoslovakia after Munich by the British could be used by these organizations—and by them alone— to finance Jewish emigration. Finally, these local organizations served as an address for Jewish groups in other countries concerned with the welfare of their brethren in distress.

As for the destruction of Jewish records, it appears that this would have been of no avail. The Nazis had at their disposal detailed data on all the Jews in the Protectorate, including those not registered in the Jewish community but falling under the Nuremberg laws. These records were available to them from two sources under non-Jewish control: (1) the governmental central record offices, which contained exact personal data on every inhabitant of Czechoslovakia, including his religion, and (2) the local offices of vital statistics (*Matrikelämter*), whose records included the religion of the parents. These local offices were administered by the religious communities, acting under governmental authority and supervision. It was not in the power of the Jews to destroy these two recording systems. It might be added that in the ordinance of the Czech

"Protectorate" government concerning the genealogy of all inhabitants[207] (obviously directed against the Jews), the Ministry of the Interior was instructed to look for pertinent material in three types of official documents, none of which was under the control of Jews.

The situation was not basically different in other countries. In Germany the help of the *Reichsvereinigung* in establishing the addresses of the Jews was not necessary. The Nazi Government had at its disposal the addresses of all Jews owning property with value greater than 5,000 reichsmark, since such holdings had to be declared by virtue of the required Property Declaration (*Vermögenserklärung*).[208] Furthermore, the government had the addresses of Jewish businesses (*Gewerbebetriebe*), the identification cards with "J,"[209] and the Ration Card Lists (*Lebensmittellisten*) of Jews, for whom special hours for purchasing food were fixed.[210] Finally, the census of May 17, 1939, covering Germany, Austria, and the Sudeten Region, supplied the German Government with a complete file of special cards titled "Supplementary Card Concerning Origins (*Abstammung*) and Education." The main item on these cards was the question, "Was (or is) one of the grandparents a full Jew by race?"[211]

Concerning The Netherlands, Dr. Louis de Jong, the Director of the *Rijksinstituut voor Oorlogsdocumentatie* (State Institute for War Documentation), had this to say on the possible consequences of destruction of records:

. . . The Jewish population was doubly registered in this country. First, there were the ordinary registration cards which were kept in each population register. Secondly, early in 1941 a special registration of Jews was effected and the cards of this together with the cards containing the data on everyone's "persoonbewijs" (identity card) were kept at the central population register at The Hague. It would have been impossible to destroy the registers of people of Jewish descent without at the same time destroying all population registers. In 1940, it would have been wise on the part of the officials of the Jewish communities if they had destroyed all their books of membership which did not form part of the official registers. Very few people urged that this should be done. It is so easy to be wise after the event. Many Jews who had no particular Jewish consciousness complied with the duty to be registered separately because in acting otherwise they would have felt ashamed of themselves. Isn't it a general characteristic of the period of Nazi persecution that in many cases even people's best and noblest impulses served the persecutor's end? In this country the population registers formed one of the most important foundations of the entire society. In fact, a normal, highly integrated society is unthinkable without these registers. The ration system is based on them. The complete destruction of the population registers would have led to a crumbling away of normal society.[212]

To the best of our knowledge, there was one place only—Athens—where the Jewish records were deliberately destroyed by the leadership of the Jewish community. This happened on September 24, 1943, a few days after the Italian capitulation and at the beginning of the German occupation. The Nazis, however, did not follow their usual procedure in getting hold of the Jewish population in Athens. Athenian Jews were simply seized by the Nazis in the synagogues at the Friday services and deported along with their families. Nine hundred Athenian Jews perished in this way.[213]

The Jewish population in Nazi Europe was practically exempt from the authority of the local administrations and physically separated from the outside world. Under the conditions of the directed war economy of the Nazi regime, the elementary day-to-day needs of millions of men, women, and children would have remained unattended to if the Jewish people had been left without any communal organization. Miss Arendt writes that "the whole truth was that if the Jewish people had really been unorganized and leaderless, there would have been chaos and plenty of misery but the total number of victims would hardly have been between four and a half and six million people" (p. 111). However, in the Soviet Union, the one place where there was no organized Jewish community—and where none had existed for more than two decades—hundreds of thousands of Jews were destroyed under the *Kommissarbefehl* in the first months of the Nazi-Soviet war, when the *Einsatzgruppen* carried out their mass murders immediately after the occupation of the Soviet territories.[214]

Jewish Resistance and the Will To Live

Miss Arendt characterizes Attorney General Hausner's question "Why did you not rebel?," asked of eyewitnesses, as a "cruel and silly question" (p. 9); one that "served as a smoke screen for the question that was not asked" (p. 110). None of the witnesses, however, felt that this question, or others, such as "Why did you not protest?" "Why did you board the train?" were "cruel and silly." On the contrary, they were anxious to give the real picture of what it meant to live under the Nazis. Perhaps no other aspect of the Jewish tragedy was so greatly in need of elaboration.

A number of features distinguished Jewish resistance movements, actual or potential, from non-Jewish resistance movements. Foremost among these was the possibility of maintaining contact with the outside world. Local resistance movements in the occupied territories of most of Europe maintained contact with their governments-in-exile, who with the help of Great Britain (and later the United States) could supply the *résistants* with information and arms.[215] In the East the most effective partisan movements were in direct contact with Moscow.[216] The effectiveness of the non-Jewish resistance was to a large extent due to this help given by London and Moscow.

But the situation of the purely Jewish resistance movements (and of individual partisans) in the East was different from that of the non-Jewish movements.[217] In the first place, they had no national government anywhere on which to rely. Palestine Jewry was subject to British rule. Nevertheless, the Palestine Jewish community established some important contacts with European Jews under Nazi control. But it could reach the *résistants* only through volunteer parachutists, who had no government behind them.[218]

A second difference was the ability to be supplied from the rear. In the East in particular, the non-Jewish partisans were usually aided and supplied by the local populations of the towns and villages nearest their bases in the woods. With such support, these groups could concentrate on the fight against the main enemy— Nazi Germany and its allies. Not so the Jewish partisan groups.[219] They were faced not only with the Nazi enemy but also with a number of hostile nationalist partisan groups (for example, in the Ukraine, Poland, Byelorussia, and Lithuania) who had also contributed to the murder of Jews. Even the Soviet-controlled partisan movement was infected by anti-Semitism. In addition, the civilian population in the Nazi-occupied territories of the U.S.S.R. was—to a degree that varied from one region to another—anti-Jewish.[220] It is true that wherever individual Jewish *résistants* (and they were a high percentage of the Jewish population)[221] were willingly accepted into the general resistance movements (for example, the *Maquis* in France), they enjoyed the same privileges as the others.

But such acceptance was infrequent in the East: Only Jews who could come with arms were admitted to non-Jewish groups. This attitude of the non-Jewish partisans was aggravated by the unwillingness of the Jewish partisans to leave their families behind at the mercy of the Nazis.[222]

Miss Arendt sees a contradiction between (1) reports of contacts between Jewish resistance fighters and partisans and (2) the feeling of the Jews that (as quoted by her) "the whole population" was "against us" (p. 108). She reproaches the defense for not having used testimony of "close contacts between Jewish partisans and the Polish and Russian underground" as "justification" for the "wholesale slaughter of civilians" (p. 108). This argument is precisely the one used by the killers in the *Einsatzgruppen* reports to "justify" the "wholesale" slaughter of Jews. (See earlier in this chapter, under Origins of the Jewish Councils.) It hardly needs to be pointed out that the Nazi attempt to combat the partisans had nothing in common with the extermination of the entire Jewish community.

A third difference between Jewish and non-Jewish resistance movements was one of overall purpose. The non-Jewish resistance was "a patriotic fight for the liberation of the entire country."[223] Jewish resistance, however, was aimed either at physical survival (for those who took up arms in the woods), or at avenging Jewish blood and rescuing Jewish honor (for those in the ghettos, who could not hope to survive).

The yearning for revenge, coupled with a poignant hope of survival, found eloquent expression in the August 1943 appeal of the Jewish resistance groups in the Vilna Ghetto:

Vilna Jews! The hour of the final liquidation has arrived. Soon the German and Lithuanian murderers will invade the ghetto to murder us; soon, they will deport us in groups through the gates. In this way hundreds of Jews were deported on the Day of Atonement, on "the night of the white, yellow and pink certificates"; in this way too were deported our brothers and sisters, our mothers and fathers, and our children. We shall not submit and go like sheep to the slaughter. Jews, defend yourselves with arms! Don't believe in the mendacious assurances of the murderers! Don't believe the words of the traitors! He who passes through the gates of the ghetto has only one direction—Ponary, and Ponary means death. Jews, anyway we can lose nothing, we are doomed. Who among us here still believes that he will survive, seeing how the murderer is exterminating us systematically? The hands of the hangman will reach out and catch hold of every man and woman. Escape and fear will not rescue our lives; only armed defense is likely to rescue our honor and lives. Brethren, it is better to fall inside the ghetto than to be deported like sheep to Ponary. You know that there exists in the ghetto an armed and organized Jewish power that will revolt! Join the revolt! Don't hide in hideouts and bunkers; you will finally fall like mice into the hands of the murderers. Jewish masses, take to the streets! If you have no arms, take an ax; if you have no ax, take an iron bar or a cane! For your parents! For your murdered children! Revenge for Ponary! Beat the murderers, on every street, in every yard and every room, inside the ghetto and outside, beat the dogs! Jews, we have nothing to lose! We will rescue our lives only if we destroy the murderers! Long live Freedom! Long live armed defense! Death to the murderers![224]

A different tone, without any illusion of survival through resistance, is found in a letter written by Mordecai Anielewicz, the commander of the Jewish Fighting Organization, to Izhak Zuckerman on April 30, 1943, during the Warsaw Ghetto uprising:

I have only one expression fit for my feelings and my friends' feelings: something happened which, perhaps, surpassed our most daring dreams. The Germans fled twice from the ghetto . . . So far we have had only one casualty. Yechiel. He met a soldier's death—he was killed by machine-gun fire. . . .

I cannot describe to you the constrictions under which Jews are living. Only selected ones will be able to hold out. Fate has decided that all the rest will perish. Sooner or later. The die has been cast.

The main thing is, the dream of my life came true. I was fortunate enough to witness Jewish self-defense in the ghetto in all its greatness and glory.[225]

An important distinction that should be drawn in any discussion of armed Jewish resistance is that between resistance in the ghettos and resistance outside the ghettos, mainly in the "woods" (partisans). The difference between these two types of resistance arises from the different expectations of the individual *résistant*. Those in the ghettos were generally aware of the hopelessness of their undertaking (in a military sense), while the *résistants* outside the ghettos, escaping direct Nazi control (though still exposed to Nazi "anti-bandit-troops" [*Banditenbekämpfung*] and local enemies), had a fair chance to survive, together with their families. It has been estimated that as many as 70 per cent of the Jewish partisans survived, while the number of surviving ghetto fighters is very small.[226]

Miss Arendt quotes the *plaidoyer* of Henry Torrès[227] in the Schwartzbard case, approving of what she takes to be his point that the Jews "had never defended themselves" (p. 244). Torrès is hardly an authority on Jewish history, nor did he intend to appear as such. A careful reading of pages 24-25 and page 26 of his *plaidoyer* reveals that his was a polemical point dealing with the special case at issue: It was intended to refute Petlyura's statement that his violent actions against the Jews were an act of defense against a *"gendarmerie juive."* Miss Arendt appears to know nothing about the glorious chapter of the Jewish *samooborona* (self-defense) in prerevolutionary Russia and during the civil war, following the October 1917 revolution. Under the shock of the Kishinev pogrom (1903), a widespread movement for self-defense arose; it gave a remarkable account of itself during the two series of pogroms 1905-1906 and the civil war period. There is a substantial literature on this subject,[228] including Rachlis' book *The Jewish Self-Defense in Ukraine under Petlyura*,[229] which deals specifically with the history of the Jewish defense against the Petlyura bands.

Miss Arendt notes that the *résistants* were "a minority, a tiny minority" (p. 108). It is difficult to follow her point that the defense should have forced the prosecution to admit "how pitifully small these resistance groups had been, how incredibly weak and essentially harmless" (p. 108). How could the defense derive advantage from the alleged "weakness" of the resistance, which was one of the direct consequences of Nazi terror? Anyway, the facts of the Jewish resistance do not bear out her statement. The first armed revolt involving open warfare (other than Yugoslav partisan activity) against the Nazi machine of terror in Europe was by Jews. This was the Warsaw Ghetto uprising of April 1943, which even Miss Arendt extols as the "glory of the uprising in the Warsaw ghetto" (pp. 9-10).

The savage reaction of the Nazis to Jewish rebellions proves that these rebellions were far from ineffectual. The Warsaw Ghetto uprising is a case in point. Himmler's order to destroy the Warsaw Ghetto completely, with "exceptional ruthlessness" (*grössere Härte*) and "relentless toughness" (*unnachsichtliche Zähigkeit*), was given on April 22, 1943—that is, on the fourth day of the revolt. "The more severely we act the better it is. Events show how dangerous the Jews are," he concluded.[230] Acting under this order, General Stroop attacked the ghetto with artillery, tanks, and flame throwers, using *Nebelkerzen* (smoke-candles) to cut off retreat through the sewers. The regular fighting lasted four weeks but lingered on among the rubble for another three months.[231] The Warsaw Ghetto uprising had considerable impact on the Nazis, although its exact nature and extent are not yet known. At least on two occasions Eichmann claimed that the uprising accelerated the pace of the deportations. He stated in the Sassen Papers that he was surprised that "ghetto-ized Jews could fight in such a way" and that Himmler "was doubt-less influenced by this event when he sent me to Hungary to deal ruthlessly with its Jews." He added that elsewhere too (i.e., in western and southeastern Europe) "the advisors on Jewish matters were urged to speed up all measures necessary to obtain jurisdiction over the remaining Jews still living there." Under the impact of the uprising, German agencies concerned with the industrial war effort stopped their interventions on behalf of the preservation of Jewish man-power for the war industry. According to Eichmann, the assignment of railroad transportation for deportations was given high priority for fear that "a second Warsaw" might occur. In his own words, "I don't have to say what a sacrifice it was for Germany to make available the rolling stock for this purpose, for there was not a single railroad car that was allowed to be empty."[232]

When questioned on this subject by Judge Halevi, Eichmann testified in court that the uprising affected "at least" the deportations from Holland and from Hungary; in the former case because of the expectation of an invasion, in the latter because of the reversals on the Eastern front. In both cases, the Germans feared that anticipated contact with Allied forces might set off Jewish uprisings.[233]

Perhaps Eichmann exaggerated when he made these statements, and perhaps Himmler and the Security Police used the uprising as a pretext to convince those in dire need of workers for the German war machine that the deportations ought to have priority over military considerations. There seems to be no question that the organized, concerted Jewish resistance in Warsaw caused a great deal of worry to the Germans. Whether or not we believe Eichmann—and there seems to be no reason why he should have lied to Sassen—the influence which the Warsaw Ghetto uprising had on Nazi anti-Jewish policies appears to have been far greater than has heretofore been realized.

The final report of Fritz Katzmann, the SS and Police Leader in Galicia, written on June 30, 1943, after describing the crushing of Jewish armed resistance, adds:

Since ever more alarming news about the increasing arming of the Jews reached us, the strictest measures for the destruction of Jewish bandits were taken simultaneously in all parts of the District of Galicia during the last two weeks of the month of June 1943. Special measures were necessary for the liquidation of the Jewish ghetto in Lemberg [Lwów], where the already described dugouts had been built. Here, in order to avoid casualties of our own, we had to proceed with brutality from the start, blowing up several houses or destroying them by fire.[234]

These actions and testimonies do not lead to the conclusion that the Jewish resistance was "incredibly weak and essentially harmless."

In her discussion, Miss Arendt suggests to the defense that it should have considered "how little they [*the résistants*] had represented the Jewish population, who at one point even took arms against them" (p. 108). This statement, referring (III, 44) to Vilna in 1943, contradicts (and may be a misreading of) the testimony of Abba Kovner at the Eichmann Trial.[235] He told the court that the SS demanded the delivery of a leader of the resistance, Izhak Witenberg (who went by the code name of Leon), to the Germans under the threat of destruction of the Vilna Ghetto. The people of the ghetto *intended* to attack the resistance group if they failed to deliver Witenberg. Faced with the Nazi threat of destruction of the ghetto and the possibility of internal strife within the Jewish community, the resistance committee decided that Witenberg should deliver himself to the Nazis, and Witenberg accepted this decision. Obvious in this tragic incident is the feeling of communal responsibility displayed by the resistance movement and its awareness of its representative character. This was a manifestation of the principle that "All Jews are responsible for one another,"[236] and not proof of the low standing of the *résistants* in the Jewish communities. The fact is that along with the deterioration of the situation in the ghettos, and the gradual decline of the authority of the *Judenräte*, the resistance movements, encompassing a new breed of leadership that matured under Nazi terror, came to the fore. In the Warsaw Ghetto, for example, the real Jewish authority in 1943 was the organized Jewish Resistance Movement.

Early in 1943, Marek Lichtenbaum, the chairman of the Jewish Council, advised the Germans that the Council had no power and that a different authority was governing the ghetto.[237]

Miss Arendt's statement that the Jewish Councils "played such a great and disastrous role in their [the *résistants*] own heroic efforts" (p. 107) is unsupported by the facts, as is her observation that "Jews inevitably found themselves confronted with two enemies—the Nazi authorities and the Jewish authorities" (p. 56). Actually, cooperation between Jewish Councils and resistance groups was not infrequent.[238]

A striking example of the identification of the official Jewish leadership with the Jewish underground can be found—of all places—in Auschwitz in the special camp for the Theresienstadt Jews. All the Jewish chiefs of blocks (*Blockälteste*), under the leadership of Fredy Hirsch, the chief of the camp and the director of its educational institution, participated in the preparations for a revolt, having learned of the threat of extermination of the camp population. This same Fredy Hirsch represented the Theresienstadt camp vis-à-vis the SS commanders, whose help he solicited in organizing Jewish life and in the construction of the camp. The abortive revolt was savagely suppressed. The first to fall were the chiefs of blocks. Fredy Hirsch committed suicide. And the survivors were led to the ovens, singing Hatikva and the Czech national anthem.[239]

The identification of resistance with armed resistance is an oversimplification. This is true of all groups and nationalities that were subject to Nazi rule. For example, Polish resistance during the first five years of occupation did not consist mainly of armed revolt; it comprised such activities as smuggling men of military age to the West, where they could join the Polish or Allied armies.[240] Jewish resistance consisted primarily of a virtually universal attempt to preserve human life and human dignity in the face of Nazi terror. This form of resistance had deep roots in Jewish tradition. It found expression in areas extending from economics to health care; in intellectual, educational, and religious activities; and in the underground press.

One of many nonmilitary forms of resistance was the preservation of records for posterity. The anti-Jewish policy of the Nazis was directed not only toward the physical destruction of European and, after victory, world Jewry. The Nazis also made a great effort to silence their victims for good by obliterating all traces that might tell the true story of the Jewish Catastrophe. A victorious "Greater Germany" could then present the world with a falsified history of events. In fact, Heinrich Himmler, in his famous Poznań speech of October 4, 1943, before leading SS men, in which he extolled the SS for its part in the extermination of the Jews, stated confidently: "This is a glorious chapter of our history which was never written and should never be written."[241] To a large extent he proved to be right: We are missing six million witnesses. But the survivors, and many of the victims, were eager to put their experiences on paper, aware of the Nazi attempt to efface all traces of their crimes. The last call sent out by the martyred sage of Jewish historiography, Simon Dubnov, was *Farschreibt!* (Write it down for the record!).[242] Somehow his plea made itself heard throughout all the areas of Nazi persecution, and many of the victims left diaries and hid documents.[243] In some places Jewish scholars organized teams which systematically collected data on aspects of Jewish life under Nazi domination. Some of these materials have been preserved. The clandestine Warsaw Ghetto Archives, containing documents collected by Dr. Emmanuel Ringelblum, are the most important of such collections. These records were hidden from the Nazis and were found in caches in 1946 and 1950.[244] Their value for historical research is inestimable. Among other important underground archives are those of the Białystok Ghetto, which are now preserved in Israel.[245] The records of Yehoshua Moshe Aaronson, the rabbi at the Konin Labor Camp (Poland) are now in the Ghetto Fighters House.[246] The *Centre de Documentation Juive Contemporaine,* now in Paris, was established by Isaac Schneersohn under the very nose of the German occupation authorities in Grenoble in 1943.[247]

The reactions of the religious sector of the Jewish population (which in certain areas constituted the majority) deserve special mention, especially since this aspect of Jewish behavior during the war has not been given sufficient attention.[248] Jews often continued to pray and study in makeshift houses of prayer, despite strict rules against collective worship.[249] Typical was the occasion in Cracow when, following an edict forbidding beards and sidelocks, the members of the religious community circumvented the order by tying scarves around their faces so that only their eyes and noses could be seen, on the pretext that they (all of them!) were suffering from toothaches.[250] Nor was there a stop in the constant need for new interpretation of rabbinical law, to which eloquent testimony can be found in the contemporary *Responsa* literature.[251]

Generally speaking, rabbis remained with their communities up to the very end.[252] One of the numerous examples of the deep attachment of these leaders to their followers is described in the following story, told by the journalist Marian Żyd, on the basis of an interview with Rabbi David Szapiro, one of the rabbis involved:

. . . From the highest ranks of the Roman Catholic hierarchy suddenly came the proposal to save the last three rabbis who still remained in the Warsaw Ghetto: Rabbi Menahem Zemba, Rabbi Samson Stockhamer, and Rabbi David Szapiro. The high Roman Catholic clergymen suddenly decided to hide the three rabbis in a safe place. The proposal was submitted to the three rabbis, and they now had to decide what to do, whether to accept or to reject. They had to make the decision quickly, and no time was to be lost, since the Nazis constantly kept asking the members of the Community Council whether there were still some rabbis in the ghetto.

So the last three Warsaw rabbis were sitting in a room and discussing the Roman Catholic offer. "Discussing" . . . in reality they were sitting silent, and did not utter a word. Time was running out dangerously fast. From the outside you could actually hear the steps of death . . .

Suddenly the silence was interrupted, and it was Rabbi Szapiro who broke it, uttering the following words:

"I am the youngest among you, and therefore my words are not binding on you. We already know that we cannot help them any longer, but by staying with them and by not abandoning them, we encourage them and strengthen their hopes, and this is the only encouragement we are able to give the last Jews. I simply do not have the strength to abandon these wretched people."

Thus spoke Rabbi Szapiro in a murmuring voice. And thus ended the dramatically silent conference. They felt as though a heavy burden were taken off their shoulders, off their hearts. At last they had found the right solution. God, who is above, is also down here.

And again silence hovered over the three rabbis. Only sobbing burst from their hearts, the sobbing of turmoil, and the sobbing of happiness, that they could withstand the temptation . . .

The end is well known. Rabbi Zemba and Rabbi Stockhamer went the way of annihilation. Only Rabbi David Szapiro was not burned. He could be saved. And he wears now the ghostly and tragic crown of the "last Warsaw rabbi," the last rabbi of a city of rabbis.[253]

Spiritual resistance to Nazi oppression permeated every community. The widespread reaction of the Jewish masses to the Nazi terror has been ably interpreted by a student of the Catastrophe, Dr. Shaul Esh, in the following words:

What was the general reaction of the Jewish masses, especially in Eastern Europe, to the Nazi horror? It was fundamentally what might be called *kiddush ha-hayyim*, the sanctification of life, the overwhelming impulse to preserve life in the midst of death. This expression is taken from one who heard it as the epigram of the late Rabbi Isaac Nissenbaum, one of the known leaders of Polish Jewry, in the years 1940-1941, in the Warsaw Ghetto: "This is a time for *kiddush ha-hayyim*, the sanctification of life, and not for *kiddush ha-shem*, the holiness of martyrdom. Previously the Jew's enemy sought his soul and the Jew sacrificed his body in martyrdom [i.e., he made a point of preserving what the enemy wished to take from him]; now the oppressor demands the Jew's body and the Jew is obliged therefore to defend it, to preserve his life." That *kiddush ha-hayyim* was to all accounts and purposes the general feeling is borne out by all the evidence. It explains the enormous will to live that was emphasized at all times and in all places, in the midst of the basest degradation, a will best expressed by the Yiddish word that was on the lips of the majority of the survivors of the Holocaust—*iberleybn*, to survive, to remain alive. The Jews of Eastern Europe felt in fact that victory over the enemy lay in their continued existence, for the enemy desired their extinction. (. . . "However wretched existence may be, it is a *mitzvah* to exist.") There is so much evidence in the documented literature for this desire to stand up under increasingly harsh persecution that there is no need to adduce further examples here. A description of *kiddush ha-hayyim* would not however be entirely faithful if we see it only as the arousing of "a mighty will to live . . . of which there is no equivalent in normal life," without adding that this strong will was often directed toward *Jewish* life, each man according to his understanding of the term. One can recognize at every level this desire of the Jewish communities to preserve a life of Jewish quality in the face of persecution and in the midst of oppression.[254]

Concluding Remarks

Miss Arendt's argument that the Jewish Councils cooperated with the Germans, were indispensable in the process of deportation, and had a decisive influence on the ultimate outcome of the Final Solution, is negated in the light of available information. No member of the Jewish Councils offered his services to the Nazis; but when a Jew accepted appointment to a Council, he did so as a rule out of a feeling of responsibility to those in his community. There were wide areas of Jewish slaughter (e.g., in the U.S.S.R., France, Italy, Bulgaria, Yugoslavia, Romania, and Greece) where the Jewish Councils had no part in compiling lists of potential deportees, or where no Jewish Councils existed. Even where Councils were involved with compilation of lists, the ultimate results were not demonstrably influenced by their activities. Finally, the "wielding of the fatal instruments" by Jewish "special commandos," alleged by Miss Arendt to have been widespread, has no basis in fact.

The real subject of the present chapter is Jewish survival under conditions of total Nazi terror. What were the best methods of coping with the condemnation to death of a whole people? What could the condemned and their "leaders" (genuine, self-styled, or appointed by the Germans) do? As a historical people par excellence, the Jews looked to history for guidance. Three comments are offered here on the theology and philosophy of survival in the thousands of years of Jewish history:

1. When the first encounter between Jacob and Esau was imminent, Jacob prepared himself with three means to achieve his survival, according to the interpretation of the commentators.[255] They were, in this sequence, *doron* (gift), *tefilah* (prayer), and *milhama* (war). This formula has been applied in the same order with amazing consistency through the thousands of years of Jewish plight.

2. It is not *Am Yisrael Chai* ("the Jewish people lives on")— of recent secular origin—that was the main source of solace of our people, as Miss Arendt says on page 137, but the belief that a remnant would return, *Shear Yashuv*.[256] There have always been in our history remnants who continued the "golden chain" of Jewish life and thought. The philosophy that guided our people, "He who preserves a single Jewish life is as one who preserves the whole world"[257] proved as valid in tranquil times of Jewish history as in the times of turbulence.

3. Jewish lore stresses the time factor in human affairs. The concept of "the present hour of life" (*Hayei shaa*) as being different from "eternal life" (*Hayei olam*) had important implications for Jewish behavior, individual and communal. This attitude is expressed with simplicity in the story about a Jewish tenant of a Polish landowner. In order to have his lease renewed he had to agree to teach the landowner's dog to speak within one month. When his wife vehemently protested he replied: "During this

month, who knows? The landowner may die . . . the dog may die . . . "

The overriding purpose of Jewish activity everywhere in Nazi Europe was survival with dignity. From his unique vantage point as the only non-Jew who witnessed life in a ghetto at close range, from its inception up to its liquidation, Tadeusz Pankiewicz put his thoughts in these words:

People who did not live in the ghetto could not understand this [the realities of life in the ghetto] just as they did not grasp other things. Many a time I was asked by my Polish friends whether the Jews really were so blinded as not to realize what was in store for them. Why during the deportation that ended in death did the Jews still carry their belongings? Why did they endure so much suffering on their last journey, and why was there no revolt, and why did they allow themselves to be led like sheep to the slaughter? Such questions could come only from people who did not witness these happenings; they were only told what had happened, or watched from secure places, or had listened to stories emanating from the ghetto that were usually distorted at that. He who did not himself watch the happenings in the ghetto or who was not witness to the uncanny theater of horror there cannot understand or perceive the conditions under which these people lived, nor will he grasp the perfidy and the lies used [by the Germans] to deceive the Jews on the eve of their death. If only those who spoke with me could have spent two hours in the atmosphere of the "actions" when at every few steps someone was shot to death or people were humiliated, beaten, and degraded. If such persons would know the behind-the-scenes goings-on of the crimes; if they had watched the executors and how they whipped up terror and fear by indiscriminate shooting without mercy or how, at other times, they gave false hopes to the deportees that they would survive, and how, at still other times, they used to threaten with collective responsibility and vengeance the closest members of the family of someone who escaped, performed acts of sabotage, or showed the slightest resistance—they would not ask "why?" any more. And we should bear in mind that the situation in the Cracow ghetto, contrary to the situation in the Warsaw ghetto, for instance, was such that it was absolutely impossible to take any defensive action. Reduced to only a few streets, the Cracow ghetto was surrounded by German guards who closely watched what was going on in the ghetto, so that to prepare any military action was out of question. As if this were not enough, the Germans organized each deportation in such a way as to safeguard their own security; they brought in strong military detachments, armed from head to toe, that were authorized to fire at will and at random.

Last but not least, each inhabitant of the ghetto still entertained a spark of hope to survive. "To survive" was a word of great meaning in those times. What more potent word is there for a slave than the words freedom and survival in times of mass murder? This hidden thought wrought miracles, gave superhuman strength and endurance to people. Because of such thoughts people gritted their teeth and swallowed degradation. Not the fear of death but the will to live was predominant. This was my impression then and this is my opinion now about people and events I encountered during my years in the ghetto.

I have tried to understand and grasp the mentality of individuals and groups I used to meet at that time and have come to the conclusion that, had it been different from what I have said, those who were shot would have either asked for mercy or simply cried or made attempts to escape. Without doubt, this would have shown their fear and cowardice. However, this was not evident in the Cracow ghetto. Except for only a few cases which I happened to notice, I did not hear people begging for mercy. I did not see people crying. People calmly looked death in the eye, resigned but also proud. The Germans did not succeed in seeing these people show sorrow or ask for mercy; and this aroused their brutality still more.[258]

Unutterably tragic was the position of the Jewish leaders. The cunning of the Nazis, their skill in the arts of psychological warfare, had thrown off balance even experienced politicians. Once Jewish leaders began to suspect the awful truth, they found themselves in a desperate race against time. Through bribery and procrastination, they invoked the traditional ways which had enabled their fathers and forefathers to survive the hostility of surrounding populations. They were convinced that the scales of war would soon turn, and in their heart of hearts they still believed that should the outside world only become aware of the atrocities it would somehow stop them. Hence the frantic efforts to send out the news, to let the world know that murder of a people was being committed.

An evaluation of the Jewish and non-Jewish reaction to the Nazi mass murders and persecution is a difficult task, involving as it does the basic question of man's responsibility for the life of his fellow man. It can only be carried out within the framework of a careful scholarly study of the Catastrophe and of the war as a whole, coupled with an investigation of the particular circumstances surrounding each individual case or community.

5

The Fate of Jews in Specific
Areas and Periods

The subject of Nazi extermination of Jews in specific countries of Europe is introduced by Miss Arendt in these words: "The end of the world, though carried out with remarkable monotony, took almost as many different shapes and appearances as there existed countries in Europe" (p. 138).

The German persecution and extermination policy was carried out not according to countries, but according to the political organization emerging from the double process of military occupation and vassalization of Axis Europe.[1] For example, as far as anti-Jewish measures were concerned, Romania was not a single entity but five different areas: the Regat (Kingdom of Moldavia-Valachia), Transylvania, Bessarabia, Bucovina (North and South), and Transnistria (insofar as it became a destination for Jews deported from certain areas of Romania). Furthermore, in certain areas of military occupation much depended on which country—Germany or Italy—was the occupying power.

A recurring aspect of Miss Arendt's treatment of regions is a comparison between indigenous and German anti-Semitism. In this connection, it is necessary to recall certain events that preceded Hitler. In the countries of Central and Eastern Europe, the rights of minorities were legally guaranteed under a series of minorities treaties[2] drawn up and signed after the First World War.[3] Germany and Italy, as major powers, were not required to sign such a treaty. In the countries bound by treaty, the affected minorities benefited from the legal and moral protection afforded by the treaties, though not in the full measure guaranteed.[4] From 1933 on, however, the world was treated to the spectacle of Germany's openly flouting accepted norms of behavior toward minorities in her anti-Jewish legislation. When Germany was seen to be getting away with her policies, the treaty-bound countries, egged on by hate-mongers, were quick to follow the same pattern. Aided and encouraged by Germany, they began to adopt anti-Jewish legislation of their own, unafraid of possible sanctions. As a result, the distinction between indigenous and German-imported anti-Semitism came to lose some of its validity.

The discussion in the present chapter follows, for the most part, the order of areas in Miss Arendt's book. Her treatment of the geographical domain of Eichmann's jurisdiction—that is, Eichmann's involvement in the fate of Jews in different countries—excludes from consideration the fate of the Jews in Poland, the Baltic States, and the U.S.S.R.

AUSTRIA

The demography of the Jewish population in Austria—and Eichmann's role in the process of forced emigration of Jews from Austria—is presented by Miss Arendt without factual basis.

She says on page 39 that "in less than eighteen months [from the Anschluss to the outbreak of war], Austria was 'cleansed' of close to a hundred and fifty thousand people, roughly fifty per cent of its Jewish population . . . " and "even after the outbreak of the war, some sixty thousand Jews could escape." These figures presume that at the time of the Anschluss (March 1938) Austria had a Jewish population of 300,000, and that a total of 210,000 of this number emigrated.

The facts are otherwise. The total number of persons in Austria considered by the Nazis to be Jews (Geltungsjuden) in March 1938 was 220,000.[5] By December 31, 1942 (after a final halt to all emigration had been decreed), 149,124 of these had emigrated.[6]

Miss Arendt characterizes Eichmann's account of his activities in Vienna as "grotesque" (p. 51), an epithet which is quite fitting. She paraphrases Eichmann to the effect that he "had saved hundreds of thousands of Jews" (p. 52), but calls his claim "preposterous" (p. 56) and a "foolish and stubborn contention" (p. 172). However, she also "finds strange support" for it in "the considered judgment of the Jewish historians, the Kimches: 'Thus, what must have been one of the most paradoxical episodes of the entire period of the Nazi regime began: the man who was to go down in history as one of the arch-murderers of the Jewish people entered the lists as an active worker in the rescue of Jews from Europe.'"

Eichmann's assignment to Vienna in 1938 represented a significant stage not only in his career as Himmler's and Heydrich's specialist for the solution of the "Jewish question" but also in the overall history of the Nazi war against the Jews. It was the beginning of forced emigration, carefully organized on a large scale. Eichmann admitted to being the chief planner and organizer of forced emigration,[7] and he devised the methods used to make it a success for the Nazis—namely, threat and blackmail. In the months following the *Anschluss,* thousands of Austrian Jews were thrown into concentration camps to speed up their emigration. Many others crossed the border without passports. Individual Jewish leaders were arrested as a means of intimidation, and the Jewish Community Organization of Vienna was put under severe pressure to make it cooperate in the Nazi emigration plan.[8]

How Eichmann felt about his task is shown in the following excerpt from a handwritten letter dated May 1, 1938, which he sent from Vienna to his friend and co-worker, Herbert Hagen, in Berlin:

I sure made those guys shake a leg (*habe ich die Herrschaften auf den Trab gebracht*), you can believe me. That's why they are already hard at work. I have asked the Jewish Community Organization (*Kultusgemeinde*) and the National Zionist Union (*Zionistischer Landesverband*) to supply 20,000 destitute Jews for the period from May 1, 1938, to May 1, 1939, and they promised to take care of it. . . .

Tomorrow I'll check up again on those outfits (*Laden*)—the Jewish Community and the Zionists. I do that at least once a week. I have them completely in my power (*Ich habe sie hier vollständig in der Hand*); they don't dare to make a single step without asking me first. That's the way it ought to be; they can be better controlled this way.[9]

THE "PROTECTORATE" AND THERESIENSTADT

The history of Theresienstadt is richly documented in the literature and in the trial records.[10] Miss Arendt lists three volumes on Theresienstadt in her Bibliography, two by H. G. Adler and one by Lederer,[11] but her account does not correspond with known facts about the purpose of the establishment of Theresienstadt, its chronology and statistics, Eichmann's relationship with the Jewish "leaders," and the legal aspects of the deportation of German Jews to Theresienstadt.

In her serial version, Theresienstadt was described as "the concentration camp for privileged German Jews" (II, 42; omitted in her book). In the book she writes: "We know from better sources than Eichmann's faulty memory that Theresienstadt, from the beginning, was designed by Heydrich to serve as a special ghetto for certain privileged categories of Jews" (p. 75).[12] Later (p. 140) she advances the hypothesis that "It was probably at this moment [in the fall of 1940] that Heydrich realized how important it would be to separate Jews with connections from the anonymous masses, and decided, with Hitler's agreement, to establish Theresienstadt and Bergen-Belsen." (The decision to establish the "residential camp" Bergen-Belsen was made by Himmler in the spring of 1943, one year after Heydrich had been assassinated.[13])

The earliest known document referring to Theresienstadt is the record of a meeting held on October 10, 1941, in which both Heydrich and Eichmann participated. According to this record, which constituted part of the Eichmann trial documentation and can also be found in Adler's volume,[14] Theresienstadt was to serve as a transit camp (vorübergehendes Sammellager) for the Jews of Bohemia and Moravia. Not a word about "Jews with connections" or German Jews. Fully fifteen months after the deportation of German Jews from Baden and Saarpfalz to France, Theresienstadt is mentioned for the first time (in the Wannsee Conference) as a destination for German Jews.[15] The idea that Theresienstadt might serve as an Altersghetto ("ghetto for the aged") belonged to Himmler, according to Eichmann.[16]

Miss Arendt writes that "Theresienstadt . . . came to serve . . . [as] a showplace for the outside world—it was the only ghetto or camp to which representatives of the International Red Cross were admitted" (p. 77). Actually, an IRC representative was admitted to Auschwitz too, in September 1944.[17] Miss Arendt gives the impression that in Theresienstadt the IRC enjoyed full freedom of inspection during its visits. This is misleading. As far as the visit in June 1944 is concerned—and there are published official reports on two visits only[18]—the judgment of the District Court quotes the following testimony of the witness Ansbacher:

There were some areas in which a complete curfew was imposed . . . and only people whose faces looked more or less human were allowed to show themselves. . . . They painted the houses on the outside. They prepared large signs which read: "Central School" . . . "Ghetto Theatre" . . . They made lovely toys . . . They brought the children there in little beds with a heart carved on them. Just as in some palace.[19]

Miss Arendt writes: "Theresienstadt was officially classified as a concentration camp, and the only people who did not know this . . . were the inmates" (p. 142). The second part of this statement requires no comment. The first part is false. Indeed, in the course of a correspondence between the German Red Cross and the Association of Exporters of Fish Preserves, the German Red Cross insisted that Theresienstadt was not a concentration camp.[20] Though no particular relevance can be assigned to Nazi nomenclature—names were often intentionally misleading, as in the case of the *Aufenthaltslager* ("residential camp") of Bergen-Belsen—Theresienstadt was not officially a concentration camp. There is no mention of it in official documents as being a concentration camp. It was a transit camp, and within the first few weeks of its establishment the inmates knew that it was a temporary stopping place in the course of deportation to the East (the Nazi decision on the physical annihilation of the Jews was still a secret).[21] To outsiders, Theresienstadt was presented as "a permanent Jewish settlement."[22]

While discussing Eichmann's initiative on Theresienstadt and referring to his words, "Give enough room into which to transfer the Jews of the Protectorate, who now live dispersed," Miss Arendt—in full knowledge that the fate of the Theresienstadt inmates was from the very start to be physical extermination—defines the camp as "A Jewish homeland, a gathering-in of the exiles in the Diaspora" (pp. 74-75).

Regarding the establishment of Theresienstadt, Eichmann's testimony,[23] misquoted by Miss Arendt with additions and deletions, to the effect that there was "immediate evacuation of the native Czech population" (p. 75), is not truthful. In fact, more than eight months elapsed before the evacuation was completed.[24]

Miss Arendt reports also that "Jewish technicians had built gas chambers in Theresienstadt" (p. 109). What happened was that Otto Hunsche, a lieutenant of Eichmann, asked Eichmann, in the last days of the ghetto, what to do with the last inmates in the event of the arrival of the Red Army. Eichmann instructed him that in such a contingency the Jews, all of them, should be exterminated,[25] and he ordered the construction of buildings similar to gas chambers. The inmates got restless and suspicious. Benjamin Murmelstein, the chairman of the Jewish Council, protested to Karl Rahm, the commandant of the ghetto. Thereupon Eichmann ordered that the buildings be used for different purposes.[26] The extermination program had anyway already been stopped by order of Himmler.

Miss Arendt presents these statistics: "For about fifty thousand Czech Jews, Theresienstadt indeed became a transfer camp on the way to Auschwitz, while an estimated twenty thousand more reached the same destination directly" (p. 75). Actually, of the 88,000 Jews in the "Protectorate," 73,608 were transported into Theresienstadt. Of these, 60,399 were deported to various extermination camps, including 30,000 to Auschwitz. Seven thousand were deported directly to the East.[27] There was no direct mass deportation of Jews from the "Protectorate" to Auschwitz.

According to Miss Arendt, the transports to Auschwitz began in 1943, "about a year after its [Theresienstadt's] establishment" (p. 75). This does not correspond with the facts. The deportations started immediately after the establishment of the Theresienstadt Ghetto and were continued, with brief interruptions, until October 1944. About 44,000 Jews, more than half of the total number deported from Theresienstadt, had already been deported by the end of 1942; in 1943, the number of deportees was 17,000. The final deportations (26,000 persons) took place in 1944.[28]

Regarding the Jewish "leadership" in the ghetto, Miss Arendt writes: "During the Eichmann trial, one witness pointed out the unfortunate consequences of this kind of 'humanity' [Dr. Baeck's policy][29]—people volunteered for deportation from Theresienstadt to Auschwitz and denounced those who tried to tell them the truth as being 'not sane'" (p. 105). This suggests that Baeck's policy was the decisive factor in the voluntary movement to Auschwitz. Actually, the reasons for volunteering for deportation were different. First, in Theresienstadt, the Jews did not know what would be in store for them when they reached Auschwitz; even after having spent some time in Auschwitz, they refused to believe the truth.[30] A second reason for "volunteering" was a desire to rejoin members of the family who had left on earlier transports. Letters coming from Auschwitz, from the so-called "family camp," contributed to their optimism.[31]

Miss Arendt assumes that the Jewish Council in Theresienstadt was the sole party authorized to prepare lists of deportees. The facts, as presented by H. G. Adler (on whom she allegedly relies), are different. There were at least two periods during which the lists were prepared by Eichmann's men.[32] More important, even though the lists were usually prepared by a special department of the Council, they were drawn up on the basis of express instructions of the commandant of Theresienstadt or of Eichmann's special emissaries. These instructions specified not only the number of deportees required but also such particulars as age, fitness for work, geographical origin (Czech or other), and the like. In addition, the Council had before it "internal" principles accepted by the various groups living in the ghetto—for example, the preservation of family unity and the retention of people having essential functions in the ghetto. Consequently the authority of the Council was limited, sometimes nonexistent, and when exercised was far from arbitrary. The lists were subject to appeal and internal supervision.[33]

No fair evaluation of this function of the Jewish Council is possible without giving its genesis. It all started in Prague, where the Jewish Community Administration was ordered to prepare lists for deportation to Theresienstadt. The members of the Administration were well aware of the destination of the deportees, and knew that it was not an extermination camp. This system was continued in Theresienstadt. The difference was that in Theresienstadt the Council knew only as much about the destination of the deportees as the Nazis chose to tell them, or as much as the soothing postal cards from deportees in the "family camp" in Auschwitz (written at Nazi orders) told.[34]

Miss Arendt implies that Eichmann was considerate in his relations with the Jewish leadership in Theresienstadt (p. 109). Actually, the leaders were under constant pressure of orders and threats, and the slightest disobedience or even suspicion of disobedience resulted in arrest and murder, as in the cases of Jakob Edelstein[35] and Paul Eppstein. Eppstein was shot on September 27, 1944—not in Theresienstadt (as Miss Arendt says on page 58) but in the nearby police prison called the "small fortress." The sources appear to confirm the view that he was shot because he plotted with the inmates of Theresienstadt for self-defense in the eventuality that the Nazis would decide to exterminate the inmates on the spot or to evacuate them en masse.[36]

The description by Miss Arendt (p. 142) of the legal basis for, and practical implementation of, the denationalization of German Jews destined for Theresienstadt, and of the confiscation of their property, is also inaccurate. Miss Arendt writes that the form the

candidates for deportation to Theresienstadt were forced to sign
was based on a "regulation, issued in March 1942"—that is, the
Executive Order of the Minister of the Interior concerning the
confiscated property of enemies of the Reich,[37] issued April 9, 1942
—but in fact it was based exclusively on a 1933 law as amended and
supplemented up to May 1941.[38] Insofar as the deportees were able
to grasp the meaning of the forms, they (contrary to Miss Arendt's
speculations on page 142) certainly realized that they were being
denationalized and that their property was being confiscated.[39] As
for the transfer of property to the Jewish *Reichsvereinigung*, this
was not done because of the lack of any legal basis for confiscation,
nor was it designed to lull suspicion on the part of the deportees
(p. 142). Its purpose was to convey control of the property to
the Gestapo through the subordinate *Reichsvereinigung*. Under the
1933 law such property fell to the Ministry of Finance, and
the Gestapo wanted to prevent this from happening.[40] It should be
noted that the majority, though not all, of the deportees had to
commit themselves in writing to the transfer of their property.[41]

FRANCE

In the section on France Miss Arendt tends to exculpate Eichmann at the expense of Pétain and Laval.[42] She writes (pp. 146-147)
that the Vichy government "had introduced, on its own initiative, a
great deal of anti-Jewish legislation; it had even established a special
Department for Jewish Affairs [*Commissariat Général aux Questions
Juives*] headed first by Xavier Vallant" (should be Xavier Vallat).
This is not so. Though Vichy exhibited initiative in the realm of anti-
Jewish legislation, the commissariat was established not at Vichy's
behest but under incessant pressure from Eichmann's representative,
Theodor Dannecker. Since Vichy was nominally independent, Eich-
mann's men remained in the background and acted through the
German Embassy and the military administration. But they threatened direct intervention if results were not satisfactory. When
Vichy was found to be procrastinating, Dannecker threatened the
German diplomats with a personal trip to Vichy in order to compel
the Frenchmen "to lay their cards on the table."[43] This threat
brought the immediate solution of the impasse, in the establishment of the commissariat. Later it was again Dannecker who made
repeated efforts to enlarge the commissariat's powers, something

that the French themselves did not request.[44] The German military administration in France was unable to stem Dannecker's demands.[45] The way Dannecker treated Vallat in February 1942 is a striking illustration of what an emissary of Eichmann could permit himself, protocol notwithstanding.[46]

There were two periods of anti-Jewish action in France: the period of internment and the period of deportation. The first is not mentioned at all by Miss Arendt. The driving force behind the internment was again Dannecker, who, via the military administration, obtained the agreement of Vichy for the establishment of concentration camps in the occupied zone.[47] As to deportations, Miss Arendt seems to minimize Eichmann's role by failing to mention his visit to Paris at the end of June 1942, his instructions to his subordinates, and his contacts with the Higher SS and Police Leader Knochen at that time.[48]

Typical of Eichmann's role in the deportation of French Jews was the so-called Bordeaux Incident. What happened was that, contrary to Eichmann's expectations, his representatives were unable to find enough victims to fill up a special train to Auschwitz. Eichmann, enraged by this failure, threatened "to consider whether France should not be dropped altogether as far as evacuation was concerned."[49] Eichmann's subordinate Röthke replied: "I request that this should not be done," adding that "it was not the fault of our office if this train had to be canceled . . . the subsequent trains will leave according to plan"—as indeed they did.[50]

Although this incident does not prove that Eichmann had the authority to discontinue the French deportation, it shows that Eichmann's subordinates thought he did have such authority. In the words of the court,[51] the incident is "evidence of Eichmann's determination and of his status in the eyes of his subordinates."[52]

Miss Arendt exculpates Eichmann from responsibility for shipping a group of four thousand Jewish children in France to Auschwitz. She accepts uncritically Servatius' claim that the "persons affected were determined neither by the accused nor by any members of his office" and concludes that the fate of these children was "the outcome of an agreement between France and Germany, negotiated at the highest level" (p. 148), a statement for which there is not a shred of evidence. This is the story of this tragic episode:

On June 11, 1942, the *Judenreferenten* for France, Belgium, and

The Netherlands met in Eichmann's Department IVB4 of the RSHA to discuss the forthcoming deportation of Jews from these countries to Auschwitz.[53] They decided that the population groups to be deported would consist of able-bodied persons of both sexes, 16 to 40 years of age,[54] with the additional stipulation that 10 per cent of the deportees could be Jews unfit for work. After Eichmann's appearance in Paris, intensive consultations on deportation of Jews from Paris took place on various levels, on July 2, 4, and 8, climaxed by a meeting held by Eichmann's emissaries on July 17, 1942, in the General Commissariat for Jewish Questions, with the participation of high officials of the commissariat and of the French police.[55] This was with the approval of Pierre Laval, who expressed the wish that the children of deportees from the nonoccupied zone should not be separated from their parents. At the same time he stated that he was not interested in the children of the occupied zone.[56] The fact is that children were arrested in the nonoccupied zone, but many were released or freed through the intervention of the Organization for the Protection of the Health of the Jews (OSE).[57] On July 6 Dannecker informed Eichmann of what Laval had said and, in the same telegram, urgently requested Eichmann's decision as to whether children under 16 could be deported.[58] Four days later, in a teletype[59] to IVB4, marked "urgent, for immediate attention,"[60] Dannecker reported that arrests of "stateless" Jews in Paris were scheduled for the period July 16 to 18. He anticipated that after the roundups 4,000 children would stay behind, who, for the time being, were to be cared for by the French *Assistance Publique*, and again asked for a decision on their deportation, "since an extended stay of these Jewish children with non-Jewish children is not desirable" and the *Union Générale des Israélites de France* (UGIF) could not accommodate more than 400 children in their own children's homes. The same day, Dannecker met with representatives of the French police. The raids were to start at 4 A.M. on July 16. The captured Jews were to be taken to the Velodrôme d'Hiver.[61] In two days of roundups 12,884 Jews were arrested, including 4,051 children, but, as Röthke complained, some were warned by French police officials and managed to escape. In a meeting with Röthke and Hagen, the representatives of the *Commissariat Général aux Questions Juives* (Darquier de Pellepoix and Pierre Gallien) suggested that the Jewish children be put in children's homes in Paris and its suburbs, but they were overruled, and it was decided that the children along with their parents should be taken from the Velodrôme d'Hiver to the camps of Pithiviers and Beaune-la-Rolande.[62] The Velodrôme d'Hiver was an inferno. Most of the people had no food, and conditions were shockingly unsanitary. There were cases of scarlet fever and measles, and subsequently, after the internees had been shipped to Pithiviers and Beaune-la-Rolande, a triple epidemic of scarlet fever, measles, and diphtheria broke out among the children, many of whom died.[63]

On July 20 Eichmann called Dannecker from Berlin to inform him of his decision. "He has decided," Dannecker recorded, "that as soon as [deportation] transports to the Government-General are again possible, children's trains (Kindertransporte) can roll."[64] The ten days that had passed between Dannecker's urgent request for a decision and Eichmann's response to the request were apparently used to make the necessary arrangements for the deportation of the children with Höss and the Ministry of Transportation. When Eichmann informed Dannecker of his decision, the children were still with their parents. It took the Germans another three weeks to arrange for their transportation to Auschwitz.[65] During this interval, the parents were deported. The children stayed behind in Pithiviers and Beaune-la-Rolande. UGIF and individual French Jews and non-Jews made frantic attempts to obtain the release of the children so they could be placed in orphanages and with families, but the efforts failed.[66] The children, many of them infants, were taken to Drancy and from there deported. The first deportation train containing children left Drancy on August 14.[67]

Miss Arendt gives 52,000 as the total number of Jews deported from France (p. 149), and leaves the impression that the deportations ended in the summer of 1943. In fact, eighteen more transports, some of them carrying more than a thousand deportees, left France in the period between July 1943 and the liberation, bringing the estimated total to approximately 80,000 persons.[68]

BELGIUM

On Miss Arendt's single page on Belgium (p. 149-150), the general picture of administration and "collaboration," and the status of the police and of Eichmann's outfit, are presented without regard for facts and documents (even those expressly mentioned by her). She uses the Belgian story to demonstrate that in the absence of Jewish Councils no deportation could take place. The facts are otherwise.

Miss Arendt writes that "the country was ruled exclusively by German military authorities." This is untrue, as the following passage from *Hitler's Europe* illustrates:

. . . Although at the highest level German control was complete and all-embracing, the actual administration of the country continued to be carried out by the old machinery of the Belgian State, that is, the civil service acting under the Secretaries-General of the various government departments. On the other hand, the Secretaries-General had now assumed powers which under the lawful Constitution they were never intended to exercise. From being the permanent heads of state departments responsible to a Minister of the Crown and without any executive authority on their own account, they had assumed the status and attributes of Ministers with wide powers which they exercised in the exclusive interest of the occupying Power. It is true that their position had been rendered somewhat equivocal by a law which had been passed on the very day of the German invasion (May 10, 1940), confirming an earlier law (October 5, 1935), which laid it down that certain officials should remain at their posts in the event of an enemy occupation, and delegating certain powers to these officials which would ordinarily have belonged to their superiors. But these powers were only to be exercised in case of urgency and where the officials concerned were cut off from all communication with the higher authority to whom they are [normally] responsible. Moreover, under the Hague Convention, such officials were still only obliged to assist the occupying Power insofar as the latter respected the laws in force in the country.

In spite of these admonitions the majority of the original Secretaries-General were at first content to continue in office, though one or two immediately refused or else were forced to resign by the Germans . . . After this the Secretaries-General of certain key departments could be known for what they were—the willing tools of German policy.[69]

Despite this, Miss Arendt writes: "Native collaborators, moreover, existed only in Flanders: there were hardly any among the French-speaking Walloons, and hence hardly any in Brussels." The implication that Brussels is purely Walloonian is both *de facto* and *de jure* incorrect. Brussels is bilingual in its population and in its administration. In addition, the statement concerning the weakness of the Nazi movement among the Walloons is not borne out by facts. There was even an active *Wallonische SS-Sturmbrigade*.[70]

According to Miss Arendt, the Belgian Government's report, submitted in the Eichmann trial,[71] stated that "the police [in Belgium] did not have the same influence upon the other German administration services that they enjoyed in other places." The question of the influence of the Gestapo is dealt with twice in the government report. The first time is in connection with "the Jews in the Antwerp area," about which the report says: "In this region, more than elsewhere, the Gestapo had gained the ascendancy (*avait assuré son ascendant*) over the other services of the German administration."[72] The second time is in connection with Brussels, where, the report says, the Gestapo "did *not* possess the ascendancy that it had elsewhere over the services of the German administration."[73] Miss Arendt does not realize that the expression "elsewhere" refers to the distinction between the Antwerp region and Brussels, and not to any distinction between Belgium and other countries.

She further declares that "Eichmann had his usual 'adviser' in Belgium, but the adviser seems not to have been very active in these operations." This, too, is incorrect. The June 1943 report of the German Military Administration notes that after having eliminated the Jews from the social and economic life of the country, the next stage was deportation, but that this belonged to the "competent service of the Reich."[74] Eichmann's representative was thus directly in charge of the deportation.

Returning to her proposition of the indispensability of Jewish Councils for registering Jews, "one of the most important prerequisites for their seizure," she says that in Belgium "there was no Jewish Council to register the Jews." But the Belgian Government report cited by Miss Arendt contains the statement that "on November 25, 1940, the occupying power established the *Association des Juifs de Belgique*"[75] and that "in Brussels the German authorities pushed their machiavellianism to the limit of forcing the Jewish Association to distribute the summonses [for deportation]."[76]

In connection with the alleged absence of a Jewish Council, Miss Arendt says: ". . . it is not surprising that not a single Belgian Jew was ever deported." The fact is that in addition to 25,000 "foreign" Jews who were deported at least 793 Belgian Jews were also deported, on September 19, 1943. Contrary to promises given to Queen Elisabeth and Cardinal Van Roey by General Alexander von Falkenhausen and the chief of the Military Administration, Eggert Hans Reeder, the Gestapo invaded the homes of

Belgian Jews in Antwerp and shipped them and their belongings, destined for "the East," to the concentration camp of Malines.[77] (Details on the deportation and extermination of Belgian Jews are available elsewhere.[78]) This happened following an about-face by the German Foreign Office, which finally accepted the demand of the RSHA to deport Belgian Jews.[79]

THE NETHERLANDS

Miss Arendt's account of the situation in The Netherlands abounds in inaccuracies.[80]

On page 150 she mentions Jewish refugees from Germany, "whom the prewar Dutch government had officially declared to be 'undesirable.'" This never happened. Although the Dutch established a camp at Westerbork for illegal immigrants, The Netherlands admitted a larger number of Jewish refugees, in proportion to its population, than any other country, with the exception of Belgium. The status of these refugees was also more favorable than elsewhere.[81] Furthermore, it was due to The Netherlands' initiative that the Assembly of the League of Nations entered the field of care for Jewish refugees from Germany.[82]

According to Miss Arendt, "there existed a very strong Nazi movement in Holland" (p. 152). As a matter of fact, the Nazi movement in Holland was no stronger than similar movements in Belgium, France, Denmark, and Norway. In a population of about nine million people, there were about 100,000 Nazis.[83]

In seeking to explain the Catastrophe of the Dutch Jews, she adds to the "strong Nazi movement" one more factor: "There existed an inordinately strong tendency among the native Jews to draw a line between themselves and the new arrivals. . . . This made it relatively easy for the Nazis to form their Jewish Council, the *Joodsche Raad*, which remained for a long time under the impression that only German and other foreign Jews would be victims of the deportations, and it also enabled the S.S. to enlist, in addition to Dutch police units, the help of a Jewish police force" (p. 152). These are the facts:[84] (1) There was a certain antagonism between the Dutch Jews and the German Jews in Holland, but there is no evidence that the policy of the *Joodse Raad* was determined by it. (2) As soon as the deportations started, no distinction was made between Dutch and German Jews. By that time, the hierarchy of the Westerbork transit camp consisted mostly of German Jews, who tried to hold on to their posts, as a result of which the antagonism between Dutch and German Jews was intensified. (3) The Jewish camp police of Westerbork was commanded by a German Jew. This police did not take part in deportations.

Miss Arendt further states that "in Holland, Sephardic Jews, of Spanish origin, had been exempted [and] . . . for God knows what reasons, some three hundred and seventy Sephardic Jews remained unmolested in Amsterdam" (p. 152). What really happened in regard to the Sephardic (Portuguese) Jews constitutes one of the most fantastic rescue attempts ever undertaken. A move was started in 1942, by members of certain resistance groups, to present the Sephardim as non-Jews racially. Quasi-scientific memoranda were drawn up, among them a historical one by Professor J. F. van Bemmelen and an anthropological one by Professor C. V. Ariens Kappers, the latter supposedly based on research by Dr. A. de Froe (now a professor), who contributed a great deal toward preparing these memoranda.[85] The results were not unexpected; while the specialist on the Jewish question (*Judenreferent*) of the RSHA was not deceived, another branch of the German administration, the Commissariat-General for Administration and Justice (*General-kommissariat für Verwaltung und Justiz*), and in particular Dr. H. G. Calmeyer of that branch (who knew the fate of Jews that were deported), was willing to grant exemption on a considerable scale, though not without struggles with the specialist. As a result, about one quarter of the Sephardic Jews were at first exempted from deportation. However, in February 1944 this exemption was canceled, and most of what was left of the group were sent to Auschwitz by way of Theresienstadt. The handful of Sephardic Jews who were allowed to stay in Amsterdam owed their exemption to reasons other than alleged non-Jewish descent.[86]

Miss Arendt makes the following statement on the German approach to the "Jewish Question" in The Netherlands: "The small nation was utterly at the mercy of the Germans and of the S.S. Eichmann's 'adviser' in Holland was a certain Dr. Günther [corrected to Willi in the paperback edition, pp. 14, 167] Zöpf (recently arrested in Germany, while the much more efficient adviser in France, Mr. Dannecker, is still at large), but he apparently had very little to say and could hardly do more than keep the Berlin office posted. Deportations and everything connected with them were handled by Obergruppenführer Hanns Rauter and Ferdinand aus der Fünten, two Higher S.S. and Police Leaders, who conferred directly with Himmler and took no orders from the R.S.H.A., though they kept Eichmann's office informed of their activities" (p. 151).

This statement is inaccurate. In the first place, there was only one Higher SS and Police Leader, SS-*Obergruppenführer* Hanns (not Hans) Rauter. The *Befehlshaber der Sicherheitspolizei und des S.D.,* Dr. Wilhelm Harster, was formally one of his assistants. The office of Eichmann's IVB4 was attached to Harster's staff; it was headed by SS-*Sturmbannführer* Wilhelm Zöpf. Since most Dutch Jews lived in or near Amsterdam, a special office was established there, the *Central Office of Jewish Emigration,* which was in the charge of SS-*Hauptsturmführer* F. H. Aus der Fünten. This office was formally controlled by Harster's representative in Amsterdam, the *Aussendienststellenleiter,* Willi Lages. Orders were passed directly from Zöpf to Aus der Fünten, and Zöpf in his turn received orders from Eichmann's office in Berlin.[87] How does Miss Arendt know that Zöpf was less efficient than Dannecker? If the basis for evaluation were the percentage of Jews deported to the East, surely Zöpf in The Netherlands was more efficient than Dannecker in France. There is no evidence of any significant independent behavior on the part of Rauter, or of any serious conflict with Eichmann's office.

In the paperback edition (pp. 167-168) Miss Arendt attributes the supervision of the Nazi anti-Jewish program in Holland to "Erich Rajakowitsch, Eichmann's former legal adviser in Vienna and Prague, who was admitted to the S.S. upon Eichmann's recommendation." She writes that it is "highly unlikely" that during Rajakowitsch's stay in Holland he "was still taking orders from Eichmann." But he did receive instructions from Eichmann while in Holland, just as he had been receiving instructions from Eichmann before then.[88]

Summing up the section on The Netherlands, Miss Arendt says: "Of the twenty ["ten" in the paperback edition, p. 170] thousand Jews who survived in hiding, fifteen thousand ["about seventy-five per cent" in the paperback edition] were foreigners—a percentage that testifies to the unwillingness of Dutch Jews to face reality" (p. 153). The authoritative estimate[89] is that about 20,000 Jews went into hiding, of whom about 10,000 were discovered by the

Germans before the liberation of Holland.[90] Proportionately, there were probably more German Jews among the survivors, but they certainly did not constitute a majority. If anything, this testifies to the fact that the German Jews, who had already been uprooted once, had become more mobile and knowledgeable in means of escape. It is also significant that the German Jews were mostly members of the middle classes; it was especially difficult for the Dutch-Jewish proletariat to find hiding places.[91]

Another example of Miss Arendt's lack of care in quoting statistics is her statement (p. 152) that 113,000 Jews were deported, "most of them to Sobibór." In fact, 34,000 Jews were sent to Sobibór, while 60,000 were deported to Auschwitz.[92]

NORWAY

Miss Arendt states that "the bulk of Norway's seventeen hundred Jews were stateless, refugees from Germany" (p. 153). However, of the total, only 200 were refugees (from all over Central Europe); the rest were Norwegian citizens. She states further that "they ["refugees from Germany"] were seized and interned in a few lightning operations in October and November, 1942." In fact, 770 Jews, including 100 refugees from Central Europe, were deported to Auschwitz from Norway. The majority of Norwegian Jews (930) were smuggled to Sweden and returned to their homes after the end of the war. There is no evidence to confirm Miss Arendt's statement, that "some of Quisling's own men resigned their government posts" in protest. A vigorous protest did come from the hierarchy of the Lutheran church in a letter to Quisling.[93]

DENMARK

The glory of the behavior of the Danish people toward their Jewish countrymen is marred in Miss Arendt's presentation by numerous errors of fact, some of which have been discussed in Chapter 4. In addition, Eichmann's role is not mentioned.

Miss Arendt claims that "Denmark . . . was respected [by the Germans] as a neutral state, until the fall of 1943" (p. 153). Formally, Denmark was considered neutral, at least until August 1943. However, there were in Denmark German occupation forces, and independence, as far as it existed, was internal only. Thus, Denmark was forced on November 23, 1941, to join the Anticomintern Pact upon German "invitation" given on three days notice.[94]

Miss Arendt asserts that "It was decisive in this whole matter that the Germans did not even succeed in introducing the vitally important distinction between native Danes of Jewish origin . . . and the fourteen hundred German Jewish refugees" (p. 154). This is not true. The real situation was outlined in a report submitted in 1947 to the Parliamentary Commission of Inquiry by Per Feder-spiel, formerly a leader of the Danish resistance, at that time Minister for Special Issues. The report deals, *inter alia*, with the problems of "detainment and internment, expulsion and extradition of foreign subjects." It describes the compliance of the Danish authorities with German demands concerning foreigners, refugees, etc., and explains the Danish behavior: "It must be added, that after the occupation Denmark could not go on providing asylum for foreign subjects, at least not for people who were still German subjects or were Germans by origin and had become stateless. It could be expected that Germany would honor Denmark's sover-eignty in respect to Danish subjects, but it did not seem reasonable to object against extradition of the occupation powers' own subjects in the occupied territory."[95] In spite of this, the Germans did not ask for the Jewish refugees' extradition.

According to Miss Arendt, "When the Germans approached them [the Danes] rather cautiously about introducing the yellow badge, they were simply told that the King would be the first to wear it . . . " (p. 154). This story, like many others about the Danish King, is as widespread (in different versions) as it is untrue. There is no evidence, either, that the Germans ever made such an approach to the Danes.[96] What actually happened, however, was as courageous as the story about the badge. When the King heard, early in the morning of October 1, 1943, about the preparations for an "action" that evening against the Jews in Denmark, he immedi-ately sent a sharp note to Best, the German Ambassador. In the note, the King wrote that he was vigorously protesting the German intentions "out of human preoccupation with the citizens of my country," and went on to warn that serious consequences would follow any "special measures in regard to a group of human beings who have enjoyed full citizenship rights in this country for 100 years."[97]

Miss Arendt describes the disturbances that occurred in the

summer of 1943: "Thereupon, the Danish workers decided that they could help a bit in hurrying things up; riots broke out in Danish shipyards . . . " (p. 155). In fact, tension was high in the summer of 1943 throughout Denmark. Disturbances occurred in several provincial towns, the main disturbance in the coastal town of Odense, where a German officer wounded a Danish boy and was beaten up by an angry crowd. The people reacted to German reprisals for the incident by proclaiming strikes. Best was summoned to Hitler's headquarters and returned with an ultimatum that was rejected by the Danish Government.[98] Thereupon martial law was proclaimed on August 29, 1943. Government and Parliament were dissolved, the King became a virtual prisoner, and the Germans assumed direct control of the country over the heads of Danish civil service officials running the day-to-day affairs.[99]

Miss Arendt is careless in citing figures on Jews sought out by the Germans: "They [the Germans] found exactly 477 people . . . at home and willing to let them in" (p. 156). The facts are that in Copenhagen they found exactly 202 Jews on the night of October 1 and 2, who were sent by ship to Stettin, as stated by Mildner and transmitted by Best on October 2 in his cable No. 1194.[100] Eighty-two more Jews were seized elsewhere in Denmark on the same night.[101] About 200 additional Jews, most of them caught in flight, were sent by railway on October 13 and November 23 (according to Danish police records).[102] Miss Arendt also claims that "The Swedes received 5,919 refugees, of whom at least 1,000 were of German origin, 1,310 were half-Jews, and 686 were non-Jews married to Jews" (p. 157). The following are the correct figures:[103] There came to Sweden, as a consequence of the persecution of Jews in Denmark, 7,906 people. Among them were 686 non-Jews and 7,220 Jews. The latter consisted of 4,543 Danish Jews, 1,301 (not 1,310) Danish "half-Jews,"[104] and 1,376 refugees from Germany and elsewhere. If the Jews deported to Theresienstadt are added, the total is about 7,700 Jews living in Denmark at the time of the German "action." Subtracting a round figure of 1,400 refugees, we find for the total number of Danish Jews a figure of 6,300, which agrees with the figure given in all the sources. Miss Arendt does not indicate where she found the Jews she refers to when she writes: "Almost half the Danish Jews seem to have remained in the country and survived the war in hiding" (p. 157).

The following statement by Miss Arendt is at variance with the conditions that prevailed at the time: "They might have remained in hiding until the end of the war . . . It seemed reasonable to ship the Jews to Sweden" (p. 156). To everybody, Danes and Jews alike, it became clear very quickly that it was quite impossible to keep the Jews safely hidden for a long period. Hence the dramatically swift action to ship them to Sweden, which, luckily, was now ready to accept refugees from Denmark, Jewish and non-Jewish. The newly organized Freedom Council, the central organ of the Danish underground, published a proclamation in October 1943 denouncing the Germans and calling for resistance in general and help to Jews in particular. The proclamation reads: "The Council asks the Danish population to help in every possible way those Jewish fellow citizens who did not yet escape abroad."[105] The ultimate solution was escape. In all descriptions of those days,[106] one of the outstanding and urgent factors was the need to send the people across the water as quickly as possible, because their lingering behind meant danger to the Jews and to their rescuers alike.

Except for stating (pp. 155-156) that Rolf Günther of Eichmann's Office was sent to Copenhagen (where he "made no impression on his colleagues"), Miss Arendt does not mention Eichmann's name in her four and a half pages on Denmark. There is nothing about the role Eichmann played in the Nazi *Aktion* against the Jews in Denmark, although his involvement can easily be traced in the documents and proceedings of the trial.[107] Thus when, shortly before the operation was to get under way, the commander of the German forces in Denmark, General von Hannecken, refused to make available the military police units (*Geheime Feldpolizei und Feldgendarmerie*) which Best had requested for the occasion, von Thadden of the Foreign Office proposed that Eichmann intercede with the High Command of the Armed Forces (OKW) in order to change von Hannecken's mind.[108] Eichmann was furious about the poor results of the *Aktion*, and, as one of his subordinates told von Thadden at the time, "Eichmann has already made a report to the *Reichsführer* and will ask for the head of the saboteur" responsible for the failure.[109] And when—in response to pressure exerted by the Danish Administration and public opinion—the German Foreign Office approached the RSHA to obtain the release of certain categories of deportees and the permission for the Danish Red Cross to visit Theresienstadt, Eichmann became involved personally. In the course of the German-Danish negotiations he was sent by Müller to join Best on the German side.[110] The agreement finally reached (with Eichmann's concurrence) was subsequently endorsed almost to the full by the RSHA.[111]

ITALY

Playing down the racial legislation in Italy, whitewashing Mussolini, distorting the nature of the deportations, erring in chronology and statistics, Miss Arendt presents a false picture of the Jewish situation in that country during the anti-Jewish action.

She minimizes the seriousness of racial legislation in Italy. Her list of categories of the *discriminati* Jews—i.e., those Jews who were exempted from the effects of the Fascist racial legislation—is full of errors. It is not true that "former members of the Fascist Party, together with their parents and grandparents, their wives and children and grandchildren" were exempted from the operation of the racial legislation (p. 160). First, the exemptions were not all automatic, as she suggests; most were left to the discretion of the Ministry of Interior. Second, the categories of Jews exempted were the following four: Jews who had joined the Fascist Party in the 1919-1922 period and in the six months immediately following the assassination of Giacomo Matteotti in 1924; Jews who were wounded or decorated in the four wars waged by Italy since 1911 (the conquest of Libya in 1911, World War I, the conquest of Ethiopia, the civil war in Spain); Jews who had been wounded while participating in the fights of the Fascist gangs, or who had taken part in D'Annunzio's coup against Fiume; families of Jews who fell in these wars or in pro-Fascist activities or in D'Annunzio's legion. The fourth category is the only one where the exemption was automatic in regard to the family of the person concerned. In all other categories the exemption applied to the person alone, and the Ministry of Interior could extend this privilege to parents, to wives, and to children, but not, as Miss Arendt writes, to grandparents or grandchildren.[112] On the basis of her erroneous information, she concludes that "the great majority of Italian Jews were exempted" (p. 160). In fact, in the first period of the racial legislation only 2,069 exemptions were granted,[113] and for the whole duration of the legislation an authoritative estimate places the maximum number at 3,000.[114] Finally, such exemptions as were granted were only partial. Important restrictions remained even for the *discriminati*. They were not allowed to continue their service in governmental or other official institutions; to work in the field of journalism, in the movie industry, in banks, or in insurance companies; to teach in schools for "Aryans" or to send their children to such schools, and the like.[115] *De facto*, the restrictions on the *discriminati* were even more severe.[116] Her statement that "Roberto Farinacci, head of the Italian anti-Semitic movement, had a Jewish secretary in his employ" (p. 160) presumably means that even he did not take the racial law seriously. The fact is, however, that the secretary in question, Miss Jole Foà, was dismissed at the start of the racist campaign, and was arrested in 1944 by the Fascists, never to return.[117]

Miss Arendt is also in error in her statement (p. 159) concerning Mussolini's moderating influence in Jewish affairs in the German-led coalition. Actually, the positive and practical influence (rescue of Jews in Italian-occupied France and the admission of refugees from Croatia to the Italian-occupied parts of Yugoslavia) came from Army officers and from high-ranking members of the Foreign Office without Mussolini's knowledge and sometimes even against his explicit instructions. A striking proof of this is contained in a case reported in the documentation of the Italian Foreign Office:[118] Following the generous admission by Italian occupation authorities of Jewish refugees from Croatia to the Italian Zone of occupation in Yugoslavia, the German Foreign Minister, von Ribbentrop (in a cable dated August 17, 1942, addressed to the Italian Foreign Office) demanded that these refugees be turned over to the German occupation authorities. Asked by the Foreign Office for instructions, Mussolini personally ordered the surrender of these Jews to the Germans, despite the efforts of the Foreign Office people to explain to Mussolini what was in store for them. This explicit order by Mussolini was defied by the Foreign Office officials (headed by Leonardo Vitetti and Luigi Vidau of the *Direzione Generale degli Affari Generali, Ufficio IV*) and the Army commanders in occupied Yugoslavia; they did not hand over the Jews to the Germans.

The tragic events that accompanied the deportation of the Italian Jews are also misrepresented by Miss Arendt. She writes that "the first blow was to fall upon eight thousand Jews in Rome, who were to be arrested by German police regiments . . . They were warned in time, frequently by old Fascists, and seven thousand escaped" (p. 162). The facts: Out of the more than ten thousand Jews in Rome, 1,024 were seized in the "action" of October 16, 1943, and deported to Birkenau. Of these, only 16 returned. In the following months, 1,067 more Jews were seized in Rome and shipped to Auschwitz. Of the altogether 2,091 Jews deported from Rome, only 102 returned.[119] Seventy-five more were murdered in the *Fosse Ardeatine*.[120]

Roman Jews were first transported to Auschwitz in October 1943; at the end of 1943 and the beginning of 1944, Jews from the provinces began to be shipped to the same destination. (The Italian-Jewish writer Primo Levi was deported in February 1944.[121]) The Fascist Republic, established on November 17, 1943, apparently intended to arrest all the Jews (proclaiming them to be "hostile foreigners"), concentrate them in special camps, and postpone the final decision on their fate to the postwar period. The order of November 30, 1943, issued by the Minister of Interior, Guido Buffarini-Guidi, outlined this policy.[122] Miss Arendt writes that "The Germans . . . now agreed that Italian Jews . . . should not be subject to deportation but should merely be concentrated in Italian camps" (p. 162). There are no available facts on the existence of such an agreement. On the contrary, the Germans had never given up their intention of deporting the Italian Jews to the East. While being careful not to spell out their ultimate objective to the Fascist Government, the Germans used the Fascist decree ordering that all Jews be placed in concentration camps as a welcome preparatory step toward deportation. Thus Horst Wagner, head of Section *Inland II* of the German Foreign Office, wrote to Eichmann's immediate superior, *Gruppenführer* Müller, on December 14, 1943 (after a discussion of the issue with *Sturmbannführer* Bosshammer, the *Judenreferent* in Italy, and with Dannecker, Eichmann's representative who handled the deportations):

On the basis of the above-mentioned conference, Ambassador Rahn has been instructed: to express to the Fascist Government the satisfaction of the Reich Government with the law for the internment (*Rückführung*) of all Jews in Italy in concentration camps so direly needed for security reasons (*aus abwehrmässigen Gründen*); to point to the fact that an accelerated execution of this law and the establishment of concentration camps in Northern Italy appears necessary in the interest of the immediate protection of the operational zones from unreliable elements; and that for the execution of these measures the Reich Government would be glad to make advisors available. On the other hand, the Foreign Office considers as not feasible the plan suggested by SS-*Sturmbann-führer* Bosshammer to request, at the same time, that the Jews collected in concentration camps be made available for deportations to the Eastern Territories. For tactical and political reasons, such a request should be put off until the seizure (*Erfassungsaktion*) of the Jews by the Italian organs has been brought to conclusion. As has already been expressed at the earlier conference, the Foreign Office, on the basis of its experiences, feels that if the request to hand over these Jews is made now, the seizing operation will be greatly impaired or perhaps even fail altogether.[123]

In accordance with the policy expressed in Wagner's letter, the Germans, with the help of irregular Fascist groups, continued their "actions" without coordination with the Fascist authorities—killing on the spot or transporting to Auschwitz every Jew they could lay their hands on.[124] There is no basis for Miss Arendt's statement that "In the Spring of 1944 . . . the Germans broke their promise and began shipping Jews from Italy to Auschwitz" (p. 162). There had been no promise—only a German tactical maneuver. A change in the official Fascist policy occurred on March 15, 1944, when Giovanni Preziosi was appointed head of the Central Office for Racial Questions (*Ispettorato Generale per la razza*) in the Prime Minister's office. The Jewish camp, Fossoli, was turned over to the Germans, and all the Jews were deported without opposition from the Fascists.[125]

Two other errors: Miss Arendt refers (p. 158) to "the Badoglio *coup d'état*"—though it is generally accepted that the downfall of the Fascist regime was not brought about on Badoglio's initiative.[126] On page 160 she says that "in the fall of 1943, when Italy declared war on Germany, the German army could finally move into Nice." The sequence of events was actually the following: Italy capitulated to the Allies on September 8, 1943; the declaration of war on Germany followed on October 13; the invasion of Italian-occupied France by the German Army occurred between these two events, on September 10, 1943.[127]

Miss Arendt claims that "considerably less than ten per cent of all Jews then living in Italy" perished (p. 162). This statement seems to be based on the fantastic figure of more than 75,000 Jews living in Italy. The best estimate is that in the process of the Final

Solution Italian Jewry lost not less than 7,500 Jews (the figure probably lies between 7,750 and 8,000) out of a total of 35,000— that is, at least 22 per cent, or more than double Miss Arendt's figure.[128]

YUGOSLAVIA

Of the various parts into which Yugoslavia was dismembered during the war by the Nazis and Fascists, Croatia and Serbia alone are discussed by Miss Arendt. (The fate of the Jews of Macedonia, which was annexed by Bulgaria, is discussed in the section on Bulgaria.)

Concerning Croatia, Miss Arendt asserts that the characterization of "honorary Aryans" was conferred on "all Jews who made contributions to 'the Croat cause'" (p. 165). On the best authority, it can be stated that their number did not exceed sixteen families.[129] Nor is there any evidence that "the number of these Jews had . . . greatly increased during the intervening years" (p. 45). It is further not true that "the very rich . . . who parted voluntarily with their property were exempted" (pp. 165-166). All Jewish property was confiscated.[130] Among the Jews that survived the Catastrophe were a few hundred in mixed marriages. It was the Catholic Church that succeeded in rescuing this group.[131]

There is no basis for the "tempting" (Miss Arendt's word) conclusion that "assimilation in the East . . . offered a much better chance for survival than it did in the rest of Europe" (p. 166). No evidence is available to support this speculation. Insofar as Croatia was concerned, it was not the fact of "assimilation" but the non-Jewish spouse that was the cause of survival. Not every mixed marriage was necessarily a marriage of an assimilated Jew or Jewess.

The situation in Serbia, which was under German military occupation, is presented by Miss Arendt as one in which "Eichmann's office was not involved at all ["although asked, had refused to become involved;" IV, 86] . . . because no Jews were deported" (p. 166). Though the Jerusalem court said that "the usual channels of command in dealing with the Jews of Serbia were not made clear to us,"[132] it went on to accept the testimony of the commandant of the Einsatzgruppen in Serbia, Wilhelm Fuchs, that "it was known to him that a Standartenführer named Eichmann assigned to special duties in the RSHA used to transmit to them [the German authorities in Serbia] the instructions for dealing with the Jews."[133] Miss Arendt also does not mention the fact that it was Eichmann who was supposed to go to Belgrade to settle the matter of the shooting of Jews, but that it was finally decided to send two other men from his office, Suhr and Stuschka.[134]

Serbia occupied a special position in the Eichmann trial because of the so-called *Erschiessen* (shooting) episode. In April 1941, Germany attacked Yugoslavia, and Serbia became German-occupied territory. In the late summer of 1941, 8,000 male Jews were rounded up in Belgrade. On September 12, 1941, the representative of the German Foreign Ministry in Belgrade, Felix Benzler, reiterated by wire[135] his and Veesenmayer's earlier request of September 8[136] that the Jews be sent to one of the islands in the Danube delta, or to the Government-General, or to occupied U.S.S.R. On this telegram Franz Rademacher, the German Foreign Office adviser on Jewish Affairs, made the following notation: "According to information from . . . Eichmann . . . reception in Russia and in the Government-General is impossible. Even Jews from Germany cannot be received there. Eichmann proposes killing by shooting (*Eichmann schlägt Erschiessen vor*)."

Miss Arendt, having recorded without objection Eichmann's protestation that he "had nothing to do" with "the killing of Jews" (p. 19), and charging that "Eichmann, as usual, chose the most complicated and least likely explanation" (p. 20), has the following to say about Rademacher's note: "This turned out to be the only 'order to kill,' if that is what it was, for which there existed even a shred of evidence" (p. 19). She declares the "categorical denial" of Eichmann to have been "very ineffective" (pp. 19-20), but says nothing about Eichmann's original admission to the police: "I did not give the shooting order on my own initiative, but, as in all such matters, I went through channels, and the instructions of my superiors happened to be: to kill by shooting."[137] Later, Eichmann claimed that Rademacher's note was a forgery on the part of Rademacher.[138] The court had this comment on the forgery excuse: "This version is neither based on facts, nor logical, as the forgery could have been discovered immediately, and then (a few days later) the truth would very easily have been established. Under the circumstances, it is inconceivable that Rademacher would have taken such a risk upon himself."[139]

Miss Arendt rejects Rademacher's testimony of 1952 before a German court, that "the Army was responsible for order in Serbia and had to kill rebellious Jews by shooting" (p. 21)—rebellious Jews numbering a total of eight thousand! But she does not mention Rademacher's earlier statement in Nuremberg,[140] quoted in the judgment:

I still remember distinctly that I sat facing him [Luther] when I telephoned the Reich Security Head Office and that I made note in my own handwriting of Eichmann's reply and passed it over to Luther during the telephone conversation. In substance Eichmann said that the military was responsible for order in Serbia and would simply have to shoot (erschiessen) the rebel Jews. In answer to my question, he repeated 'to kill by shooting' (Erschiessen) and hung up.[141]

All this evidence is in Miss Arendt's words "questionable"—even "more questionable than it appeared to be during the trial" (p. 19). She offers no explanation for this statement.

Her attempt to account for the extermination of the Serbian Jews as an element of the fight against the partisans is not founded on fact. She writes: "The Army had been plagued by partisan warfare ever since [the German occupation of Serbia], and it was the military authorities who decided to solve two problems at a stroke by shooting a hundred Jews and Gypsies as hostages for every dead German soldier" (p. 20). Actually, the concentration of the Serbian Jews in Topovske Šupe (in Belgrade) by the Gestapo started in August 1941 and was carried out with great speed. Some of the Jewish inmates were shot during the following months. Though this was the largest Jewish camp in Serbia, it was not the only one. There was a camp in Sabac for some 400 Austrian and German refugees, and the camp of Banjica (in Belgrade) where Jews and Serbs were detained. The camp of Topovske Šupe was not a camp of hostages but of Jews qua Jews; but it also served as a reservoir for Jewish hostages. Under the order of General Bader, of October 13, 1941, concerning the suppression of Communist partisans, hostages were to be taken in the proportion of 100 to 1 from among Communists and Jews, and also from among democrats and Waldgänger (anti-Nazi fighters in the woods).[142] An earlier similar order on hostages by General Franz Böhme is dated October 10, 1941.[143]

Further, it is inexact to claim that the Army acted on its own.

The Foreign Office had its representative there (Minister Benzler), and through him the Army kept constant contact with the Foreign Office. Nor was contact with the SS lacking, as can be seen from the report of *Oberleutnant* Walther of November 1, 1941,[144] which starts: "I picked up the Jews and the Gypsies from the Belgrade prison camp in agreement with the SS office . . . " All this notwithstanding, Miss Arendt continues as follows: "In any event, if Eichmann actually did 'propose shooting,' he told the military only that they should go on doing what they had done all along, and that the question of hostages was entirely in their own competence" (p. 20). Here again the question of the extermination of Jews is presented in terms of the fight against the partisans and the seizure and execution of hostages. Contrary to Miss Arendt's statement, Eichmann did not "tell the military" anything, but did advise Rademacher, the competent official of the Foreign Office. Rademacher had turned to Eichmann as a matter of course for instructions on dealing with Jews.

BULGARIA

The Jerusalem Court had before it fifteen documents—all a matter of record—concerning the pressures exerted by the "Eichmann organization" on Bulgarian authorities. With disregard for these and other available facts, Miss Arendt presents (pp. 167-170) an account of the operation of the Final Solution in Bulgaria, the Bulgarian political situation, and the attitude of the King, the Parliament, and the people. The German side of the operation is depicted without mentioning Eichmann's personal role (attributed instead to "Berlin").

Miss Arendt deduces from the Bulgarian Government's opposition to the *Ratnizi* (a Fascist splinter group) and from Bulgaria's failure to declare war on Russia that the remaining political factors were non-Fascist (p. 167). The fact is that the Bulgarian Government during World War II was committed to the Axis Anti-Comintern Pact.[145] Bulgaria did not declare war on Russia—primarily because of the Bulgarian people's traditional affection for Russian culture and for the Russian people, and because of the danger of civil war in the event of a governmental anti-Russian policy (or even anti-Soviet policy, notwithstanding cruel persecution of Communists).[146]

The local population in Macedonia and Thrace was, contrary to Miss Arendt's statement and to Nazi documentation,[147] *not* anti-Semitic. Jewish-Macedonian and Jewish-Greek relations were in general friendly under all regimes.[148] What is more important, the attitude of the local population toward Jews was no factor at all in the deportation of the Jews from these areas. The Germans conquered Macedonia and Thrace and turned them over to Bulgaria. The Bulgarian occupation authorities were indifferent to the views of the local population on what to do to the Jews.

Miss Arendt writes that "the population of Sofia tried to stop Jews from going to the railroad station and subsequently demonstrated before the King's palace" (p. 169). This story has scant basis in the sources. It is not mentioned in Grinberg's book,[149] published in 1945, which placed special emphasis on the help given by the Bulgarian people to the Jews. Nor is it mentioned in the report of the German police attaché Otto Hoffmann, of June 7, 1943, on the deportation from Sofia, though an attempt by demonstrators to proceed to the King's palace in order to protest the deportation is mentioned.[150] Apparently Miss Arendt drew her information from an article by Jacques Sabille,[151] who gave no source.

Miss Arendt tries to connect the murder of Bulgaria's King Boris III with German dissatisfaction at his "keeping Bulgaria's Jews safe" (p. 169). There is no substantial evidence that he was assassinated by the Nazis as a result of his attitude toward the "Jewish question." The chronology does not bear out this speculation. The Jews were deported, with the King's consent, from Sofia to the provinces in May, 1943, but as late as June 1943 he still opposed deportation to the East.[152] The King went to Germany in August 1943, and a few days after his return he died. Nineteen hundred forty-three was the year of the beginning of the fall of the "thousand-year Reich." It is possible that the King was asked to give active assistance to the Axis and refused.[153] The relative parts played by the King and the people in the rescue of Bulgarian Jewry are a matter of controversy. In a monograph published in 1952, Benjamin Arditi presented the view that the rescue was due exclusively to the intervention of the King,[154] but in his standard work he wrote that it was the King together with certain circles of Bulgarian society who shared the responsibility for this act.[155] Not so Nathan Grinberg, who has denied that the King had a role in the rescue. According to him, the King had done everything to implement the Nazi-planned deportation to the East, but he was frustrated by the efforts of the progressive elements of Bulgarian society, the Communist underground, and the victories of the Soviet armies on the Eastern front.[156] No final judgment on this issue can be expected before the opening of the Bulgarian archives, provided the archives still exist. There is no doubt, however, that the Bulgarian intelligentsia—the societies of writers, lawyers, and doctors, individual members of Parliament, the Greek Orthodox Church, and personalities within the Government—had displayed a high degree of courage and humanity in the tragedy of Bulgarian Jewry.[157]

Contrary to Miss Arendt, "Parliament" did not remain "clearly on the side of the Jews" (p. 169). The Law for the Protection of the State, directed against the Jews, was adopted by a majority of the Parliament at the end of December 1940 and promulgated in January 1941.[158] In 1943 the majority of the members of the Parliament supported the deportation of the Jews, and the Vice-President of the Parliament, Dimiter Peshev, who objected to the deportation, was deprived of his office by a majority vote,[159] a fact duly reported to Eichmann.[160]

Miss Arendt's speculation (p. 168) on the "high priority given to the task of making Bulgaria *judenrein*," which allegedly was dictated by Berlin's information of the need for "great speed," is not substantiated by documents. Concerning the deportation of the Jews, Luther's note of June 19, 1942, to the German Embassy in Sofia gave the following instructions: "You have to give a positive answer to the question whether Germany is prepared to receive Jews from Bulgaria and to transport them to the East. But if you are asked to fix an exact date for their reception it is advisable to evade an answer and to point to the engagement of all transportation facilities in this year for the deportation of the Jews from Germany, the Protectorate, Slovakia, and Romania. Consequently, there is no possibility of receiving the Bulgarian Jews this year."[161] A note of August 21, 1941, from Under Secretary Luther to Ambassador von Rintelen, gave the following instruction: ". . . if on the Bulgarian side the question of Germany's readiness to deal with the transportation of Bulgarian Jews to the East should be raised, the answer should be positive, but an answer to the question of the time of the transportation should be evaded."[162]

As for the "five thousand more Jews," who allegedly "received special privileges" (p. 167), the only source for this statement is the aforementioned report of the police attaché, Otto Hoffmann, dated June 7, 1943. According to his report, however, only some two to three thousand Jews were to remain in Sofia after the deportation. There is no evidence for Miss Arendt's opinion that Hoffmann "seems not to have been very enthusiastic about his work" (p. 168).

Especially unreliable is her information concerning the persecution of the Bulgarian Jews carried out by the Bulgarian Government. It is not true that "all baptized Jews, regardless of the date of their conversion, were exempted" from anti-Jewish legislation (p. 167). The relevant legal sources (Law for the Protection of the State of January 1941, Art. 33, as amended by Art. 52 of the Decree of August 27, 1942),[163] state that only Jews converted before September 1, 1940, were exempt. A later amendment introduced a further restriction to the exemption: Bulgarian citizens of Jewish origin in mixed marriages performed before September 1, 1940, who had been converted before January 23, 1941, were to be exempt from the operation of the discriminatory legislation; however, this exemption was withdrawn in case of divorce if there were no living children born from the marriage.[164] Miss Arendt states that as a result of the exemption from the operation of the anti-Jewish legislation of baptized Jews "regardless of the date of their conversion, . . . an epidemic of conversions broke out" (p. 167). No evidence can be found in available sources to support this claim that a great number of conversions took place. On the authority of a former member of the Jewish Consistory in Sofia, it can be stated that 348 Sofia Jews out of a total of 25,000 were converted to Christianity, but this happened much later—namely, at the beginning of 1943, on the eve of the deportation of Sofia Jews to the provinces.[165]

It is also not true (pp. 167-168) that the *numerus clausus* for Jewish physicians and businessmen was based on the percentage of Jews in the cities. Article 25 of the Law for the Protection of the State was based on the percentage of the Jewish population in the country as a whole. Nor did stabilization occur "to everybody's satisfaction" following the 1941-1942 measures, as Miss Arendt implies (p. 168). On the contrary, new measures were taken by the legislative and executive bodies, including the Commissariat of Jewish Affairs and the local authorities. In Ruse, Dupnitsa, and other places, it was the *local* authorities that forbade Jews to walk in certain streets, to leave their houses during air-raid alarms, to buy food in the market at certain hours, and the like.[166]

Miss Arendt's account of the introduction of the "Jewish badge" is also wrong. The badge was introduced in October 1942. Whether it was "a very little star" (p. 168) is beside the point. Contrary to Miss Arendt, who says that "most Jews simply did not wear it," all Jews did wear it. Perhaps in the first months there was some laxity in enforcing the wearing of the badge, but not in 1943-1944.[167] The badge was supposed to be sewed on in a specified way.[168] Raids were made in order to make sure that the badges were worn and sewed on as prescribed.[169] Contrary to Miss Arendt's statement (p. 168) that "those who did wear it received . . . 'manifestations of sympathy' . . . whereupon the Bulgarian government revoked the decree," the decree was revoked in August 1944—one month before the entry of the Red Army into Bulgaria, and almost two years after the badge had been introduced.

Miss Arendt uses incorrect figures: The number of Jews deported to the East from Macedonia, Thrace, and Pirot was not 15,000 (p. 167) but 11,363,[170] and the number of those mobilized for forced labor was not 6,000 (p. 167) but between 9,000 and 11,000.[171]

ROMANIA

Miss Arendt begins the section on Romania in her book by recounting Eichmann's claim that the "coordination of evacuations and deportations achieved by his office, had in fact helped his victims; it had made their fate easier" (pp. 171-172)—a claim to which "no one, not even counsel for the defense, paid any attention." She adds: "In the light of what took place in Rumania, one begins to wonder."

What actually took place in Romania only remotely resembles Miss Arendt's presentation. The situation was complicated. There were two converging anti-Jewish policies: a policy that developed locally by virtue of the indigenous Romanian anti-Semitism, which was capable of cruel atrocities against Jews; and Nazi Germany's "program." There were also factors arising from internal Romanian politics, and from the delicate relationship between Romania and Germany, the two powers occupying Transnistria. Miss Arendt presents a picture in which the Germans appear to be almost the

saviors of the Jews, and the Romanians to be the real butchers:
"In Rumania even the S.S. were taken aback, and occasionally
frightened, by the horrors of old-fashioned, spontaneous pogroms
on a gigantic scale; they often intervened to save Jews from sheer
butchery, so that the killing could be done in what, according to
them, was a civilized way" (p. 172). While there might have been
on the part of some Germans private expressions of disapproval of
the Romanian atrocities, Miss Arendt's statement, for which no
source is indicated, does not stand scrutiny. It is nonsense to call
the pogroms in Romania "spontaneous"; they were all organized,
either by local groups or at the instigation of the Nazis. For example, the pogrom of June 29, 1941, in Jassy, the headquarters of
the German military authorities, was the result of cooperation (in
its initiation and execution) between the Nazi military and the
Romanian military and police forces.[172] It is also historically false
to call such pogroms as those that took place in Dorohoi,[173] Jassy,
or Bucharest[174] "old-fashioned." There are no precedents for this
type of pogrom in Romania. And to speak of "pogroms on a gigantic
scale" is an unwarranted exaggeration. To be sure, the Odessa
pogrom carried out by the Romanian Army was accomplished on
"a gigantic scale."[175] But in Odessa the Romanian Army was subordinated to the German Army, and here the Germans quite
neglected to indicate their preference for "civilized" killings. The
"contrast" between German and Romanian butcheries is illustrated
in the following exchange: The General Headquarters of the 11th
German Army sent a protest, on July 14, 1941, to Romanian Army
Headquarters against criminal acts committed against Jews by
Romanian soldiers.[176] The Romanians, by the order of Marshal
Antonescu himself, retorted by forming a commission to investigate
the atrocities against Jews committed by *Germans*.[177]

The *Einsatzgruppen* and their activities in Transnistria, the
area of joint German-Romanian occupation, are not mentioned by
Miss Arendt. The Cernăuți Synagogue was set on fire by Commando
10b of Ohlendorf's *Einsatzgruppe D*. The chief rabbi and other
personnel of the synagogue were shot.[178] According to Ohlendorf,[179]
there were a total of 90,000 victims of his unit's activities, which
ranged over Southern Ukraine and Crimea (including Transnistria).

Germany's role vis-à-vis Romania's anti-Jewish policies is inac-
curately presented by Miss Arendt. First she says that "Richter
reported that Antonescu now wished to ship a hundred and ten

thousand Jews into 'two forests across the river Bug,' that is, into German-held Russian territory, for liquidation" (p. 173).[180] Then comes a description of how "the Germans were horrified [at this prospect of anarchy; IV, 99], and everybody intervened: the Army commanders, Rosenberg's Ministry for Occupied Eastern Territories, the Foreign Office in Berlin, the [German] Minister to Bucharest . . ." The source for her account of this major effort on the part of the Germans is not indicated. Actually, Richter received his information from Radu Lecca, the Romanian Commissar for Jewish Affairs, on October 10, 1941. On the basis of this information, Richter filed a report on October 17, 1941. Eichmann's intervention "to stop these unorganized and premature Rumanian efforts" (p. 173) took place on April 14, 1942, six months later.[181] By ignoring the chronology, Miss Arendt depicts the intervention as an immediate reaction stemming from German horrification. The fact is that the Lecca scheme never came near to execution. As for Eichmann's intervention, it should be noted that Eichmann's job was the solution of the "Jewish question" in all of Europe, according to plans worked out by his office. He did not allow unauthorized action from any quarter to interfere with his own plans. Nothing can better illustrate the fact that it was for Eichmann and not for local authorities to decide the timing of individual actions.

Dr. Martin Broszat of the Institute of Contemporary History in Munich commented on this incident as follows: "The information conveyed by Lecca [to Richter] . . . was in no way in accordance with the facts and had obviously an ulterior motive."[182] Indeed, no Jews from the *Regat* (Kingdom of Moldavia-Valachia) were deported by the Romanians across the Bug River to the German destruction area. On the other hand, on August 19, 1942, SS men penetrated into Romanian-administered Transnistria and abducted thousands of Jews, transporting them from there to physical destruction in the East.[183] The extermination of the Jews in Transnistria (a political-geographical term not mentioned by Arendt) was carried out by German special detachments of Mobile Killing Unit D. The deportation of the Jews from Bucovina, Bessarabia, and Dorohoi was carried out in accordance with Hitler's instructions (*Richtlinien*).[184] On the other hand, the administration of the Jewish concentration camps in Transnistria was entrusted to the Romanians (with certain qualifications) by virtue of the Tighina

Agreement of August 30, 1941, between the Romanian General Staff and the German *Oberkommando*. In those camps the Jews were to be held and assigned to forced labor, pending the conclusion of the military operations, following which they were to be shipped to the East.[185]

Concerning the part of the Romanians in the persecution of the Jews, Miss Arendt has this to say: "Deportation Romanian style consisted in herding five thousand people into freight cars and letting them die there of suffocation while the train traveled through the countryside without plan or aim for days on end; a favorite follow-up to these killing operations was to expose the corpses in Jewish butcher shops" (p. 173). In these statements Miss Arendt confuses two different events: Freight cars in which "Jews died of suffocation" were an element of the Jassy pogrom; the cars were used to transport the victims to the Romanian concentration camp (itself a transit camp in the process of deportation to the German-held East) in Calaraşi harbor, on the Danube.[186] (The German role in the Jassy pogrom has been discussed previously.) The worst pogrom, however, took place in Bucharest in January 1941, and it was then that the corpses were exposed in the Jewish slaughterhouses.[187] Miss Arendt's generalization of these two tragic instances has no foundation in fact.

About Antonescu, Miss Arendt says that he was "always a step ahead of German developments. He had been the first to deprive all Jews of nationality, and he had started large-scale massacres openly and unashamedly at a time when the Nazis were still busy trying out their first experiments" (p. 174).[188] The "first experiments" of the Nazis were made in Poland in 1939-1940; the large-scale massacres in Romania began in 1940 and reached a crescendo following Romania's entry into the war in 1941. These massacres were carried out by the German *Einsatzgruppen*—assisted by the Romanian military, who, according to the German report, "were satisfied with looting everything [so that] no pogrom could be achieved."[189] In general, the Germans were not satisfied with the degree of thoroughness with which the Romanians carried out their massacres,[190] but Miss Arendt does not state this. And when she discusses the willingness of the Romanians to allow emigration for a price, she does not mention that the Germans opposed this action as an undesirable partial solution of the "Jewish question."[191]

There is not a word in Miss Arendt's book about German influences on the political situation in Romania. The first openly anti-Semitic government of Romania (1937-1938), which lasted only six weeks, came into existence as a result of the efforts of the Foreign Policy Office (*Aussenpolitisches Amt*) of the German Nazi Party.[192] In October 1940, Romania—a German satellite—was occupied by German troops.[193] The anti-Jewish policies of Romania were henceforth determined by the Instructions for the Treatment of the Jewish Question (*Richtlinien für die Behandlung der Judenfrage*), personally handed over by Hitler to Antonescu[194] before the German-Romanian war against the Soviet Union.

There is no basis for Miss Arendt's statement (p. 175) that Gustav Richter, Eichmann's adviser on Jewish affairs in the Bucharest German Mission (contrary to her statement on page 11, he was never arrested) "had never had a chance to get into the act." He was sent to Bucharest as early as April 1, 1941, not in October 1941, as stated in IV, 99 (in her book, the beginning of his mission is given no date). Her postdating of his arrival to October has the effect of minimizing German influence in Romania's *Judenpolitik*. During this half year (April through October 1941), in which Adolf Eichmann according to Miss Arendt had not yet started personally to direct the anti-Jewish operation in Romania, the following events took place: "actions" by the *Einsatzgruppen*, the Jassy pogrom, and the deportation of the Jews from Bessarabia and Bucovina. Richter's mission was to bring Romanian anti-Jewish legislation "up" to the level of German legislation. He was ordered to remain in Romania until the final solution of the "Jewish question" had been achieved, which he did.[195] It was he who dealt with the deportation of Romanian Jews, acting without the knowledge of the German Minister in Romania, Killinger,[196] who—contrary to Miss Arendt's statement (p. 173) that "on this matter, however, they were all [including Killinger] in agreement"—complained about the "action," saying that he knew all too well "the methods of the gentlemen of the SS."[197] Richter acted under instructions from Eichmann, who himself admitted during the cross-examination that Killinger "could not know what was going on in Berlin."[198]

Miss Arendt also gives incorrect information on the citizenship status of Jews in Romania before and during the Nazi period. On page 172 she says that "in 1878, the great powers had tried to intervene, through the Treaty of Berlin, and to get the Rumanian

Government to recognize its Jewish inhabitants as Rumanian nationals—though they would have remained second-class citizens." This is apparently a reference to Article 44 of the Berlin Treaty of 1878, which reads as follows:

The difference of religious creeds and confessions shall not be alleged against any person as a ground for exclusion or incapacity in matters relating to the enjoyment of civil and political rights, admission to public employments, functions and honours, or the exercise of the various professions and industries in any locality whatsoever.

The freedom and outward exercise of all forms of worship are issued to all persons belonging to Romania as well as to the foreigners, and no hindrance shall be offered either to the hierarchical organization of the different communions, or to their relations with their spiritual chiefs.[199]

This is not an attempt to intervene, as Miss Arendt would have it, but an international treaty creating rights and duties for States. Nor is there anything in Article 44 that can be considered as sanctioning the continuation of Jewish status on the level of "second-class citizens." On the contrary, Article 44 is explicitly against religious discrimination of all kinds, and of all gradations.

The citizenship status of Romanian Jews is reported by Miss Arendt as follows: ". . . at the end of the First World War all Rumanian Jews—with the exception of a few hundred Sephardic families and some Jews of German origin—were still resident aliens" (p. 172). The fact is that there were almost no Jews of German origin in Romania at that time. Miss Arendt may have confused the appellation "Ashkenazim" (which means, in substance, "of Occidental origin") with "Germans." The Ashkenazim in Romania were not of German origin, but hailed from Galicia and the Ukraine. Their emigration to Old Romania (also called Regat-Kingdom) had been going on for generations, and those born in the country were considered indigenous (pământeni) as distinguished from foreign-born Jews under consular jurisdiction. Furthermore, after the Berlin Congress, 885 Jews received, as a group, Romanian citizenship, for having taken part in the war against Turkey in 1877, and by Parliament's decision (in implementation of Article 7 of the Romanian Constitution)[200] 30 Jews per year received citizenship; this process continued until World War I.[201] There is no basis for Miss Arendt's claim that Sephardic families were privileged and possessed Romanian citizenship. The tendency to distinguish the *Sephardim* at the expense of the *Ashkenazim* has no basis in Romanian history, but was first emphasized by the anti-Semitic Romanian historian N. Iorga.[202]

Miss Arendt's account of how Romanian Jews were deprived of their citizenship is inaccurate. She writes: "This concession to world opinion [the signature by Romania of a treaty for the protection of minorities] was withdrawn in 1937 and 1938, when, trusting in the power of Hitler Germany, the Rumanians felt they could risk denouncing the minority treaties as an imposition upon their 'sovereignty,' and could deprive some two hundred and twenty-five thousand Jews, roughly a quarter of the total Jewish population, of their citizenship" (p. 172). The reference is apparently to the Citizenship Revision law[203] of Goga-Cuza's Government (it held office from December 29, 1937, to February 10, 1938). This decree was modeled after the German law of July 14, 1933, concerning the revocation of naturalizations (*Gesetz über den Widerruf von Einbürgerungen und die Aberkennung der deutschen Staatsangehörigkeit*).[204] The government that enacted the Revision law was promoted by Nazi Germany and the law itself was modeled after a German law. However, despite passage of the law, no group of Romanian Jews was deprived of citizenship, nor was the Minorities Treaty ever denounced. Miss Arendt continues on page 172: "Two years later, in August, 1940, some months prior to Rumania's entry into the war on the side of Hitler Germany, Marshal Ion Antonescu, head of the new Iron Guard dictatorship, declared all Rumanian Jews to be stateless, with the exception of the few hundred families who had been Rumanian citizens before the peace treaties. That same month, he also instituted anti-Jewish legislation that was the severest in Europe, Germany not excluded." In August 1940, Ion Gigurtu (in whose Cabinet were also Iron Guard men) was head of the government. The dictatorship of Antonescu started on September 6, 1940. Gigurtu had met with Hitler on July 26, 1940, and had then told Hitler that solution of the "Jewish question" in Romania would come about after the *Führer* had seen to the solution of this "question" in Europe as a whole.[205] Subsequently, on August 8, 1940, Gigurtu's government adopted two anti-Jewish decree-laws, neither of which dealt with the Romanian citizenship of the Jews.[206] In the explanatory note to the second law, explicit reference is made to the racial theories of the Third Reich, and the Nuremberg Laws are mentioned as a model.[207] More anti-Jewish legislation was passed during the months of August, October, and November. On August 14, 1940, Jewish functionaries were dismissed from their jobs;[208] on August 30, 1940, a list of debarred Jewish lawyers was published;[209] on October 4, 1940, expropriation of Jewish landowners took place;[210] and so on. The harshest law was the expropriation of the property of all Jewish houseowners in towns; this appeared on March 27, 1941,[211] the very day Rosenberg's *Institut zur Erforschung der Judenfrage* in Frankfurt am Main was inaugurated. The Vice-Prime Minister, Mihai Antonescu, declared on the occasion that this law was a token of esteem for A. Rosenberg.[212] German influence thus played a key role throughout. The Germans however were still not satisfied: Luther reported that *Judenberater* Gustav Richter's mission was to obtain anti-Jewish laws equal to the German ones.[213] Killinger cabled on September 1, 1941, that the Romanian Government had agreed to publish the laws that Richter proposed.[214]

Concerning the postwar measures taken in Romania against war criminals, Miss Arendt claims that "the Rumanian murderers were *all* duly executed" (p. 175). In fact, there was one trial of twenty-four major war criminals ("major traitors"), including Ion Antonescu (Chief of State), Mihai Antonescu (Prime Minister and Foreign Minister), Gheorghe Alexianu (Governor of Transnistria), Constantin Pantazi (Minister of War), Constantin Vasiliu (Minister of Interior), and Radu Lecca (Director-General for Jewish Questions).[215] Only the two Antonescus, Pantazi, and Vasiliu were executed.[216] In addition to the major war criminals, there were apparently a total of 287 persons of Romanian nationality listed by the postwar government as war criminals. There is almost no information available on the fate of these people.[217]

HUNGARY

Miss Arendt devotes about fourteen pages in two sections (pp. 123-128, 176-184) to the Jewish Catastrophe in Hungary and to Eichmann's part in it. Some aspects of her account have been discussed in other chapters: in Chapter 1, Eichmann's attitude toward Hitler's agreement to allow emigration of some 40,000 Jews, the Kistarcsa case, and his part in the deportations and in the *Fussmarsch*; in Chapter 4, the Jewish Council in Budapest. The present chapter takes up Miss Arendt's overall approach to events in Hungary.

Miss Arendt writes: "The safety . . . [of the] Jews newly acquired by Hungary was due to the Germans' reluctance to start a separate action for a limited number" (p. 124). This statement calls for the following comments: (1) It was a concrete person, Eichmann, who was reluctant "to start a separate action for a limited number" and not some unidentified, abstract entity (Germans). (2) Eichmann's letter to Klingenfuss,[218] on which Miss Arendt may have relied, deals with refugees from Poland and Slovakia only, and not with the "three hundred thousand Jews" in the annexed territories (Southern Slovakia, part of Subcarpathian Russia, Northern Transylvania, and Bacska) whom Miss Arendt includes. (3) Two months after Eichmann wrote the Klingenfuss letter, Himmler referred to the solution of the "Jewish question" in Hungary in a letter to Ribbentrop of November 30, 1942, and, apparently on the advice of Eichmann, was already willing and eager to "clear" Hungary of Jews, and to send Wisliceny to that country for this purpose.[219]

Eichmann's mission in Hungary is characterized by Miss Arendt (pp. 124-125) as a "gliding down" in his career. On the contrary, it was the crowning act of an infamous career. Prior to the Hungarian Special Action (*Sonderaktion*), Eichmann had supervised the operations from afar, mostly from behind his desk in Berlin, although he had been involved at first hand during his frequent visits to the areas of his jurisdiction, and during the "forced emigrations" in Austria and the Protectorate. In Hungary, Eichmann had the first opportunity to direct at close quarters all the stages in the smooth operation of a well-tested death machine, a *Blitz* operation against the one Axis-controlled but still relatively intact Jewish community destined for deportation and extermination.

The job of carrying out the Final Solution in Hungary was very important to Hitler. The idea of having in the midst of his empire an island of Jews was something he could not accept. Hungary's "soft" treatment of the Jews was a constant source of friction between him and the Horthy regime.[220] In early 1944, things were ripe for settling this affair once and for all. Horthy was "invited" to Klessheim on March 17, where the raging *Führer* told him of the imminent occupation of Hungary by German troops. Horthy protested, but was told that it was too late. Hitler gave as one of his chief reasons for the occupation the fact that Hungary was sheltering the Jews instead of following German demands for a total solution. The Regent arrived home on March 19, when the German occupation of Hungary was almost complete.[221]

The destruction of Hungarian Jewry had to be done with speed and expertise, because time was running out on Nazi Germany. Eichmann was selected by Himmler personally to complete this giant task.[222] As for Eichmann himself, he felt the weight of this enormous "mission." Already, about March 10, he had met with other Gestapo officers at Mauthausen, to prepare a detailed plan of action in Hungary.[223] He arrived in Hungary on March 19. He wasted not one minute. Even before his arrival his two chief aides, Wisliceny and Krumey, went to the headquarters of the Jewish community in Budapest, commanding the Jewish leadership to convene the next morning.[224] Shortly thereafter he proceeded to order the establishment of the *Judenrat* and to promote anti-Jewish legislation. The Jewish leaders were so shocked and overwhelmed by his methods that they went for protection to the Hungarian Ministry of Religions (in charge until then of matters concerning religious minorities), which in turn—at a loss for an answer—sent them to the Prime Minister's Office, where they were told that they must obey the orders of the Germans—that is, of Eichmann.[225] Eichmann was thus recognized even by top Hungarian authorities as the unchallenged manager of the Jewish destruction, with Hungarian Lieutenant Colonel László Ferenczy serving as liaison officer with him.

Miss Arendt errs when she states that Rolf Günther, Eichmann's deputy in Berlin, also came to Budapest as a member of the *Sondereinsatzkommando* (p. 178). He stayed in Berlin, where he took charge of the IVB4 office in Eichmann's absence.[226] Just as inaccurate is Miss Arendt's information concerning other assistants of Eichmann (pp. 177-178). She says that Eichmann "called . . . Brunner from . . . Greece, . . . Dannecker from Paris and Bulgaria, Siegfried Seidl from . . . Theresienstadt and, from Vienna, Hermann Krumey." In fact, Brunner was at that time not in Greece (where Burger was in charge) but in Paris;[227] Dannecker left Paris in August, 1942, and had been in Italy since October 1943;[228] Seidl had been Commander of Bergen-Belsen since June or July 1943, and came to Hungary from there;[229] and there is no record of Krumey's being posted in Vienna prior to the Hungarian action.

While it is true that the Hungarian Lieutenant-Colonel Ferenczy "was directly in charge of deportations" (p. 181), a study of the "various materials which the trial authorities handed to the press" (p. 259) reveals that Eichmann's associates actually controlled every facet of this operation.[230] Eichmann was convinced that during the first stage of the deportations, when the overwhelming majority of the Jews had no idea that the concentrations were indeed going to lead to deportations, it was best for him to function in the background.[231] He wanted to keep the Nazi uniform out of the sight of Jewish eyes at least until the ghettoization was completed. Once the Jews were concentrated and subsequently loaded in freight cars, Hungarian gendarmes accompanied the train till Košice (Kassa), where SS men took over and ensured the surrender of the victims into the hands of their executioners in Auschwitz.[232]

Miss Arendt's statement that "Hungary was the only Axis country to send Jewish troops—a hundred and thirty thousand of them, in auxiliary service but in Hungarian uniform—to the Eastern front" (p. 177), not only is false but is an insult to the memory of the victims, the thousands of labor battalion draftees who suffered a fate often worse than that of prisoners in the concentration camps in Germany. The literature on their fate is abundant.[233] The total number of Jews mobilized, beginning in 1939, for labor service may even have exceeded the figure of 130,000, but only part of these men were sent to the "East"—that is, to the Ukrainian front. In February 1942 there were 14,000 Jewish laborers in the Ukraine. The most was 50,000 in January 1943.[234] The tragic truth is that some of these "Jewish troops" were between 40 and 60 years of age, others were rejects from previous drafts, unfit for service because of lameness, semiblindness, mental disturbance, or heart trouble. Their "uniforms" consisted of their civilian rags, a yellow armband, and a military cap. Often barefooted, they dug trenches and picked up mines with their bare hands. They were beaten, robbed of their food rations, and murdered by their non-Jewish officers and guards (the so-called *Keret*), who were instructed to make sure that their charges did not return alive from the Ukraine. Death from freezing became an everyday matter and was used by the *Keret* as a means of execution. (Many of these murderers were sentenced and hanged after the war; hundreds received severe prison terms.[235]) The Jewish community of Hungary collected clothing and footwear and sent it to the slave laborers, but most of it was stolen on the way. Small wonder that of the nearly 50,000 slave laborers sent to the Ukrainian front only some 6,000 to 7,000 returned alive.[236] The Hungarian Minister of Defense,

Vilmos Nagy, sympathetic to the plight of these Jews, went to the front personally on October 16, 1942, to investigate the situation and returned with the strong feeling that something had to be done immediately. He admitted the terrible truth before Parliament and attempted to improve the lot of the Jewish "troops." His orders of December 19, 1942, were, however, mostly sabotaged by the local Hungarian commanders on the fronts, and soon Nagy was relieved of his duties.[237]

There are many other errors in Miss Arendt's account,[238] of which the following will serve as examples. The statement that the "few 'able-bodied men' " who were selected for labor upon their arrival in Auschwitz worked in Krupp's fuse factory at Auschwitz (p. 182) is incorrect. The record shows that the Hungarian Jews who were selected for labor at Auschwitz were dispersed to no less than 386 different camps and factories, including the Krupp factory.[239] The statement (p. 180) that "the Zionist movement had always been particularly strong in Hungary" is not true. Hungary had been the weakest area in the European Zionist movement. For years the organization had to fight for legalization, its membership was scanty, and its representation in the Zionist congresses negligible.[240] The statement that the "so-called Arrow Cross men" followed the example of Italy "by passing their first anti-Jewish legislation" (p. 177) is inaccurate. In the first place, the extreme Fascist Arrow Cross Party had already been outlawed when the debates on the anti-Jewish law took place in the Hungarian Parliament. Arrow Cross sympathizers remaining in Parliament were few, and the leader of the movement, Ferenc Szálasi, was in jail. Secondly, the anti-Jewish law reflects the interaction of indigenous anti-Semitism and German pressure and was modeled after German as well as Italian legislation.[241] Finally, the statement that "forty-five members of the Weiss family emigrated to Portugal" (p. 127) is not true. Using false passports supplied by the Nazis (after they had taken over the industrial empire of the family), some of the members entered Portugal via Spain; others went to Switzerland via Stuttgart; still others remained in Hungary as hostages.[242]

SLOVAKIA

In Miss Arendt's section on Slovakia (pp. 184-187), the general political background is misrepresented, Jewish resistance activities are distorted, and chronology and statistics are muddled.

Miss Arendt states that Slovakia "was primitive, backward, and deeply Catholic" (p. 184) but does not reveal the sources for her judgment. Nor does she seem aware that Slovakia, during its association with the Republic of Czechoslovakia, made considerable progress in various fields.[243] She is confused about the structure of the Slovak Fascist party, identifying the Fascist movement with the Hlinka Guard (p. 184). The Slovak Fascist movement, however, was organized in the Slovak People's Party; the Hlinka Guard was a semimilitary uniformed party corps, modeled on the SS and the SA.[244] She states that "there was only one modern anti-Semite in the Slovak government, and that was . . . Sano Mach . . . All the others were Christians . . ." (p. 184; see also p. 76). If by "modern" anti-Semitism she understands racial, as distinct from religious, anti-Semitism (she nowhere explains her usage), then there was far more than "one modern anti-Semite." To mention only two from the gallery of the main culprits: Prime Minister Vojtech Tuka, the ideologist of "Slovak National Socialism," who led the negotiations on the deportation of Jews, signed an agreement with the Germans, and even in 1943, when some of the Ministers sought to block renewal of the deportations, appealed for German cooperation to overcome the opposition of his Cabinet;[245] and Dr. Anton Vašek, Mach's subordinate and chief of Department No. 14 for Jewish Affairs in the Ministry of Interior, who was nicknamed (to his delight) "king of the Jews" (židovský král) and was sentenced to death by the Bratislava People's Tribunal.[246] Mach, who was sentenced to 30 years in prison, was the only one who publicly repented for his part in the Jewish tragedy.[247]

Miss Arendt is no more accurate in regard to Monsignor Josef Tiso (President of Slovakia). She says (p. 186) that "in June, 1944, Veesenmayer, now Reich plenipotentiary in Hungary, appeared again, and demanded that the remaining Jews in the country be included in the Hungarian operation. Tiso refused again." There is no evidence for Miss Arendt's report of a second visit by Veesenmayer to Bratislava, in June 1944, or for her report of Tiso's refusal to deport the remaining Jews.

Miss Arendt writes that Wisliceny "also proposed the so-called Europe Plan" (p. 186). The idea of the Plan Europa, a plan to ransom Jews from the Germans, was conceived by Rabbi Michael Beer (Dov) Weissmandel, a member of the active core of the Jewish underground movement known as the "Working Group."

The Working Group came into existence with the aim of rescuing those Jews who were still left. Among its first acts was the dissemination abroad and among the local Slovakian leaders and clergy of the reports of escapees from Majdanek, Bełżec, and Sobibór, in order to destroy the "resettlement" legend and gain support in the struggle to rescue the remaining Jews.[248] It was headed by the renowned Zionist leader, Gizi Fleischmann, though it was not a Zionist organization, but rather an all-inclusive underground organization. Most of its members were at the same time members of the Jewish Council (Ústredňa Židov). Its leaders included two rabbis—Weissmandel, Orthodox and non-Zionist, and Armin Frieder, Progressive and Zionist—and two assimilated Jews, Dr. Tibor Kovács and Engineer Andrej Steiner, both non-Zionists. It was the Working Group that proposed the Plan Europa and suggested that Wisliceny act as its mediator.[249]

The role of the Catholic Church in the struggle against the Final Solution in Slovakia is described the wrong way around by Miss Arendt: "But it was just at this moment that the Vatican informed the Catholic clergy of the true meaning of the word 'resettlement'" (p. 186). What happened was just the reverse: The clergy and the Nuncio of Bratislava supplied the information to the Vatican.[250]

Miss Arendt's chronology of the Jewish Catastrophe in Slovakia is wrong. She states that except for the passage of "some anti-Jewish legislation . . . nothing much happened" to Slovakian Jews "until March, 1942, when Eichmann appeared in Bratislava . . ." (p. 185). As a matter of fact, quite a lot happened, partly admitted by Miss Arendt on the same page. With the assistance of Wisliceny, who arrived in Slovakia in September 1940 (together with his staff) as "adviser for Jewish affairs,"[251] the Aryanization of Jewish property was put into effect during the period in question, and transfer of the larger Jewish enterprises to non-Jews and mobilization of Jews for forced labor were carried out.[252] Exactly at that period, the Jewish Code was passed, on September 9, 1941, by the Slovak Parliament. It contained 270 paragraphs and was in some respects even more severe than the Nuremberg Laws. It served to prepare the ground for the subsequent deportation.[253] Furthermore, Eichmann did not appear in Bratislava in March 1942. His visit was announced on March 13, 1942,[254] but he arrived in the last week of May 1942.[255]

Miss Arendt asserts (p. 187) that "there were perhaps twenty thousand Jews left who had survived the catastrophe." The number of Jews in Slovakia in 1944, according to German sources (Veesenmayer's report of December 22, 1943), was 16,000 to 18,000 Jews and about 10,000 baptized Jews.[256] Hanns Ludin (the German Minister in Slovakia) reported that in the summer of 1944 there were 15,000 officially registered Jews and about 2,000 in hiding.[257] From Jewish sources we learn that in August 1944 (before the outbreak of the uprising) there were about 22,000 Jews, 4,000 of them in hiding. After the suppression of the Slovak national uprising, about 12,000 Jews were deported. There were no more than 3,000 to 5,000 Jews left in Slovakia when the Red Army arrived there.[258]

Contrary to Miss Arendt's statement (p. 130), Wisliceny was not prosecuted and executed in Prague, but stood trial before the People's Tribunal in Bratislava, was sentenced to death by hanging on May 4, 1948, and was executed there.[259]

FINLAND

On page 153 of her book Miss Arendt speculates as to the reason why "the Nazis never ['hardly ever" in the paperback edition, p. 170] even approached [Finland] on the Jewish question." The political archives of the German Foreign Office, however, include a dossier labeled "Jews in Finland" containing evidence of several "approaches" by the Nazis to the Finns.[260]

Dependent as she had become on Germany, and dominated by German forces, Finland refused to give up her 2,000 Jews "for resettlement." "We are an honest people," declared Witting, the Finnish Foreign Minister. "We would much rather die with the Jews than give them up." Himmler was furious. "The Finns will have to choose between hunger and delivering up their Jews," he said, before proceeding to Helsinki for talks. Still, he did not get the Jews of Finland after all.[261]

GERMANY

On the Germany of 1935, Miss Arendt makes generalizations that do not conform with reality. Thus she writes (p. 33) that already in 1935 "Hitler was admired everywhere [I, 88: "almost everywhere"] as a great national statesman." This is hardly true.

Neither Roosevelt's United States nor Stalin's Soviet Union felt or expressed such admiration, to name only two exceptions. The situation was somewhat different in England, but here Miss Arendt's chronology is inexact. While it is true that eminent politicians and intellectuals from England had visited Hitler from 1933 on, the first signs of admiration appeared late in 1936 from David Lloyd George in his famous article in the *Daily Express* of September 17, 1936. There he tried to convince England that "the Germans have definitely made up their minds never to quarrel with us again." Somewhat earlier he had pleaded with England to take seriously Hitler's offer (made in the *Reichstag*, March 7, 1936, the day of the occupation of the Rhineland) of a twenty-five-year nonaggression treaty.[262] Approximately at the same time, Arnold Toynbee, after an interview with Hitler, declared himself "convinced of his sincerity in desiring peace in Europe and close friendship with England."[263]

Miss Arendt writes (p. 33) that in 1935 unemployment in Germany "had been liquidated." It is true that unemployment was reduced from approximately five to two and a half million, but this can hardly be termed liquidation. Moreover, Miss Arendt ignores the slowdown in the rate of reduction of unemployment: On December 31, 1935, German unemployment stood at 2.51 millions, slightly less than the 2.6 millions of the preceding year.[264]

In 1935, too, according to Miss Arendt, Germany "prepared neither quietly nor secretly the occupation of the demilitarized zone of the Rhineland" (p. 33). The question of the Rhineland occupation in 1936 was intensively investigated by the International Military Tribunal. The results of the investigation showed conclusively that in 1935 preparations for the occupation of the Rhineland were kept a guarded secret.[265]

Miss Arendt believes that only with the outbreak of the war did the Nazi State become "openly totalitarian and openly criminal" (p. 63). The Nazi State became "openly totalitarian" by virtue of some of its earliest legislation. The Ordinance for the Protection of People and State of February 28, 1933, the so-called *Gleichschaltungsgesetze* of March 3, 1933 and of April 7, 1933, the ban on parties (spring and summer 1933), and the take-over of trade unions (May 1933) created an elaborate system of totalitarian government long before the outbreak of the war.[266] On the other hand, the Nazi State was never "openly criminal," not even during the war. It always tried to cast a veil of secrecy over its criminal activities, and were it not for the mass of material that fell into the hands of the Allies, and the large number of victims who either were discovered after the war to be missing or survived to bear witness, most of the horrors perpetrated by the Nazi regime never would have been revealed.

Miss Arendt has no notion of the function of legislation under the Nazi regime. She accepts Eichmann's version that "the war against Russia . . . marked . . . 'the end of an era in which there existed laws, ordinances, decrees for the treatment of individual Jews' " (p. 73). (She writes, however, on page 142, that even as late as March 1942 "the Nazis took their own legislation quite seriously.") In the first place, laws were not the only tools for attaining the regime's will. Often, direct action was employed instead. In the Government-General, no anti-Jewish laws were passed after 1942. In the occupied territories of the Soviet Union, hardly any anti-Jewish legislation was passed except for the Provisional Instructions (*Richtlinien*) concerning the Jews in Ostland, issued on August 13, 1941, by Hinrich Lohse,[267] which constituted a sort of codification of extant Nazi legislation in areas under Nazi domination; and two ordinances in the Ukraine prohibiting ritual slaughter and introducing forced labor for the Jewish population.[268] Even the Lohse instructions included the reservation that their validity was subject to future measures of the Final Solution. Second, where laws were passed, many of them were not published in the official gazettes until after their contents were communicated to those charged with their implementation by telephone or other means.[269] In some cases, laws concerning certain types of direct action were passed when more drastic methods of action were already in operation.[270] It must be added that the Nazis did not recognize the basic principle of the nonretroactivity of law. They often promulgated laws which were ostensibly designed to regulate certain acts, but were in reality *post factum* "legislation" governing acts already accomplished.[271] Finally, most of the actions of the Final Solution (deportations and mass murder) were ordered not in published laws but in top-secret oral or written orders and were considered "secret Reich business" (*geheime Reichssache*).

With reference to "the Führer's words" (*Führerworte*) Miss Arendt declares (p. 132) that "whole libraries of very 'learned' juridical comment have been written, all demonstrating that the Führer's *words* [Miss Arendt's italics], his oral pronouncements, were the basic law of the land." From these nonexistent "libraries," Miss Arendt summons Theodor Maunz (p. 21), whom she quotes as having said that "the command of the Führer . . . is the absolute center of the present legal order." This quotation is neither accurate nor pertinent to the argument. Maunz wrote: "The mandate of the Führer . . . is . . . in itself the core of the legal system in force. . . ." (*Der Auftrag des Führers . . . ist schlechthin das Kernstück des geltenden Rechtssystems*).[272] The "mandate" to which Maunz refers is not some abstraction, but is, in his own words, "the Führer's general mandate to the police to be the 'Corps for the Protection of the State'—a mandate called the 'institutional authorization'" (*Den allgemeinen Auftrag des Führers an die Polizei, Staatsschutz- korps zu sein, nennt man die "institutionelle Ermächtigung der Polizei"*).[273] The whole discussion in Maunz is a highly technical examination of the sources of police law in the Third Reich (as *Führerstaat*), but does not deal with *Führerworte*.

In fact, the only *Führerworte* that had immediate practical consequences were the secret *Führer* orders (*Führerbefehle*), and these were taboo in juridical literature. In Nazi legal works there is no trace of any discussion of the secret *Führerbefehle*, one of which, the *Kommissarbefehl*, has already been discussed.[274] The two other drastic *Befehle* were those of September 16, 1941, on the suppression of revolts in occupied territories (authorizing the shooting of hostages at the ratio of 30 to 100 "communists" for each German killed)[275] and Hitler's *Kommandobefehl* of October 18, 1942 (authorizing the slaughter of soldiers engaged in sabotage).[276] The legal implications of Hitler's *written* orders were discussed at length in the Subsequent Trials.[277] The only order for which no written trace has been found is the order for the Final Solution.[278] (The Euthanasia Order of September 1, 1939, was also kept secret but was formulated in writing.[279])

Not only is there no "juridical comment" on the secret *Führer* orders, but it was widely held (although far from generally accepted in doctrine and practice) that promulgation is the very essence of the binding force of law. Thus Werner Weber, in his 1942 monograph *Die Verkündung von Rechtsvorschriften* (The Promulgation of Legal Provisions), stated that laws obtained their force always and necessarily through promulgation. He specifically extended the application of this principle to the *Führer* orders (*Führererlasse*).[280] As late as 1944 another legal expert, Ernst Rudolf Huber,[281] argued that "promulgation" is "the formal minimum without which we cannot do" (*das Minimum von Form, auf das nicht verzichtet werden kann*). Consequently, even in Nazi legal theory and practice, the secret *Führerbefehl* on the extermination of the Jews constitutes nothing but an illegal secret promise of the *Führer* of immunity from prosecution for violation of Sections 211 and 212 of the Criminal Code (punishment of murder and manslaughter) insofar as the acts were in implementation of the Final Solution.[282]

On the Jewish situation in the prewar Nazi period, Miss Arendt writes that the regime in 1935 "had not yet shifted entirely to persecution of the Jews qua Jews" (p. 34). Were the murders and physical violence directed against Jewish judges and attorneys in March 1933 not directed against Jews qua Jews?[283] Was the boycott of April 1, 1933, anything but an act of persecution of Jews qua Jews? And the removal of Jews from the civil service (which included the teaching profession, in institutions of learning on all levels), an action she herself mentions on page 34, was that, too, not directed against Jews as Jews?[284]

Miss Arendt adds that "private business and the legal and medical professions were not touched until 1938" by Nazi restrictive measures (p. 34; redrafted in the paperback edition, p. 38, to read: "private business remained almost untouched until 1938, and even the legal and medical professions were only gradually abolished"). She contends that there were only individual actions putting Jews under pressure to sell their businesses and real estate at low prices, and that these actions usually occurred only in small towns before the *Kristallnacht*, in November 1938. But by April 1934, about 4,000 Jewish lawyers had been disbarred; 3,000 physicians, 2,000 civil servants, and 2,000 actors and musicians had lost their jobs; and, in Prussia alone, 1,199 notaries had lost their licenses. Already in 1933, physicians and dentists were excluded from the public sick funds (*Krankenkassen*); under pressure from the Nazi Party, the spoliation of Jewish industry and commerce was in full swing, not to speak of the total exclusion of Jews from German cultural activities.[285] Miss Arendt's information concerning individual actions forcing Jews to sell business and land is at variance with the extensive Aryanization that took place all over Germany. On April 26, 1938, all Jews were ordered to register their property in excess of 5,000 reichsmark. The same month, lists of well-to-do Jews were drawn up in the police precincts and revenue offices. On June 9 the Munich synagogue was destroyed. On June 14 Jewish businesses had to be marked *Jüdisches Geschäft*. On June 15 the so-called "June Action" took place: 1,500 Jews were arrested and taken to concentration camps. On July 25 all Jewish physicians lost their licenses. On August 17 all Jews whose first names were not considered to be sufficiently Jewish were to assume the middle name of "Israel" (for men) or "Sara" (for women). The Nuremberg synagogue was destroyed on August 10. On October 5 passports were withdrawn from Jews. Those that were reissued were marked with a conspicuous "J." On October 28, 15,000 to 17,000 Polish Jews, longtime residents of Germany, were expelled.[286] These were the most important events that happened in 1938 before the *Kristallnacht*. The list does not include what happened during the wave of terror in Austria immediately following the *Anschluss* in March 1938.[287]

Miss Arendt declares that "Emigration of Jews in these years proceeded in a not unduly accelerated and generally orderly fashion" (p. 34). Actually, in this period, 143,000 Jews, having lost their vocations and at least part of their property, left Germany[288]— fully one quarter of the total Jewish population. This is hardly an exodus "not unduly accelerated."

Concerning negotiations between the Germans and Jews, Miss Arendt says: "[The Jews'] conviction of the eternal and ubiquitous nature of anti-Semitism [has] been the most potent ideological factor in the Zionist movement since the Dreyfus Affair; it was also the cause of the otherwise inexplicable readiness of the German Jewish community to negotiate with the Nazi authorities," and "produced their dangerous inability to distinguish between friend and foe" (p. 8). With whom should German Jews have negotiated? Should they never have made any effort at all? And these "friends" whom they could not distinguish from foe, who were they?

Miss Arendt writes of the "in no way Nazi appointed" *Reichsvertretung* which she says was "the national association of all communities and organizations . . . founded . . . on the initiative of the Berlin community" (p. 35). The initiative for the establishment of the *Reichsvertretung* came not from Berlin (the initiators and their friends had to fight the opposition of the Berlin Jewish community) but from Essen—namely, from Dr. Georg Hirschland, the president of the Jewish community there and Dr. Hugo Hahn, the rabbi. They did, however, have the cooperation of Ernst Herzfeld of Berlin, one of the leaders of the Central Association of German Jews.[289] Elsewhere (p. 54) she says that "it was in those years a fact of everyday life that only Zionists had any chance of negotiating with the German authorities." She produces no proof for this statement, except for her remark that the chief adversary of the Zionists among Jewish organizations, the "Central Association of German Citizens of Jewish Faith," was "by definition an organization 'hostile to the state'" and as such not qualified to negotiate with the Germans (p. 54). Actually, the *Reichsvertretung* negotiated regularly with the German government, and its Presidium (*Praesidialausschuss*) consisted originally of three members—two non-Zionists and one Zionist. The Zionist was Siegfried Moses; the non-Zionists were Leo Baeck and Otto Hirsch, both members of the Central Association that Miss Arendt claims was inactive in this respect. If Miss Arendt has evidence that Moses, because of his Zionism, was more successful in these negotiations than the others, she fails to present it. Nor was there any Zionist domination in the *Reichsvereinigung* (successor to the *Reichsvertretung*), where Leo Baeck and Otto Hirsch continued their activities for the good of the community while subject directly to the Gestapo.[290] Miss Arendt writes: "the Zionists could, for a time, at least, engage in a certain amount of non-criminal cooperation with the Nazi authorities" (p. 54). Does she intend to imply that there was "criminal cooperation" between Zionist and Nazi authorities? She submits no evidence.

Miss Arendt's treatment of the *Ha'avara* (Transfer) agreement, concluded primarily between Palestine Jewish institutions (Anglo-Palestine Bank) and the Nazi authorities, is hardly a fair one. She writes on page 55: "The result [of the agreement] was that in the thirties, when American Jewry took great pains to organize a boycott of German merchandise, Palestine . . . was swamped with all kinds of goods 'made in Germany.'" The *Ha'avara* agreement resulted not only in the presence of German goods in Palestine but also in the grant of permits allowing some 50,000 Jews to emigrate and settle in Palestine at a time when each certificate or visa meant rescue for a person or a family. Even the terms of the *Ha'avara* were not understood by Miss Arendt. She writes (p. 55) that the emigrant could "take all his money with him" (II, 41). The truth was that he could transfer only a portion of his wealth, in goods, and even this allowance was handicapped by the imposition of various emigration taxes.[291]

On the subject of world Jewish reactions to prewar German anti-Jewish policies, Miss Arendt writes: "International Jewish organizations therefore promptly tried to obtain for this newest minority the same rights and guarantees that minorities in Eastern and Southeastern Europe had been granted at Geneva" (p. 246). Such an attempt was never made, nor was the objective ever considered attainable. Jewish organizations did three things: (1) They pressed for the adoption of a resolution by the Assembly of the League of Nations confirming the principle of the protection of minorities and obliquely condemning Germany for her treatment of the Jews.[292] (2) They initiated the Bernheim case, whose successful conclusion suspended, for the period of the Polish-German Upper-Silesia Convention (expired July 15, 1937), the operation of the racial laws in that province.[293] (3) They pressed for action by the Assembly of the League of Nations in favor of "refugees from Germany, Jewish and others" and the appointment of a High Commissioner to protect these refugees and to look into possibilities for their emigration.[294]

Miss Arendt is no more accurate in many of her statements concerning wartime Germany than she is in her statements on prewar Nazi Germany. On page 141 she declares that a "shower of new anti-Jewish legislation descended upon the Reich's Jews only after Hitler's order for the Final Solution had been officially handed down to those who were to implement it." Nothing of the sort happened. The "shower" started as early as spring of 1938 and was intensified at the beginning of the war.[295] Only two regulations of any significance were issued after the order for the Final Solution. One was the Eleventh Implementing Regulation to the Reich Citizenship law (published on November 25, 1941; this was not a "change in the nationality law," as Miss Arendt writes on p. 141), which decreed that Jews living outside Germany (including deportees) could not be considered German subjects (*Staatsangehörige*) and had forfeited *ipso facto* their property to the Reich.[296] The second was the Thirteenth Implementing Regulation to the Reich Citizenship law (published on July 1, 1943), which transferred jurisdiction over criminal offenses committed by Jews in the Reich from the courts to the police.[297] Miss Arendt's account of this second regulation is inaccurate. According to her, "the preparations [of a legal basis for the Final Solution] culminated in an agreement between Otto Thierack, the Minister of Justice, and Himmler whereby the former relinquished jurisdic-

tion over 'Poles, Russians, Jews, and Gypsies' in favor of the S.S."
(p. 141). In the first place, the Final Solution was at that time
already in full swing. Moreover, Miss Arendt's statement confuses
two separate actions:

1. The *physical transfer* to the *Reichsführer-SS*, for exploitation
as expendable manpower, of all Jews, as well as certain other
people, who had been convicted by a court and were serving a
term in a penal institution. This measure was "legalized" by the
Thierack-Himmler Agreement of September 18, 1942, which in
the words of Thierack's memorandum provides for the following:

Delivery of asocial elements (*asozialer Elemente*) serving out
penal sentences to the Reich Leader SS, in order to be worked to death
(*zur Vernichtung durch Arbeit*).

Persons under security detention: Jews, Gypsies, Russians, and
Ukrainians; Poles with more than 3-year sentences; and Czechs and
Germans with more than 8-year sentences, will be turned over without
exception, according to the decision of the Reich Minister of Justice.[298]

2. The *transfer of jurisdiction* from the courts to the police, of
Jews accused, or to be accused, of a crime. This far-reaching, and
far more ominous, transfer of jurisdiction was provided for only
about nine months later, in the regulation cited above, which states
in the first paragraph: "Punishable acts committed by Jews will be
punished by the police."[299]

Miss Arendt asserts that "the final rounding up of Jews in Berlin
was, as I have mentioned [where?], done entirely by Jewish police"
(p. 104). Again, she cites no evidence. We have it on the authority
of Norbert Wollheim, a former staff member of the *Reichsvertretung*, that no such police ever existed.[300] There were plenty of
local German police for these operations. On the other hand, there
were the so-called *Ordner*—Jews whose original function was to
assist Jews dislodged from their apartments.[301] During the deportations of November-December 1942 (known as the *Brunner-Aktion*)
they—elderly, reasonable, well-bred, and well-educated persons—
sometimes had to be rough with their panicky charges in order to
protect them from maltreatment by Brunner's men. They assisted
the deportees in collecting their movables, and occasionally accompanied them to the central collection point. They had no uniforms
and carried out no police functions, but they wore a red armband
which exempted them from deportation as long as they remained
Ordner. In due course they too were deported.[302]

Concluding Remarks

A balanced account of the Jewish Catastrophe ranges from its internal Jewish aspects to its relationships with worldwide events. The foregoing survey, presenting the results of research in vast documentation and literature, may help set straight the history of a tragic and difficult period of our times.

Notes on Chapters 1 to 5

The judgment delivered by the Jerusalem District Court in the Eichmann trial is referred to as "Judgment"; that delivered by the Israel Supreme Court in Eichmann's appeal is referred to as "Supreme Court Judgment." Since there are no official English versions, I have translated all extracts from the official Hebrew texts.

In general, extracts from sources—except for those written originally in English or published in official English translations—have been translated by me or under my supervision from the original languages in which they appeared.

The records of a particular trial session are referred to by the number of the session. Since the official records have not yet been published, it was necessary to use the unofficial transcripts of these sessions. The documentation of the trial is referred to by the official symbols *T* for documents submitted by the prosecution and *N* for those submitted by the defense. Special attention is called to document T/37, the 3,564-page record of the pretrial interrogation of Eichmann, and to the Sassen Papers (see note 52 of Chapter 3).

The documents of the International Military Tribunal (IMT) and of the Nuremberg Military Tribunals (NMT) are cited by their Nuremberg numbers. For those which have been published, the facts of publication are given. These sources are usually referred to as the *Blue Series,* the *Red Series,* and the *Green Series.* The *Blue Series* is the official record of the IMT, *Trial of the Major War Criminals Before the International Military Tribunal,* 42 volumes (Nuremberg, 1947-1949). The documents in this series are printed in their original languages—for the most part in German. The *Red Series* contains documents collected by the American and British prosecuting staffs in preparing their case for the IMT. The documents were published in English translation by the Office of United States Chief of Counsel for the Prosecution of Axis Criminality, *Nazi Conspiracy and Aggression,* 11 volumes (Washington, D.C.: Government Printing Office, 1946-1948). The *Green Series* is a selection from the record of the twelve Subsequent Trials before the NMT, *Trials of War Criminals Before the Nuremberg Military Tribunals Under Con-*

trol Council Law No. 10, 15 volumes (Washington, D.C.: Government Printing Office, 1949-1953). The documents in this series are all published in English translation.

Chapter 1

1. Judgment, Section 59, *passim.*

2. The Nisko episode and the Madagascar plan are described later in this chapter.

3. The basic journalistic vocabulary in a Yiddish newspaper contains far more than a "few dozen" words of Hebrew origin, not to mention words of Slavic origin. Even the elements of "old German dialect" are usually unintelligible to a modern German who has not been specially trained. For a scholarly account of the origins and present structure of the Yiddish language, see Max Weinreich, "History of the Yiddish Language: The Problems and Their Implications," *Proceedings of the American Philosophical Society* (New York), Vol. 103, No. 4, August 15, 1959, pp. 563-570. See also Uriel and Beatrice Weinreich, *Yiddish Language and Folklore. A Selective Bibliography for Research* (The Hague: Mouton & Co., 1959), 66 pp. (Janua Linguarum, Studia Memoriae Nicolai van Wijk Dedicata, No. X).

4. The "proof" offered for this statement is the fact that letters of his department to the Foreign Office were signed by Kaltenbrunner or Müller. But this is no proof at all. (See the discussion later in the chapter.)

5. T/37, p. 2339.

6. T/1113 (*Der Bericht des jüdischen Rettungskomitees aus Budapest, 1942-1945,* mimeogr.), p. 43. This document is usually referred to as the *Kasztner Report.* The printed version is *Der Kastner-Bericht über Eichmanns Menschenhandel in Ungarn* (Munich: Kindler, 1961), p. 104.

7. Eichmann was cross-examined in Session 98 on his use of this expression in the Sassen Papers.

8. Session 103. This statement was made by Eichmann in connection with the "blood for goods" episode (see note 15 of this chapter). According to his account, he participated in the negotiations merely because he wanted to help his friend, a commander of the 22nd SS Cavalry Division, obtain trucks. For these he was ready to offer in exchange one million Jews, although in his heart he felt "he would rather see every single 'enemy of the Reich' dead than alive."

9. Quoted from Eichmann's testimony in Session 90.

10. Joachim Schwelien, *Jargon der Gewalt* (Frankfurt am Main: Ner Tamid, 1961), p. 6.

11. The statement about Eichmann having been fed up with anonymity refers to the article in *Life* Magazine (Nov. 28, 1960, p. 21), where he is quoted as having said: "I have slowly tired of living as an anonymous wanderer between two worlds." The statement does not appear in the sections of the Sassen Papers accepted by the Jerusalem Court. See also *Der Stern* (Hamburg), No. 28, July 9, 1960, submitted in Court as T/46.

12. The characterization of Eichmann as being "incapable of telling right from wrong" is nowhere repeated or alluded to in the rest of Miss Arendt's book, and indeed would run counter to her entire thesis. In addition, it would imply that he was morally insane, which again contradicts her thesis and has never been advanced as a defense of Eichmann.

13. When questioned by Sassen on this subject (Sassen Papers, transcript of tape 47, p. 11), he denied that he had ever tried to get away from his job. Here is what was said:

Q. Since you found this task, physical extermination, so monstrous, didn't you try to get out of this job?

A. No, never.

14. For a man who was horror-stricken when he came in direct contact with the machinery of extermination—as he claimed he was—Eichmann had a remarkably hard time remembering his visits to Auschwitz. The first time he was asked, in the course of the pretrial interrogation, he admitted three such visits (T/37, p. 219); when the subject came up again in the same context (T/37, pp. 371-372), his answer was lost in a maze of explanatory phrases that were inconclusive. During cross-examination in court, he first acknowledged "four or perhaps five" trips to the camp (Session 93) and five days later (Session 99) "about five or six" visits. One cannot but infer from his attitude that the number of visits to Auschwitz that he was ready to acknowledge was in direct proportion to the amount of incriminating evidence with which he was confronted.

15. This refers to negotiations between Jewish communal leaders and Himmler's agents for the exchange of Jewish lives in return for goods required by the Germans, especially trucks. The court, having analyzed all the circumstances of the case, concluded (Judgment, Section 116): "We are of the opinion that this attempt [of Eichmann] to appear now before this Court as the initiator of the above transaction is nothing but a lie."

16. See note 149 of this chapter.

17. Judgment, Section 243.

18. Should read: "Sure, sure."

19. Testimonies of Pinhas Freudiger (Sessions 51 and 52) and Dr. Alexander Brody (Sessions 52 and 53).

20. T/691 (Nuremberg Document: Veesenmayer-216).

21. Raul Hilberg, *The Destruction of the European Jews* (Chicago: Quadrangle Books, 1961), 788 pp.

22. *Green Series*, V, p. 981. The fact that the WVHA was not directly responsible for the physical destruction of concentration camp inmates should not be interpreted to mean that it dealt humanely with them. Its attitude toward camp prisoners is revealed in a document—published in Reimund Schnabel's *Macht ohne Moral: Eine Dokumentation über die SS* (Frankfurt a. M.: Röderberg, 1957), p. 203—in which profits and expenses are listed (RM stands for reichsmark):

Estimated Profit

[From Exploitation of Inmates of Concentration Camps. Prepared by the SS (WVHA)]

Average daily income from hiring out [an inmate]	RM 6,..
less food	RM ..,6o
less amortization for clothes	RM ..,1o
Average life expectancy 9 mos. = 270 × RM 5.30 =	RM 1431,..

Income from an efficient (*rationelle*) utilization of the corpse:

(1) gold from the teeth	(3) valuables
(2) clothes	(4) money

less cost of burning [the corpse]   RM 2,..

Average net profit	RM 200,..
Total profit after 9 months	RM 1631,..

to which must be added income from utilization of the bones and the ashes

23. T/294.

24. T/37, pp. 3424 ff. and 3441 ff.

25. Judgment, Section 72.

26. *The Spectator* (London), April 21, 1961. The Attorney General of Frankfurt has opened a case against Martin Bormann (Js11/61) and a reward of 100,000 D.M. has been posted for information leading to Bormann's arrest.

27. *Newsweek*, Atlantic Edition, July 1, 1963.

28. Private communication of Robert M. W. Kempner to the author, dated Sept. 23, 1963.

29. Judgment, Section 137. Novak was tried in Vienna in 1964, and was found guilty of arranging the transportation of the Jews to the camps.

30. Judgment, Section 179.

31. *Ibid.*, Section 154 *in fine*.

32. T/37, p. 227. Also cited in Judgment, Section 143.

33. T/37, pp. 229-230. This section of the tape (from which T/37 was transcribed) was played back in Session 10.

34. Session 93.

35. T/37, pp. 210-212, played back in Session 10.

36. T/37, p. 215, played back in Session 10.

37. Judgment, Section 132. This discussion extends from Section 132 through Section 140, and is not concerned with the previously established facts regarding victims from the Western and Central European countries who were rounded up and deported to the East by Eichmann and his subordinates, to be killed there.

38. *Ibid.*, Section 137, *in fine.* See also Sections 132-134, dealing with Eichmann's activities in the annexed Polish territories.

39. T/296 (compare Nuremberg Document 347-EC, reproduced in *Blue Series*, XXXVI, pp. 331-355) and T/297 (Nuremberg Document NO-4882).

40. A stenographic record of General Lahousen's testimony before the IMT can be found in *Blue Series*, II, pp. 440-478 and III, pp. 1-31. References to the Jews appear in II, pp. 446-449, 478 and III, pp. 20-22. The conference of September 12, 1939, in which Hitler participated, is mentioned in II, pp. 446, 478 and III, pp. 7, 21. In the paperback edition (p. 216), Miss Arendt quotes Lahousen as having said before the IMT: "As early as September, 1939, Hitler had decided the murder of Polish Jews." This sentence does not appear in the stenographic record of Lahousen's testimony.

41. T/186: Letter dated Jan. 26, 1942; reproduced in Robert M. W. Kempner, *Eichmann und Komplizen* (Zurich, Stuttgart, Vienna: Europa Verlag, 1961), p. 150.

42. Judgment, Section 133. See also Section 163.

43. T/37, p. 3083. Miss Arendt is uninformed about the political geography of the Nazi conquests. On page 82 she writes of "the Western Regions of Poland that had been incorporated into the Reich, called the Warthegau," and on page 138 she refers to "the annexed Polish Western Regions . . . the so-called Warthegau" (see also page 188). In fact, *Reichsgau Wartheland* was only one of the Districts (*Gaue*) of Northern and Western Poland that were incorporated (*eingegliedert*) into the Reich. *Gau Danzig-Westpreussen* was another separate District; Katowice, Będzin, and Sosnowiec were incorporated into Silesia to constitute the special administrative unit *Ostoberschlesien*; and three other Polish areas were incorporated into *Ostpreussen.* See Arnold and Veronica Toynbee, eds., *Hitler's Europe* (London, New York, Toronto: Oxford University Press, 1954), p. 91.

44. Judgment, Section 137.

45. *Ibid.*, Section 139.

46. The *Einsatzgruppen* were among the most important instruments of the Final Solution. On p. 93 Miss Arendt writes that "the troops of the *Einsatzgruppen* had been drafted from the Armed S.S., a

military unit with hardly more crimes in its record than any ordinary unit of the German Army." But further on (p. 194) she asserts that the "troops [of the *Einsatzgruppen*] were either criminals or ordinary soldiers drafted for punitive duty."

47. T/37, p. 387.

48. Judgment, Sections 166-169. See also T/37, p. 2274.

49. Rudolf Hoess, *Commandant of Auschwitz* (Cleveland and New York: World Publishing Co., n.d.), p. 206. The book was submitted to the court as T/45. In the paperback edition (p. 86) Miss Arendt writes: "Concerning the doubtful reliability of Höss's testimony see also R. Pendorf, *Mörder und Ermorderte*, 1961." Pendorf's only comment on Höss's reliability as a witness appears on page 97 of his book, where he expresses some doubt about Höss's testimony concerning Eichmann's direct contacts with Himmler (over the heads of Heydrich and Müller). Except for this single reservation, Pendorf writes that Höss had an "unusually precise memory" and that "his testimonies and writings are justly considered to be almost as valuable as original documents."

50. T/1306 to T/1315, T/1375; N/94 (Testimony of defense witness Dr. Konrad Morgen before the International Military Tribunal, *Blue Series*, XX, pp. 487-515, in particular pp. 494-495) and N/95 (Nuremberg Document SS-67, reproduced in *Blue Series*, XLII, pp. 563-565, in particular pp. 563-564).

51. Judgment, Sections 141 and 166.

52. Judgment, Sections 166 to 169.

53. Nuremberg Documents 185-L and 219-L, reproduced in *Blue Series*, XXXVIII, pp. 1-24, 60-85.

54. *Geschäftsverteilungsplan und Geschäftsordnung der Ministerien*, 1958 (T/1423). As stated in its preface, this official publication of the Federal Republic of Germany is practically identical with the corresponding regulations published during the Weimar Republic and in use during the Nazi regime.

55. T/297.

56. Session 92.

57. Session 106. Making recommendations on matters pertaining to his assigned field of activities is, of course, an essential, if not the most essential, function of a *Referent*.

58. T/469.

59. These suggestions were incorporated in a IVB4 secret note to the Foreign Office, signed by Kaltenbrunner (T/310; Nuremberg Document NG-183).

60. T/271.

61. T/779 (Nuremberg Document NG-2652-E). For von Thadden's apologetic and reserved attitude toward Eichmann's proposals, see

T/781. For Eichmann's exchanges with the Foreign Office concerning preparation of his proposals, see T/766, T/769 (Nuremberg Document NG-2652-B), T/767, T/770, T/772, T/775, T/774 (Nuremberg Document NG-2652-C), and Nuremberg Document NG-2652-D. For Eichmann's exchanges with the Foreign Office subsequent to his letter containing his proposals, see T/781 and Nuremberg Document NG-2652-L, in which more drastic measures against foreign Jews were suggested by Eichmann.

62. T/782 (Nuremberg Document NG-2652-F).

63. T/784 (Nuremberg Document NG-2652-H).

64. See note 54 of this chapter.

65. See, for example, T/212, T/246, T/395, T/437, T/462, T/552, T/553, T/593, T/728, T/732, T/733, T/764, T/771, T/772, T/779, T/837; Nuremberg Documents NG-2652-L, NG-4817, Steengracht 064; and the letters reproduced in Randolph L. Braham, *The Destruction Of Hungarian Jewry: A Documentary Account* (New York: World Federation of Hungarian Jews, 1963), pp. 5-6, 36-37, 42. Miss Arendt writes on p. 135 that Luther "died in a concentration camp"; in the paperback edition, p. 151, this is changed to "put into a concentration camp." Luther died as a free man toward the end of the war during the bombing of Berlin. See Robert M. W. Kempner in *Aufbau* (New York), Vol. 29, No. 21, May 24, 1963, p. 11. According to Paul Seabury, *The Wilhelmstrasse: A Study of German Diplomats Under the Nazi Regime* (Berkeley and Los Angeles: Univ. of California Press, 1954), p. 133 and note 43 on p. 196, Luther, having been imprisoned in various camps, "attempted suicide, was hospitalized, and released just before the Russian capture of Berlin. He apparently died shortly thereafter of a heart attack." Contrary to Miss Arendt's assertion (p. 135), Eberhard von Thadden was not Luther's successor. That position was held by the *Vortragende Rat*, Horst Wagner. Eberhard von Thadden was one of Wagner's subordinates.

66. T/37, pp. 429-432. Despite Eichmann's rank, he did on occasion communicate directly with Under Secretary of State Martin Luther, as in Nuremberg Document NG-183.

67. Session 106. Quoted in Judgment, Section 174.

68. Judgment, Section 174, *in fine*.

69. See the Jenny Cozzi and Hanni Klepper examples presented later in this chapter.

70. T/84.

71. N/97 (Nuremberg Document 2376-PS). The exhibit consists of two substantially identical documents: (*a*) a declaration, dated June 22, 1945; (*b*) an affidavit, dated Nov. 16, 1945. The declaration is reproduced in part in *Blue Series*, XXX, pp. 290-291; the affidavit is reproduced entirely, in English translation, in *Red Series*, V, pp. 3-4.

72. *Blue Series*, XLII, p. 556.

73. Reproduced in *Blue Series*, XLII, pp. 551-565.

74. N/94 to N/96 (Nuremberg Documents SS(A)65 and SS(A)67; the latter is reproduced in *Blue Series*, XLII, pp. 563-565). The close connection of Eichmann with the deportation of the Jews to the death camps is also expressed by Höss—in the original German edition of his book, *Kommandant in Auschwitz* (Stuttgart: Deutsche Verlags-Anstalt, 1958), p. 171—when he speaks of "Eichmann's shipments" (*Transporte von Eichmann*). The American edition, *loc. cit.*, p. 211, speaks of "Jews transported to Auschwitz on the authority of Eichmann's office."

75. Testimony taken in Germany, referred to in Session 93.

76. T/1168. Published in part as *Nuremberg Diary* (New York: New American Library, 1961), 430 pp.

77. G. M. Gilbert, *Nuremberg Diary*, *loc. cit.*, p. 102.

78. Session 55.

79. Dr. Tibor Ferencz' testimony in Session 54.

80. T/1245 (Nuremberg Document NO-1874).

81. Judgment, Section 176.

82. Judgment, Section 117.

83. Judgment, Sections 54b and 176.

84. N/104.

85. L.M.I.L. van Taalingen-Dols, *De strijd om een mensenleven* (Goes: Oosterban & Le Cointre, 1960), p. 215. Submitted to the court as N/105.

86. *Documents sur l'activité du Comité international de la Croix-Rouge [CICR] en faveur des civils détenus dans les camps de concentration en Allemagne* (Third edition, Geneva: April 1947). Pages 99-100 contain a description of the visit made to the camp on April 5, 1945; pages 130-133 contain a report of the visit of April 21, 1945, subsequent to which one delegate remained till the liberation of the camp on May 10, 1945.

87. This is apparently a reference to the records of the conference of Sept. 21, 1939. See T/164 and T/165 (Nuremberg Document EC-307-1). The minutes of that meeting do not mention Nisko or Madagascar or any territorial schemes for the "solution of the Jewish question."

88. Judgment, Section 115.

89. Quoted in Session 104.

90. Referred to during Eichmann's cross-examination in Session 104.

91. *Kasztner Report*, p. 109. See also T/37, p. 291, and Sassen Papers, transcript of tape 17, p. 62; both referred to in Session 104.

92. For a summary of these initiatives, see Supreme Court Judgment, Part III.

93. T/1214, T/1215.

94. T/1215, T/1216.

95. Judgment, Section 155e.

96. T/1214 to T/1216.

97. Transcript of tape 46, page 12.

98. Session 100.

99. Curt Rothenberger, "Die Rechtsquellen im neuen Staat," *Deutsche Juristenzeitung* (Munich and Berlin), Vol. 41, 1936, pp. 22-26. See also Chapter 5, under Germany.

100. Sassen Papers, transcript of tape 5, pp. 3-4, referred to in Session 104. This statement was made in reference to Eichmann's assertion that the Jewish press called him the Czar of the Jews.

101. Judgment, Section 176, referring to document T/1393/a.

102. Judgment, Sections 238 and 239. Eichmann's statement "I will jump into my grave laughing, because the fact that I have the death of five million Jews . . . on my conscience gives me extraordinary satisfaction" is discarded by Miss Arendt as "preposterous, as he knew very well" (p. 42). She tries to mitigate this damning sentence by saying that "it gave him 'an extraordinary sense of elation to think that (he) was exiting from the stage in this way'" (p. 42; the source of her citation is not indicated). She maintains that this sentence belongs to the same category as his expressed desire to hang himself as a warning to anti-Semites (p. 48), though this desire was expressed after his capture.

103. T/689: Interrogation No. 929-B (in the presence of Dr. Rudolf Kasztner), July 10, 1947, p. 12. In a previous interrogation, No. 929 (also in the presence of Kasztner), July 7, 1947, p. 17, Becher said: "I believe I have never in my life met a person who could lie so convincingly as that fellow Eichmann."

104. Eichmann's cross-examination in Session 98.

105. Quoted in Session 98; earlier referred to in Session 95 and later in Session 106.

106. *Vierteljahrshefte für Zeitgeschichte* (Stuttgart), Vol. 9, 1961, pp. 286, 292-293 for a characterization of Eichmann; pp. 295-298, 303-304 for the history of the persecution (posthumously published). The same views on Eichmann were expressed by Loesener in 1941 (T/526) and in 1948 (T/693). A propos, Loesener's story on the Central Emigration Office in Vienna coincides with Franz Meyer's testimony in the Eichmann trial (Session 17).

107. Session 102. See also T/37, pp. 249 ff.

108. Judgment, Sections 222-230.

109. No. 28, July 9, 1960, submitted to the Court as T/46.

110. Gerhard Boldt, *Die letzten Tage der Reichskanzlei* (Hamburg, Stuttgart: Rowohlt, 1947), 95 pp.

111. T/37, pp. 2670-2671, 2682-2683.
112. Rudolf Hoess, op. cit.
113. Sassen Papers, transcript of tape 17, pp. 5 ff.
114. Session 95.
115. Rudolf Hoess, op. cit., pp. 242-243.
116. Ibid., p. 172.
117. Judgment, Sections 136 and 178; and T/212, T/246, T/462, T/488, T/499, T/547, T/548, T/549, T/552, T/553, T/593, T/728, T/732, T/733, T/764, T/771, T/837.
118. Especially because of the fear that she would reveal the nature of Nazi behavior in occupied territories. Eichmann never referred to this pretext in the entire course of his correspondence concerning the affair.
119. T/349.
120. T/354. Quoted in Judgment, Section 138.
121. Jochen Klepper, Unter dem Schatten deiner Flügel. Aus den Tagebüchern der Jahre 1932-1942 (Stuttgart: Deutsche Verlags-Anstalt, 1962). See in particular pp. 971-974, 1126-1127, 1130-1133.
122. T/1215.
123. Eichmann's cross-examination by the presiding judge, Session 107.
124. Eichmann told of his own "instructions" on the "Jewish question" in T/37, pp. 64 ff.
125. Eichmann's alertness during the cross-examination was amazing. "Eichmann's voice was calm and clear, his enunciation careful and impersonal, as if he were addressing a classroom of not overbright pupils. There was a certain precision in the marshaling of his points and the formulation of his phrasing."—Moshe Pearlman, The Capture and Trial of Adolf Eichmann (New York: Simon and Schuster, 1963), p. 419. "On any showing that performance had been remarkable. He had come in fighting, and he fought up to the end."—Ibid., p. 528.
126. The Jerusalem District Court was fully aware of the sui generis nature of Eichmann's type of crime and criminality (see Chapter 3, under The Judgment and Its Execution). The Attorney General in his opening statement—Gideon Hausner, 6,000,000 Accusers; Israel's Case Against Eichmann (Jerusalem: Jerusalem Post, 1961), p. 30—had the following to say on this subject: "In this trial, we shall also encounter a new kind of killer, the kind that exercises his bloody craft behind a desk. . . . But it was his word that put gas chambers into action; he lifted the telephone, and railway trains left for the extermination centers; his signature it was that sealed the doom of thousands and tens of thousands. He had but to give the order, and at his command the troopers took to the field to rout Jews out of their homes, to beat and torture them and chase them into ghettos, to pin the badge of shame

on their breasts, to steal their property—till finally, after torture and pillage, after everything had been wrung out of them, when even their hair had been taken, they were transported en masse to the slaughter."

127. *Blue Series*: The final pleas of the defense counsels can be found in Volumes XVII, XVIII, and XIX; the final statements of the defendants in XXII; Jahrreiss's speech in XVII, pp. 458-494.

128. For example, Keitel, in *Blue Series*, XVIII, pp. 3-5; Albert Speer, *ibid.*, XVI, pp. 521, 581.

129. T/164.

130. T/219. This is a report on discussions in the Office of the *Reichsstatthalter* of *Reichsgau Wartheland* in Posen, sent to Eichmann apparently by SS *Sturmbannführer* Hoeppner in July 1941.

131. Judgment, Sections 163 to 165.

132. Summarized in the Judgment, Section 76.

133. *Ibid.*

134. See Nuremberg Document NG-5764, pp. 1-5, 7-8. See also Himmler's memorandum of May 1940 on the treatment of alien (*fremdländisch*) peoples in the East, in *Vierteljahrshefte für Zeitgeschichte* (Stuttgart), Vol. 5, 1957, pp. 194-198, especially p. 197.

135. Miss Arendt writes (p. 100) that at the Wannsee Conference Eichmann "was by far the lowest in rank and social position of those present." Eichmann's rank was SS-*Obersturmbannführer,* while the rank of Rudolf Lange, another participant in the conference, was only SS-*Sturmbannführer.*

136. See the sections on these countries in Chapter 5.

137. See note 68 of Chapter 2.

138. Sassen Papers, Folder 17, p. 20.

139. The following may serve as an example: A report on a meeting of the Specialists on Jewish Affairs (*Judenreferenten*) for France, Belgium, and The Netherlands, on June 11, 1942, at Department IVB4 of the RSHA, during which the deportation of Jews from these countries to Auschwitz was discussed, mentions as slated for deportation persons of both sexes, between 16 and 40 years old, 10 per cent of the total being Jews unfit for work (*nicht arbeitsfähige Juden*). (T/419; Nuremberg Document RF-1217.) In a letter dated June 22, 1942, in which Eichmann informs the Foreign Office of this project, he speaks only of able-bodied Jews. There is no mention of those unfit for work. (T/422; Nuremberg Document NG-182. Also Session 97.)

140. Nuremberg Document 3762-PS, reproduced in *Blue Series,* XXXIII, pp. 68-69 (affidavit of Becher).

141. See the account of Hitler's orders on earlier pages.

142. According to a private communication of Dr. Robert M. W. Kempner, dated March 6, 1964, even *Ministerialdirektor* Kritzinger of

the Reich Chancellery, once a member of the German Nationalist Party (*Deutschnationale Volkspartei*), had joined the Nazi Party in 1938. And there were at least nine SS officers (including State Secretaries Neumann and Stuckart) among the fifteen participants: Gauleiter Dr. Alfred Meyer, Deputy Minister for the Occupied Eastern Territories; Dr. Georg Leibbrandt, Department Head of the Reich Ministry for the Occupied Eastern Territories; Dr. Wilhelm Stuckart, Secretary of State, Ministry of Interior; Erich Neumann, State Secretary, Office of the Plenipotentiary for the Four Year Plan; Dr. Roland Freisler, State Secretary, Reich Ministry of Justice; Dr. Joseph Bühler, State Secretary, Office of the Governor General; Martin Luther, Under Secretary of State, Foreign Ministry; SS Colonel Dr. Gerhard Klopfer, Party Chancellery; Friedrich Wilhelm Kritzinger, Ministerial Director, Reich Chancellery; SS Major General Otto Hofmann, SS Race and Settlement Head Office; SS Major General Heinrich Müller, RSHA; SS Lieutenant Colonel Adolf Eichmann, RSHA; SS Senior Colonel (*SS-Oberführer*) Dr. Eberhard Schöngarth, Commander of the Security Police and the SD in the Government-General, representing the Security Police and the SD; SS Major Dr. Rudolf Lange, Commander of the Security Police and the SD for the *Generalbezirk* Latvia, representing the Commander of the Security Police and the SD for *Reichskommissariat Ostland*. The Chairman was Reinhardt Heydrich.

Of the participants in the Wannsee Conference, Freisler, Luther, Kritzinger, Stuckart, and Neumann died natural deaths; Heydrich was assassinated in Prague; Meyer committed suicide; Müller's fate is unknown; Schöngarth, Bühler, and Eichmann were sentenced to death and executed; Hofmann was sentenced to 25 years imprisonment by an American Military Commission but released in 1951; Klopfer was investigated, and the investigation discontinued; Leibbrandt has been freed from criminal prosecution.

143. Quoted in Eichmann's cross-examination in Session 96.

144. See the correspondence between Himmler and Greiser in Folder 94 of the Himmler Files, preserved in the Manuscript Division of the Library of Congress. Part of the correspondence is reproduced by Hilberg, *op. cit.*, pp. 142-144.

145. Judgment, Section 75. Miss Arendt considers the Stettin deportation—together with the deportation from Baden and Saarpfalz, discussed in note 42 of Chapter 5—to have been "test cases." She writes: "The objective seems to have been a test of general political conditions—whether Jews could be made to walk to their doom on their own feet, carrying their own little valises, in the middle of night, without any previous notification; what the reaction of their neighbors would be . . ." (p. 139). She does not explain why the Nazis had to test what had

already been tested time and again, by other regimes against other victims throughout history, and by the Nazis themselves—for example on the *Kristallnacht* in 1938, when thousands of Jews were thrown into concentration camps, and a few weeks later, when fifteen to seventeen thousand Polish Jews residing in Germany were dumped into Poland, then at peace with Germany.

146. Published in Max Weinreich's *Hitler's Professors* (New York: YIVO Institute for Jewish Research, 1946), pp. 153-154. The original is in the Archives of the YIVO Institute.

147. In the same letter, Kube complained to Lohse that the arrivals in Minsk from Germany included half Aryans and even one three-quarters Aryan. This should be compared with Miss Arendt's statement that "nothing was ever done about the *Mischlinge*, or about Jews who had made mixed marriages" (p. 143). There is no evidence that any of the *Mischlinge* mentioned in Kube's letter ever returned to Germany (Hilberg, *op. cit.*, p. 333). Indeed, Müller instructed all *Stapoleitstellen* to include *Mischlinge* of the first degree in the deportation and destruction process (Hilberg, *op. cit.*, p. 296, n. 184).

148. Nuremberg Document NO-2262 (the so-called Kube-Mappe of the Himmler Files).

149. See also the last in a series of three articles published in *Aufbau* (New York), Vol. 12, Nos. 34, 35, and 36 (Aug. 23 to Sept. 6, 1946), reproducing excerpts, not published before, from written statements made in Nuremberg by the former Higher SS and Police Leader of *Russland-Mitte* (Central Russia), Erich von dem Bach-Zelewski: ". . . Kube tried to save the German-Jewish intellectuals . . . by employing them in his administration. After Kube's death Himmler told me that his death was a blessing for Germany, since anyhow he would have had to put him into a concentration camp again because his policy toward the Jews had bordered on treason."

150. *Akademische Jahresfeier 1940 der Technischen Hochschule München. Vortrag von Reichsminister Generalgouverneur Dr. Hans Frank: Technik des Staates* (Munich, 1940), 6 pp. See in particular p. 3, left column. In abbreviated form also in *Zeitschrift der Akademie für Deutsches Recht* (Berlin), Vol. 8, No. 1, 1941, pp. 2-6.

151. The bizarre attempt to link Kant with the extermination of European Jewry calls to mind the prophetic words of Heinrich Heine written in 1834: "Do not fear, you German republicans, the German revolution will not turn out to be gentler and more lenient [*milder und sanfter*] because Kant's *Critique*, Fichte's transcendental idealism, and, above all, Nature Philosophy preceded it. Because of these doctrines, revolutionary forces have evolved, which are only waiting for the day that they can break forth to fill the world with terror and awe. Kantians

will emerge who will refuse to feel reverence even with respect to the world of visible phenomena (*Erscheinungswelt*); who will, without pity, use sword and ax to plow through the soil of our European life in order to eradicate even the last roots of the past. . . . For . . . the hand of the Kantian strikes hard and without flinching, because his heart is not moved by any kind of traditional reverence." From *Zur Geschichte der Religion und Philosophie* in *Sämtliche Werke*, Vol. 5 (Hamburg: Hoffmann & Campe, 1873), pp. 264-265.

152. Judgment, Section 228, quoted earlier in the text of this chapter (see note 108).

153. F. M. Dostoevsky, *The Diary of a Writer*. Translated and annotated by Boris Brasol (New York: Scribner's, 1949), Vol. I, p. 16. The Diary discusses numerous criminal cases, and contains reflections on crime and punishment (e.g., pp. 172 ff., 206 ff., 210 ff., 312 ff., 459 ff., 527 ff., 690 ff., 763 ff.).

154. This refers to one Bertold Storfer from Vienna, who became involved in illegal emigration and was shipped to Auschwitz. At his request, Eichmann actually went to Auschwitz to pay him a visit. Storfer perished there, and Miss Arendt claims (p. 58) that his "fate . . . was not Eichmann's fault," since he was deported on an order from Himmler. It follows that Eichmann could not ask Himmler to reconsider the fate of one Jew, though he was eager to ask Hitler to reconsider his decision to spare the lives of 40,000 Hungarian Jews. Incidentally, an example of how Miss Arendt creates "Jewish leaders" is presented by her on page 45, where she calls Storfer "one of the representatives of the Jewish community." But on page 58 she states that Storfer "had shown no interest in Jewish matters prior to the arrival of the Nazis in Austria"— that is to say, he was an appointee of Eichmann.

155. See note 15 of this chapter.

156. Gideon Hausner, *op. cit.*, p. 71.

157. The Book of Esther, 7:6.

158. Sassen Papers, transcript of tape 34, pp. 4-5, referred to in Session 104.

159. Contained in an exchange of letters between Gershom Scholem and Miss Arendt in *Mitteilungsblatt* (Tel Aviv), Vol. 31, No. 33, pp. 3-5. The exchange is reproduced in abbreviated form in *Der Zeitgeist*, Supplement to *Aufbau* (New York), No. 208, Dec. 1963, pp. 17-18. An English translation appears in *Encounter* (London), Vol. 22, No. 1, Jan. 1964, pp. 51-56.

160. Yitzhak Katznelson, *The Poem of the Murdered Jewish People*, in his *Last Writings* (Tel-Aviv: Hakibbutz Hameuhad, 1956), pp. 339-383 (Yiddish); Hebrew translation by M. S. Volfovski, pp. 387-431.

161. Transcript of tape 67, p. 9.

Chapter 2

1. See, for example, *History of the United Nations War Crimes Commission and the Development of the Laws of War* (London: UNWCC, 1948, 592 pp.) and notes 29 to 32 of this chapter.

2. The testimony was given in Case XI (the Ministries Case), pp. 15424-15491, 15603-15671, 15831-15879 (August 10-12, 1948) of the record (mimeogr.).

3. *Green Series*, VI, p. 1188.

4. Nuremberg Document NG-2586-G, published in part in *Green Series*, XIII, pp. 210-217; and in full in Robert M. W. Kempner's *Eichmann und Komplizen* (Zurich, Stuttgart, Vienna: Europa Verlag, 1961), pp. 170-180.

5. *Green Series*, XIV, pp. 868-870. In the paperback edition (p. 129), Miss Arendt reversed herself, writing: "The Nuremberg court, in possession of the minutes of the Wannsee Conference, may not have believed that he [Stuckart] had known nothing of the extermination program, but it sentenced him to time served on account of ill health."

6. Pp. 132 ff., 151 ff.

7. T/185.

8. The defense was based, among other things, on Sauckel's loyalty to Hitler and his "good intentions." (*Blue Series*, XVIII, pp. 466-506.)

9. Hess is not considered here because of his plea of amnesia.

10. *Blue Series*, I, p. 284; XXII, p. 382.

11. *Ibid.*, XXII, p. 383.

12. For Göring's counsel's attacks on Hitler, see *Blue Series*, XVII, pp. 513, 548, 550.

13. *Blue Series*, I, pp. 366-367.

14. They, too, are declared to be "failures" (p. 251).

15. Denys P. Myers, "Human Rights in Europe," *The American Journal of International Law* (Washington, D.C.), Vol. 48, 1954, pp. 299-302.

16. Denys P. Myers, "The European Commission on Human Rights," *The American Journal of International Law* (Washington, D.C.), Vol. 50, 1956, pp. 949-951. Contrary to Miss Arendt (p. 228), France did sign the Convention on Nov. 4, 1950 (see *United Nations Treaties Series*, Vol. 213, pp. 221-271), but has failed so far to ratify it. In the paperback edition, p. 250, Miss Arendt deleted the sentence sketching the origins of the Convention.

17. L. Oppenheim and H. Lauterpacht, *International Law* (London: Longmans, Green & Co., 1952, 7th edition) Vol. II, pp. 880-883.

18. *Ibid.*, p. 882.

19. *Ibid.* In the *Handbook of the International Red Cross* (Geneva: International Committee of the Red Cross and the League of the Red Cross Societies, 1953, 10th edition), p. 302, the U.S.S.R. is listed as being a party to the Fourth Hague Convention of 1907; see, however, the footnote on p. 300.

20. *Blue Series,* XXII, p. 497.

21. L. Oppenheim and H. Lauterpacht, *op. cit.,* p. 881.

22. *Blue Series,* XXII, p. 497.

23. Resolution 260(III)A of December 9, 1948, in: *Official Records of the Third Session of the General Assembly. Part I. Resolutions* (Paris: United Nations, 1949), pp. 174-177. See also Nehemiah Robinson, *The Genocide Convention: A Commentary* (New York: Institute of Jewish Affairs, 1960), p. 27.

24. Robinson, *op. cit.,* p. 139.

25. *Ibid.,* pp. 86-89.

26. With the turn of the fortunes of war, the Allies undertook a concerted action among the neutrals (including Argentina) to receive their cooperation in preventing "fugitives from justice to escape just punishment." After Sweden, Turkey, Switzerland, and Spain had given such assurances, Argentina advised the U.S. Department of State by the end of September 1944 that "in no event would persons accused of war crimes be allowed into Argentine territory." From *History of the United Nations War Crimes Commission, loc. cit.,* p. 428. More details can be found in Keesing's *Contemporary Archives* (London), Vol. 5, 1943-1945, p. 6784.

27. An English translation of the law can be found in the *Israel Government Yearbook, 5710/1950* (Jerusalem: Government Printer, 1951), pp. 296-297.

28. For the legal basis of the Eichmann trial, see the text of this chapter.

29. *Tratado de derecho penal internacional e internacional penal* (Madrid: Consejo Superior de Investigaciones Cientificas, Instituto "Francisco de Vitoria"), Vol. I, 1955, 676 pp.; Vol. II, 1957, 406 pp.

30. *Die Verantwortlichkeit der Staatsorgane nach dem Völkerstrafrecht. Eine Studie zu den Nürnberger Prozessen* (Bonn: Ludwig Röhrscheid, 1952), 420 pp.

31. "Le nouveau Droit pénal international," *Revue de Droit International* . . . (Geneva), Vol. 35, 1957; continued in quarterly installments through Vol. 41, 1963.

32. *Introduction à l'étude du droit international pénal* (Brussels: Bruylant; Paris: Sirey, 1954), 207 pp. See also *Infraction internationale. Ses éléments constitutifs et ses aspects juridiques. Exposé sur la base*

du droit pénal comparé (Brussels: Bruylant; Paris: Librarie Générale de Droit et de Jurisprudence, 1957), 225 pp.

33. See, for example, John Alan Appleman, *Military Tribunals and International Crimes* (Indianapolis: Bobbs-Merrill, 1954), 422 pp.; Georg Dahm, *Zur Problematik des Völkerstrafrechts* (Göttingen: Vandenhoeck and Ruprecht, 1956), 86 pp.; Robert K. Woetzel, *The Nuremberg Trials in International Law* (London: Stevens; New York: Praeger, 1962), 287 pp.; Gerhard Hoffmann, *Strafrechtliche Verantwortung im Völkerrecht. Zum gegenwärtigen Stand des völkerrechtlichen Strafrechts* (Frankfurt am Main: Metzner, 1962), 211 pp.

34. Ganshof van der Meersch in *Revue de l'Université de Bruxelles* (Brussels), Vol. 14, 1961, pp. 50-104.

35. Justice Jackson wrote:

International Law is more than a scholarly collection of abstract and immutable principles. It is an outgrowth of treaties or agreements between nations and accepted customs. But every custom has its origin in some single act, and every agreement has to be initiated by the action of some state. Unless we are prepared to abandon every principle of growth for International Law, we cannot deny that our own day has its right to institute customs and to conclude agreements that will themselves become sources of a newer and strengthened International Law. International Law is not capable of development by legislation, for there is no continuously sitting international legislature. Innovations and revisions in International Law are brought about by the action of the Governments designed to meet a change in circumstances. It grows, as did the Common-Law, through decisions reached from time to time in adapting settled principles to new situations. Hence I am not disturbed by the lack of precedent for the inquiry we propose to conduct.

Trial of War Criminals. Documents: Report of Robert H. Jackson to the President (Washington, D.C.: U.S. Department of State Publication No. 2420, 1945), p. 9. The question of the growth of international law is complex, but no jurist has ever proposed solving it by means of the trial judge's feeling of right and wrong.

36. On Lauterpacht's contribution to international criminal law, see, for example, *Studies in Public International Law in Memory of Sir Hersch Lauterpacht* (Jerusalem: Hebrew University, 1961), pp. 84-91 (Hebrew). His article, "The Law of Nature and the Punishment of War Crimes," *British Year Book of International Law* (London), Vol. 21, 1944, pp. 56-95, was a milestone in the development of international criminal law.

37. The principle is recognized in traditional Jewish law: *Ein*

onshin ela im ken mazhirin (No punishment may be delivered without previous warning). The earliest version is found in *Tosefta Avodah Zarah*, chapter 8.

38. *Report of the International Law Commission Covering the Work of Its Sixth Session, 3 June–28 July 1954, General Assembly, Official Records: Ninth Session, Supplement No. 9 (A/2693)* (New York: United Nations, 1954), pp. 9-12.

39. Miss Arendt's quotation from Stone is inaccurate: "if they" should read "who." Julius Stone, *Legal Controls of International Conflict* (London: Stevens and Sons, 1954), p. 361, n. 67.

40. *History of the United Nations War Crimes Commission, loc. cit.,* pp. 191-204. The original English version of Art. 6(c) had a semicolon after "before or during the war"; consequently, the clause "in execution of or in connection with any crimes within the jurisdiction of the Tribunal" did not apply to the more drastic crimes listed in the beginning of the Article, but only to "persecutions" not covered by the first part of the Article. See *Report of Robert H. Jackson, United States Representative to the International Conference on Military Trials, London, 1945* (Washington, D.C.: Department of State Publication No. 3080), p. 423. This was the text as adopted on August 8, 1945. Two months later it was discovered that in the Russian text (unlike the English and French) there was not a semicolon after "before or during the war," but a comma, which would suggest the applicability of the clause "in execution of or in connection with any crimes within the jurisdiction of the Tribunal" also to the crimes in the first three lines. A Protocol was drawn up on October 6, 1945, to adjust the English and French texts to the Russian (*Report of Robert H. Jackson, loc. cit.,* p. 429). See also note 69 of this chapter.

41. Convention (IV) Respecting the Law and Customs of War on Land (1907), reproduced in Kurt Heinze and Karl Schilling *Die Rechtsprechung der Nürnberger Militärtribunale* (Bonn: Girardet, 1952), pp. 295-300.

42. Her statement that this crime "had so little to do with war that its commission actually conflicted with and hindered the war's conduct" (p. 237) calls for the following comment: Hitler's war was not the classical war of Clausewitz with a single purpose (destruction of the armed forces of the enemy) but a war with multiple aims, partly conflicting, partly parallel—for example, a war for the liquidation of the Versailles Treaty, a war against the historic enemy (*Erbfeind*) France, a war against Communism, a war for German *Lebensraum* at the expense of other nations, a war for the supremacy of the German race in the world, *and* a war against the Jews. It cannot be overlooked that physical mass extermination of a people generally becomes possible only in con-

ditions of war. This is true not only for the Jewish tragedy but also for other examples of crimes against humanity (and genocide) in the past. The perpetration of these crimes was facilitated by conditions of war.

43. The relevant section reads: (c) *Crimes against Humanity.* Atrocities and offences including but not limited to murder, extermination, enslavement, deportation, imprisonment, torture, rape, or other inhumane acts committed against any civilian population, or persecutions on political, racial or religious grounds whether or not in violation of the domestic laws of the country where perpetrated. (See note 70 of this chapter.)

44. *Law Reports of Trials of War Criminals.* Selected and prepared by the United Nations War Crimes Commission, Vol. XV, Digest of Laws and Cases (London, 1949), pp. 136-138.

45. Henri Meyrowitz, *La Répression par les tribunaux allemands des crimes contre l'humanité et de l'appartenance à une organisation criminelle en application de la loi no. 10 du Conseil de Contrôle Allié* (Paris: Librarie générale de droit et de jurisprudence, 1960), 514 pp.

46. General Assembly Resolutions 95 (I) of 11 December 1946 in: *United Nations Resolutions Adopted by the General Assembly During the Second Part of its First Session* (New York: United Nations, 1947), p. 188; and 488 (V) of 12 December 1950 in: *Resolutions Adopted by the General Assembly During the Period 19 September to 15 December 1950* (New York: United Nations, 1951), p. 77.

47. "Inhuman acts such as murder, extermination, enslavement, deportation or persecutions, committed against any civilian population on social, political, racial, religious or cultural grounds by the authorities of a State or by private individuals acting at the instigation or with the toleration of such authorities."—*Report of the International Law Commission, loc. cit.,* p. 11.

48. "Crime against humanity means any of the following acts: murder, extermination, enslavement, starvation or deportation and other inhumane acts committed against any civilian population, and persecution on national, racial, religious or political grounds."—Nazis and Nazi Collaborators Punishment Law 5710/1950, Section I(b).

49. See, for example, *Njurenbergski Protses* (Moscow: Gosiurizdat, 1957), Vol. I, p. 67.

50. See, for example, *Amtsblatt des Kontrollrats in Deutschland* (Berlin), No. 3, Jan. 31, 1946, pp. 50 ff.

51. For a detailed discussion of these terms see A. Ripollés, *op. cit.,* Vol. I, pp. 641-656.

52. Judgment, Section 16.

53. Raphael Lemkin, *Axis Rule in Europe. Laws of Occupation. Analysis of Government Proposals for Redress* (Washington, D.C.: Carnegie Endowment for International Peace, 1944), pp. 79-95 *passim.*

54. International Court of Justice, *Reports* (Leyden: Sijthoff, 1951), pp. 15 ff. (Reservations Case of May 28, 1951. See the text of this chapter.)

55. See Chapter 1, under Attitude Toward His Work.

56. The only extensive history of genocide is the statistically inexact, historically unreliable, and nationalistically biased book by Gerhard Ludwig, *Massenmord im Weltgeschehen* (Stuttgart: Friedrich Vorwerk, 1951), 104 pp. The book contains numerous references, many of them correct, to the wholesale slaughter of Jews in the past.

57. International Court of Justice, *Reports, ibid.*, p. 23.

58. This is an unusual expression. "Comity" in international law (*comitas gentium; convenance et courtoisie internationales*) means the rules of politeness, convenience, and good will observed by States in their mutual intercourse without being legally bound by them. Miss Arendt apparently meant the community of nations, the international community.

59. Nathan Feinberg, *The Jewish Action Against Hitler in the League of Nations: The Bernheim Petition* (Jerusalem: Mosad Bialik, 1957), 186 pp. (Hebrew). Chapter I is also available in English in *Yad Washem Studies* (Jerusalem), Vol. I, 1957, pp. 67-83.

60. A. Leon Kubowitzky, *Unity in Dispersion. A History of the World Jewish Congress* (New York: World Jewish Congress, 1948), p. 35.

61. A resolution of the Assembly of the League of Nations expressing an opinion, and having moral force only.

62. *League of Nations. Protection of Linguistic, Racial or Religious Minorities by the League of Nations. Resolutions and Extracts from the Minutes of the Council, Resolutions . . . adopted by the Assembly . . .* (Second edition, Geneva, 1931), p. 240.

63. Permanent Court of International Justice, *Advisory Opinions*, No. 4 of Feb. 7, 1923, p. 24.

64. See, for example, Article 7 of the (minorities) treaty between the United States of America, the British Empire, France, Italy, Japan (the victorious powers after World War I), and Poland, of June 28, 1919. This article was reproduced verbatim (with change of nationality) in all other similar instruments:

> All Polish nationals shall be equal before the law and shall enjoy the same civil and political rights without distinction as to race, language or religion.
>
> Differences of religion, creed or confession shall not prejudice any Polish national in matters relating to the enjoyment of civil or political rights, as for instance admission to public employment, functions, and honors, or the exercise of professions and industries.

No restriction shall be imposed on the free use by any Polish national of any language in private intercourse, in commerce, in religion, in the press, or in publications of any kind, or at public meetings.

Notwithstanding any establishment by the Polish Government of an official language, adequate facilities shall be given to Polish nationals of non-Polish speech for the use of their language, either orally or in writing, before the courts.

Jacob Robinson and Others, *Were the Minorities Treaties a Failure?* (New York: Institute of Jewish Affairs, 1943), p. 315.

65. *Ibid.,* pp. 247-260.

66. Karl Dietrich Bracher, Wolfgang Sauer, and Gerhard Schulz, *Die nationalsozialistische Machtergreifung. Studien zur Errichtung des totalitären Herrschaftssystems in Deutschland 1933/34* (Köln u. Opladen: Westdeutscher Verlag, 1960), p. 166.

67. In addition to the Fourth and Fifth Hague Conventions 1907, the Covenant of the League of Nations (Art. 10), the General Act for the Pacific Settlement of International Disputes of October 2, 1926 (Art. 10), the Declaration of the Eighth Assembly of the League of Nations of September 24, 1927, concerning the Prohibition of War of Aggression, the Briand-Kellogg Pact of August 27, 1928, and the Geneva Convention on the Treatment of Prisoners of War of July 27, 1929. See K. Heinze and K. Schilling, *op. cit.,* pp. 295-309.

68. Louise W. Holborn, *War and Peace Aims of the United Nations* (Boston: World Peace Foundation), Vol. I, 1943, pp. 7-8, 14; Vol. II, 1948, pp. 10-11, 144-145.

69. *Blue Series,* I, pp. 8-18 (includes Protocol rectifying discrepancy in texts of Charter, pp. 17-18). And *Green Series,* I, pp. ix-xvi; also available in Vols. III, IV, VI, X, XII, XV.

70. *Green Series,* I, pp. xvi-xix; also in Vols. III, IV, VI, X, XII, XV.

71. *History of the United Nations War Crimes Commission, loc. cit.,* pp. 461-475.

72. See note 124 of Chapter 3.

73. See note 46 of this chapter.

74. See the 1951 Convention Relating to the Status of Refugees, Art. 5(a), in the *United Nations Treaty Series,* Vol. 189, pp. 137-222; and the 1954 Convention Relating to the Status of Stateless Persons, Art. 1, par. 2(iii), in the same *Series,* Vol. 360, pp. 117-207.

75. See note 38 of this chapter.

76. She lists the Benton-Grimm Anthology in her Bibliography, on p. 261.

77. Miss Arendt also characterizes the *Israel* court as a "court of the victors" (pp. 233, 251) and as such incompetent. If we had not been

confronted with the tragedy of Hitler's war against the Jews—"the war that Hitler won" (*De oorlog die Hitler won*, the title of H. Wielek's book on the Catastrophe that befell the Jews in The Netherlands)—this statement could have been dismissed without comment.

78. The wartime coalition of the United Nations of some 50 members (including dependent territories) out of some 60 sovereignties existing at that time. Karl Jaspers, respectfully mentioned by Miss Arendt on pages 91, 230, 247, wrote in his book *The Question of German Guilt* (New York: Capricorn, 1961): "If a war ends in victory for one side, it is the absolute prerogative of the victor, who has staked his life, to decide on the political responsibilities" (p. 42). A bit further on, he added: "And the jurisdiction, which in the peaceful order of a state rests in the courts, can after a war rest only in the victor's tribunal" (p. 56).

79. In this connection, Jaspers wrote: "Had the victors named a German tribunal, or appointed Germans as associate judges, this would make no change at all. The Germans would not sit on the court by virtue of a German self-liberation but by the grace of the victors. The national disgrace would be the same. The trial is due to the fact that we did not free ourselves from the criminal regime but were liberated by the Allies." (*Ibid.*, pp. 54-55.)

80. For a legal discussion of this aspect of Nuremberg, see Solon Cleanth Ivrakis, "International Military Justice and Neutral Judges," *Revue Hellénique de Droit International* (Athens), Vol. 9, 1956, pp. 231-244. Concerning neutrals, Jaspers asked: "Does a neutral have any right to judge in public, having stayed out of the struggle and failed to stake his existence and his conscience on the main cause?" (*Op. cit.*, pp. 42-43.)

81. See the discussion earlier in the text of this chapter on precedent and the emergence of new law.

82. See note 68 of this chapter.

83. *Blue Series*, XXII, pp. 461-469.

84. "Being permanent in its nature and purpose and representing a fundamental change in the legal structure of international society, the Pact of Paris must be regarded as continuing in being and as one of the corner-stones of the international legal systems."—L. Oppenheim and H. Lauterpacht, *op. cit.*, p. 197.

85. *Blue Series*, XXII, p. 463. For notes 86-98 see also Kurt Heinze and Karl Schilling, *op. cit.*, items 601-612.

86. *Blue Series*, XXII, p. 558.

87. *Ibid.*, p. 559.

88. *Ibid.*, p. 563.

89. *Green Series*, III, p. 970.

90. *Ibid.*, XIV, p. 317.

91. *Ibid.*, XI, p. 482.
92. *Ibid.*, XI, p. 534.
93. *Ibid.*, XIV, pp. 322-323.
94. *Ibid.*, IV, p. 457.
95. *Ibid.*, pp. 466-467.
96. *Ibid.*, XI, p. 1317.
97. *Ibid.*, p. 587.
98. *Ibid.*, p. 685.
99. Nehemiah Robinson, *op. cit.*, p. 80. See also the discussion on pp. 80-86.
100. Judgment, Section 22.
101. Miss Arendt does not tell where one would find an international criminal court. The International Military Tribunal has never been dissolved and its charter is still valid. See Article 7 of the London Agreement of August 8, 1945, which provides that the agreement shall continue in force subject to the right of any signatory to give one month's notice of intention to terminate it. There is no record of such a "notice of intention" ever having been given.

No great imagination is required to see how unrealistic it would have been to try to reassemble this Tribunal under the conditions of the Cold War. Furthermore, the United Nations phase of the Israel-Argentine conflict provided a clear demonstration of the unfeasibility of setting up a new international tribunal which, if convened, would surely have been turned into a battlefield in the conflict between East and West. The Security Council, whose composition reflects world power relationships, offered almost a full-dress preview of what such a trial would have been like. See the Security Council's Verbatim Records of June 22-23, 1960 (S/P.V. 865-868), and Documents S/4334, S/4336, S/4338, S/4341, S/4342, S/4345, S/4346, S/4349. These documents are partly reproduced in *Security Council Official Records* (United Nations), *Fifteenth Year, Supplement for April, May, and June 1960*, pp. 24-35.

102. Judgment, Section 12.
103. Publications of the Permanent Court of International Justice. Series A, No. 10, September 7, 1927. The Case of SS *Lotus* (Leyden: Sijthoff, 1927), pp. 18-19.
104. *Ibid.*, p. 20.
105. *Ibid.*, p. 23.
106. *Ibid.*, p. 35.
107. *Ibid.*, p. 63. See also the dissenting opinions of Judge Weiss on p. 45 and Judge Altamira on p. 95.
108. *Loc. cit.*, Vol. I, pp. 239-240.
109. Lotus Judgment, p. 57. See note 104.
110. Vol. I, pp. 331-332.
111. Miss Arendt does not have a clear conception of the nature

and extent of the criteria for jurisdiction in criminal cases of international scope. She charges that the principle of "universal jurisdiction" (see the Supreme Court Judgment quotations in the text of the present chapter, cited in note 118) was "in flagrant conflict with the conduct of the trial as well as with the law under which Eichmann was tried," and argues that it was not applicable in any case because "Eichmann . . . was accused chiefly of crimes against the Jewish people" and not against humanity (p. 240). The conduct of the trial and its conformity to the highest standards of civilization and international law are discussed in Chapter 3. The lack of conflict between the Israel law under which Eichmann was tried and international law is discussed in the present chapter; also the relation between crimes against the Jewish people and crimes against humanity. From these passages, and the sources cited therein, it becomes clear that Miss Arendt's charges lack foundation. The same goes for her contention that the invocation of the universality principle was to excuse the kidnaping. (See Chapter 3.)

No less misinformed is Miss Arendt's discussion of the passive personality principle of jurisdiction. She states that the Jerusalem Court relied on this principle, and that this principle "implies that criminal proceedings are initiated by the government in the name of the victims, who are assumed to have a right to revenge" (p. 239). The fact that the state maintains a monopoly in the administration of criminal justice, and has the right to act instead and on behalf of victims, is not at all based on the assumption that the victim has a "right to revenge." The exact opposite is true: The monopolization of the administration of criminal justice by the state is a substitute for the individual right to revenge. However, *communal* revenge remains the basis of at least two of the four classical purposes of criminal justice: "as punishment, life imprisonment—the supreme noncontroversial punishment—is assumed to satisfy and channel the community's need to express feelings of vengeance; as restraint, it is assumed . . . to provide a structure for satisfying vengeance." (J. Goldstein and J. Katz in *Daedalus* (Boston), summer 1963, p. 557.) Miss Arendt's contrasting of justice and "vengeance" is based on her indiscriminate use of the term "vengeance" in its opposite meanings: (1) Individually implemented, nonregulated, and uncontrolled vengeance, which is certainly the antithesis of justice, and (2) implemented community vengeance, regulated and controlled by the state, which is characteristic of criminal justice.

Finally, the extent to which she understands the principle of active nationality is revealed by her statement (p. 14) that "every sovereign state is jealous of its right to sit in judgment on its own offenders." This principle of active nationality is far from accepted by "every state," and stands in contradiction to the territoriality principle.

Miss Arendt states that the court asserted its jurisdiction over Eichmann on the basis of all three principles—universal jurisdiction, passive personality, and active nationality—and she continues, "as though merely adding together three entirely different legal principles would result in a valid claim" (p. 241). The court asserted its jurisdiction solely on the basis of the Israel law; but even if it had used three criteria, it would simply be fulfilling its obligations to justice in considering all the possibilities.

112. Session 117 (May 24, 1960) in the official records of the Bundestag (*Verhandlungen des deutschen Bundestages, 3. Wahlperiode, Stenographische Berichte,* Bonn), Vol. 46, pp. 6681C, 6684D, 6694B; Session 128 (October 21, 1960), *ibid.,* Vol. 47, p. 7384A; Sessions 147 (March 8, 1961) and 156 (April 21, 1961), *ibid.,* Vol. 48, pp. 8319D, 8946. See also the interpellation of the Social-Democratic Party on June 10, 1960 (*Verhandlungen . . . , Anlagen,* Vol. 68, *Drucksache* 1913) and the reply of the Minister of Justice, Dr. Fritz Schäffer, on June 22, 1960 (*ibid., Drucksache* 1951).

113. Dr. Schäffer, in a written statement dated June 22, 1960, said: "If Israel were to return Eichmann to Argentina, the Federal Government would without delay request the extradition of Eichmann from Argentina to the Federal Republic of Germany. As far as is admissible under international law, the Federal Government has asked foreign governments to extradite persons who are strongly suspected of having committed murder in Germany. Furthermore, in accordance with the provisions of the Passport Law, such persons are in all cases denied a passport or [if they have a passport, it is] withdrawn."

In Session 128, on October 21, 1960, Dr. Schäffer informed the Bundestag of the intention of the German judicial authorities "to ask the Israeli authorities to interrogate Eichmann in the presence of a German investigating judge (*Untersuchungsrichter*)" for the purpose of obtaining information needed in the preparation of the trial against Hermann Krumey, one of Eichmann's former subordinates. He further stated that steps had been taken to send an attorney from the staff of the *Zentrale Stelle der Landesjustizverwaltungen* in Ludwigsburg to Israel, who, "to the extent the Israel Government would authorize, would collect the necessary information in order to make the results of the Israeli investigations as far as possible available for utilization by the German prosecuting authorities." See note 112 for the sources of these two citations.

114. Decision of the Administrative Court of Cologne of April 4, 1961, in the case of Adolf Eichmann vs. the Federal Republic of Germany (not published, photocopy in my possession).

115. Julius Stone, *The Eichmann Trial and the Rule of Law* (Sydney, Australia: International Commission of Jurists, Australian Section, 1961), pp. 17-18.

116. Judgment, Sections 10 to 11.

117. *Ibid.*, Section 16.

118. Judgment of the Supreme Court, Section I(10).

119. Gideon Hausner, *6,000,000 Accusers: Israel's Case Against Eichmann* (Jerusalem: Jerusalem Post, 1961), pp. 309-313.

120. Transcript of tape 3, pp. 2-3.

121. Penal Law Revision (Abolition of the Death Penalty) Law, 5714/1954, in *Israel Government Yearbook 1954/5715* (Jerusalem: Government Printer, 1955), p. 249.

122. §§211 and 212 of the German Criminal Code.

123. 1 StR 179/61. Decision of June 13, 1961.

124. This was the label given to those German political parties which agreed, particularly after the occupation of the Ruhr District by the French, to comply with the provisions of the Versailles Treaty concerning German reparations.

125. Albert Krebs, *Tendenzen und Gestalten der NSDAP. Erinnerungen an die Frühzeit der Partei* (Stuttgart: Deutsche Verlags-Anstalt, 1959), p. 46.

126. Edmond Paris, *Genocide in Satellite Croatia 1941-1945: A Record of Racial and Religious Persecution and Massacres* (Chicago: American Institute for Balkan Affairs, 1961), 306 pp.

127. Nuremberg Document NO-3732: Die Frage der Behandlung der Bevölkerung der ehemaligen polnischen Gebiete nach rassenpolitischen Gesichtspunkten. Reproduced in Karol Marian Pospieszalski, *ed.*, *The Hitler "Law" of Occupation in Poland. Selected Documents. Part I: Incorporated Territories* (Poznań: Instytut Zachodni, 1952), pp. 2-28 (Polish). (*Documenta Occupationis*, Vol. V.) Himmler's memorandum "Über die Behandlung der Fremdvölkischen im Osten," is published in *Vierteljahrshefte für Zeitgeschichte* (Stuttgart), Vol. 5, 1957, pp. 194-198.

128. See Martin Broszat, *Nationalsozialistische Polenpolitik, 1939-1945* (Stuttgart: Deutsche Verlags-Anstalt, 1961), 300 pp. (*Schriftenreihe der Vierteljahrshefte für Zeitgeschichte*, No. 2.)

129. *Statement on War Losses and Damages of Poland in 1939-1945* (Warsaw: Presidium of the Council of Ministers, War Indemnities Office, 1947), p. 43.

130. Nuremberg Document USSR-172 in *Blue Series*, XXXIX, pp. 426, 427, 428, and, in particular, p. 429. For the *Volksliste* and re-Germanization see *Green Series*, IV, pp. 639-645, 714-816.

131. Broszat, *op. cit.*, p. 25.

132. The text, which is available in the Polish State Archives, is reproduced in part in Artur Eisenbach, *The Hitler Policy of the Extermination of the Jews* (Warsaw: Żydowski Instytut Historyczny, 1953), p. 107 (Polish).

133. Nuremberg Document NG-2325. Reproduced in *Vierteljahrshefte für Zeitgeschichte* (Stuttgart), Vol. 6, 1958, pp. 297-324.

134. Available in the original in the YIVO archives, Berlin Collection (Occ/E2-74).

135. Alexander Dallin, *German Rule in Russia, 1941-1945. A Study of Occupation Policies* (London: Macmillan; New York: St. Martin's Press, 1957), pp. 444-450. See also Broszat, *op. cit.*, pp. 114-117.

136. Broszat, *op. cit.*, p. 22.

137. On Nazi actions against Jewish intellectuals, see the following sources. For Warsaw: Emmanuel Ringelblum, *Notes from the Warsaw Ghetto* (Warsaw: Yiddish Bukh, Vol. II, 1963), pp. 53-74. For Częstochowa: L. Brener, *Resistance and Death in the Ghetto of Częstochowa* (Warsaw: Jewish Historical Institute [1951]), pp. 101-103. For Kaunas (Kovno): J. Gar, *The Destruction of Jewish Kovno* (Munich: Union of Lithuanian Jews, 1948), pp. 54-56. (All in Yiddish.)

138. See Jonas Turkow, *It Happened This Way* (Buenos Aires: Union of Polish Jews in Argentina, 1948), pp. 149-151, 269, 270, 494-495. Same author, *In the Struggle for Life* (Buenos Aires: Union of Polish Jews in Argentina, 1949), pp. 221-230. (Both in Yiddish.)

139. *Green Series*, X, pp. 1054 ff. Miss Arendt (p. 94) confuses the Commissar Order with another secret order of Hitler's, dated Sept. 16, 1944, concerning the suppression of uprisings in the occupied territories. See note 295 of Chapter 5.

140. We know that it had already been planned. Miss Arendt herself—quoting from Viktor Brack's testimony at Nuremberg—states that by March 1941 "it was no secret in higher Party circles that the Jews were to be exterminated" (p. 79).

141. Nuremberg Document NO-3414, *Green Series*, IV, pp. 123-132.

142. *Ibid.*, especially p. 130. However, from the reports of the *Einsatzgruppen* and the practice in regard to Russian prisoners of war, it is evident that these categories were applied without regard to the restrictions in the order.

143. Nuremberg Document NO-3414.

144. Alexander Dallin, *op. cit.*, pp. 426-427.

145. *Ibid.*, pp. 450-453.

146. *Vierteljahrshefte für Zeitgeschichte* (Stuttgart), Vol. 6, 1958, pp. 281-325, and Vol. 8, 1960, p. 119.

147. See, for example, Benedikt Kautsky, *Teufel und Verdammte* (Zurich: Büchergilde Gutenberg, 1946), pp. 129-133.

148. So Göring in his *Aufbau einer Nation*, quoted in Gerd Rühle, *Das Dritte Reich: Dokumentarische Darstellung des Aufbaus der Nation* (Berlin: Hummelverlag, 1933), p. 49. See also pp. 47, 48, 357.

149. Kautsky, *op. cit.* Kautsky knew the situation well. While a

prisoner, he had, with the exception of the last ten weeks prior to the liberation of Buchenwald, "always lived among Jews, for 4¾ years as a Jew and for two years as a German political prisoner" (*ibid.*, p. 11).

150. *Blue Series*, XXIX, pp. 133, 145.

151. Testimony of Raya Kagan in Session 103.

152. Hans-Joachim Döring, *Die Zigeuner im nationalsozialistischen Staat* (Hamburg: Kriminalistik-Verlag, 1964), pp. 18, 32, 38, 40-42, 56, 58, 60, 62-64, 67, 68-70, 82, 96-99, 105, 110-111, 117-118, 129-130, 139, 140-142, 143-145, 153, 155, 159, 160-161, 166-169, 170, 175, 179-188, 189-196. For official texts, see pp. 197-219. See also Richratl, *Sammlung der auf dem Gebiete der vorbeugenden Verbrecherbekämpfung ergangener Erlässe und sonstigen Bestimmungen. Vertraulich. Schriftenreihe des Reichskriminalpolizeiamtes Berlin No. 15* (Berlin: Reichssicherheitshauptamt, n.d.). This contains all provisions concerning Gypsies in the period from December 8, 1938, to January 30, 1943. (No pagination.)

153. Jerzy Ficowski, *The Polish Gypsies* (Warsaw: State Publishing Institute, 1953), p. 162 (Polish). Even Himmler had a soft spot for Gypsies, as told by Höss: "The Reichsführer SS wanted to insure that the two main Gypsy stocks [the Sinte and Lalleri Gypsies, according to the editor of the book] be preserved. I cannot recall their names. In his view they were the direct descendants of the original Indo-Germanic race, and had preserved their ways and customs more or less pure and intact." Rudolf Hoess, *Commandant of Auschwitz* (Cleveland and New York: World Publishing Company, n.d.), p. 137.

154. Hans-Joachim Döring, *op. cit.*, p. 144.

155. According to an oral communication (Nov. 24, 1964) from Professor Jan Sehn of Cracow University, the leading authority on Auschwitz, 30,000 Gypsies, all listed by name, were killed in Auschwitz.

156. For some sweeping views on the fate of Gypsies, see Döring, *op. cit.*, p. 191, n. 9.

157. J. Ficowski, *op. cit.*, p. 182. I was unable to find a reliable source for the number of Gypsies in prewar Poland.

158. Judgment, Sections 212 and 213.

159. See also Eliezer Yerushalmi, *Shavli Diary. A Diary from a Lithuanian Ghetto* (Jerusalem: Yad Washem, 1958), p. 302, for an account (in Hebrew) of a *Kinderaktion* in Šiauliai on Nov. 5, 1943; and Isaiah Trunk, *Ghetto Lodz. A Historical and Sociological Study* (New York: YIVO–Yad Washem, 1962), pp. 271-273, for an account (in Yiddish) of such an "action" in Lodz from Sept. 5 to 12, 1942. Estimates of the total number of Jewish children murdered by the Nazis during the war vary from 1,000,000 to 1,500,000.

160. Ilya Ehrenburg, *Murderers of Peoples* (Moscow: Emes, 1944), First collection, p. 45 (Yiddish).

161. The "Vlasov men" were members of a corps of disaffected Soviet prisoners of war under General Vlasov, himself a disaffected prisoner of war.

162. Joseph Gar, *op. cit.,* pp. 207-208.

163. Mark Dworzecki, *The Jerusalem of Lithuania in Struggle and Destruction: Memoirs of the Vilna Ghetto* (Paris: Jewish National Far-band, 1948), p. 490.

Chapter 3

1. Judgment, Sections 1 and 2.

2. See also the discussion on the court's jurisdiction in Chapter 2, under The Legal Basis for War Crimes Trials.

3. Sections 41 to 52 of the judgment deal with the legal implications of the act of abduction.

4. Statute of International Court of Justice, Art. 38(1)c. Art. 38 lists the sources of international law to be applied by the International Court of Justice; one of these sources is described by the quotation cited in the text.

5. Kurt R. Grossmann, *Ossietzky—ein deutscher Patriot* (Munich: Kindler, 1963), pp. 441-448.

6. See, for example, *The Great Soviet Encyclopedia,* 2nd edition, Vol. 41, p. 548 (Russian).

7. Henry Torrès, *Le Procès des pogromes* (Paris: Editions de France, 1928), 270 pp.

8. *Divrei Haknesset* [*The Records of the Knesset*] (Jerusalem: Government Printer, 1960), record of 98th meeting of May 23, 1960.

9. *New York Times,* May 24, 1960.

10. *New York Herald Tribune,* May 24, 1960.

11. *Haaretz* (Tel-Aviv), May 24, 1960.

12. The tape is deposited in the archives of Kol Israel, the Israel radio station. The first part of the session was played back to me at my request.

13. Records of the 865–868 meetings of the Security Council (June 22-23, 1960). See also note 101 of Chapter 2.

14. "In re Eichmann: A Dilemma of Law and Morality," *American Journal of International Law* (Washington, D.C.), Vol. 55, 1961, pp. 307-358.

15. Felix Luna, *Dialogos con Frondizi* (Buenos Aires: Editorial Desarolles, 1963), p. 131.

16. Discussing the problem of extradition of Eichmann to Germany,

Miss Arendt states that Fritz Bauer, the Attorney General of Hesse, in suggesting that Germany start negotiations with Israel for a special arrangement in the Eichmann Case (not "extradition proceedings," as Miss Arendt thinks), had acted not in his capacity as the competent Attorney General but in pursuance of his "feelings of a German Jew" (p. 14). She presents no evidence that he acted with this motivation, or that this motivation, if present, must necessarily have resulted in a desire to have Eichmann tried in Frankfurt.

17. J. Robinson and P. Friedman, *Guide to Jewish History Under Nazi Impact* (New York: Yad Washem–YIVO, 1960), pp. 119-121.

It should be noted that despite the excellence of the Yad Washem archives, the Israel police searched for material in other research institutes (Jewish and non-Jewish) and also in such collections as the World War II Archives in Alexandria, Va., where they found the record of the crucial meeting of Sept. 21, 1939, of the *Einsatzgruppen* commanders, under the chairmanship of Heydrich, with the participation of his aides, including Eichmann.

18. See the interview with Ben-Gurion in the *New York Times Magazine*, Dec. 18, 1960.

19. Session 26.

20. Session 67.

21. Session 27.

22. Session 7. Also in Gideon Hausner, *6,000,000 Accusers, Israel's Case Against Eichmann* (Jerusalem: Jerusalem Post, 1961), p. 32.

23. *Ibid.*, pp. 44-89.

24. T/164.

25. T/166.

26. T/185.

27. T/676 (Nuremberg Document NG-300).

28. T/312 to T/338.

29. The following is an account of what became of those officials concerning whom we have information:

> Dr. Werner Best. Condemned to death (1946) in Copenhagen. Sentence commuted to 5 years imprisonment. Released 1951. Lives in Germany.

> Ernst Biberstein, Chief of *Einsatzkommando 6* of *Einsatzgruppe C*. Condemned to death in *Einsatzgruppen* case (NMT, Case IX). Sentence commuted to life imprisonment by Clemency Board. Released May 1959.

> Dr. Walter Blume, Chief of *Sonderkommando 7a* of *Einsatzgruppe B*. Condemned to death in *Einsatzgruppen* case. Sentence commuted to 25 years imprisonment.

> Dr. Werner Braune, Chief of *Sonderkommando 11b* of *Einsatz-*

gruppe D. Condemned to death in *Einsatzgruppen* case and executed in 1951.

Dr. Joseph Bühler, *Staatssekretär* (the highest official, generally a career civil servant, on the staff of a German Minister) in the Government-General. Condemned to death in Poland and executed in 1948.

Dr. Roland Freisler, Presiding Judge of the People's Court. Killed 1944 in an air raid in Berlin.

Dr. Hans Globke, Ministry of Interior, Expert on Citizenship Problems. After the war, *Ministerialdirektor*, Chancellor's Office, 1950; *Staatssekretär*, 1953. Retired 1963.

Dr. Walter Haensch, Chief of *Sonderkommando 4b* of *Einsatzgruppe C.* Condemned to death in *Einsatzgruppen* case. Sentence commuted to 15 years imprisonment by Clemency Board.

Waldemar Klingelhöfer, Member of *Sonderkommando 7b* of *Einsatzgruppe B,* Chief of *Vorkommando Moskau.* Sentenced to death in *Einsatzgruppen* case. Sentence commuted to life imprisonment by Clemency Board.

Rudolph Lange, *Befehlshaber der Sicherheitspolizei* (*BdS*), Latvia. Allegedly shot in Russia (where he was held as a prisoner of war). According to a statement by the *Landgericht Hamburg,* dated May 24, 1961, he was killed in Poznań.

Dr. Karl Lasch, Governor of Radom District in the Government-General. Arrested for corruption early in 1942 and killed while in prison (see Martin Broszat, *Nationalsozialistische Polenpolitik, 1939-1945* [Stuttgart: Deutsche Verlags-Anstalt, 1961], p. 73 n.). According to other sources, he committed suicide.

Gustav Nosske, Chief of *Einsatzkommando 12* of *Einsatzgruppe D.* Sentenced to life imprisonment in *Einsatzgruppen* case. Sentence reduced to 10 years imprisonment by Clemency Board. Now free.

Otto Ohlendorf, Chief of *Einsatzgruppe D.* Condemned to death in *Einsatzgruppen* case. Executed 1951.

Dr. Erich Rajakovic, Gestapo legal expert. Arrested in Vienna in 1963; tried and sentenced to 2½ years imprisonment.

Dr. Otto Rasch, Chief of *Einsatzgruppe C.* Indicted in *Einsatzgruppen* case. Too ill to be tried (Parkinson's disease).

Dr. Martin Sandberger, Chief of *Einsatzkommando Ia* of *Einsatzgruppe A.* Sentenced to death in *Einsatzgruppen* case. Sentence commuted to life imprisonment by Clemency Board. Released May 1958.

Dr. Eberhard Schöngarth, *Befehlshaber der Sicherheitspolizei* (*BdS*), Government-General; *BdS*, Holland. Condemned to death by British military court and executed 1946.

Willy Seibert, Deputy Chief, *Einsatzgruppe D*. Condemned to death in *Einsatzgruppen* case. Sentence commuted to 15 years imprisonment by Clemency Board. Released 1955.

Dr. Franz Six, Chief, *Vorkommando Moskau* of *Einsatzgruppe B*. Sentenced to 20 years imprisonment in *Einsatzgruppen* case. Reduced to 10 years imprisonment by Clemency Board. Released 1952.

Eugen Steimle, Chief of *Sonderkommando 7a* of *Einsatzgruppe B*; Chief of *Sonderkommando 4a* of *Einsatzgruppe C*. Sentenced to death in *Einsatzgruppen* case. Sentence commuted to 20 years imprisonment by Clemency Board.

Dr. Wilhelm Stuckart, *Staatssekretär*, Interior Ministry. Sentenced in the Ministries case to time served because of ill health. Fined 500 mark by denazification court. Killed in automobile accident in 1953.

30. See, for example, the indictments in the Ulm and Auschwitz trials. Among evidence submitted by the prosecution in the Ulm trial (case against Bernhard Fischer-Schweder *et al.*) were documents dealing with persecution of the Jews before the outbreak of the war, and with such events as the *Kristallnacht*. Also submitted were the order of Göring on the "total solution of the Jewish problem," the Poznań speech of Himmler, and photographs of executions by *Einsatzkommandos* (*Anklageschrift*, dated June 25, 1957, *Aktenzeichen* Js 1/56). The indictment in the Auschwitz trial, dated April 16, 1963 (*Aktenzeichen* 4 Js 444/59) contains numerous references to the SS and to concentration camps. Three scholars from the *Institut für Zeitgeschichte* testified as expert witnesses on such subjects as Nazi persecution of the Jews in general (Dr. Helmut Krausnick); the SS and the police in the Third Reich and the general question of "superior orders" (Dr. Hans Buchheim); and German *Polenpolitik* (Dr. Martin Broszat).

31. *Saturday Evening Post*, Vol. 235, No. 39, Nov. 3, 1962, p. 20.

32. Professor Lipot Szondi, who devised the test named after him, is the author of professionally well-known works such as *Experimental Diagnostic of Drive* (New York, 1952); *Schicksalsanalyse*, 2nd edition (Basel, 1948); *The Szondi Test: Its Diagnosis, Prognosis, and Treatment* (Philadelphia, 1959).

33. The Szondi test was administered to Eichmann by psychiatrists of the Israel Health Department; his responses to the test were sent to Professor Szondi for evaluation. Szondi did not know who the person tested was. For further details see the article cited in note 31.

34. For a recent discussion of *mens sana* and legal insanity, see J.

Goldstein and J. Katz in *Daedalus* (Boston), summer 1963, pp. 549-563, and in *Yale Law Journal* (New Haven), Vol. 72, 1963, pp. 853-876, with numerous references.

35. H. G. Adler, *Theresienstadt 1941-1945: Das Antlitz einer Zwangsgemeinschaft. Geschichte, Soziologie, Psychologie* (Tübingen: J. C. B. Mohr [Paul Siebeck], 1960), 892 pp.

36. Session 45. At Session 44 Mr. Bar-Or submitted to the court an affidavit by Dr. Adler (T/852).

37. According to the files of the Israel Ministry of Justice *re* Eichmann, Dr. Servatius asked for the book on behalf of his client, and the request was honored.

38. T/3.

39. Art. 15 [of the Israel law]: (a) In an action for an offense under this law, the Court may deviate from the rules of evidence if it is satisfied that this will promote the ascertainment of the truth and the just trial of the case; (b) Whenever the Court decides to deviate, under subsection (a), from the rules of evidence, it shall place on record the reasons which prompted its decision.

40. Julius Stone, *The Eichmann Trial and the Rule of Law* (Sydney, Australia: International Commission of Jurists, 1961), p. 17.

41. Judgment, Section 3. The "slight deviations . . . from the narrow path which the court found itself obliged to designate" is an apparent reference to the exchange between the presiding judge and the Attorney General on the relevance of Jewish Resistance to the subject matter of the trial. This took place in connection with Abba Kovner's testimony (Session 27).

42. *Blue Series*, XXII, pp. 493, 496.

43. This is an obvious typographical error. Eichmann's final rank was *Obersturmbannführer*.

44. *Blue Series*, XXII, p. 509.

45. T/37, containing 3,564 pages.

46. Sessions 88-107.

47. For example, the records of the Wannsee Conference of January 20, 1942, and those of the sterilization conferences of March 6, 1942, and October 27, 1942, were submitted to the NMT in the Ministries case (Case No. XI) without the accompanying letters discovered by the Israel police. Another example is the correspondence between Ribbentrop's personal office (then on the special railroad train "Westfalen") and the German Foreign Office in February 1943 in connection with German dissatisfaction with Italian policies toward Jews in occupied France and the Balkans (NG-4956; T/610, T/611). The Israel police discovered this correspondence (T/612 to T/614).

48. T/164.

49. T/1395 to T/1398, and T/1400 (a selection of documents from those files).

50. T/142, T/144, T/145, T/148. Miss Arendt errs, however, when she writes that the "Löwenherz" memorandum was "one of the few new documents produced by the trial" (pp. 57-58). What Miss Arendt calls the "Löwenherz" memorandum was actually compiled by Wilhelm Bienenfeld, an official of the Vienna Community (*Kultusgemeinde*), in 1946 for the case against Baldur von Schirach. At that time Löwenherz was no longer in Vienna. The memorandum, far from being new, had already been known to the prosecution at the IMT (Nuremberg Document 3934-PS). It was analyzed by H. G. Adler, *op. cit.*, pp. 772-774 (a book listed in Miss Arendt's Bibliography).

51. T/1107 and T/1116.

52. The Sassen Papers are the typewritten transcripts of tapes containing Eichmann's story as it was told to Willem Antonius Maria Sassen, a former Dutch National Socialist newspaperman, now living in Buenos Aires. The original set consisted of 67 such transcripts (one transcript per tape), numbered from 1 to 67. Five of the transcripts are missing in my set. The transcripts were bound in 17 folders (*Leitz* binders), with each volume containing from three to seven transcripts. It appears that Eichmann read all the transcripts, for throughout the set there are corrections in his handwriting. In some cases the transcript is preceded by a list of numbered corrections (transcripts 11 and 12), each referring to a specific word or sentence in the transcript. In other instances, there are handwritten (e.g., transcript 51) or, more frequently, typewritten additions of one or more pages located either at the beginning or at the end of a transcript. These additions—which may have been either part of the tape or added to the typed transcript—are sometimes called *Bemerkungen am Rande* ("marginal notes") or *Extrablatt* ("additional page"). Each of the transcripts is individually paginated.

53. The court admitted in evidence only one complete folder, the last (17th) one, which carries the exhibit number T/1393. T/1393a is a collection of fragments from the 16 folders on whose authenticity both parties agreed. Twenty-four other fragments from the 16 folders are contained in T/1432.

54. It is regrettable that those in possession of the tapes did not find themselves in a position to submit them to the court.

55. Chapter 1, under Attitude Toward His Work.

56. Chapter 5, under Germany.

57. *Aliyah Beth* is the Hebrew name for the "illegal" immigration of Jews to Palestine.

58. Chapter 5, under The "Protectorate" and Theresienstadt.

59. Chapter 4, under Jewish Resistance and the Will To Live.

60. *Blue Series*, I, pp. 6, 7.

61. *Green Series*, I, p. 7; V, p. 199; XII, pp. 10, 11.

62. See note 78 of Chapter 1, and the text to which that note refers.

63. *Guide to Captured German Documents*, prepared under contract with the Bureau of Applied Social Research, Columbia University, by Gerhard L. Weinberg and the War Documentation Project staff under the direction of Fritz T. Epstein (Maxwell Air Force Base, Alabama: Air University Human Resources Research Institute, Dec. 1952), 90 pp. (mimeograph). (Research Memorandum No. 2, Vol. 1, HRRI, "War Documentation Project"). And *Supplement to the Guide to Captured German Documents*, prepared by Gerhard L. Weinberg (Washington, D.C.: The National Archives, the American Historical Association, Committee for the Study of War Documents, 1959), 69 pp. (mimeograph).

64. *Guides to German Records Microfilmed at Alexandria, Va.* Prepared by the American Historical Association, Committee for the Study of War Documents (Washington, D.C.: The National Archives, 1958 *et seq.*). See in particular Guides Nos. 32, 33, 39.

65. No comparable inventories are available of the documents captured by the U.S.S.R. and by formerly occupied countries. Individual documents emanating from Leipzig (T/647), Potsdam (T/811), and Frankfurt an der Oder (T/644) were available in the documentation of the Eichmann trial. Some documents captured by the Poles in Poznań, Lodz, and Danzig were also put at the disposal of the prosecution.

66. He made two such comments in the opening of the case for the defense (Session 75); see also his reactions to the files of the Gestapo (*Leitstelle* Düsseldorf (T/1395-T/1398) in Session 74 and to T/649 in Session 37.

67. See note 71 of Chapter 1. Miss Arendt is apparently referring to the declaration dated June 22, 1945. In this declaration Mildner states that he had heard from others that Himmler's orders concerning the killing of Jews in concentration camps were channeled through Pohl and Glücks of the WVHA.

68. *Green Series*, V, p. 981.

69. Chapter 1, under Background and Character.

70. Ka-tzetnik 135633, *House of Dolls* (New York: Simon & Schuster, 1955), 245 pp.; *Piepel* (London: Anthony Blond, 1961), 285 pp.; *Atrocity* (New York: Lyle Stuart, 1963), 217 pp. (this is the American title of the British *Piepel*).

71. Session 68.

72. Ben-Zion Dinur, author of numerous books and articles on various problems of Jewish history, including the voluminous *Sources of Jewish History*, now in progress. In the paperback edition, p. 204, the characterization of the name as "unlikely" is omitted.

73. Judgment, Section 119.

74. In the secret indictment (*Anklageschrift*) of October 16, 1941, of Herschel Feibel (Hermann) Grynszpan (case 8 J 393/41 g) by the Attorney General of the Nazi People's Court (*Der Oberreichsanwalt beim Volksgerichtshof*), the following is said about homosexuality: "In the course of further interrogations, he [Grynszpan] even went so far as to make the brazen and false claim that he had met Embassy Counselor vom Rath already some time before [the shooting] and that he had been used by him several times for homosexual purposes." A photocopy of the indictment and its annexes is available in the *Centre de Documentation Juive Contemporaine* (Paris). A brief survey of the documentation is offered by Lucien Steinberg in *Le Monde Juif* (Paris), April-June, 1964.

75. Judgment, Section 57.

76. Transcript of tape 4, p. 1.

77. T/37, pp. 2464 ff.

78. Eichmann's conclusion: "there were apparently no men behind Grynszpan . . . he committed his deed on his own." (Transcript of tape 4, p. 1).

79. Session 27. Miss Arendt's selectivity in identifying positive types is reflected in her failure to mention the Swiss Consul General, Carl Lutz, and the Swedish diplomat, Raoul Wallenberg, who in a courageous, systematic effort rescued thousands of Hungarian Jews. Wallenberg was seized by the Soviets and has not been heard from. (Kasztner Report [T/1113], 230 ff., 236; Philip Friedman, *Their Brothers' Keepers* [New York: Crown Publishers, 1957], pp. 83, 159-168, 217-218.)

80. Session 22.

81. Session 30.

82. Session 28.

83. Session 65.

84. See the survey of the 1,500 witnesses heard before the IMT and NMT, *Catalogue of Nuremberg Documents* (London: Wiener Library, 1961), pp. 79-139 (mimeograph).

85. Göring, Ribbentrop, Rosenberg, Schirach, Sauckel, and Fritzsche pleaded in this manner before the IMT (*Blue Series*, II, pp. 97-98).

86. See also Judgment, Section 119.

87. Session 41.

88. *Ibid.* According to Wisliceny (T/84), Eichmann was "brutal to his subordinates and without interest in their personal welfare."

89. Session 41.

90. *Ibid.*

91. *Green Series*, V, p. 1129. In the same Pohl case, Eichmann's personal file (Doc. NO-2259) and excerpts from the Wisliceny testimony before the IMT were introduced in evidence by the defense (*Green Series*, V, pp. 689-692, 810-811).

92. *Green Series*, IV, p. 114. In the official transcript of Case IX

of the Subsequent Trials, the *Einsatzgruppen* case (mimeographed), Judge Musmanno's questioning of defendants and their counsels concerning Eichmann can be found on pages 3498-3501. In the same case, Wisliceny's testimony before the International Military Tribunal regarding Eichmann's status was introduced at the request of Ohlendorf's attorney.

93. *The New Yorker*, April 27, 1963, p. 108.

94. *Green Series*, IV, p. 3.

95. Sessions 39, 40.

96. Judgment, Section 54.

97. Erich von dem Bach-Zelewski, Richard Baer, Hermann Krumey (in the Federal Republic of Germany); Franz Novak and Franz Slavik (in Austria); Herbert Kappler (in Italy).

98. Kurt Becher, Hans Jüttner, Max Merten, Franz Six, Eberhard von Thadden, Edmund Veesenmayer, Otto Winkelmann, Horst Grell.

99. Wilhelm Höttl and Walter Huppenkothen.

100. The Judgment (Section 54) says:

> Most of the evidence submitted in this case falls into five categories . . .
>
> b) Declarations, on oath and not on oath, and records of evidence given in previous trials by persons who are no longer alive, including war criminals who were punished, and also by living persons. We admitted this evidence by virtue of the special authority which is given to this court by Section 15 of the Nazis and Nazi Collaborators (Punishment) Law, 5710/1950 [see note 39 of this Chapter], and in every such instance we gave our reasons for admitting the evidence, as required by that Section. Obviously, the weight which is to be given to evidence admitted in this way still remains a matter for careful consideration by the court, depending upon the man who gave the evidence or the declaration, whether he was an accomplice in the crime, any special interest he might have had in diverting blame from himself to the accused, the lack of opportunity for cross-examination by the accused, etc.

See also Section 176.

101. *Bulletin of the International Commission of Jurists* (Geneva), No. 14, October 1962, pp. 13-19. Compare Miss Arendt's ridicule of the Eichmann trial as a "historic trial" on her page 85.

102. Miss Arendt finds fault with the court for having "followed the definitions of 'criminal organizations' established at Nuremberg" (pp. 142-143) and pleads for inclusion in this category of more organizations which participated in the Jewish Catastrophe. This criticism is without foundation. The function of the court was to try not organizations but

only Adolf Eichmann, though sometimes in his capacity as member of certain organizations; not one of those to which Eichmann belonged was left out. (See points 13-16 of the Conclusions of the judgment.)

103. Judgment, Section 34.

104. Judgment, Section 137.

105. Judgment, Sections 138 and 132.

106. Judgment, Section 180.

107. Judgment, Section 190.

108. Judgment, Sections 192-194.

109. Judgment, Section 197. This sentence should be translated: "In such an enormous and complex crime . . . in which many people participated . . . there is not much point in using the ordinary concepts of aiding and abetting the commission of a crime."

110. Supreme Court Judgment, Section I(5).

111. Sessions 39, 40.

112. Supreme Court Judgment, Section I(5).

113. *Nach dem Eichmann Prozess. Zu einer Kontroverse über die Haltung der Juden* (London-Jerusalem-New York: Council of Jews from Germany, 1963), p. 100. Also private communication from Martin Buber, dated September 3, 1964. A similar argument was developed by Gershom Scholem in his article "Eichmann," *Amoth* (Tel-Aviv), Vol. I, 1962, pp. 10-11 (Hebrew).

114. *Mishna Avot* 5, 8 and *Sanhedrin* 11, 4. There was no reason for delay. His wife had already seen him before he was sentenced, and no other member of his family had expressed the wish to see him before the execution.

115. For a general survey, see M. Muszkat, "Reactions to the Eichmann Trial," *Yad Washem Bulletin* (Jerusalem), No. 13, October 1963, pp. 48-53. For the United States, see the two reports published by the American Jewish Committee: *The Eichmann Case in the American Press* (New York, n.d.), 87 pp. (listed in Miss Arendt's Bibliography); and George Salomon's "The End of Eichmann: America's Response" in the *American Jewish Year Book* (New York), Vol. 64, 1963, pp. 247-259. See also Irving Crespi, "Public Reaction to the Eichmann Trial," *The Public Opinion Quarterly* (Princeton), Vol. 28, 1964, No. 1, pp. 91-103. For Germany, see Hans Lamm, *Der Eichmann-Prozess in der öffentlichen Meinung* (Frankfurt a.M.: Ner Tamid, 1961), 73 pp.

116. See, for example, Ilse Staff, *Justiz im Dritten Reich. Eine Dokumentation* (Frankfurt, a.M.: Fischer-Bücherei, 1964), p. 95. The following *Führerworte* are quoted by Miss Staff (p. 61): "Wer Landesverrat übt, soll nicht bestraft werden nach dem Umfang und Ausmass seiner Tat, sondern nach seiner zutage getretenen Gesinnung." ("He

who commits treason shall not be punished in accordance with the scope and extent of his deed but on the basis of the convictions he manifested.") (Originally published in *Völkischer Beobachter* [Berlin], July 14, 1934.)

Miss Arendt categorically declares that "not . . . racism" was "on trial" (p. 3). But she asserts that Eichmann deserved the death penalty because (p. 255) he "supported and carried out a policy of not wanting to share the earth with the Jewish people."

117. *International Affairs* (London), Vol. 38, 1962, p. 423. This authoritative statement of an expert in law stands in direct contradiction to Miss Arendt's prophecy (pp. 249-250) that "it is safe to predict that this last of the Successor trials will no more, and perhaps even less than its predecessors, serve as a valid precedent for future trials of such crimes."

118. *The Spectator* (London), Jan. 5, 1962.

119. *Current Legal Problems* (London), Vol. 15, 1962, p. 265.

120. Section 2, *in fine*.

121. The information in this paragraph is based on an unpublished paper by Dr. Leni Yahil, Jerusalem.

122. *Yedioth Yad Washem* (Jerusalem), No. 28, December 1961, pp. 8-10, and No. 29, July 1962, pp. 49-50 (Hebrew).

123. Moshe Bar-Nathan, "The Authors and the Party," *Jewish Frontier* (New York), November 1963, pp. 4-7 (analysis of the discussion as presented in the Tel-Aviv daily *Maariv*).

124. Erwin Schüle, "Die Justiz der Bundesrepublik und die Sühne nationalsozialistischen Unrechts," *Vierteljahrshefte für Zeitgeschichte* (Stuttgart), Vol. 9, 1961, pp. 440-443. For a detailed survey of trials (mainly German) of Nazi criminals against the background of Nazi crimes and for an analysis of the German legal problems involved, see Reinhard Henkys, *Die nationalsozialistischen Gewaltverbrechen. Geschichte und Gericht* (Stuttgart-Berlin: Kreuz-Verlag, 1964), pp. 25-266; Jürgen Baumann, "Die strafrechtliche Problematik der nationalsozialistischen Gewaltverbrechen," in the foregoing title, pp. 267-321; also Baumann's article in *Neue Juristische Wochenschrift* (Munich and Berlin), Vol. 17, 1964, pp. 1398-1405. For a Jewish survey of (mostly) German trials, see Emmanuel Brand, "The Handling of Nazi Criminals after World War II," *Bitfutsoth Hagolah* (Jerusalem), No. 1(28), 1964, pp. 18-27 (Hebrew). A tabular survey of the German trials can be found in Hermann Langbein's thoughtful book, *Im Namen des deutschen Volkes: Zwischenbilanz der Prozesse wegen nationalsozialistischer Verbrechen* (Vienna, Cologne, Stuttgart, Zurich: Europa Verlag, 1963), pp. 149-197. For an official account published by the Federal Republic

NOTES ON CHAPTER 3

of Germany see: *Die Verfolgung nationalsozialistischer Straftaten im Gebiet der Bundesrepublik Deutschland seit 1945* (Bonn: Bundesjustiz-ministerium, 1964), 108 pp. A list of cases is given on pp. 71-103. See also the report of the Federal Minister of Justice (German Bundestag, Printed Matter IV/3124, February 26, 1965), 37 pp., and the March 10, 1965, debate in the Bundestag (Official Records, pp. 8516-8571). The introduction of the specific term "crimes of Nazi violence" instead of "war crimes" is welcome. War crimes may be attributed to all parties in a war, not so the "crimes of Nazi violence."

125. Private communication of Dr. Erwin Schüle of the Central Agency of the Ministries of Justice in the *Länder* (Germany), dated Jan. 14, 1964.

126. §§67 and 68 of the German Criminal Code. See also Hans Welzel, *Das Deutsche Strafrecht* (Berlin: Walter de Gruyter, 1958), pp. 219-220.

Chapter 4

1. On page 110 Miss Arendt quotes Eichmann as using the phrase "the very cornerstone" in characterizing the place of alleged Jewish cooperation in the overall framework of Nazi anti-Jewish policy. Neither Eichmann nor any witness, judge, or counsel ever used this or a similar phrase, or ever implied that without "Jewish cooperation" the Nazi program would have foundered.

2. Oral communication of Professor G. M. Gilbert in July 1963; confirmed in writing June 9, 1964.

3. G. M. Gilbert, *Nuremberg Diary* (New York: New American Library, 1947), p. 28.

4. *Ibid.*, p. 74.

5. *Ibid.*, pp. 28-29.

6. Charles Wighton, *Heydrich: Hitler's Most Evil Henchman* (Philadelphia–New York: Chilton Co., 1962), pp. 270-279.

7. Gerald Reitlinger, *The Final Solution: The Attempt to Extermi-nate the Jewish People of Europe 1939-1945* (New York: Beechhurst Press, 1953), p. 100, and British edition (London: Vallentine, Mitchel, 1953). German translation: *Die Endlösung* (Berlin: Colloquium Verlag, 1960), 3rd edition, p. 111. Reitlinger refers the reader to Willi Frischauer, *Himmler, the Evil Genius of the Third Reich* (Boston: Beacon Press, 1953), p. 195: "As Heydrich expiated his sins and died with

a sneer on his lips . . . " See also Eugen Kogon, *Der SS-Staat. Das System der deutschen Konzentrationslager* (Frankfurt a.M.: Europäische Verlagsanstalt, 1959), p. 35.

8. G. M. Gilbert, *op. cit.*, pp. 24-25 and *passim*.

9. *Blue Series*, XII, p. 13.

10. *Ibid.*, XXII, p. 385. The Introduction to *Guide to Jewish History Under Nazi Impact* (New York: Yad Washem–YIVO, 1960), by Jacob Robinson and Philip Friedman, contains the story of Frank's recantation in the first paragraph. (This book is listed in Miss Arendt's Bibliography.)

11. Personal file of Heydrich in Berlin Document Center (available in *Yad Washem*). No serious counterevidence has been presented against the genealogy in this file.

12. Berlin-Leipzig: Max Hesse, 1916, p. 467.

13. The allegedly Jewish origin of Heydrich is mentioned by Felix Kersten in his *Totenkopf und Treue: Himmler ohne Uniform* (Hamburg: Robert Mölisch, 1952), pp. 127-131; and, on Kersten's authority, also by Charles Wighton, *op. cit.*, pp. 21-27. Robert M. W. Kempner, in his *Eichmann und Komplizen* (pp. 36-38), seems at first to have accepted the view that Heydrich was not free of Jewish blood, but in the 1964 Hebrew edition of his book (Tel-Aviv: Schocken) he dropped all mention of this. Eichmann told Sassen that he heard of this allegation, but it was all "a lie and a smear" (*Lüge und Verleumdung*). See transcript of tape 4, p. 4; and transcript of tape 64, p. 3.

14. The author is indebted to Josef Wulf for checking the personal file of Hans Frank in the Berlin Document Center.

15. Arnold and Veronica Toynbee, eds., *Hitler's Europe* (London, New York, Toronto: Oxford University Press, 1954), p. 119. Published for the Royal Institute of International Affairs, as part of its Survey of International Affairs, War-time Series (1939-1946).

16. *Ibid.*, pp. 480-481.

17. *Ibid.*, pp. 120-121.

18. *Ibid.*, p. 103.

19. Decree on the administration of Polish communities of Nov. 28, 1939, and decree on the formation and administration of communal associations in the Government-General of June 27, 1940, both reproduced in *Documenta Occupationis* (Poznań: Western Institute, 1958), Vol. VI, pp. 73-78.

20. Toynbee, *op. cit.*, pp. 93-95 and *passim*.

21. *Ibid.*, p. 93 and *passim*.

22. *Ibid.*, p. 125.

23. *Ibid.*, p. 480, footnote 2.

24. *The Institute Anniversary Volume: 1941-1961* (New York: Institute of Jewish Affairs, 1962), pp. 106-108, 111.

25. Toynbee, *op. cit.*, pp. 233-234, 237-238, 240-241.

26. See E. Brodsky's account of the resistance group called "The Fraternal Association of Prisoners of War," *Novy Mir* (Moscow), August 1957, pp. 188-201, and June 1964, pp. 258-276.

27. See note 7 of this chapter.

28. Raul Hilberg, *The Destruction of the European Jews* (Chicago: Quadrangle Books, 1961), 788 pp.

29. See, for example, Joseph Melkman's review of Hilberg, *op. cit.*, in *Kiryat Sefer* (Jerusalem), Vol. 39, 1963, pp. 212-214 (Hebrew).

30. *Encyclopedia of the Jewish Diaspora. A Memorial Library of Countries and Communities.* Poland Series (Jerusalem: Encyclopedia Publishing House, 1953-1957), 6 volumes (Hebrew). Also *Towns and Cities in Israel. A Sacred Monument of the Communities of Israel Destroyed by the Unholy Tyrants in the Last World War* (Jerusalem: Mosad Harav Kook, 1946-1955), 6 volumes (Hebrew). Accounts of the Catastrophe do not constitute a major part of the latter series. By contrast, the former series contains detailed description of the life and death of such communities as Warsaw (Vol. I, columns 601-816; Vol. VI, columns 29-48, 331-360, 489-650), Brest-Litovsk (Vol. II, pp. 453-547), Tarnopol (Vol. III, pp. 377-426), Lwów (Vol. IV, pp. 593-730), and Lublin (Vol. V, pp. 655-752).

31. Rachel Auerbach, "Yizkor Books," *Tsukunft* (New York), Vol. 63, 1958, pp. 186-189, 388-391 (Yiddish). Also Nachman Blumental, "Memorial Books of Remnants of Communities," *Yad Washem Bulletin* (Jerusalem), No. 15-16, 1958, pp. 22-24 (Hebrew), and the Yiddish edition, No. 3, 1958, pp. 26-28. And Blumental's "A New Literary Genre—The Memorial Books," *Lebensfragen* (Tel-Aviv), Vol. X, 1960, Nos. 99, 100, 102-103, 105, 108-109, 110; Vol. XI, 1961, Nos. 113-114, 117 (Yiddish).

32. Bernard Mark, *The Struggle and Destruction of the Warsaw Ghetto* (Warsaw: Ministry of National Defense, 1959), 509 pp. (Polish). German translation: *Der Aufstand im Warschauer Ghetto, Entstehung und Verlauf* (Berlin: Dietz, 1959), 479 pp., 3rd ed., revised and enlarged.

33. Mark Dworzecki, *The Jerusalem of Lithuania in Struggle and Destruction. Memoirs of the Vilna Ghetto* (Paris: Jewish National Labor Farband, 1948), 515 pp. (Yiddish); (Tel-Aviv: Israel Labor Party, 1951), 431 pp. (Hebrew).

34. Leib Garfunkel, *The Destruction of Jewish Kovno* (Jerusalem: Yad Washem, 1959), 330 pp. (Hebrew). Also Joseph Gar, *The Destruction of Jewish Kovno* (Munich: Association of Lithuanian Jews, 1948), 424 pp. (Yiddish).

35. Nachman Blumental, *Conduct and Actions of a Judenrat. Docu-*

ments from the Białystok Ghetto (Jerusalem: Yad Washem, 1962), 561 pp. (Hebrew and Yiddish), with Introduction in Hebrew and English.

36. Isaiah Trunk, *Ghetto Lodz: A Historical and Sociological Study, Including Documents, Maps and Tables* (New York: Yad Washem–YIVO, 1962), 528 pp. (Yiddish).

37. Aryeh Bauminger, Meir Busak, and Nathan Michael Gelber, eds., *The Book of Cracow* (Jerusalem: Mosad Harav Kook, 1959), pp. 381-429 (Hebrew). Tadeusz Pankiewicz, *The Pharmacy in the Cracow Ghetto* (Cracow: Świat i Wiedza, 1947), 151 pp. (Polish).

38. Eliezer Yerushalmi, *Shavli Diary. A Diary from a Lithuanian Ghetto* (Jerusalem: Yad Washem, 1958), 420 pp. (Hebrew).

39. Liber Brener, *Resistance and Destruction of the Częstochowa Ghetto* (Warsaw: Jewish Historical Institute [1951]), 176 pp. (Yiddish).

40. Philip Friedman, *The Destruction of the Jews in Lwów* (Munich: 1947), 39 pp. (Polish). See also note 30 of this chapter.

41. The literature must be read critically, using generally accepted historiographic methods, including careful comparison of materials on the same subject emanating from more than one source. For instance, we have contradictory evaluations of personalities like Czerniakow and Gens by their contemporaries. Bernard Mark, in *Bleter far Geshikhte* (Warsaw), Vol. 4, 1951, No. 1, p. 11; Melekh Neustadt (Noy), *Destruction and Revolt in the Warsaw Ghetto* (Tel-Aviv: Histadrut, 1948), p. 80; and Bernard Goldstein, *Five Years in the Warsaw Ghetto* (New York: Unser Tsait, 1947), p. 255 (all Yiddish) are sharply critical. A different view is expressed by Bernard Mark in an earlier book, *The Book of Heroism* (Lodz: Dos naie leben, 1947), p. 38. On the other hand, Nathan Eck, *Wandering on the Roads of Death* (Jerusalem: Yad Washem, 1960), pp. 54-56 (Hebrew) is sympathetic toward Czerniakow. On Gens, see the survey of his activities and personality by Philip Friedman, in *Bitsaron* (New York), Vol. 29, 1954, pp. 151-158, 232-239 (Hebrew), with many references.

42. T. Brustin-Berenstein, "Research on the Jewish Councils," *Yedies: Bulletin of the Jewish Historical Institute in Poland* (Warsaw), November 1949, pp. 9-10 (Yiddish).

43. *The Wiener Library Bulletin* (London), Vol. 9, 1955, p. 21.

44. Philip Friedman, "Preliminary and Methodological Problems of the Research on the Jewish Catastrophe in the Nazi Period," *Yad Washem Studies* (Jerusalem), Vol. II, 1958, pp. 95-113.

45. Judgment, Sections 63 to 67.

46. T/164.

47. It is symptomatic of the Germans' arbitrary polyarchic methods in dealing with the Jews that the German police chief in Warsaw, in establishing the Warsaw Ghetto in October 1939, did not wait for a

"general" proclamation of the Governor General, Hans Frank, whose ordinance on the establishment of Jewish Councils was dated five weeks later (November 28, 1939) and published afterward in the Official Gazette (*Verordnungsblatt des General-Gouverneurs für die besetzten polnischen Gebiete*, No. 9, December 6, 1939, pp. 72-73).

48. *Nowa Gazeta Warszawska* (Warsaw), October 28, 1939. On Czerniakow's title of "Senator," see note 60 of this chapter.

49. T/165 (Nuremberg Document 3363-PS, reproduced in English translation in *Red Series*, Vol. VI, pp. 97-101).

50. For Eichmann's interpretation of this word, see Chapter 1, under Eichmann's Conscience and "The New Type of Criminal."

51. *Zygelboim Book*, compiled by J. Sh. Herz (New York: Unser Tsait, 1947), pp. 120-121 (Yiddish).

52. *Ibid.*, pp. 126-130.

53. Philip Friedman, *Yad Washem Studies* (Jerusalem), Vol. II, 1958, p. 106.

54. Emmanuel Ringelblum, *Notes from the Ghetto* (Warsaw: Yiddish Bookh, 1961), Vol. I, p. 234, note 110 (Yiddish).

55. Jonas Turkow, *It Happened This Way. The Destruction of Warsaw* (Buenos Aires: Central Union of Polish Jews in Argentina, 1948), pp. 58-69, 291-292 (Yiddish). For a lively account of the Tenants' Committees see Nathan Eck, *op. cit.*, pp. 20-29.

56. Livia Rotkirchen, *Destruction of the Slovak Jews* (Jerusalem: Yad Washem, 1961), pp. 227-242 and *passim*. (Hebrew; Introduction also in English).

57. Th. Lavi (Löwenstein), "Documents on the Struggle of Rumanian Jews for Their Rights during the Second World War," *Yad Washem Studies* (Jerusalem), Vol. IV, 1960, pp. 261-315. A more comprehensive account is contained in the same author's *Rumanian Jewry in World War II: Fight for Survival* (Jerusalem: Yad Washem and Union of Romanian Jews, 1965), 149 pp. (Hebrew, with an English summary).

58. *Kasztner Report* (see note 6 of Chapter 1), submitted to the court as T/1113.

59. *Zygelboim Book, loc. cit.*, p. 127.

60. Apolinary Hartglass, in *Yad Washem Bulletin* (Jerusalem), No. 15, 1964, pp. 4-7 (an excerpt from Hartglass' extensive [unpublished] diary).

61. See, for example, *Grodno Echoes* (Buenos Aires), No. 2, 1949, p. 13 (Yiddish). Also Herman Kruk, *Diary of the Vilna Ghetto* (New York: YIVO Institute for Jewish Research, 1961), p. 10 (Yiddish).

62. Benjamin Mintz and Israel Klausner, eds., *The Book of Horrors* (Jerusalem: Rubin Mass for United Rescue Committee of the Jewish Agency, 1945), Vol. I, pp. 67-68 (Hebrew).

63. Isaiah Trunk, *op. cit.*, p. 362. Also Artur Eisenbach, *The Lodz Ghetto*, Vol. 3 of the Series "Documents and Materials Relevant to the History of the German Occupation of Poland" (Warsaw-Lodz-Cracow: Central Jewish Historical Commission), p. 21 (Polish).

64. Michael Molho, *In Memoriam. Hommage aux victimes juives des Nazis en Grèce* (Saloniki: N. Nicolaides, 1948), Vol. I, p. 3.

65. *Ibid.*, pp. 92-93.

66. *Ibid.*, pp. 34, 40, 57-58.

67. *Ibid.*, p. 92.

68. Gerald Reitlinger, *op. cit.*, p. 425 (German edition).

69. Transnistria (meaning "beyond the river Dniester," which used to be the frontier between Russia and Romania) embraced the Soviet territories between the rivers Dniester and Bug. The Jewish population of this occupied area consisted of local Jews (including those of Odessa) and Jews deported from Romania in 1941 and 1942. Almost half of the Jewish population of Bessarabia, Bucovina, and the Moldavian county of Dorohoi had already been exterminated before the establishment of short-lived Transnistria in October 1941. It is estimated that out of a total of 450,000 Jews concentrated in Transnistria in October, 350,000 were exterminated. Matatias Carp, *Cartea Neagră. Suferinţele Evreilor din România, 1940-1944*, Vol. III: Transnistria (Bucharest: Societatea Nationala de Editura Şi Arte Grafice "Dacia Traiană," 1947), pp. 8-9 (Romanian). Also Meir Teich, "The Jewish Self-Government in Ghetto Shargorod (Transnistria)," *Yad Washem Studies* (Jerusalem), Vol. II, 1958, pp. 219-255. For a scholarly account of Transnistria, see Alexander Dallin, *Odessa 1941-1944: A Case Study on Soviet Territory Under Foreign Rule* (Santa Monica: Rand Corporation, 1957), pp. 45-109.

70. Matatias Carp, *op. cit.*, pp. 15-16.

71. Shaul Barkli (ed.), *Eyszyszki: Its History and Destruction* (Jerusalem: Committee for the Survivors of Eyszyszki in Israel, 1950), p. 61 (Hebrew), p. 96 (Yiddish). On the reluctance of the leaders of the Jewish communities to accept membership in the Councils in the period following the Nazi invasion of the U.S.S.R. see: for Grodno, *Grodno Echoes* (Buenos Aires), No. 2, 1949, p. 13; for Vilna, Herman Kruk, *op. cit.*, pp. 10-12; for Białystok, Nachman Blumental, *Conduct and Actions of a Judenrat*, *loc. cit.*, pp. 219-221; for Lwów, Philip Friedman, *Encyclopedia of the Diaspora*, *loc. cit.*, Vol. IV, p. 614.

72. Almost everywhere the Jewish Councils had to collect contributions and supply the Germans with slave labor in order to prevent cruel repressions from the Nazis. For typical discussions on the attitudes of members of the Councils, see *Byten Book. The Emergence and Destruction of a Jewish Community* (Buenos Aires: Byten Countrymen in

Argentina, 1954), pp. 221-222, 224, 413 (Yiddish); *Records of Five Destroyed Communities* (Buenos Aires: Union of Countrymen of These Communities, 1958), pp. 624-625 (Yiddish); *Grodno Echoes, loc. cit.* (Yiddish).

73. For Rumkowski's concept of "rescue through work" (in Lodz), see Isaiah Trunk, *op. cit.*, pp. 437-438; for Białystok, see Haike Grossman, *The Men of the Underground* (Merhaviah: Sifriyat Poalim, 1950), pp. 163-164 (Hebrew); for Vilna, see Herman Kruk, *op. cit., passim.*; for Kovno, see J. Gar, *op. cit.*, pp. 83-84, 100-111, 312-344.

74. Peter-Heinz Seraphim, *Das Judentum im osteuropäischen Raum* (Essen: Essener Verlagsanstalt, 1938), 736 pp. See in particular pp. 56-67.

75. See J. Gar, *op. cit.*, pp. 277-394.

76. See, for example, *Verordnungsblatt des Generalgouverneurs für die besetzten polnischen Gebiete* (Cracow), Part II, 1940, No. 32, May 1, 1940, p. 249; No. 45, July 4, 1940, p. 387; *Verordnungsblatt für das Generalgouvernement* (Cracow), 1941, No. 35, April 23, 1941, pp. 211-212.

77. H. G. Adler, *Die verheimlichte Wahrheit. Theresienstädter Dokumente* (Tübingen: J. C. B. Mohr [Paul Siebeck], 1958), pp. 27, 67-68, 77-85.

78. For Lodz: I. Trunk, *op. cit.*, p. 285. For Warsaw: *Bleter far Geshikhte* (Warsaw), Vol. IV, 1951, No. 2, pp. 183-185.

79. See, for Warsaw, the *Report of the United Jewish Underground Organizations to the Polish Government-in-Exile of 15 November 1942*, reproduced in *Bleter far Geshikhte* (Warsaw), Vol. IV, No. 2, April-June 1951, pp. 190, 195, 198 (Yiddish). For Lwów, see Philip Friedman in *Encyclopedia of the Jewish Diaspora, loc. cit.*, Vol. IV, Lwów (first part), cols. 644, 655. For Cracow, see Tadeusz Pankiewicz, *op. cit., passim.* For Lublin and Częstochowa, see Nathan Eck, *op. cit.*, pp. 102-106.

80. See, for example, *The Brzeziny Memorial Book* (New York-Israel: The Brzeziny Book Committee, 1961), p. 139 (Yiddish); *Drohiczyn. Five Hundred Years of Jewish Life* (Chicago: Book Committee, 1958), p. 295 (Yiddish); *Memorial Book of Czyżewo* (Tel-Aviv: Union of Czyżewo Countrymen, 1961), p. 927 (Yiddish and Hebrew).

81. Isaiah Trunk, "Toward a Study of the History of the Jews in the Warthe District in the Period of the Catastrophe (1939-1944)," *Bleter far Geshikhte* (Warsaw), Vol. II, 1949, p. 92 (Yiddish).

82. Dated February 10, 1942, and consisting of 41 typewritten pages containing 2,072 names. The list is available in the Yad Washem Archives in Jerusalem, No. 06/4-1.

83. See, for Warsaw, the *Report* in note 79, pp. 184 and 189. For

Lodz see I. Trunk, *Ghetto Lodz, loc. cit.*, pp. 270-272. See also indictment by the *Staatsanwaltschaft bei dem Landgericht Hannover*, of October 22, 1962 (2 Js 376/60) in the Fuchs-Bradfisch case (mimeographed), in particular p. 2, and the Judgment (*Strafurteil*) Fuchs-Bradfisch of November 18, 1963 (*Landgericht* Hannover, 2Ks 1/63, 28a 12/62), in particular pp. 18-32, 73-123 (mimeograph).

84. In fact, even before Eichmann's arrival. See the section on Hungary in Chapter 5.

85. Jenö Levai, *The Black Book on the Martyrdom of Hungarian Jewry* (Zurich: Central European Times, 1948), pp. 97-98 (listed in Miss Arendt's Bibliography). The original Hungarian text of the manifesto can be found in the same author's *Jewish Fate in Hungary* (Budapest: Magyar Téka, 1948), pp. 81-82.

Having accused the Jewish leadership of being power-hungry, Miss Arendt enigmatically comments: "We know how the Jewish officials felt when they became instruments of murder—like captains 'whose ships were about to sink and who succeeded in bringing them safe to port *by casting overboard a great part of their precious cargo*'" (p. 105). The ominous phrase in italics is Miss Arendt's own invention. The use of the definite article in this context ("the Jewish officials") is indefensible. How does Miss Arendt know what was going on in the minds and hearts of these people? The comparison of the Jewish officials with sea captains appears to be her version of Dr. Eppstein's statement on the eve of Rosh Hashana 5704 (1944), which reads in full as follows:

... We are like people on a ship which is lying in front of a harbor which it cannot enter because of densely mined waters. Only those in charge of the ship (*Schiffsleitung*) know that narrow lane that leads to the safety of the land. They must not pay attention to the misleading signs and signals given from the shore. The ship has to stay outside and wait for instructions. You must (*Man muss*) have confidence that your leaders will do all that is humanly possible to secure your survival.—H. G. Adler, *Theresienstadt 1941-1945. Das Antlitz einer Zwangsgemeinschaft: Geschichte, Soziologie, Psychologie*, second edition (Tübingen, J. C. B. Mohr [Paul Siebeck], 1960), p. 191. (Miss Arendt lists the 1955 edition in her Bibliography.)

Two other versions of this passage are reported by Adler:

The ship still has to struggle but our friends are already standing on the shore (p. 746). We are like people on a ship who see from afar the longed-for harbor. We believe that we can already recognize our friends on the shore, but we still have to steer through uncharted rocks, and premature hand-waving and greeting must not deceive us about the dangers which we still have to overcome (p. 814).

For purposes of comparison with the Jewish situation in Hungary, another "manifesto" of the Prague "Jewish Council" is quoted here: By decree, the Prague Jewish Community is now headed by a governing body (*Leitung*) to whose jurisdiction all communities in the country are subordinated as well. The authority [to be] exercised by this body derives from the competence of the [German] Central Agency (*Zentralstelle*) [for Jewish Emigration]. The very existence of such an authority is new in the history of the Jewish Diaspora. It is the sincere (*tiefe*) wish and the firm hope of the governing body that this authority shall operate only for the benefit of the community.—*Jüdisches Nachrichtenblatt, Židovské Listy* (Prague), No. 30, July 26, 1940.

Great courage was needed by the Jewish Council in Prague to make this statement and to have it published in the Nazi-censored *Jüdisches Nachrichtenblatt.*

86. Düsseldorf *Stapoleitstelle* archives (T/1395 to T/1398), sheets 61-64. T/1400 is a selection from these four volumes.

87. Raul Hilberg, *op. cit.,* p. 767.

88. In this figure are included all deportees from all areas of Germany, including such areas as Stettin (see Chapter 1, under Eichmann's Conscience and "The New Type of Criminal") and Baden and Saarpfalz (see note 42 of Chapter 5), where the Jewish community had no role in the deportation.

89. According to archival evidence deposited in *Yad Washem* (Slovakia collection), this number should be 58,000.

90. The information following in the text is taken from *The Institute Anniversary Volume: 1941-1961, loc. cit.,* pp. 109-110.

91. Dr. Hans Buchheim, in an unpublished opinion dated June 12, 1961, and prepared for the *Institut für Zeitgeschichte,* estimates the total number of guards of concentration camps for the period 1934-1945 at 65,000 men and 5,000 women. The number of guards who themselves were actively engaged in the mass murder was, according to him, a fraction of these 65,000. This number does not include doctors. Dr. Buchheim's estimates do not embrace the death camps (except Auschwitz).

92. Another estimate for the Government-General has been offered by Reinhard Henkys in *Die nationalsozialistischen Gewaltverbrechen* (Stuttgart-Berlin: Kreuz, 1964), p. 89: "It is probable that among the 25,000 German police and non-German subsidiary policemen, a large part was engaged, in one way or another, in the liquidation of the Polish Jews." The present state of research does not yet enable us to provide exact figures. Robert Pendorf, in his generally reliable book *Mörder und Ermordete* (Hamburg: Rütten & Loening, 1961), writes on

pp. 111-112: "On their entire path to death, Polish Jews saw hardly more than a handful of Germans." (This passage is cited by Miss Arendt in the paperback edition, p. 117, in support of her thesis of the indispensability of Jewish cooperation to the Nazi extermination program. On p. 218 of the paperback edition, Miss Arendt writes that in Poland, and throughout the East, "the Jewish bureaucracy . . . played no part in the seizure and the concentration of the Jews." Miss Arendt nowhere explains who it was who did carry out the extermination program.) Pendorf's statement is contradicted by hundreds of Jewish witnesses who identified large numbers of Germans in trials of Nazi criminals involved in the Polish extermination program. See also the accounts of "resettlements" in Lodz and Cracow, under The Behavior of the Victims, in this chapter.

There was, of course, a great deal of overlapping in the membership of the organizations mentioned here. For example, the RSHA was an amalgamation of SS and State organs: the SD was originally part of the SS, while the Kripo and the Gestapo were originally State agencies. A large majority of the personnel in all departments of the RSHA were or became SS members. Another example is the membership of the *Einsatzgruppen*. Officers (commissioned and noncommissioned) were members of the Gestapo, Kripo, or SD on loan, while the ranks were largely made up of emergency service draftees (*Notdienstverpflichtete*) and of companies or battalions of the Waffen-SS and Regular Police (Ohlendorf affidavit in *Green Series*, IV, p. 93).

93. For example, see "Testimony of M. Garfunkel, the former chairman of the Zamość Jewish Council" (YIVO Archives, testimonies, No. 1043, p. 3); *Memorial Book of Baranowicze* (Tel-Aviv: Union of Baranowicze Immigrants, 1958), pp. 512-513 (Hebrew and Yiddish); *The Book of Kleck* (Tel-Aviv: Union of Kleck Immigrants, 1959), p. 368 (Yiddish); *Book of Horrors, loc. cit.*, pp. 8-12 (Hebrew, report of former Senator M. Kerner); *The Skierniewice Book* (Tel-Aviv: Union of Skierniewice Immigrants, 1955), pp. 550, 576; *Grodno Echoes, loc. cit.*

94. *Memorial Book of Baranów* (Jerusalem: Yad Washem, 1964), p. 208 (Hebrew and Yiddish).

95. *Memorial Book of Baranowicze, loc. cit.*, p. 527.

96. *Yiskor Book Ratno* (Buenos Aires: Ratno Countrymen in Argentina and North America, 1954), pp. 488-489 (Hebrew and Yiddish).

97. Philip Friedman in *Encyclopedia of the Jewish Diaspora, loc. cit.*, Vol. IV, pp. 613-614 (Hebrew).

98. Shloyme Mayer, *The Destruction of Złoczów* (Munich: Ibergang, 1947), p. 32 (Yiddish in Latin letters).

99. *Memorial Book of Mława* (New York: World Union of Mława Jews, 1950), p. 405 (Yiddish).

100. *Towns and Cities of Israel, loc. cit.*, Vol. V, pp. 397, 400 (Hebrew).

101. *Ibid.,* p. 401.

102. Philip Friedman, *Encyclopedia of the Jewish Diaspora, loc. cit.,* pp. 614, 662, 663, 664 (Hebrew).

103. *Memorial Book of Nowogródek* (Tel-Aviv: Relief Committee . . . 1963), p. 254 (Yiddish and Hebrew).

104. Bauminger and Others, *The Book of Cracow, loc. cit.,* pp. 389, 390, 409.

105. *Ibid.,* pp. 398, 399. See also the quotation from Pankiewicz, *op. cit.,* cited on the following pages of this chapter.

106. Eck, *loc. cit.,* pp. 78-79.

107. Leopold Marx, "Otto Hirsch: Ein Lebensbild," *Bulletin des Leo Baeck Institute* (Tel-Aviv), Vol. 6, 1963, pp. 295-312.

108. *Bleter far Geshikhte* (Warsaw), Vol. III, No. 3-4, 1950, p. 80.

109. Testimony of Szlama Lubowicz in YIVO Archives, confirmed in *Memorial Book of Mława, loc. cit.,* pp. 406-407.

110. *Rohatyn and Its Neighboring Communities* (Tel-Aviv: Union of Immigrants from Rohatyn, 1962), p. 228 (Hebrew and Yiddish).

111. J. Gar, *op. cit.,* pp. 205-206, 216-217; also pp. 305-306 on the services of the Jewish police to the ghetto community.

112. Bar-On and Dov Levin, *The Story of an Underground* (Jerusalem: Yad Washem, 1962), pp. 233-234 (Hebrew).

113. Testimony of Eliezer Kerstadt in Session 29. See also Max Kaufman, *Churbn Lettland. Die Vernichtung der Juden Lettlands* (Munich: Selbstverlag, 1947), pp. 177-181. It should be noted in this connection that, when the Nazis first organized the ghettos, joining the police was considered a public duty (without pay). As their functions became more and more distasteful the composition of the police changed. In addition, the situation was different in big cities and small and medium-sized ones. Finally, the situation differed with respect to the place of origin of the policemen (locally recruited or coming from other places) and with respect to ideological loyalties or lack of them on the part of policemen.

114. *Memorial Book of Baranowicze, loc. cit.,* p. 469.

115. *Ibid.,* p. 544.

116. Werner Warmbrunn, *The Dutch under German Occupation* (Stanford: Stanford University Press; and London: Oxford University Press, 1963), pp. 173-184. The *Joodse Raad* is discussed in greater detail by Abel J. Herzberg, *Kroniek der Jodenvervolging* (Arnhem: van Loghum Slaterus, and Amsterdam: J. M. Meulenhoff, n. d.), pp. 143-196 and by J. Presser, *Ondergang: De Vervolging en verdelging van het Nederlandse Jodendom 1940-1945* ('s-Gravenhage: Staatsuitgeverij/ Martinus Nijhoff, 1965), Vol. I, pp. 81-84, 287-297, 402-416, 452-526.

117. Joseph Gar, "Liberated Jews," in *From the Recent Past* (New York: Yiddisher Kulturkongress, 1957), Vol. 3, p. 129 (Yiddish).

118. English translation in *Israel Government Yearbook* 1951/2 [5712] (Jerusalem: Government Printer, 1952), pp. 189-192. The crimes that are listed are common law crimes committed "by a persecuted person against a persecuted person," or by a person "exercising some function in a place of confinement . . . against a persecuted person" (Articles 2 and 4), and such specific crimes as assisting in delivering a persecuted person to an enemy administration (Article 5); receiving or demanding a benefit from a persecuted person under threat of delivering him or another persecuted person to an enemy administration; receiving or demanding a benefit from a person who had given shelter to a persecuted person under threat of delivering him or the persecuted person that was sheltered by him to an enemy administration (Article 6). The Israel legislator was not unaware (Article 10) of the possibility that such a person might have acted or failed to act in order to save himself from the danger of immediate death or with the intention to avert consequences more serious than those which resulted from his act or omission. Mitigating circumstances are allowed for (Article 11).

119. Pinhas Freudiger.

120. *Op. cit.*, p. 292.

121. *Reconstructionist* (New York), March 22, 1963.

122. *Aufbau* (New York), Vol. 29, No. 13, March 29, 1963. Reproduced in *Nach dem Eichmann-Prozess. Zu einer Kontroverse über die Haltung der Juden* (London-Jerusalem-New York: Council of Jews from Germany, 1963), pp. 25-30. Despite these criticisms, Miss Arendt did not respond to Leschnitzer's call for correction of the wrong she did to the memory of Leo Baeck, and left the whole passage unchanged in the hardcover book (adding only "former" before "Chief Rabbi of Berlin").

123. Ernst Simon, *Aufbau im Untergang* (Tübingen: J. C. B. Mohr [Paul Siebeck], 1959), pp. 39-41 (*Schriftenreihe wissenschaftlicher Abhandlungen des Leo Baeck Institute of Jews from Germany, No. 2*). The Baeck prayer was read in Session 14 of the trial.

124. Sessions 51 and 52. In the paperback edition (p. 125) Miss Arendt writes: "According to Freudiger's calculations about half of them [the "between four and a half and six million" victims mentioned in the previous sentence] could have saved themselves if they had not followed the instructions of the Jewish Councils." Nowhere in his testimony in the Eichmann trial, or in any other oral or written statements, did Freudiger make such a "calculation" or claim.

125. T/1116. Freudiger explained in his testimony that one of the reasons he did not recommend unorganized mass escape was that some 50 percent of those who fled were caught and killed. On this Miss Arendt comments (p. 110), "as compared with ninety-nine per cent" killed of

those who did not try to escape. In fact, out of some 400,000 Jews of Trianon Hungary, some 45 percent survived, including the majority of the Budapest Jews. The number of survivors in Northern Transylvania was approximately 30,000 out of 150,000; in Subcarpathian Russia, approximately 15,000 out of 100,000. An insignificant number of Jews escaped by fleeing. Thus for all of Hungary about 65 percent of the Jewish population was killed, and 35 percent—not 1 percent—survived.

126. The original Hebrew of Freudiger's testimony is conversational and grammatically loose. The phrase "Wisliceny geireish et kol hayehudim mislovakia" is ambiguous and can be taken to mean either "Wisliceny was the one who deported all the Jews in Slovakia" or "Wisliceny was the one who was in charge of all deportation in Slovakia." Read in the context of Freudiger's testimony, the second version is the only acceptable one, clearly indicating that he knew—as he explicitly stated earlier—that as of March 20, 1944 (the date of his meeting with Wisliceny) not all the Jews had been deported.

127. This is by no means the total number of Jews rescued as a result of the efforts of the Kasztner committee. Rather, it is the number of Jews saved in one operation, the transfer to Switzerland via Bergen-Belsen (*Kasztner Report, loc. cit.*, pp. 133, 252-254). Other rescue operations carried out on the initiative of the Kasztner committee were: (1) The transfer of 15,000 Jews to Austria (to be "frozen" there), of whom 13,500 survived (*Ibid.*, pp. 18, 115, 147, 270, 276ff.). (2) The placement of 5,000 Jewish children in shelters of the International Red Cross (*Ibid.*, pp. 202-205). (3) The issuance by the Swedish and Swiss consulates of approximately 15,000 protective passports to Jews (*Ibid.*, pp. 218-221). Thus, at least 35,000 Jews owed their lives to the efforts of this committee.

128. This number is incorrect. See note 125 and Gerald Reitlinger, *Die Endlösung, loc. cit.*, pp. 563, 567, 568.

129. Isaiah Trunk, *Ghetto Lodz, loc. cit.*, pp. 303-304. Many more such cases could be listed, and I may be forgiven for mentioning the case of Kovno, with whose population I was and remain intimately connected. When, in the wake of the Soviet offensive in June 1944, the ghetto was on the eve of liquidation, and its inmates—ten thousand remnants of a once glorious Jewish community—were deported to Germany (men to Dachau, women to Stutthof), they could all have been rescued if the tempo and direction of the offensive had continued as it had begun. In the event, only a few thousand survived in the concentration camps (J. Gar, *The Destruction of Jewish Kovno, loc. cit.*, p. 291).

130. E. Ringelblum, *op. cit.*, Vol. I, p. 137.

131. Wolf Jasny, *The Extermination of the Lodz Jews* (Tel-Aviv: Union of Immigrants from Lodz, 1950), pp. 66-67 (Yiddish). For addi-

tional details, see also Jakub Poznański, *Notes from the Lodz Ghetto* (Lodz: Lodz Publishing House, 1960), p. 224 (Polish).

132. E. Yerushalmi, *op. cit.*, p. 315.

133. M. Dworzecki, *op. cit.*, p. 308. It is interesting to note that the same readiness to be judged by a Jewish court was expressed by Rumkowski. See Nathan Eck in *Haaretz* (Tel-Aviv), Sept. 7, 1962, p. 10.

134. M. Dworzecki, *op. cit.*, p. 312.

135. H. G. Adler, *Theresienstadt, op. cit.*, pp. 19-20.

136. R. Kasztner, *op. cit.*, pp. 67-68 (mimeogr.).

137. He discovered that the Jews took over from the Germans the use of mead (*Met*) which is an old German Christmas beverage (*Weihnachtstrank*). The Jews continued using the beverage after their expulsion from Germany to the East, while in Germany the ways of brewing it were forgotten. The pretext he used to get to Lodz was consultation with Jewish scholars there concerning the drink. See Friedrich Hielscher, *Fünfzig Jahre unter Deutschen* (Hamburg: Rowohlt, 1954), p. 355.

138. *Ibid.*, p. 362. The conversation apparently took place during the second visit, in May 1942. This was Hielscher's answer: "You have done right. So help me God. Go on as before. There is no other way. You are absolved before God if you follow it. I would not act differently myself" (p. 365). See also *Green Series*, II, p. 30. Hielscher's complete testimony of April 15-16, 1947, is available in Subsequent Trials, Case No. 1, pp. 5926-5994. For more details and further references, see Shaul Esh, "A German in the Lodz Ghetto," *Amot* (Tel-Aviv), No. 11, April-May 1964, 34-46.

139. Tadeusz Pankiewicz, *op. cit.*, pp. 62-63.

140. Benedikt Kautsky, *Teufel und Verdammte* (Zurich: Büchergilde Gutenberg, 1946), pp. 292-294.

141. E. Ringelblum, *op. cit.*, Vol. I, p. 365.

142. *Hilkhot Yesodei Hatorah*, Chapter 5, par. 5.

143. Philip Friedman, in *Yad Washem Studies* (Jerusalem), Vol. II, 1958, p. 111, footnote 4.

144. S. Glube, "Rabbinical Judgment," *Fun letstn Khurbn* (Munich), No. 6, August 1947, pp. 44-47 (Yiddish).

145. Ephraim Oshri, *The Book of Ephraim's Sayings* (New York: Waldon Press, 1949), p. 96 (Hebrew).

146. M. Dworzecki, *op. cit.*, p. 294 (Yiddish).

147. Friedman, *ibid.*, p. 109.

148. *Łomża: Its Rise and Destruction* (New York: American Committee for the Łomża Memorial Book, 1957), pp. 284, 286 (Yiddish).

149. Elieser Unger, *Remember* (Tel-Aviv: Masada, 1945), pp. 51-

53, 54-59 (Hebrew). See also Shlomo Bickel, ed. *Kołomyja Book* (New York: Kołomyja Memorial Book, 1957), pp. 420-424 (Yiddish).

150. *Records of Five Destroyed Communities, loc. cit.,* pp. 421, 690, 691 (Yiddish).

151. Adolf and Barbara Berman, "The Destruction of the Warsaw Ghetto," *Bulletin of the Jewish Historical Institute* (Warsaw), No. 45-46, 1963, pp. 138-158 (Polish). Czerniakow's diary is now in the possession of *Yad Washem.*

152. *Underground Report* (note 79 of this chapter), p. 188.

153. T. Berenstein, A. Eisenbach, B. Mark, and A. Rutkowski, eds., *Faschismus, Getto, Massenmord: Dokumentation über Ausrottung und Widerstand der Juden in Polen während des zweiten Weltkrieges* (Berlin: Rütten & Loening, 1960), p. 286.

154. Tadeusz Pankiewicz, *op. cit.,* pp. 34-48.

155. The reference is to the 80 transports from Cracow to other Jewish communities in the period between November 29, 1940, and April 2, 1941. See Dora Agatstein, *Bleter far Geshikhte* (Warsaw), Vol. I, No. 1, 1948, pp. 170-171.

156. Tadeusz Pankiewicz, *op. cit.,* pp. 55-58.

157. *Ibid.,* pp. 75-76.

158. Evidence given by Mordecai Żuravski in Session 65 and Shimon Srebnik in Session 66 of the Eichmann trial. See also Władysław Bednarz, "Extermination Camp in Chełmno [Kulmhof]," in *German Crimes in Poland* (Warsaw: Central Commission for the Investigation of German Crimes in Poland, 1946), Vol. I, pp. 109-121, in particular pp. 118 and 121; the same author's Polish-language pamphlet *The Extermination Camp in Chełmno* (Warsaw: State Publishing Institute, 1948), pp. 65 and 66; and Miriam Novitch, *The Jewish Resistance and the Allies* (Milan: Second International Conference on the History of the Resistance, 1960), p. 3 (mimeogr.).

159. Miss Arendt even implies that *all* Jews kept alive and forced to work in the camps were undesirable elements of the population. She writes (p. 109): "The selection and classification of workers in the camps was made by the S.S., who had a marked predilection for the criminal elements; and, anyhow, it could only have been the selection of the worst." It is well known that the only criterion for selection was physical fitness. In fact, since the selection was always made immediately at first sight, without the aid of papers or records, it would have been impossible for the SS men in charge of selection to use anything but physical criteria. (See Judgment, Section 144.) Miss Arendt goes on to write: "This was especially true in Poland, where the Nazis had exterminated a large proportion of the Jewish intelligentsia . . ." Note how she equates the morally "worst" elements with those not part of the "intelligentsia."

160. Jan Sehn, *Concentration Camp Oświęcim-Brzezinka* (Warsaw: Wydawnictwo Prawnicze, 1960), pp. 137, 143 (Polish).

161. Yankel Wiernik, *A Year in Treblinka* (New York: Unser Tsait, 1944), 46 pp.

162. *Observer* (London), April 7, 1963; reported in the *Day-Morning Journal* (New York), April 8, 1963 (Yiddish).

163. A. Pechorsky, *The Uprising in Sobibór* (Moscow: Emes, 1946), 64 p. (Yiddish).

164. See note 161 of this chapter.

165. Ota Kraus and Erich Kulka, *The Mills of Death—Auschwitz* (Jerusalem: Yad Washem, 1960), pp. 231-236 (Hebrew). German translation: *Die Todesfabrik* (Berlin: Kongress-Verlag, 1958), pp. 221-226. Both are translated from the original Czech version.

166. See note 158 of this chapter.

167. Nuremberg Document NO-3408. Miss Arendt may have drawn her information on the behavior of the *Sonderkommandos* from Hoess's macabre description in *Commandant of Auschwitz* (Cleveland and New York: World Publishing Co., n.d.), pp. 164-169. But Hoess nowhere says that the *Sonderkommandos* "actually wielded 'the fatal instrument with their own hands.'" Of course, he does not reveal his own methods to force the inmates to join the *Sonderkommandos* and to break their attempts to refuse to do so or to resist (see Kraus and Kulka, *op. cit.*, pp. 143-145). The only source that suggests something like Miss Arendt's account is N/94 (see note 50 of Chapter 1), pp. 493-494 (English); this is the testimony of Konrad Morgen, in which he reported at second hand what Wirth (of the Lublin camp) had told him.

168. *Aufbau* (New York), Vol. 29, No. 26, June 28, 1963. Text in German.

169. *Newsweek* (New York), Vol. LXI, No. 24, June 17, 1963, p. 95.

170. Hans Frank's order of October 15, 1941, imposing the death penalty on persons hiding Jews outside the ghetto, par. 4b(1), reproduced in *The Destruction of the Jews in Poland during the Hitlerian Occupation* (Warsaw: Jewish Historical Institute, 1957), p. 122 (Polish). These were no empty threats. See the detailed study by Kazimierz Leszczyński, "The Extermination of the Population in Polish Lands in the Years 1939-1945," published in *Biuletyn Głównej Komisji Badania Zbrodni Hitlerowskich w Polsce* (Warsaw), Vol. VIII, 1956, pp. 115-204; Vol. IX, 1957, pp. 113-255; Vol. X, 1958, pp. 89-192; Vol. XI, 1960, pp. 209-286 (Polish). See also Tatiana Berenstein and Adam Rutkowski, *Assistance to the Jews in Poland, 1939-1945* (Warsaw: Polonia Publishing House, 1963), 83 pp.; Isaiah Trunk, "Polish-Jewish Relations During World War II," *Tsukunft* (New York), Vol. LXIX, 1964, pp. 151-157

(Yiddish). For a survey of Polish-Jewish relations during World War II by an acute and knowledgeable contemporary, see E. Ringelblum, *op. cit.*, Vol. II, 1963, pp. 237-283 (Yiddish translation); Polish original with English summary in the *Biuletyn Żydowskiego Instytuta Historicznego* (Warsaw), No. 28 (1958) pp. 1-37; No. 29, pp. 3-39; No. 30, pp. 50-86; No. 31, pp. 26-37.

In Berlin some 5,000 Jews "submerged," of whom approximately 75 per cent were discovered. See Siegmund Weltlinger, *Hast Du schon vergessen? Erlebnisbericht aus der Zeit der Verfolgung* (Frankfurt am Main: Gesellschaft für christlich-jüdische Zusammenarbeit, 1954), p. 26.

The case of Tuczyn, a town in Western Ukraine, is especially illuminating. There the Jewish community burned its homes and fled to the woods. But the local Ukrainian population hunted it down and delivered its members to the Germans. Fifteen survivors are all that remained of this community of seven hundred families. See Shalom Cholawski, "The Story of Tuczyn," in *Yalkut Moresheth* (Tel-Aviv), No. 2, May 1964, pp. 81-95 (Hebrew); and *Yalkut Volhynia* (Tel-Aviv), No. 1, p. 25 (Hebrew).

171. As for The Netherlands, non-Jews who gave shelter to Jewish escapees were often not punished at all; in other cases, perhaps the majority, they were arrested and usually sent to the concentration camp Vught for a period of six months. There they were severely maltreated and a number of people died. In some other cases these non-Jews were sent to concentration camps in Germany, especially to Dachau or Sachsenhausen. (Private communication of Dr. L. de Jong, dated July 3, 1964.)

See, for France, J. Lubetzki, *La Condition des Juifs sous l'occupation allemande 1940-1944* (Paris: Centre de Documentation Juive Contemporaine, 1945), pp. 185-186. On French practice, see Joseph Billig, *Le Commissariat Général aux Questions Juives (1941-1944)* (Paris: Editions du Centre, Vol. I, 1955, Vol. II, 1957, Vol. III, 1960), Vol. II, pp. 114-119.

172. Miss Arendt mistakenly writes (p. 157) that about half the Danish Jews survived in hiding. See Chapter 5, under Denmark, for an account of what actually happened.

173. See Chapter 5, under The Netherlands.

174. E. Ringelblum, *op. cit.*, p. 382.

175. For source material concerning Denmark, see notes 93-111 of Chapter 5.

176. Session 106. Judge Halevi's questions on this aspect of the Catastrophe and Eichmann's answers:

Q. You already mentioned Himmler's orders to cover things up?
A. Yes.

Q. By misleading the victims, these orders made the job easier, and also made it possible to put the Jews to work toward their own destruction?

A. Yes, that goes without saying.

177. *How Did It Happen? Data and Documents Relating to the Tragedy of Hungarian Jewry* (Budapest: Renaissance, 1947), 252 pp. (Hungarian). Pp. 28-33 of this book (in German translation) were submitted to the court by Dr. Ernö Boda (T/1156). This is a record of the meeting of the Jewish Council with Eichmann in Budapest, Hotel Majestic, on March 31, 1941.

178. Judgment, Section 237.

179. *Green Series*, IV, p. 299.

180. See Chapter 1, under Authority and Activities.

181. *Blue Series*, XLII, p. 559.

182. *Centre de Documentation Juive Contemporaine* (Paris), Archives, Document XLIX-42.

183. New Haven, Yale University Press, 1949, pp. 292-293.

184. See note 122 of this chapter.

185. Arieh Tartakower and Kurt R. Grossmann, *The Jewish Refugee* (New York: Institute of Jewish Affairs, World Jewish Congress, 1944), pp. 26 ff. This volume contains a 60-page bibliography (pp. 597-658).

186. See, for example, Tadeusz Pankiewicz, *op. cit.*, pp. 34-35.

187. See, for example, *ibid.*, p. 116.

188. For example, Hungary served for a certain time as haven for Jews fleeing from Poland and Slovakia; Italy, for Jewish refugees from France, Yugoslavia, and Greece.

189. The implications of this situation were early recognized by Dr. Joachim Prinz in his article "Life Without Neighbors," *Jüdische Rundschau* (Berlin), April 17, 1935, Vol. 40, No. 31/32, p. 3.

190. The controversy is at present centered around the drama by Rolf Hochhuth, *The Representative*, translated from the German with a preface by R. D. Macdonald (London: Methuen, 1963), 331 pp. For collections of reviews and other reactions, see Fritz J. Raddatz, ed., *Summa Iniuria oder Durfte der Papst schweigen? Hochhuths "Stellvertreter" in der öffentlichen Kritik* (Reinbek bei Hamburg: Rowohlt, 1963), 235 pp.; *Der Streit um Hochhuths "Stellvertreter"*, a special issue of *Theater unserer Zeit. Kritische Beiträge zu aktuellen Theaterfragen* (Basel-Stuttgart), Vol. 5, 1963, 169 pp.; and Eric Bentley, ed., *The Storm over The Deputy: Essays and Articles about Hochhuth's Explosive Drama* (New York: Grove Press, 1964), 254 pp., with an extensive Bibliography. Critical of Hochhuth are Walter Adolph, *Verfälschte Geschichte; Antwort an Rolf Hochhuth. Mit Dokumenten und authentischen Berichten* (3rd ed., Berlin: Morus, 1963), 112 pp.; Joseph L.

Lichten, *Pius XII and the Jews. A Question of Judgment* (Washington, D.C.: National Catholic Welfare Conference, 1963), 35 pp., with a bibliography; Nathan Eck, "What Would Have Happened, Had Not the Pope Kept Silent?," *Tsukunft* (New York), Vol. 69, 1964, pp. 299-303 (Yiddish). An official reply to Hochhuth is given in a special issue of *L'Osservatore della Domenica* (Città del Vaticano), Vol. XXXI, No. 26, June 28, 1964, 80 pp. Generally favoring Hochhuth's attitude are Guenther Lewy, "Pius XII, the Jews and the German Catholic Church," *Commentary* (New York), February 1964, pp. 23-29 (with 105 footnotes), and comments by readers in the June 1964 issue, pp. 6-12; the same author's book, *The Catholic Church and Nazi Germany* (New York-Toronto: McGraw Hill, 1964), pp. 297-308 *passim.*; Léon Poliakov, "Pope Pius XII and the Nazis," *Jewish Frontier* (New York), Vol. 31, No. 3, April 1964, pp. 7-13. See also Saul Friedlander, *Pie XII et le IIIᵉ Reich: Documents* (Paris: Editions du Seuil, 1964), pp. 91-100, 103-140, 185-217. For a survey of the controversy around Hochhuth, see Jacques Nobécourt, *"Le Vicaire" et l'Histoire* (Paris: Editions du Seuil, 1964), 382 pp.

For an earlier discussion on the Vatican and the Jewish Catastrophe, see Léon Poliakov's articles in *Le Monde Juif* (Paris), No. 38, December 1950, and No. 40, February 1951. The Catholic position on the questions raised by Poliakov was given by Roberto Leiber S. I., "Pio XII e gli ebrei di Roma 1943-1944," *La civiltà cattolica*, 1961, Vol. I, pp. 449-458.

191. *Report of the International Committee of the Red Cross on Its Activities during the Second World War* (Geneva, 1948), Vol. I, p. 641. See also pp. 642-657; Vol. II, pp. 299-303; Vol. III, pp. 73-84 and 513-525. For a critical review of certain statements in this Report, see N[athan] E[ck], "Misrepresentation by the International Red Cross," *Yad Washem Bulletin* (Jerusalem), No. 3, July, 1958, p. 21; Joseph Tenenbaum, "Red Cross to the Rescue," *ibid.*, No. 4-5, October 1959, pp. 7-8.

192. *Jewish Population Figures, Memento Statistic* (Bucharest: World Jewish Congress, Romanian Section, 1945), pp. 40-42 (Romanian).

193. Eberhard Kolb, *Bergen-Belsen* (Hannover: Verlag für Literatur und Zeitgeschehen, 1962), p. 316.

194. See, however, a preliminary report in: *The Governments-in-Exile and Their Attitudes Towards the Jews.* [Documents] edited by Z. H. Wachsman (New York: The Resistance, 1943), VIII, 96 pp.

195. Communication of Dr. Leni Yahil, Yad Washem, Jerusalem.

196. See Chapter 5, under Denmark and Norway.

197. *La politique pratiquée par la Suisse à l'égard des réfugiés au cours des années 1933 à 1955. Rapport adressé au Conseil fédéral à l'intention des conseils législatifs par le professeur Carl Ludwig* (Bern:

Chancellerie fédérale, 1957), 411 pp. Also *Die Flüchtlingspolitik der Schweiz in den Jahren 1933 bis 1955. Bericht an den Bundesrat zuhänden der eidgenössischen Räte von Professor Dr. Carl Ludwig* (Bern, 1957), 416 pp. The published version includes comments by Eduard von Steiger, Chief of the Department of Justice and Police (1941-1951).

198. See Chapter 5, under Hungary.

199. *Documenti Diplomatici Italiani*, Nona Seria, 1939-1943. The Soviet collections of diplomatic correspondence (in Russian), such as the three-volume *Foreign Policy of the Soviet Union in the Period of the Patriotic War* and the two-volume *Stalin-Roosevelt-Churchill Correspondence*, are mostly selective and of poor yield. Only the third volume of the U.S. Foreign Relations Series [*Foreign Relations of the United States: Diplomatic Papers* (Washington, D.C.: U.S. Government Printing Office)] for 1943 contains substantial material on the Jewish situation in regard to the possibilities of shelter for a small number of potential victims (see pp. 28-30, 38-39, 314, 321-322, 327-328, 344, 388, 650-651, 656, 680). See also Ira A. Hirschmann, *Life Line to a Promised Land* (New York: Vanguard Press, 1946), 214 pp., and his *Caution to the Winds* (New York: David McKay, 1962), pp. 127-208.

200. T/1177.

201. *Times* (London), June 14, 1961, under the heading "Wartime Persecution of the Jews."

202. T/1312 and T/1404. Gerstein was the anti-Nazi who joined the SS in order to learn firsthand of their crimes. Hochhuth (*op. cit.*) deals with him in the Historical Comments to his play, as in the play itself. See also Léon Poliakov's article in *Le Monde Juif* (Paris), January-March 1964. And Helmut Franz, *Kurt Gerstein. Aussenseiter des Widerstandes der Kirche gegen Hitler* (Zurich: Evangelische Zeitbuchreihe Verlag, 1964), 112 pp.

203. See, for example, Leon Kubowitzky, *Unity in Dispersion. A History of the World Jewish Congress* (New York: World Jewish Congress, 1948), 381 pp.; *Political Report of the London Office of the Executive of the Jewish Agency Submitted to the Twenty-Second Zionist Congress at Basle, December 1946* (London, 1946), 87 pp. See also J. Robinson and P. Friedman, *Guide to Jewish History Under Nazi Impact* (New York: Yad Washem–YIVO, 1960), pp. 243-262. On the Jewish war effort, see pp. 264-265.

204. For a preliminary survey of the factors of rescue, see H. G. Adler, *Der Kampf gegen die "Endlösung" der Judenfrage* (Bonn: Bundeszentrale für Heimatdienst, 1960), 115 pp.

205. The documentation is available in the Central Zionist Archives in Jerusalem.

206. Communications of Dov Otto Kulka (*Yad Washem*, Jerusalem),

author of several studies on the "Protectorate" and Theresienstadt; and of Dr. G. Fleischmann (Jerusalem), secretary of the Supreme Council of the Unions of Jewish Communities in Bohemia-Moravia. See also Yehuda Reznichenko, ed., *Theresienstadt* (Tel-Aviv: Mapai, 1947), pp. 13-15 (Hebrew); Leo Hermann, *Bericht über den tschechischen Transfer*, Manuscript in Central Zionist Archives, Jerusalem; P. Maerz, "The Czech Transfer . . . " in Felix Weltsch, ed., *Prague and Jerusalem. In Memoriam of Leo Hermann* (Jerusalem: United Jewish Appeal in Israel, n.d.), pp. 165-176 (Hebrew); *Documents on British Foreign Policy* (London), Third Series, Vol. III, pp. 631, 633-634.

207. *Sammlung der Gesetze und Verordnungen des Protektorats Böhmen und Mähren*, No. 61, of July 17, 1939, reproduced in *Judenerlässe, Protektorat Böhmen und Mähren, 1939-1944*, p. 61 (Yad Washem Archives 0-7/3).

208. Bruno Blau, *Das Ausnahmerecht für die Juden in Deutschland, 1933-1945* (Düsseldorf: Allgemeine Wochenzeitung der Juden in Deutschland, 1954), item no. 154.

209. *Ibid.*, items no. 160, 168.

210. *Ibid.*, item no. 282.

211. "Die Juden und jüdischen Mischlinge im Deutschen Reich," *Wirtschaft und Statistik* (Berlin), Vol. XX, 1940, pp. 84 ff. Also Friedrich Burgdörfer, "Die Juden in Deutschland und in der Welt. Ein statistischer Beitrag zur biologischen, beruflichen und sozialen Struktur des Judentums in Deutschland" in *Forschungen zur Judenfrage* (Hamburg: Hanseatische Verlagsanstalt, Vol. 3, 1938), pp. 155, 193.

212. Private communication of Dr. Louis de Jong of the *Rijksinstituut voor Oorlogsdocumentatie*, Amsterdam, The Netherlands, dated October 22, 1963.

213. Communications from Mr. H. Benruby, the representative of the American Joint Distribution Committee in Athens, dated October 25 and December 10, 1963, and October 14, 1964. See also the statistics submitted in T/953.

214. Raul Hilberg, *op. cit.*, p. 767.

215. Henri Michel, "Rapport Général–Les Alliés et la Résistance en Europe," in *European Resistance Movements, 1939-1945. Proceedings of the Second International Conference on the History of the Resistance Movements Held at Milan 26-29 March 1961* (Oxford, London, New York, Paris: Pergamon, 1964), pp. 581-588, 593-597.

216. *Ibid.*, pp. 588-593.

217. Philip Friedman, "Jewish Resistance to Nazism; Its Various Forms and Aspects," in *European Resistance Movements . . . , loc. cit.*, pp. 195-214, and Miriam Novitch, *op. cit.* For an early survey (1950) on the fundamental problems of Jewish resistance and the opinions

expressed by various writers, see Isaiah Trunk, "Jewish Resistance in the Nazi Period," in his *Studies on Jewish History in Poland* (Buenos Aires: Yidbukh, 1963), pp. 298-312 (Yiddish).

218. Dorothy and Pesah Bar-Adon, *The Seven Who Fell* (Tel-Aviv: Palestine Pioneer Library, No. 11, n.d.), 198 pp.

219. Basic sources: Moshe Kahanovich, *The Struggle of the Jewish Partisans in Eastern Europe* (Tel-Aviv: Ayanot, 1954), 435 pp. (Hebrew); Zvi Bar-On, "On the Position of the Jewish Partisan in the Soviet Partisan Movement," *European Resistance Movements, 1939-1945. First International Conference on the History of the European Resistance Movements, Liège-Bruxelles-Breendonk, 14-17 September, 1958* (Oxford, London, New York, Paris: Pergamon Press, 1960), pp. 215-247. On the difficulty of contact between Lithuanian Jews and Soviet partisans in the woods and on the fate of the Jewish "reconnaissance group," see Joseph Gar, *The Destruction of Jewish Kovno, loc. cit.*, pp. 145-146.

220. On anti-Semitism in the partisan detachments, see also Yehiel Granatshtein, *I Wanted to Live* (Paris: A. B. Cerata, 1950), pp. 88, 193-194 (Yiddish); Haim Lazar, *Destruction and Revolt* (Tel-Aviv: Masuot, 1950), pp. 213-217, 252-253, 318 (Hebrew); *Baranowicze in Martyrdom and Resistance* (New York: Baranowich Union of America, 1964), Vol. I, pp. 98-100 (Yiddish).

221. See, for France, Jacques (Capitaine Jacquel) Lazarus, *Juifs au combat. Témoignage sur l'activité d'un mouvement de résistance* (Paris: Editions du Centre, 1947), 153 pp.

222. See notes 219 and 220.

223. Henri Michel, "General Report," in *European Resistance Movements 1939-1945. First International Conference on the History of the European Resistance Movements, loc. cit.*, pp. 1-2. Michel later added to his definition the following: "It [the resistance] is also a struggle for the freedom and the dignity of man against totalitarianism." In *European Resistance Movements, 1939-1945. Proceedings of the Second International Conference . . . , loc. cit.*, p. 576. He was, however, careful to indicate that the second part of this definition is not generally accepted.

224. Haim Lazar, *op. cit.*, pp. 155-156 (Hebrew).

225. *The Fighting Ghettos*. Translated and edited by Meyer Barkai. (Philadelphia–New York: J. B. Lippincott, 1962). Pp. 37-38.

226. According to Moshe Kahanovich, in *The Jewish Part in the Partisan Movement in Soviet Russia* (Rome–New York: Zionist Labor Committee, 1948), p. x (Yiddish), the casualties in Western Byelorussia and Western Ukraine constituted some 30 per cent of the total partisan Jewish force.

227. Henry Torrès, *Le Procès des pogromes* (Paris: Editions de France, 1928), 270 pp.

228. See, for example, Yehuda Erez, "Jewish Self-Defense in Russia 1903-1905," *Heavar* (Tel-Aviv), Vol. IV, 1956, pp. 82-94 (Hebrew); A. Rosental (ed. A. Ashman), *The Book of the Jewish Self-Defense*, Vol. I, Ukraine, First Issue (Tel-Aviv, n.d.), 104 pp. (Hebrew).

229. New York, n. d., 47 pp. (Yiddish).

230. Available in the YIVO collection of "The Exposition on the Twentieth Anniversary of the Uprising," mentioned also by Bernard Mark in his *Uprising in the Warsaw Ghetto* (Warsaw: Yiddish Bookh, 1963), p. 91 (Yiddish).

231. Stroop Report, Nuremberg Document 1061-PS, published in *Blue Series*, XXVI, pp. 628-694 (and 18 pages of photographs).

232. Sassen Papers. Transcript of tape 23, pp. 3-6.

233. Session 106.

234. T/215 (Nuremberg Document 018-L, reproduced in *Blue Series*, XXXVII, pp. 410 f.).

235. Session 27. Accounts of this incident can be found in *The Book of the Jewish Partisans* (Merhavia: Sifriat Poalim, 1958), Vol. I, pp. 37-39 (Hebrew); also in M. Dworzecki, *op. cit.*, pp. 440-445 (Yiddish); in *YIVO-Bleter* (New York), Vol. 30, 1947, pp. 188-213 (Yiddish); and in Haim Lazar, *op. cit.*, pp. 122-127 (Hebrew). These accounts, though differing in some details, agree in substance with Kovner's testimony. It is interesting to note that, in a recent publication (M. Rolnikaite, *I Have to Tell the Story* [Vilna: State Political and Scientific Publishing House, 1963], pp. 65-66 [Lithuanian]), Witenberg is presented as having declared that he would deliver himself to the Gestapo because he did not want to be responsible for the death of 20,000 persons.

236. *Kol Yisrael Arevim Zeh Lazeh*, a well-known Jewish saying, originating in Rabbinic times. See Babylonian Talmud, *Shevuoth*, 39a.

237. Letter of the (Polish) Jewish National Committee to London, reproduced in Melekh Neustadt (Noy), *Destruction and Revolt of the Jews in Warsaw* (Tel-Aviv: Histadrut, 1946), p. 97 (Hebrew). The reference is apparently to the ŻOB (Żydowska Organizacja Bojowa, meaning Jewish Fighting Organization). Along with this multi-party organization there was another organization of the Zionist Revisionists ŻZW (Żydowski Związek Wojskowy, meaning Jewish Military Union). On the latter organization see Haim Lazar-Litai, *The Warsaw Fortress. The Jewish Military Union in the Uprising of the Ghetto Warsaw* (Tel-Aviv: Zhabotinsky Institute, 1963), 364 pp. (Hebrew); David Wdowinski, *And We Are Not Saved* (New York: Philosophical Library, 1963), 123 pp.; Nachman Blumental in *Yediot Yad Washem* (Jerusalem), No. 33, October 1964, pp. 25-28 (Hebrew).

238. Examples have been cited earlier in this chapter, under Authority, Influence, and Activities of the Jewish Councils. See also: for

Piotrków Trybunalski, where the chairman of the Jewish Council, Tannenberg, was in contact with the underground movement of the Jewish Socialist Bund, Yaacov Kurts, *Book of Testimonies* (Tel-Aviv: Am-Oved, 1944), p. 139 (Hebrew); for Pruzana, *The Book of Five Destroyed Communities*, loc. cit., pp. 638 and 682; for Białystok, Haike Grossman, op. cit., passim; for Kovno, L. Garfunkel, op. cit., pp. 173-174; for Baranowicze, *Memorial Book*, loc. cit., p. 46.

239. Ota Kraus and Erich Kulka, op. cit., pp. 156-161, in particular p. 161, and cf. p. 149 for the testimony of a member of the *Sonderkommando*. The original report on this event is preserved in the Central Zionist Archives in Jerusalem. Incidentally, the Theresienstadt camp in Auschwitz was well known to Jews and non-Jews alike as the center of spiritual resistance there, thanks to its leadership.

240. K. Shabbetai, *As Sheep to the Slaughter* (Bet Dagan: Keshev Press, 1962), p. 27.

241. Nuremberg Document 1919-PS, *Blue Series*, XXIX, p. 145.

242. Sophie Dubnov-Erlich, *Life and Work of S. M. Dubnov* (New York: S. M. Dubnov Committee, 1950), p. 288 (Russian).

243. E. Ringelblum, op. cit., Vol. II, pp. 68-69. In addition to diaries by individuals, there were preserved such archives as the *Oneg-Shabbat* in Warsaw and the Herman Kruk archives in Vilna. See also notes 245-247 of this chapter.

244. Nachman Blumental, "The Heritage of Emmanuel Ringelblum," *Di goldene keyt* (Tel-Aviv), No. 15, 1953, pp. 235-242 (Yiddish).

245. At present they are in the possession of *Yad Washem* in Jerusalem. The story is told by Bronia Klibanski, "The Underground Archives in the Białystok Ghetto founded by [Zevi] Mersik and [Mordecai] Tenenbaum," *Yad Washem Studies* (Jerusalem), Vol. II, pp. 295-329.

246. Zvi Szner, "The Records Kept by the Rabbi of Sanniki," in *In the Dispersion*. Surveys and Monographs on the Jewish World (Jerusalem: World Zionist Organization, Winter 1963/64), pp. 16-20.

247. *Le Monde Juif* (Paris), Numéro d'anniversaire, 1943-1963, No. 34-35, July-December 1963.

248. The information on this score is scattered in hundreds of books (mostly in Hebrew and Yiddish). So far no attempt has been made to give a comprehensive picture of religious life, religious leaders, and institutions under the Nazis.

249. For references on this subject, see the *Bibliography of Books in Hebrew on the Jewish Catastrophe and Heroism in Europe*, edited by Philip Friedman (Jerusalem: Yad Washem, 1960), under "Destruction and Desecration of Synagogues and Religious Subjects." See also P. Friedman and J. Gar, *Bibliography of Yiddish Books on the Catastrophe*

and Heroism (New York: Yad Washem–YIVO, 1962), under "Religious Life."

250. Tadeusz Pankiewicz, *op. cit.*, p. 12.

251. For an incomplete list, see Philip Friedman, ed., *Bibliography of Books in Hebrew on the Jewish Catastrophe and Heroism in Europe, loc. cit.*, pp. 137-141.

252. See Friedman, *ibid.*; also Friedman and Gar, *op. cit.* See in particular Benjamin Orenstein, *Reality* (Bamberg: Historical and Literary Bureau, 1948), pp. 122-123 (Yiddish); *Mława Book* (New York: World Union of Mława Jews, 1950), pp. 53, 390 (Yiddish). For activities of rabbis in smuggling arms to the ghetto, see Hillel Seidman, *Diary of the Warsaw Ghetto* (Buenos Aires: Union of Polish Jews in Argentina, 1947), pp. 166-167 (Yiddish).

253. Marian Żyd, "Interview with Rabbi David Szapiro, a survivor of the Warsaw Ghetto, later a displaced person in Germany," in Philip Friedman's *Martyrs and Fighters. The Epic of the Warsaw Ghetto* (New York: Frederic A. Praeger, 1954), pp. 172-173. Also in Hillel Seidman, *op. cit.*, p. 282.

254. Shaul Esh, "The Dignity of the Destroyed: Towards a Definition of the Period of the Holocaust," *Judaism* (New York), Vol. II, No. 2, 1962, pp. 106-107. See also Eck, *Wandering on the Roads of Death, loc. cit.*, p. 37. For a contrary interpretation of the behavior of the Jewish masses, see Abraham Aizen, *The Spiritual Face of the Ghetto* (Mexico: Jewish Cultural Center, 1950), p. 128 (Yiddish).

255. Genesis 32:9. See Rashi's comment on this verse: "[Jacob] prepared himself for three things: gift, prayer, war."

256. Isaiah 10:21.

257. *Mishna, Sanhedrin,* 4, 5.

258. Tadeusz Pankiewicz, *op. cit.*, pp. 111-112.

Chapter 5

1. The following example is a case in point. Miss Arendt writes (p. 105) that 476,000 Hungarian Jews were killed by the Nazis. Later (p. 175), she writes that there were in Romania 850,000 Jews, of whom half survived. Hence, according to her, there were 425,000 Romanian Jews who did not survive. Taken together, Hungary and Romania are thus said by Miss Arendt to have accounted for 901,000 Jewish dead. According to Raul Hilberg, *The Destruction of the European Jews* (Chicago: Quadrangle Books, 1961), p. 670, there were a total of 630,000 victims, 430,000 from Romania and 200,000 from Hungary. It is not clear where Miss Arendt found her added 271,000 victims. Perhaps she counted Transylvania twice, inasmuch as it was under Romanian

control until 1940 and was subsequently partitioned between Romania and Hungary under the Vienna Award. See Arnold and Veronica Toynbee, eds., *Survey of International Affairs 1939-1946: The Initial Triumph of the Axis* (London, New York, Toronto: Oxford University Press, 1958), pp. 319 ff., 381. In the paperback edition, Miss Arendt writes in the Note to the Reader that "the total number of Jewish victims . . . for each of the countries concerned" is "a guess . . . that has never been verified." There are, however, areas for which we have reliable figures—Germany, Austria, Bulgaria, the "Protectorate," The Netherlands, and Belgium. There are other areas for which there are well-founded estimates—for example, France and Italy.

2. Jacob Robinson and Others, *Were the Minorities Treaties a Failure?* (New York: Institute of Jewish Affairs, 1943), 349 pp.

3. According to Miss Arendt, the victorious powers after World War I enacted an "elaborate system of minority treaties whereby the Allies had vainly hoped to solve a problem that, within the political framework of the nation-state, is insoluble," and which "came crashing down during these years" (p. 164). Actually, the "elaborate system of treaties," consisting of the special minorities treaties, the minority provisions in the peace treaties, and the declarations on minorities before the League of Nations, were practically identical in their provisions, and were phrased in very general terms. Miss Arendt claims that the minorities had been granted their protection at Geneva (p. 246). In fact, the protection under these treaties derived from the peace treaties of Versailles, Neuilly, Saint-Germain, Trianon, and Lausanne. Later, the guarantee of these treaties was assumed by the League of Nations. For an official collection of the texts see: League of Nations, *Protection of Linguistic, Racial and Religious Minorities by the League of Nations. Provisions Contained in the Various International Instruments at Present in Force* (Geneva, August 1927), 111 pp. (English and French.)

Each State had its own experience, and the experience varied greatly from State to State. A survey of the detailed situation in every country concerned can be found in Jacob Robinson and Others, *Were the Minorities Treaties a Failure?* (New York: Institute of Jewish Affairs, 1943). Conditions ranged from genuine liberalism and cultural autonomy for minorities, as in Estonia, to the oppressive police methods of Romania. The very nature of the minority problem varied considerably from country to country. In Albania, Austria, Estonia, Greece, Hungary, Lithuania, Bulgaria, and Turkey, minority populations were insignificant in numbers. The Slovaks in Czechoslovakia, whom Miss Arendt labels a minority (p. 163), did not regard themselves as such, nor did the Czechs consider them a minority; nor did they fall under the protection of the minority treaties. The same holds true, contrary to Miss Arendt (p. 164), for Croats, Slovenians, Montenegrins, Macedonians, and

Bosnians in what is now Yugoslavia and was known as *Serbsko-Horvatsko-Slovensko* after the end of World War I. Except for the Jews, who were a genuine minority population dispersed throughout these States, other minorities lived mostly concentrated in areas where they actually constituted the majority of the local inhabitants. Thus the Germans constituted the majority in the *Sudetenland*; the Byelorussians and Ukrainians constituted the majority in the eastern regions of Poland. Miss Arendt believes that "none [of the States of Eastern and South-eastern Europe] possessed anything even approaching the ethnic homogeneity of the old European nations" (p. 163). Are the "old" States of Belgium and Switzerland ethnically homogeneous? And what of the "ethnic homogeneity" of Great Britain, with its English, Scot, and Welsh components? Or Spain, with its Catalans and Basques?

For current information on European nationalities, see the quarterly *Europa Ethnica* (Vienna), 1961 *et seq.* See also Otto Junghann, *National Minorities in Europe* (New York: Covici-Friede, 1932), pp. 112-119. The situation in Poland has been studied in great detail by Stephan Horak in *Poland and Her National Minorities, 1919-1939. A Case Study* (New York: Vantage Press [1961]), 259 pp.

Miss Arendt writes: "If any proof of the political instability of these recently founded states had been needed, the case of Czechoslovakia amply provided it. When Hitler marched into Prague, in March, 1939, he was enthusiastically welcomed not only by the *Sudetendeutschen*, the German minority, but also by the Slovaks, whom he 'liberated' by offering them an 'independent' state" (p. 163). This is not true. In Prague, Hitler could have been welcomed only by the German population of the town, then numbering about forty thousand, since the *Sudetendeutschen*, inhabitants of the territory of *Sudetenland*, had already been "liberated" in October 1938, following the Munich agreement. And who are the Slovaks in Prague to whom Miss Arendt refers? It is hardly necessary to add that Hitler did not simply come up with an "offer" to the Slovaks of an "independent state." After instituting continuous pressures, acts of sabotage, and infiltration, the Slovaks obtained independence from Prague in two stages: On October 6, 1938, Slovakia became autonomous with Dr. Tiso as President; and on March 14, 1939, total independence from Prague was proclaimed. Only nine days after Slovakia was turned into a *de facto* German protectorate, under the political treaty between the two States of March 23, 1939, Germany undertook to "protect" the independence and integrity of Slovakia for a period of twenty-five years. See Arnold and Veronica Toynbee, eds., *Hitler's Europe* (London, New York, Toronto: Oxford Univ. Press, 1954), pp. 597-598. The text of the agreement can be found in *Reichsgesetzblatt* (Berlin), 1939, Part II, p. 607. See in particular Article 5.

Czechoslovakia's ethnic problems became acute when hostile Nazi and pro-Nazi forces began to engulf the Republic from the outside. Only then was the intense cohesiveness of the country threatened. Moreover, second to the *Sudetedeutschen*, not the Slovaks but the Hungarian ethnic group, concentrated in part in a small region of Southern Slovakia, proved to be the main disruptive force. (Compare the Hungarian slogan *ném, ném, soha!* [no, no, never!], in regard to the boundaries of the Trianon Treaty.) One must distinguish between the dissatisfied ethnic groups, such as the *Sudetedeutschen* and the Hungarian minority, both of which had been "striving" to be annexed to the bordering homelands, and the discontented groups of the Slovaks and Ruthenian "autonomists" who aspired for autonomy within a federal Czechoslovak State.

On pages 163-164 Miss Arendt says: "Exactly the same thing happened later in Yugoslavia, where the Serbian majority, the former rulers of the country, was treated as the enemy, and the Croatian minority was given its own national government." The temporary dismemberment of Czechoslovakia—a process substantially completed before World War II—was hardly "exactly the same thing" as the dismemberment of Yugoslavia, during the war, into six distinct units. She also confuses the minorities problem with the constitutional problem of the coexistence of Southern Slavs in one State. As already indicated, the Croats, the Slovenians, the Montenegrins, and the Macedonians did not consider themselves minorities but *Staatsvolk*.

As for the condition of the Jews in Central and Southeastern Europe, Miss Arendt declares that "the Jews were an officially recognized minority in all Successor States" (p. 164). This is untrue. The minorities provisions protected *individuals* of all races, religions, and languages, but conferred no rights on *groups*. Nowhere had the Jewish minority—or for that matter any other—any special standing as a group in public law. The Polish treaty contained provisions for Jewish schools and Sabbath privileges (see Articles 7 and 8 of the minorities treaty in note 64 of Chapter 2). Identical provisions are contained in Articles 7 and 8 of the Lithuanian Declaration of May 12, 1922. Sabbath privileges were provided for in Article 10 of the Peace Treaty of Neuilly-sur-Seine. The *ipso facto* citizenship for all Jews inhabiting any Romanian territory was provided in Article 10 of the treaty of the victorious powers in World War I with Romania. As it happened, even though Jewish initiative and influence had been instrumental in obtaining the Polish treaty, the Jews rarely used their right of petition to the League of Nations. Information on these questions can be found in Nathan Feinberg, *La question des minorités à la Conférence de la paix 1919-1920 et l'action juive en faveur de la protection internationale des minorités* (Paris: Comité des Délégations Juives, 1929). See also Oscar Janowsky, *The Jews and Minority Rights* (New York: Columbia Univ. Press; London: Kingston,

1933), 419 pp. And Herbert Truhart, *Völkerbund und Minderheiten-petitionen* (Vienna: Braumüller, 1931), pp. 86-92. Supplemented in *Nation und Staat* (Vienna), Vol. 8, 1934/5, p. 238.

Miss Arendt says that "legalized discrimination had been practiced by all Balkan countries" (p. 247). What she apparently means is that there was discrimination against Jews in those countries under local law. Actually, however, only Hungary and Romania had such laws; later, in 1941-1942, Bulgaria too passed discriminatory legislation. Neither Greece nor Yugoslavia (except for Croatia) had such laws. Such discrimination based on local laws was a flagrant violation of the valid minorities treaties, and consequently was illegal from the viewpoint of international law. See Bernard D. Weinryb, *Jewish Emancipation Under Attack* (New York: Research Institute on Peace and Post-War Problems, American Jewish Committee, 1942).

Miss Arendt also presents incorrectly the history of the Jewish efforts to secure rights for Jews in Europe within the framework of the Versailles peace negotiations. According to her, "to the surprise, and also sometimes to the dismay, of the Western-educated Jewish 'notables' it had turned out that the large majority of the people desired some sort of social and cultural . . . autonomy" (p. 164). There was no "surprise" and no "dismay." The Memorandum on this question presented to the Versailles Peace Conference on May 10, 1919, was submitted by the *Comité des délégations juives auprès de la Conférence de la Paix* which represented Jewish groups at the Conference. (See Jacob Robinson, *op. cit.*, pp. 323-325.) The *Comité* was presided over by Justice Julian W. Mack of the American Jewish Congress and later by Louis Marshall of the American Jewish Committee. To a large extent it was owing to these two "Western-educated notables" that the efforts of the *Comité* were so fruitful. Only the Joint Foreign Committee (of the Board of Deputies of British Jews and the Anglo-Jewish Association) and the *Alliance Israélite Universelle* did not join the *Comité*, but they had a gentlemen's agreement with the *Comité* under which they undertook not to take action against its efforts. See Feinberg, *op. cit.*, and Janowsky, *op. cit.*

4. Robinson and Others, *op. cit.*, pp. 260-265.

5. This figure appears in the November 9, 1943, report of Richard Korherr, the *Inspekteur für Statistik beim Reichsführer-SS*, to Himmler, "Final Solution of the Jewish Question" (Nuremberg Document NO-5193, reproduced in Léon Poliakov and Josef Wulf, *Das Dritte Reich und die Juden: Dokumente und Aufsätze* [Berlin-Grunewald: Arani Verlag, 1955], pp. 239-248; see in particular p. 244). Although the terminology of this report was heavily censored by Himmler himself, Korherr's figures for Austria are accurate. On Korherr's reliability, and on the

sources he used, see H. G. Adler, *Theresienstadt 1941-1945. Das Antlitz einer Zwangsgemeinschaft: Geschichte, Soziologie, Psychologie* (Tübingen: J. C. B. Mohr [Paul Siebeck], 2nd edition, 1960), pp. 765-767.

6. L. Poliakov and J. Wulf, *op. cit.*, p. 245.

7. Sessions 16 and 17 (see also next note).

8. Testimonies of Moritz Fleischmann and Franz Meyer in Sessions 16 and 17.

9. T/130; see also T/111, T/129, T/132.

10. For example: T/294, T/842, T/852, T/861, T/863, T/864, and testimonies by four former inmates (Ansbacher in Session 38, Salzberger in Session 42, Diamant and Engelstein in Session 45).

11. H. G. Adler, *op. cit.* Also Adler's *Die verheimlichte Wahrheit. Theresienstädter Dokumente* (Tübingen: J. C. B. Mohr [Paul Siebeck], 1958), 372 pp. And Zdenek Lederer, *Ghetto Theresienstadt.* Translated from the Czech by K. Weiskopf (London: Edward Goldston, 1953), 275 pp.

12. By "better sources" Miss Arendt may be referring to the vague mention by Heydrich at the Wannsee Conference (T/185) of two categories of Jews—those severely wounded in World War I and those decorated with the Iron Cross First Class—to be transported to Theresienstadt.

13. Eberhard Kolb, *Bergen-Belsen* (Hannover: Verlag für Literatur und Zeitgeschehen, 1962), p. 13.

14. T/294; H. G. Adler, *Theresienstadt, loc. cit.*, pp. 720-722; see also p. 21.

15. T/185.

16. T/37, p. 254.

17. *Documents sur l'activité du Comité International de la Croix-Rouge* [CICR] *en faveur des civils détenus dans les camps de concentration en Allemagne* (3rd edition, Geneva: CICR, April 1947), pp. 91-92.

18. T/864, pp. 2-4, and H. G. Adler, *Die verheimlichte Wahrheit, loc. cit.*, pp. 312-316, and T/864, pp. 2-4; on a later visit (April 6, 1945) see T/865, and note 81 of Chapter 1.

19. Judgment, Section 151.

20. Miss Arendt apparently bases her view on Reitlinger, *op. cit.*, p. 167, who simply says that Theresienstadt was economically under Pohl and administratively under Eichmann. However, even a document of the WVHA reporting from Auschwitz on the selection for the gas chambers speaks of *Ghetto Theresienstadt* (Ota Kraus and Erich Kulka, *The Mills of Death—Auschwitz* [Jerusalem: Yad Washem, 1960], p. 153, in Hebrew); see also T/584. The correspondence between the German Red Cross and Arno Harting in Lisbon of April 15 to May 9, 1943, is available on microfilm in Yad Washem (JM/1700/4). H. G. Adler, *Die*

verheimlichte Wahrheit, op. cit., pp. 3ff., proves that Theresienstadt was set up for the purpose of deceiving the world on the real nature of the Final Solution.

21. See, for example, T/842, Section 15, pp. 8-9.

22. Dov Kulka, in *Encyclopedia Hebraica*, Vol. 17, *s.v.* Theresienstadt (Hebrew).

23. T/37, pp. 116-118.

24. H. G. Adler, *Theresienstadt, loc. cit.*, p. 103.

25. *Kasztner Report* (T/1113), p. 161; printed edition, p. 294 (see note 6 of Chapter 1).

26. H. G. Adler, *Theresienstadt, loc. cit.*, p. 201.

27. Zdenek Lederer, *op. cit.*, pp. 202-208, 215-216, 242. See also T/836 and T/840.

28. Lederer, *op. cit.*, statistical appendix.

29. The reference is to Dr. Baeck's policy of not informing the deportees of the purpose of their deportation (see Chapter 4, under The Authority, Influence, and Activities of the Jewish Councils).

30. Ota Kraus and Erich Kulka, *op. cit.*, p. 157.

31. *Ibid.*, p. 161. See also T/842, Section 15, p. 9, and postcards from Auschwitz in Yad Washem Archives 07/3-5.

32. Adler, *Theresienstadt, loc. cit.*, pp. 122, 192-194.

33. *Ibid., passim.*

34. See also the testimonies of the commandants of Theresienstadt, Seidl (T/842) and Rahm (T/864).

35. Jakob Edelstein was apparently charged by the Nazis with helping escapees; he and his family were shot in Auschwitz (Adler, *Theresienstadt, loc. cit.*, pp. 158-159, and notes 11a and 238).

36. Benjamin Murmelstein's testimony in the People's Court in Prague *in re* Rahm, Case No. Lsp 441/47, p. 27 (Czech). German translation in *Mitteilungsblatt* (Tel-Aviv), August 1, 1947, p. 5. See also Murmelstein's article in the *Neue Zürcher Zeitung* (Zurich), Morgenausgabe, Blatt 5, Nr. 5231, Dec. 14, 1963. Also Zdenek Lederer, *op. cit.*, pp. 148-150. And H. G. Adler, *Theresienstadt, loc. cit.*, pp. 191-192. See also Murmelstein's *Terezin, Il Ghetto-Modello di Eichmann* (Coppelli Editore, 1961); in particular, "Quasi un Epilogo," pp. 233-235.

37. Published in *Ministerialblatt des Reichsministeriums des Innern* (Berlin), 1942, cols. 687-690.

38. H. G. Adler, *Die verheimlichte Wahrheit, loc. cit.*, pp. 61-62.

39. *Ibid.*, pp. 16-19, 52.

40. *Ibid.*, p. 50.

41. *Ibid.*, pp. 48-52; and Adler's *Theresienstadt, loc. cit.*, p. 62.

42. Miss Arendt considers the shipment of seventy-five hundred Jews from Baden and Saarpfalz into unoccupied France, together with

the deportation from Stettin (see Chapter 1, under Eichmann's Conscience, and note 145 of Chapter 1), to have been "test cases." She writes: "The objective seems to have been a test of general political conditions—whether Jews could be made to walk to their doom . . . ; what the reaction of their neighbors would be . . . ; and, last but not least, . . . how a foreign government [Vichy France] would react to being suddenly presented with thousands of Jewish 'refugees.' As far as the Nazis could see, everything turned out very satisfactorily" (pp. 139-140).

The facts do not bear out Miss Arendt's account. On October 22 and 23, 1940, Eichmann secretly dumped some 6,000 Jews [another version: 7,450 Jews] from Baden and Saarpfalz into unoccupied France, without previous agreement with Vichy. The French authorities, vanquished but not completely conquered, started pressing for an "explanation" as early as October 27, 1940. (Letter of General Doyen, member of the French delegation to the Armistice Commission, to General von Stülpnagel, chairman of the Commission.) For the next two months, not a single negotiation between the two countries took place without the French raising a question about the operation. The Germans were instructed to apply delaying tactics. The official telegraphic agency of the Vichy government, Havas, came out on November 14, 1940, with a sharp denial of the suggestion that the "action" was undertaken with the consent of Vichy. The French Ambassador in Washington intervened. Finally, on November 18, a formal protest note was presented by General Doyen to General von Stülpnagel. The instructions to the Germans remained the same: delay answer, suggest discussion on higher level. Indeed, the problem was put on the agenda of a forthcoming meeting between Ribbentrop and Laval. Ribbentrop was ready to promise the French that no more such transports were intended. It should be added that at the end of November 1940 the Germans tried to smuggle into the unoccupied zone of France 287 Luxembourg Jews, but they were not admitted.

See Nuremberg Documents NG-4337, NG-4933, NG-4934. Also, *Recueil de documents publié par le gouvernement français*. La Délégation française auprès de la commission allemande d'armistice (Paris: Alfred Costes), Vol. II, 1950, pp. 244-245; Vol. III, 1952, pp. 16, 37, 87-89, 309-310; Vol. IV, 1957, pp. 98-99; Vol. V, 1959, pp. 216-217. In fact, no subsequent expulsions took place either to France or to any other defeated country maintaining a semblance of sovereignty.

43. Joseph Billig, *Le Commissariat Général aux Questions Juives, 1941-1944* (Paris: Editions du Centre de Documentation Juive Contemporaine, 1955), Vol. I, pp. 45-57.

44. *Ibid.*, p. 71.

45. T/400 (Nuremberg Document RF-1210, reproduced in *Blue Series*, XXXVIII, pp. 740-745).

46. Joseph Billig, *op. cit.*, pp. 221-223.

47. T/389 and T/390. T/389 was signed by Helmuth Knochen, Commander of the Security Police in Northern France and Belgium, but drafted by Dannecker.

48. T/428 (Nuremberg Document RF-1223). See also Joseph Billig, *op. cit.*, pp. 240-241.

49. T/436, quoted in the Judgment, Section 100.

50. *Ibid.*

51. Judgment, Section 100.

52. Miss Arendt's account, on pp. 147-148 of her book, bears little resemblance to the documented account given in the judgment and summarized in the text. Among her errors is her statement that Eichmann "had plainly threatened them [the subordinates concerned] with losing their very cozy war jobs." There is not a word about such threats in the evidence placed before the court, or anywhere else to my knowledge.

53. T/419.

54. The lower age limit remained the same throughout the operation; the upper limit was subsequently raised to 60 for men and 55 for women (T/440).

55. Billig, *op. cit.*, pp. 244-245, 249 (July 2 meeting); 247-248 (July 4 meeting); 249-251, 373-376 (July 8 meeting); 254-256 (July 17 meeting).

56. We do not have the exact wording of Laval's statement on this issue. We have only two sentences in a telegram Dannecker sent to Eichmann on July 6 (T/433), sentences which most likely reflect Dannecker's desire to make France *judenrein* rather than giving a true account of Laval's attitude (Billig, *op. cit.*, pp. 371-372).

57. *L'activité des organisations juives en France sous l'occupation* (Paris: Centre de Documentation Juive Contemporaine, 1947), pp. 141-143, 149 ff. See also Joseph Weil, *Contribution à l'histoire des camps de concentration dans l'Anti-France, 1940-1944* (Paris: Centre de Documentation Juive Contemporaine, 1946), p. 91.

58. Billig, *ibid.*

59. He did not phone, as Miss Arendt has it on page 148; he sent a telegram.

60. T/438.

61. T/440.

62. Henri Monneray, *La persécution des Juifs en France et dans les autres pays de l'Ouest, présentée par la France à Nuremberg* (Paris: Editions du Centre, 1947), pp. 148-151.

63. A vivid description of the ordeal of the children is given by Jacob Kaplan, the acting *Grand Rabbin* of France, in his report "French Jewry under the Occupation" published in English translation in *The American Jewish Year Book* (New York), Vol. 47, 1945-1946, pp. 83-84.

A description is also given by Professor Georges Wellers, a former detainee of Drancy (Session 32). See also Wellers' *De Drancy à Auschwitz* (Paris: Centre de Documentation Juive Contemporaine, 1954).

64. T/439 and T/443. It should also be noted that Röthke claimed that "the representatives of the French police have on several occasions expressed the wish to have the children deported along with their parents." This is a clear reference to the preoccupation of the French authorities with the thorny problem of shelters for the children (Billig, *op. cit.*, Vol. I, pp. 255-256; Vol. III, pp. 317-319), which became a factor favoring Eichmann's fatal decision.

65. T/444.

66. Jacob Kaplan in the *American Jewish Year Book, loc. cit.*

67. T/444.

68. The *Centre* in Paris has lists of 74,000 deportees for the period ending May 1944. The deportation continued till October, and the number of additional deportees was estimated at 6,000 by Joseph Billig in a private communication to the author. See also T/452.

69. Arnold and Veronica Toynbee, *Hitler's Europe, loc. cit.*, pp. 480-481.

70. *Ibid.*, p. 484. Miss Arendt's reference to Brussels is omitted in the paperback edition, p. 166.

71. T/520.

72. *Ibid.*, p. 23.

73. *Ibid.*, pp. 28-29.

74. Materials of the Falkenhausen case in the *Centre de Documentation Juive Contemporaine.*

75. T/520, p. 19.

76. *Ibid.*, p. 26. Miss Arendt's phrase, "there was no Jewish Council to register the Jews" (p. 150), was changed in the paperback edition (p. 166) to "the Jewish Council did not command any authority among native Jews." No evidence is presented for the latter statement.

77. *Ibid.* See also *Centre* Documents CXCVI-17 and CXCVI-18.

78. *Centre* Document LXXV-171 (*Tätigkeitsbericht Nr. 25 der Militärverwaltung, Juli-September, 1943, des Militärbefehlshabers in Belgien und Nord-Frankreich*).

79. Nuremberg Document NG-5219. Miss Arendt's assertion that "not a single Belgian Jew was ever deported" (p. 150) was modified in the paperback edition (p. 166) to read: "very few Belgian Jews were deported." In fact, at least one-quarter of the Jews who were Belgian citizens were deported in a number of shipments to the East. (Private communications from Dr. A. L. Kubovy of *Yad Washem*, dated April 4, 1965, and Miss Betty Garfinkels of the *Centre National des Hautes Etudes Juives* in Brussels, dated June 22, 1965).

80. In addition to those discussed in the text, there are others. For example, on page 9 of Miss Arendt's book we read that some Dutch Jews attacked a German police officer in the old Jewish quarter of Amsterdam. The fact is that the attack took place in the southern part of Amsterdam, not in the Jewish quarter, which is in the center of the city. See B. A. Sijes, *The February Strike, 25-26 February* (The Hague: The Netherlands State Institute for War Documentation, 1954), pp. 101-104 (Dutch). She depicts the fate of the people arrested in reprisal for the attack in the following language (p. 9): "they were literally tortured to death, first in Buchenwald and then in the Austrian camp of Mauthausen. For months on end they died a thousand deaths." These were accidental victims of the raids—not *résistants*, as Miss Arendt implies—passersby or inhabitants of the old Jewish quarter. Of the 425 (not 430 as she states) people arrested and sent to Buchenwald, 77 died in that camp, while 348 were sent to Mauthausen early in June 1941, most of them to die there within a few weeks. The treatment meted out to the captured Jews of Amsterdam was the usual one for the Jews under the *Reichssicherheitshauptamt* (i.e., murder: many of them were forced to jump to their death in stone quarries; others were beaten to death), while non-Jews (*résistants* or others) had a chance to survive in many camps. (Information supplied by Dr. Louis de Jong, Director of The Netherlands State Institute for War Documentation, Amsterdam, on June 23 and July 9, 1963, and on May 29, 1964.) See also Abel J. Herzberg, *Kroniek der Jodenvervolging* (Arnhem: van Loghum Slaterus, and Amsterdam: J. M. Meulenhoff, n. d.), pp. 89-96; and J. Presser, *Ondergang: De Vervolging en verdelging van het Nederlandse Jodendom 1940-1945* ('s-Gravenhage: Staatsuitgeverij/Martinus Nijhoff, 1965), Vol. I, pp. 3-18.

81. Arieh Tartakower and Kurt R. Grossmann, *The Jewish Refugee* (New York: Institute of Jewish Affairs, 1944), p. 343. See also p. 307 for the activities of the Dutch Government on behalf of German Jewish refugees.

82. *Records of the Fourteenth Ordinary Session of the Assembly. Plenary Meetings. Text of the Debates* (Geneva: League of Nations, 1933), pp. 47-49.

83. Information supplied by Dr. Louis de Jong on the basis of extensive records of the Dutch Nazi Party, held by The Netherlands State Institute for War Documentation.

84. Louis de Jong. Based on extensive researches carried out by the Institute.

85. They are available in The Netherlands State Institute for War Documentation; a copy is in the Ghetto Fighters House, Haifa.

86. Based on the Institute's holdings of records of the German administration (information supplied by Dr. Louis de Jong).

87. Information supplied by Dr. de Jong.

88. The indictment (*Anklageschrift*) of Rajakovic—now Raja—by the Attorney General of Vienna (15 St 25696/61[27 d Vr 8896/61]), dated July 17, 1964, documents in great detail his contacts with, and subordination to, Department IVB4 of the RSHA and Eichmann in particular (pp. 1, 5-8, 25-40).

89. Provided by Dr. de Jong.

90. Elsewhere Miss Arendt says that "a large number of Jews" went into hiding and that "an unusually large number of Jews living underground were eventually found" (p. 152). This statement contains references to "a large number" and "an unusually large number" without giving these phrases meaning. Compare notes 170-173 of Chapter 4.

91. Written communication of Dr. de Jong, dated June 22, 1963.

92. Dr. de Jong.

93. For information supplied in this paragraph of the text, see Hugo Valentin, in *YIVO Annual of Jewish Social Science* (New York), Vol. VIII, 1953, p. 233.

94. The first notice was given by the German Minister von Renthe-Fink on November 20, 1941. The *Rigsdag* was called into special session about the issue, the meeting being scheduled for November 23 at night (Sunday), but before it could convene, the Administration was forced to reply in the affirmative to a German ultimatum which expired on November 23, 5 P.M. See Hartvig Frisch, *Denmark—Occupied and Liberated* (Copenhagen: Fremad, 1945), Vol. I, pp. 202-210 (Danish).

95. *Appendix to the Report to Parliament (Folketing) Submitted by the Commission Established . . . with Reference to Section 45 of the Constitution.* Part VII. *The Ministry of Justice and Legal Affairs During the Occupation: Documents.* (Copenhagen: Schultz, 1950), Vol. 1, pp. 186-189 (Danish).

96. Nothing of the kind is mentioned in the essay entitled "King Christian X" in *Denmark during the German Occupation*, Børge Outze, ed. (Copenhagen, London, Chicago: The Scandinavian Publishing Company, 1946), pp. 134-147; or in Harold Flender, *Rescue in Denmark* (New York: Simon & Schuster, 1963), p. 31.

97. T/581.

98. Arnold and Veronica Toynbee, *Hitler's Europe, loc. cit.*, p. 528.

99. *Ibid.*, pp. 528-529. Also Hartvig Frisch, *op. cit.*, pp. 319-336. And "The 29 August 1943," in *Denmark during the German Occupation, loc. cit.*, pp. 32-39.

100. T/582. Also T/37, pp. 2661 ff. And Nuremberg Document NG-3907.

101. T/583; T/586 (Nuremberg Document NG-3920).

102. M. Friediger, *Theresienstadt* (Copenhagen: J. Fr. Clausens, 1946), pp. 54, 56 (Danish).

103. Hugo Valentin, *op. cit.*, pp. 224-251. See also Adler, *Theresienstadt, loc. cit.*, pp. 61, 63, 778-780.

104. These figures are taken from a statistical study made by Julius Margolinsky and quoted on pp. 224-225 of Leni Yahil's unpublished dissertation, *Danish Jews During the Catastrophe* (The Hebrew University of Jerusalem, 1964) in Hebrew. Miss Arendt probably copied the printing error of Hilberg, *loc. cit.*, p. 363, without checking the source he cites—namely, Professor Hugo Valentin's article, *loc. cit.*

105. The proclamation of the Danish Freedom Council (October 1943) in *Facts of the Period of Occupation. A Documentary Handbook* (Copenhagen: Schultz, 1945), Vol. I, p. 235 (Danish).

106. H. Flender, *op. cit.*, p. 74 and *passim*. Also Aage Bertelsen, *October '43* (New York: Putnam [1954]), 246 pp.

107. T/580, 583-584, 586-588, and T/37, pp. 251, 1749 ff., 2661 ff., 3059 ff., 3492 ff. To be sure, Eichmann did not seem to remember very much when interrogated in Jerusalem eighteen years after the event (T/37, pp. 253-254, 945-946, 1752-1759, 2649-2650). But in 1943 Eichmann was so well informed about the details of the matter that he could even discuss the fate of individual Jews: "As Eichmann added, her [Mrs. Texeira, a 102-year-old Jewess] present whereabouts are not known here. Probably she is hiding out in Denmark." (T/588.)

108. T/580.

109. T/584. For his angry remarks about Best, see Sessions 36 and 101; see also T/37, pp. 251-252 and T/585 (compare T/37, p. 3065). During the pretrial interrogation Eichmann wondered why Günther and not he had been sent to Copenhagen to conduct the deportation (T/37, pp. 2662-2666).

110. Archives of the German Foreign Office, Document D-524926 (K-211238). During this visit Eichmann also tried to find out the real reasons for the failure of the *Aktion*. Later Eichmann recalled especially his talks with his friend Mildner concerning this matter (T/37, pp. 948, 1752-1753, 2667; Session 83).

111. T/588. The conditions of the agreement, as recalled by Best, can be found in T/587.

112. Regio Decreto Legge, 17 novembre 1938-XVII, N. 1728, art. 14 (*Gazzetta Ufficiale*, No. 264, November 19, 1938).

113. *Relazione della Direzione Generale per la Demografia e Razza, Ministero dall'Interno*, Rome. Also in Renzo De Felice, *Storia degli ebrei italiani sotto il fascismo* (Turin: Giulio Einaudi, 1962), pp. 640-644.

114. Communication of Dr. Daniel Carpi of the University of Tel-Aviv, dated January 9, 1964.

115. Regio Decreto Legge, *ibid.*, parts 10-13. And Regio Decreto Legge, 29 giugno 1939-XVII, N. 1054, arts. 1-5, 21-35 (*Gazzetta Ufficiale*, No. 179, August 2, 1939).

116. In their ordinances, the secretariat of the Fascist Party and various Ministries exceeded the law. Thus Jews were forbidden to reside in resorts or to have a radio, and schools were forbidden to use textbooks whose authors were Jews. For summaries of these restrictions, see Eucardio Momigliano, *Storia tragica e grottesca del razzismo fascista* (Milan: Arnoldo Mondadori, 1946), pp. 111-118, and Antonio Spinosa, "Le persecuzioni razziali in Italia," *Il Ponte* (Florence), Vol. IX, No. 7, July 1953, p. 963.

117. Dr. Carpi has interviewed Miss Jole Foà's family in Vercelli. The testimony is in his possession. There is only one point which remained obscure, namely whether the Fascists did away with her or turned her over to the Germans.

118. Ministero degli Affari Esteri, *Relazione sull' opera svolta dal Ministero degli Affari Esteri per la tutela delle Comunità Ebraiche, 1938-1943*, pp. 18-22.

119. *Ottobre 1943: Cronaca de un' infamia* (Rome: [Comunità Israelitica di Roma], 1945), p. 29.

120. Attilio Ascarelli, *Le fosse Ardeatine* (Rome: Fratelli Palombi, 1945), 95 pp. In reprisal for the explosion of a bomb in Via Rasella, Rome, March 23, 1944, which caused the death of some German soldiers, an indiscriminate hunt was initiated by the Nazis against men, women, and children in Rome, and 322 Roman citizens (among them at least seventy-five Jews) were butchered in the *Fosse Ardeatine*, a historical place in the vicinity of the city.

121. Primo Levi, *Se questo è un uomo* (Turin: Einaudi, 1958), 194 pp.

122. Renzo De Felice, *op. cit.*, p. 503.

123. T/623. See also T/1274.

124. Attilio Milano, *Storia degli ebrei in Italia* (Turin: Giulio Einaudi, 1963), p. 404.

125. Renzo De Felice, *op. cit.*, pp. 509-510. Also Renzo Baccino, *Fossoli* (Modena: Cooperativa Tipografica di Modena, 1961), 60 pp.

126. On the coup by the Fascist Grand Council against Mussolini and Badoglio's role, see Roy Macgregor Hastie, *The Day of the Lion. The Life and Death of Fascist Italy 1922-1945* (London: Macdonald, 1963), pp. 332-341. See also Federico Chabod, *A History of Italian Fascism* (London: Weidenfeld and Nicolson, 1963), p. 96. For a Fascist evaluation of the coup, see Bruno Spampanato, *Contromemoriale* (Rome: Edizione di "Illustrato," n.d.), Vol. I, pp. 209-235.

127. *Fascismo e antifascismo*. Lezioni e testimonianze a cura del Comitato promotore per l'Universale Economica dell' Editore Feltrinelli, Vol. II, 1936-1948 (Milan: Feltrinelli, 1962), pp. 668-669. See also *Keesing's Contemporary Archives* (London), Vol. 5, 1943-1945, p. 5978.

128. These figures are from the *Comitato ricerche deportati ebrei*, Lungotevere Sanzio 9, Rome (*Schedario statistico*). As for the statistics on Jews in Italy, we rely on the leading Italian historian Gino Luzzatto, "Gli Ebrei in Italia dalla marcia su Roma alle leggi razziali: appunti sulla loro situazione economica, sociale e politica," *Gli Ebrei in Italia durante il fascismo* (Turin: [Quaderni della Federazione Giovanile Ebraica d'Italia], 1961), p. 8. According to Luzzatto, the number of Italian Jews at the end of 1943 was less than 30,000. Adding some five thousand Jewish refugees (mostly from Yugoslavia and France) the maximal figure could not have been higher than 35,000.

129. Communication of David Alcalay, Yad Washem, Jerusalem, who interviewed knowledgeable persons from Zagreb. Incidentally, the majority of these families (for example, the family of Dr. Josip Frank, one of the founders of the Croatian National Party) had long been converted to Catholicism. Some wives or mothers of leading men in "independent" Croatia were Jewish, and their relatives might have been among the few "honorary Aryans."

130. A description of the legislation depriving the Jews of their property is given in Zdenko Levntal, ed., *The Crimes of the Fascist Occupants and Their Collaborators Against Jews in Yugoslavia* (Belgrade: Union of Jewish Communities, 1952), pp. 111-113 (Serbo-Croatian).

131. Archbishop Stepinac intervened on the initiative of the Papal Nuncio, Dr. Marconi. These were, however, exceptions. (Communication of David Alcalay dated March 20, 1964.)

132. Judgment, Section 106.

133. Judgment, Section 106, referring to T/894.

134. Judgment, Section 106.

135. T/874.

136. T/870.

137. T/37, p. 2356, quoted in Judgment, Section 106.

138. *Ibid.*, pp. 2417 ff.

139. Judgment, Section 106.

140. From notes prepared by Rademacher, partly in his own handwriting and partly typed by him, which he submitted to a United States prosecutor in the Nuremberg Ministries case, Dr. Max Mandellaub, who interrogated him. The notes were introduced in evidence in the Eichmann trial with an authenticating affidavit by Dr. Mandellaub (T/875; see p. 3 in particular).

141. Judgment, Section 106.

142. Zdenko Levntal, *op. cit.*, p. 199.

143. *Green Series*, XI, pp. 977-978.

144. Levntal, *op. cit.*, pp. 203-204.

145. Toynbee, *op. cit.*, p. 606.

146. *Ibid.*, p. 605.

147. This view is repeatedly stated in the German documents. See the dispatch of German Minister Beckerle to the Foreign Office, dated March 20, 1943 (available in *Yad Washem*: the Bulgarian collection of the German Foreign Office); and German Police Attaché Hoffmann's report, dated April 5, 1944 (T/941).

148. Benjamin Arditi, *Bulgarian Jews in the Years of the Nazi Regime 1940-1944* (Holon, 1962), p. 401, note 265 (Hebrew).

149. Nathan Grinberg, *Documents* (Sofia: Central Jewish Consistory, 1945), 200 pp. (Bulgarian).

150. T/943.

151. *Le Monde Juif* (Paris), No. 31, May 1950, pp. 7-8. Sabille's book, *Lueurs dans la tourmente* (Paris: Editions du Centre, 1956) has no chapter on Bulgaria.

152. While the Bulgarian Jews were being evacuated from Sofia to the provinces, preparations were being made for their shipment by sea to the East. Already in the written agreement between the *Judenkommissar* Belev and Dannecker (T/938), it was specified that 20,000 Jews were to be deported from Bulgaria, of which 6,000 were from Old Bulgaria (See also the report of Dannecker to IVB4, dated February 23, 1943, T/939). In fact, Belev had confidentially advised the German authorities in Sofia that the resettlement of the Sofia Jews in the provinces was a preliminary measure, to be followed by the deportation of all Bulgarian Jews to the East. (Note of von Thadden to Eichmann, dated June 1, 1943, *Auswärtiges Amt*, Inland II, 1482g, available in *Yad Washem*.) The Hoffmann report (seen by Beckerle; see note 147), stated that the Germans set aside for this purpose, during June 1943, five large Danube ships and one small one, which would be able to transport 25,000 Jews in the course of one month by making ten round trips.

153. Helmut Heiber, "Der Tod des Zaren Boris," *Vierteljahrshefte für Zeitgeschichte* (Stuttgart), Vol. 9, 1961, pp. 384-416.

154. Benjamin Arditi, *The Role of King Boris in the Deportation of Jews from Bulgaria* (Tel-Aviv, 1952), 70 pp. (Bulgarian).

155. Arditi, *Bulgarian Jews, loc. cit.*, Chapter 17.

156. Nathan Grinberg, *The Hitlerian Pressure for the Destruction of Bulgarian Jews* (Tel-Aviv, 1961), pp. 127-129 (Bulgarian).

157. On this point Arditi and Grinberg agree.

158. Arditi, *Bulgarian Jews, loc. cit.*, p. 47.

159. *Ibid.*, pp. 290-294 (excerpts from the verbatim records of the 28 March 1943 session of the Bulgarian *Sobranie*).

160. T/937.

161. Documents available on microfilm in *Yad Washem*.

162. Document available on microfilm in *Yad Washem*; also reproduced in Nathan Grinberg, *The Hitlerian Pressure, loc. cit.*, pp. 38-39. The two notes of Luther were not exhibited at the trial. But page 15 of T/196 (Nuremberg Document NG-2586-J), a memorandum by Luther, dated August 21, 1942, contains, as far as Bulgaria is concerned, the same information as the above-mentioned Luther note of the same date. An extract in English translation is reproduced in *Green Series*, XIII, pp. 243-249.

163. *Drzhaven Vestnik* (Official Gazette), 64th year, Decree No. 129 of August 29, 1942 (Bulgarian). See also Petko Stainov in *Zeitschrift für osteuropäisches Recht* (Berlin), 1943, No. 1, pp. 55-56.

164. Decree No. 3 in application of Art. 33 of the Law for the Protection of the Nation of September 4, 1942, §1; *Drzhaven Vestnik*, Decree No. 210 of September 9, 1942, p. 41.

165. Private communication of Ora Alcalay, of Yad Washem, dated August 30, 1963, based on an extensive inquiry into this question.

166. Arditi, *Bulgarian Jews, loc. cit.*, pp. 252-265.

167. See note 165.

168. See Articles 14 and 15 of the decree in note 163.

169. See note 165.

170. Arditi, *Bulgarian Jews, loc. cit.*, p. 181. See also note 160 of this chapter.

171. The figure 6,000 appears in a report dated May 17, 1943, sent by IVB4 to the Foreign Office (T/942). See also Arditi, *Bulgarian Jews, loc. cit.*, p. 244. However, in the same report a further "supply" (*Einsatz*) of 8,000 slave laborers was expected; according to Arditi (*ibid.*), between 3,000 and 5,000 were actually provided.

172. *Gutachten des Instituts für Zeitgeschichte* (Munich: Selbstverlag, 1958), pp. 141-142; also Matatias Carp, *Cartea neagră. Suferintele evreilor din România, 1940-1944* (Bucharest: Dacia Traiană, 1947) Vol. II-A, Doc. 45.

173. The pogrom in Dorohoi took place on July 1, 1940 (Carp, *op. cit.*, Vol. 3, p. 26).

174. Matatias Carp, *op. cit.*, Vol. 1, pp. 219 ff. The Bucharest massacre took place on January 21 to 23, 1941 (Nuremberg Document NO-488, reproduced on pp. 116-117 of the mimeographed collection of documents on Romania published by the Central Office of the United Restitution Organization [URO], Friedrichstrasse 29, Frankfurt a. M.).

175. Alexander Dallin, *Odessa 1941-1944: A Case Study on Soviet Territory under Foreign Rule* (Santa Monica: Rand Corporation, 1957), pp. 306-321.

176. Matatias Carp, *op. cit.*, Vol. 3, Doc. 14.

177. Carp, *op. cit.*, Vol. 3, Doc. 19.

178. Mrs. Perla Mark's testimony in the Eichmann trial, Session 48; URO, *loc. cit.*, pp. 183-185.

179. *Blue Series*, IV, p. 319, reproduced in URO, *loc. cit.*, p. 155.

180. This may be based on Nuremberg Document PS-3319, published in *Blue Series*, XXXII, pp. 158-193. For this particular item, see pp. 183-184.

181. T/1013 (Nuremberg Document NG-4817).

182. *Gutachten* . . . , *loc. cit.*, p. 154.

183. Matatias Carp, *op. cit.*, Vol. 3, pp. 281-282. See also URO, *loc. cit.*, pp. 404 ff.

184. Document 212-PS published in *Blue Series*, XXV, pp. 301-306; reproduced in URO, *loc. cit.*, pp. 135-138. See also Matatias Carp, *op. cit.*, Vol. 1, pp. 455, 456, 476.

185. T/1002, quoted in Judgment, Section 110.

186. Carp, *op. cit.*, p. 26.

187. See note 174.

188. Miss Arendt states that "Hitler thought" Antonescu to be "more 'radical' than the Nazis" (p. 174). How does she know?

189. *Ereignismeldung UdSSR Nr. 19*, daily report of the *Einsatzgruppen des Chefs der Sicherheitspolizei und des SD*, dated July 10, 1941; reproduced in URO, *loc. cit.*, p. 194. The reports of the *Einsatzgruppen* are available in photocopy in the Institute of Jewish Affairs, New York, and in Yad Washem, Jerusalem.

190. See, for example, *Ereignismeldung[en] UdSSR Nr. 19* and *Nr. 52*, dated July 10, and August 14, 1941, respectively.

191. Nuremberg Documents NG-3986 (reproduced in URO, *loc. cit.*, p. 370) and NG-2200 (reproduced in URO, *loc. cit.*, pp. 370-371, 372-373).

192. Matatias Carp, *op. cit.*, Vol. 2, pp. 2-5.

193. *Ibid.*, pp. 118, 444, 452, 447. Miss Arendt writes on page 164 that "Hungary, Rumania, and Bulgaria [were] won as Axis partners by generous enlargements of their territories." Quite the opposite was the case with Romania. Under the so-called Vienna Arbitral Award (see note 1 of this chapter), Romania, while promised the return of Bessarabia after victory, had to make territorial concessions to Hungary. At the same time further concessions were made to Bulgaria, in accordance with the recommendations of Hitler and Mussolini. See *Documents on German Foreign Policy* (Washington, D.C.), Series D, Vol. X, Document No. 413, in particular p. 587. The same thing happened to another satellite, Slovakia, which had to cede part of its territory to Hungary (Toynbee, *Hitler's Europe, op. cit.*, p. 598).

194. See note 184 of this chapter.

195. T/196 (Nuremberg Document NG-2586-J, reproduced in URO, *loc. cit.*, pp. 354-361).

196. T/1029.

197. The deportation planned by Richter in cooperation with Lecca never materialized. See the text and note 182 of this chapter.

198. Session 102.

199. Lewis (and Edward) Hertslet, *A Complete Collection of Treaties* (London), Vol. IV, No. 513, pp. 2759 ff.

200. Decree-Law Concerning the Legal Status of Jewish Residents in Romania, Art. 5(b); see note 206 of this chapter.

201. Joseph Berkowitz, *La Question des Israélites en Roumanie* (Paris: Jouve, 1923), p. 725.

202. Nicolae Iorga, "Histoire des Juifs en Roumanie," *Bulletin de la Section Historique* (Academia Română, Bucharest), No. 1, 1914, pp. 33-81. See in particular pp. 37-38, 41, 47, 64, 74, 81.

203. *Monitorul Oficial* (Bucharest), No. 18, January 22, 1938.

204. *Reichsgesetzblatt* (Berlin), 1933, Part I, 480.

205. *Documents on German Foreign Policy 1918-1945* (Washington, D.C.: Government Printing Office, 1957), Series D, Vol. X, Doc. 234.

206. The first of these concerned the juridical status of the Jews in Romania, the second prohibited intermarriage between persons of "Romanian blood" and Jews. *Monitorul Oficial* (Bucharest), Part I, No. 183, August 9, 1940, pp. 4079-4088.

207. *Ibid.*, p. 4087.

208. *Timpul* (Bucharest), August 14, 1940.

209. For lists of disbarred Jewish lawyers, see *Timpul* (Bucharest), August 30, 1940. For the status of those who had not been disbarred, see the Decree-Law of October 10, 1940, reproduced in *Timpul* (Bucharest), October 18, 1940.

210. *Monitorul Oficial* (Bucharest), Part I, No. 233, October 9, 1940, pp. 5703-5705.

211. For a list of the spoliatory laws, see the Decree-Law for the Creation of a National Center for Romanization of May 2, 1941. *Monitorul Oficial* (Bucharest), 1941, No. 102, May 3, 1941, Article 2.

212. *Gutachten . . . , op. cit.*, p. 134, footnote 1.

213. See note 195 of this chapter.

214. N/58 (Nuremberg Document NG-3989, reproduced in URO, *loc. cit.*, p. 294).

215. *Procesul marii trădări naţionale. Stenograma desbaterilor dela tribunalul poporului asupra Guvernului Antonescu [The Trial of the Major National Treason. Verbatim Records of the Proceedings of the People's Tribunal in the Case of the Antonescu Government]* (Bucharest: Eminescu, 1946), 315 pp.

216. Keesing's *Contemporary Archives* (London), Vol. 6, 1946-1948, p. 8035A. See also Vol. 5, 1943-1945, pp. 6752A and 7196.

217. See Keesing's *Archiv der Gegenwart* (Essen), March 9, 1945, p. 144H. And *The Institute Anniversary Volume: 1941-1961* (New York: Institute of Jewish Affairs, 1962), p. 108. Also private communications from Dr. Bruno Fischer, United Restitution Organization, Frankfurt a. M., dated June 11, 1963; and Dr. Theodor Lavi, *Yad Washem*, Jerusalem, dated September 9, 1964.

218. T/1136.

219. Randolph L. Braham, *The Destruction of Hungarian Jewry. A Documentary Account* (New York: World Federation of Hungarian Jews, 1963). Document 48. Hereafter referred to as Braham, *Documents*.

220. Josef Goebbels, *The Goebbels Diaries* (London: Hamish Hamilton, 1948), p. 279. Also *Blue Series*, X, pp. 203-204, 409-412.

221. Toynbee, *Hitler's Europe, loc. cit.*, pp. 628-629.

222. T/37, p. 267. In her account of the Hungarian operation, Miss Arendt asserts that Eichmann "was not used to thinking big" (p. 128). This is her characterization of the man who directed an operation in which close to one-half million Jews were arrested, concentrated, and deported within a few months and who personally arranged for the forced march of 100,000 Jews.

223. Braham, *Documents*, Document 440, p. 926. Also *Red Series*, VIII, p. 614. And Randolph L. Braham, *Eichmann and the Destruction of Hungarian Jewry* (New York: World Federation of Hungarian Jews, 1961), p. 14.

224. Braham, *Eichmann and the Destruction of Hungarian Jewry, loc. cit.*, p. 16.

225. Eugene Lévai, *Black Book on the Martyrdom of Hungarian Jewry* (Zurich: The Central European Times Publishing Co., 1948), p. 79.

226. Braham, *Documents*, pp. 927, 929. Also *Red Series*, VIII, pp. 606-621.

227. T/1411 and George Wellers' testimony, Session 32.

228. T/48 and testimony of Herbert Kappler.

229. T/842 and Police Document 06/329.

230. T/1153 to T/1166. See also Judgment, Section 117.

231. The methods of Eichmann's cooperation with the Hungarians are analyzed by J. Lévai in *Yad Washem Studies* (Jerusalem), Vol. V, 1963, pp. 69-103.

232. J. Lévai, *ibid.*, pp. 88-94. Also *Kasztner Report* (T/1113), pp. 80, 117 ff., 120, 124 ff., 128, 129; printed version, pp. 159, 218 ff., 223, 230 ff., 236, 238 (see note 6 of Chapter 1).

233. Randolph L. Braham, *The Hungarian Jewish Catastrophe: A*

Selected and Annotated Bibliography (New York: Yad Washem–YIVO, 1962), Entries 26, 172, 286-312, 695.

234. Elek Karsai, ed., *They Stood Unarmed in the Mine-Fields* (Budapest: Magyar Izraeliták Orszagos kepviselete Kiadása, 1962), Vol. I, pp. 274-281 (Hungarian).

235. J. Lévai, *Black Book . . .* , *loc. cit.*, p. 475.

236. Elek Karsai, ed., *op. cit.*, p. 278. For additional statistical data, see pp. lxxv ff.

237. For a personal account, see Vilmos Nagy, *Fateful Years* (Budapest: Körmendy [1946]). In Hungarian.

238. By way of introduction to her chapter on Hungary, Miss Arendt presents on pages 176-177 some erroneous information on its historical background.

She writes that "once upon a time, the Holy Roman Emperor had been King of Hungary." The expression "Holy Roman Emperor" should be avoided. In Latin, the Empire was called holy (*sacrum*) since 1155, but not the Emperor; the German title of the Empire was *Das Heilige Römische Reich Deutscher Nation*, but *Heiliger Kaiser* is simply nonsense. In modern German the head of the Holy Roman Empire is always called *Deutscher Kaiser* or simply *Der Kaiser*, because on the European continent there was only one emperor, at least until the rise of Peter the Great or Napoleon. A learned and graceful exposition of the history of the Holy Roman Empire are the two volumes of Ricarda Huch, *Römisches Reich Deutscher Nation* (Berlin: Atlantis, 1934), 395 pp., and *Untergang des Römischen Reiches Deutscher Nation* (Berlin: Atlantis, 1954), 351 pp.

The statement that "once upon a time, the Holy Roman Emperor had been King of Hungary" creates the impression that there was some period in history during which possession of the crown of Hungary went with that of the Holy Roman Empire. These are the facts:

1. The Emperor qua Emperor (throughout the entire history of the Holy Roman Empire he remained an elected head of state) did not possess or rule directly any territory within the limits of the Empire. Moreover, Hungary never belonged to the Empire.

2. Individual dynasties or constituent parts of the Empire acquired domains outside the Empire. For example, the Elector of Brandenburg gained control over Prussia, then a territory outside the Empire, and assumed the title of King in Prussia. During the last centuries of the Empire, the Hapsburgs did usually provide the Emperor. But there was never a constitutional link between the crown of the Empire and of Hungary. The Hapsburgs, too, had possessions within the Empire as well as others outside the Empire. Maps of Europe therefore show the pre-1866 Hapsburg domains in two different colors. In 1848, only the

political units within the German Federation (*Deutscher Bund*) sent deputies to the German Parliament in the Paulskirche in Frankfurt am Main. There were, of course, none from Hungary, Galicia, etc., although they constituted part of the Hapsburg domain.

3. The relation between the Hapsburg dynasty and Hungary was based on a document whose very *raison d'être* was to stress that the Hapsburg ruler would not be identical with the Emperor. This document is the Pragmatic Sanction, issued to assure the succession of the daughter of the last male Hapsburg, the Emperor Charles VI. Hungary accepted the Pragmatic Sanction in 1723 and was declared an integral part of the Hapsburg domain. During the entire reign of the heiress (Maria Theresa, 1740-1780), she was *Hungariae Rex* (not *Regina*; Hungarian constitutional law did not recognize a reigning queen), but not Emperor. Charles VI was succeeded as Emperor by the Elector of Bavaria (under the name of Charles VII), and, after the latter's early death, by Maria Theresa's husband, Francis of Lorraine (Francis I). Only at that time did Maria Theresa have the title of Empress, but merely as Francis' consort.

Miss Arendt's statement reads in full: "Once upon a time, the Holy Roman Emperor had been King of Hungary, and more recently, after 1806, the *kaiserlich-königliche Monarchie* on the Danube had been precariously held together by the Hapsburgs, who were emperors (*Kaiser*) of Austria and kings of Hungary." The facts are quite different. Chronologically, the dualistic system was introduced not "after 1806," but in 1867. In accordance with what has been said above, the renunciation of the last head of the Holy Roman Empire, Francis II, in 1806, did not cause any change in the relations between the Hapsburgs and the various parts of their domains (*Hausmacht*). Since the time of Maria Theresa's son, Emperor Joseph II (1780-1790), a rather thorough centralization of governmental activities for all the Hapsburg possessions had taken place, and Hungary was governed from Vienna. A new order of things finally arose—to last for half a century—after defeat in the war of 1866 compelled Austria to sever completely her constitutional links with the German lands. The Hapsburgs now had to come to terms with restless Hungary, and the result was the so-called *Ausgleich* (compromise) of 1867 establishing the dualistic system that remained in force until November 1918.

Miss Arendt also errs in her terminology. The *Ausgleich* of 1867 did not establish a *kaiserlich-königliche Monarchie*. On the contrary, it established two autonomous states with different citizenship, different governments, and, at least partly, different armies (the Austrian *K.K. Landwehr* and the Royal Hungarian *Honveds*). The two *Reichshälften* now had in common only the dynasty and certain matters which had been clearly stipulated in the *Ausgleich* (chiefly foreign affairs, a joint army [the third, albeit the largest force], and navy, currency, and customs). All joint agencies, institutions, etc. were called *kaiserlich und königlich* or briefly *k.u.k.* (e.g., the Foreign Ministry, the General Staff), while *kaiserlich-königlich* (*k.k.*) exclusively designated the Austrian constituent part (e.g., *k.k. Finanzminister, k.k. Gymnasium, k.k. Staatsbahnen,* all Austrian). In addition, the term *königlich* in *kaiserlich-königlich* had nothing to do with Hungary. It referred to those Austrian lands which ranked as kingdoms: Bohemia, Galicia, and Dalmatia. Finally, it should be noted that although the title "Emperor of Austria" was officially introduced in 1804 (Francis was for two years, 1804-1806, double Emperor), according to Austrian constitutional law a country "Austria" did not in fact exist. It was officially called *"die im Reichsrate vertretenen Königreiche und Länder"* (Kingdoms and Countries Represented in the *Reichsrat*).

The basic sources for the constitutional and legal problems touched upon in the preceding discussion are compiled in *Die Staatsgrundgesetze* in Manz'sche *Taschenausgabe der österreichischen Gesetze*, Volume XIX, 6th edition, 1894, 743 pp. The volume includes also Gustav Steinbach's *Die ungarischen Verfassungsgesetze* (Vienna, 1895), 145 pp. See also Ernst C. Hellbling, *Österreichische Verfassungs- und Verwaltungsgeschichte* (Vienna: Springer, 1956), pp. 184-209, 268-270, 345, 353-354, 363-365, 396-398.

Miss Arendt states that after World War I "Hungary . . . was constitutionally a kingdom without a king." This is correct, but her continuation—"the only visible sign of royalty was an abundance of *Hofräte*"—is not correct. In fact, after the collapse of the Communist regime in 1919, practically all institutions of the royal past were restored, modified only through the disappearance of "dualism." There continued to be a House of Magnates (Upper House) in the Hungarian Parliament; titles of nobility and decorations were not abolished; a special Crown Guard watched over the Hungarian Crown (now in United States trust). And these were by no means all remaining "signs of royalty." Hungary was the only state of former Hapsburg sovereignty which did not bar the members of the Hapsburg dynasty from residence, though everywhere else they were barred unless they signed individual declarations renouncing membership in the dynasty and all claims to the Crown. Members of the dynasty who still regarded themselves as archdukes not only continued to reside in Hungary, but remained ex officio members of the House of Magnates. (One of them, the Archduke Albrecht, suggested to Gottlob Berger of the SS Main Office that Hitler should exert pressure on Horthy for more severe anti-Jewish measures. See Nuremberg Document NO-1117.) Indeed, Archduke Joseph, Field Marshal in the old army, used to appear at all public affairs together with Horthy. He was even elected temporary governor of Hungary on August 7, 1919, after the collapse of the short-lived Communist regime. He was still around at the time of Horthy's ouster in 1944. The day of the Nazi entrance into Hungary, he paid a visit to Otto Skorzeny, who describes the event in his memoirs, *Geheimkommando Skorzeny* (Hamburg: Hansa, 1950), p. 249. (The identification of the Archduke as Friedrich is obviously an error; Friedrich died in 1938.) The head of another branch of the Hapsburg family residing in Hungary was the above-mentioned Archduke Albrecht, son and heir of the immensely rich Archduke Friedrich, who once was Commander-in-Chief of the Austro-Hungarian forces (1914-1916), and was an active candidate for the succession to the throne.

On the chances of restoration of a monarchy in the period between the wars, Miss Arendt writes that this was a hopeless case since Otto von Hapsburg "would never have been accepted as King of Hungary" and "an authentically Hungarian royalty" did not exist. The reason for the failure to restore the monarchy was different. True, Otto was unacceptable, as a result of the invalidation of the Pragmatic Sanction by enactments of Austria and Hungary. However, the way was open for the election of another king and dynasty, and there were several candidates, among them Hapsburgs. None had sufficient support. But the main reason for the continuation of the regency was to be found in the field of foreign politics, particularly in view of the violent resistance on the part of the "Little Entente" (Czechoslovakia, Yugoslavia, Romania), which regarded "restoration" as a *casus belli*, and had, in this respect, the support of the Great Powers. See John Oliver Crane, *The Little Entente* (New York: Macmillan, 1931), 222 pp.

Comments on two other subjects: Miss Arendt asserts (p. 177) that the Arrow Cross was "under the influence of Italian Fascism." In fact, it was closely modeled after the German Nazi Party, on whose financial help it relied heavily. The party insigne of the Arrow Cross was a slight variation of the swastika. Another instance of misinformation is her singling out in this context (p. 177) "the strong influence of the Catholic Church." Protestantism (Calvinism) was not less of a powerful factor in Hungarian life. Quite a large number of anti-Hapsburg noblemen (and their serfs and other dependents) had embraced that faith in sizable numbers shortly after the Reformation. In the recent history of Hungary, Calvinist aristocrats have played important roles—for example, the Counts Tisza (father and son, Kálmán and István), both Prime Ministers during the time of the monarchy, and Count Bethlen, the most durable of Hungarian Prime Ministers in the period after World War I. Horthy himself was a Calvinist. On the relative importance of the

Catholic and Protestant (particularly Calvinist) elements in Hungary, see Nuremberg Document NG-5620.

239. Braham, *Eichmann and the Destruction of Hungarian Jewry*, loc. cit., p. 26.

240. See, for example, *Report of the Executives of the Zionist Organization and of the Jewish Agency for Palestine to the 21st Congress* . . . (Jerusalem, 1939), p. 76.

241. See Braham, *The Hungarian Jewish Catastrophe. A Selected and Annotated Bibliography*, loc. cit., p. 14.

242. Braham, *Documents*, Vol. II, pp. 833-892.

243. Jozef Lettrich, *History of Modern Slovakia* (New York: Praeger, 1955), pp. 62-66. Also R. W. Seton-Watson, *Slovakia Then and Now* (London: Allen and Unwin; Prague: Orbis, 1931), p. 63: "The transformation of Slovakia is one of the most remarkable pieces of cultural work which post-war Europe has seen."

244. Lettrich, *op. cit.*, pp. 115-116.

245. Livia Rotkirchen, *The Destruction of Slovak Jewry. A Documentary History* (Jerusalem: Yad Washem, 1961), Document 67. (The book is in Hebrew, with an English Introduction). This book is listed by Miss Arendt in her Bibliography.

246. Judgment in the trial of Dr. Vašek, Tnľud $17/46_{74}$, July 25, 1946. Available in *Yad Washem* Archives (Slovakian).

247. Judgment in the trial of Mach, Tnľud 6/46, April 15, 1946. Available in *Yad Washem* Archives (Slovakian).

248. Testimony of Dr. T. Kovács and Engineer A. Steiner in the trial of Vašek, before the Bratislava People's Tribunal, Tnľud $17/46_{72}$ pp. 72, 74, 130. Available in *Yad Washem* Archives (Slovakian). See also Rotkirchen, *op. cit.* On five dramatic escapes of Jewish inmates from Auschwitz for the express purpose of telling the world what was going on there, see Erich Kulka, "Five Escapes from Auschwitz and Their Echo," *Moreshet* (Tel-Aviv), No. 3, December 1964, pp. 23-38 (Hebrew).

249. M. B. Weissmandel, *Out of the Straits* (New York: Emuna, 1960), pp. 63, 75 (Hebrew). See also Oscar Neumann, *Im Schatten des Todes: Ein Tatsachenbericht vom Schicksalskampf des Slowakischen Judentums* (Tel-Aviv: Olamenu, 1956), p. 138. The affidavit given by Wisliceny in Bratislava prison on November 18, 1946, reads: "with Engineer Steiner we drafted together the Europe-Plan" (T/285). See also Livia Rotkirchen, *op. cit.*, Document 102.

250. *La civiltà cattolica* (Rome), 1961, Vol. III, p. 10.

251. *Gutachten* . . . , *op. cit.*, 425 ff.

252. Anton Vašek, *Die Lösung der Judenfrage in der Slowakei: Systematische Übersicht der anti-jüdischen Gesetzgebung* (Bratislava: Globus, 1942), 162 pp.

253. *Slovenský Zákonnik* (Slovak Code), Sept. 10, 1941, pp. 643-684. See also Nuremberg Document NG-4409, reproduced in *Green Series*, XIII, p. 230.

254. T/1079.

255. T/37, pp. 208-209.

256. Nuremberg Document NG-4651.

257. File of the German Foreign Office (Bonn), K-348359.

258. *Kasztner Report* (T/1113), pp. 157-158; printed version, p. 288. (See note 6 of Chapter 1.)

259. Judgment of the People's Tribunal in Bratislava, TK 347/48, La $^{10/48}\!/_{35}$, May 4, 1948. Available in *Yad Washem* Archives (Slovakian).

260. Files of the German Foreign Office (Bonn): *Inland IIg*, Vol. 186, Finland/Jewish Questions (1942-1944) and *Inland II A/B* 83-26 Finland (1943-1944).

261. Felix Kersten, *Totenkopf und Treue: Himmler ohne Uniform* (Hamburg: Robert Mölisch, 1952), pp. 172, 180; *The Kersten Memoirs, 1940-1945* (New York: Macmillan, 1957), pp. 144-145.

262. Thomas Jones, *Lloyd George* (Cambridge, Mass.: Harvard Univ. Press, 1951), pp. 242, 244, 247-248.

263. Thomas Jones, *A Diary with Letters, 1931-1950* (London, New York, Toronto: Oxford Univ. Press, 1954), p. 181.

264. Adolf Lande, ed. *Chronology of Adolf Hitler's Life* (Washington, D.C.: U.S. Office of War Information, Overseas Branch, 1944), p. 87 (mimeogr.).

265. The following defendants made statements on the preparation of the Rhineland occupation before the International Military Tribunal: Admiral Raeder (*Blue Series*, XIV, p. 15); Neurath ("It was one of those sudden decisions of Hitler which was to be carried out within a few days."–*Ibid.*, XVI, p. 626); Göring (The plan had to be hatched "at the most two to three weeks."–*Ibid.*, IX, pp. 505, 507); Jodl (*Ibid.*, V, pp. 28-29).

266. See the *Zeittafel* in Gerd Rühle, ed., *Das Dritte Reich. Dokumentarische Darstellung des Aufbaues der Nation.* Vol. I, *Das erste Jahr, 1933 (Berlin*: Hummelverlag, 1934), pp. 356-368.

267. Nuremberg Document 1138-PS, reproduced in *Blue Series*, XXVII, pp. 18-25.

268. Part II of the Brown Dossier: The Civil Administration in the Occupied Eastern Territories, *Reichskommissariat Ukraine*, submitted in the Trial as T/296 (Nuremberg Document 702-PS).

269. Jacob Robinson and Philip Friedman, *Guide to Jewish History Under Nazi Impact* (New York: YIVO–Yad Washem, 1960), p. 221.

270. The "Provisional Instructions" on the Jews in *Ostland*, issued

August 13, 1941, by Hinrich Lohse (see note 267), constituting a sort of codification of Nazi legislation, were issued when the actual mass murder was in full progress. On the function of "law" in the incorporated areas of Poland, see Isaiah Trunk, *Studies in Jewish History in Poland* (Buenos Aires: Yidbukh, 1963), pp. 177-181 (Yiddish).

271. After the so-called *Röhm-Putsch* and the crimes committed by the Nazis on June 30 and on July 1 and 2, 1934, a law was published on July 3, 1934 (*Reichsgesetzblatt* [Berlin], Part I, p. 529) which in substance declared these crimes to be acts of self-defense of the State. The same thing happened after the *Kristallnacht* crimes; a law was promulgated on November 12, 1938 (*Reichsgesetzblatt*, Part I, p. 1581) which in substance punished the victims and cleared the criminals.

272. Theodor Maunz, *Gestalt und Recht der Polizei* (Hamburg: Hanseatische Verlagsanstalt, 1943), p. 27.

273. *Ibid.*

274. See Chapter 2, under Crimes Against Humanity and Crimes Against the Jewish People.

275. Nuremberg Document NOKW-258. For an excerpt in English translation, see *Green Series*, XI, pp. 971-972.

276. Nuremberg Document 498-PS, reproduced in *Blue Series*, XXVI, pp. 100-102. For English translation, see *Green Series*, XI, pp. 73-74.

277. *Green Series*, XI, pp. 1248-1249, 1252, 1270, 1278, 1289, 1303, 1308; XIV, pp. 515, 527, 581, 654, 1305. See also Kurt Heinze and Karl Schilling, *Die Rechtsprechung der Nürmberger Militärtribunale* (Bonn: Girardet, 1962), items 1035-1045, 1062-1065.

278. There is no doubt that such an order existed; the only question is whether it emanated from Hitler or from Himmler. It is difficult to surmise that Himmler would have taken on himself such a far-reaching decision. Höss testified in the Trial of the Major War Criminals in Nuremberg (*Blue Series*, XI, p. 398) that he received from Himmler Hitler's Final Solution order orally in June 1941. Wisliceny claimed to have seen the Final Solution order in writing in the summer of 1942 (*Blue Series*, IV, pp. 358-359).

279. The text of the euthanasia order was written on Adolf Hitler stationery and signed by him. Apparently, the original was not made available, but photocopies were shown around. See Reinhard Henkys, *Die nationalsozialistischen Gewaltverbrechen* (Stuttgart, Berlin: Kreuz Verlag, 1964), p. 61.

280. Quoted by Welzel in *Neue Juristische Wochenschrift* (Munich and Berlin), Vol. 17, 1964, p. 521.

281. *Zeitschrift für die gesamte Staatswissenschaft* (Tübingen), Vol. 104, 1944, p. 336. The same view was taken by Maunz, *Verwaltung*

(Hamburg: Hanseatische Verlagsanstalt, 1937), p. 40 (". . . the *Führer* above anyone else is competent to . . . promulgate and to implement the law . . ."). Redeker, in *Neue Juristische Wochenschrift* (Munich and Berlin), Vol. 17, 1964, pp. 1097-1100, quotes contrary views expressed by Nazi jurists during the Third Reich.

282. See the controversy between Anton Roesen, Adolf Arndt, Hans Welzel, Konrad Redeker, Jürgen Baumann, and Walter Lewald in *Neue Juristische Wochenschrift* (Munich and Berlin), Vol. 17, 1964, pp. 133-136, 486-488, 521-523, 1097-1100, 1111-1112, 1310-1313, 1398-1405, 1658-1661, and the one-page supplement to the twelfth issue of the journal (retort by Roesen). See also Jürgen Baumann in Reinhard Henkys, *op. cit.*, pp. 295-296.

283. Horst Göppinger, *Die Verfolgung der Juristen jüdischer Abstammung durch den Nationalsozialismus* (Villingen/Schwarzwald: Ring-Verlag, 1963), pp. 21-24, 109, 121 f., and notes 1-3 on p. 31. Also G. Schoenberner, *Wir haben es gesehen, Augenzeugenberichte über Judenverfolgung im Dritten Reich* (Im Bertelsmann Lesering, 1962), pp. 19-22.

284. Wolfgang Scheffler, *Judenverfolgung im Dritten Reich 1933-1945* (Berlin: Colloquium, 1961), expanded edition for the members of the Gutenberg Book Club, p. 25.

285. Karl Dietrich Bracher, Wolfgang Sauer, and Gerhard Schulz, *Die nationalsozialistische Machtergreifung. Studien zur Errichtung des totalitären Herrschaftssystems in Deutschland 1933/34* (Cologne and Opladen: Westdeutscher Verlag, 1960), p. 28; and H. Göppinger, *op. cit.*, pp. 35, 38n. For detailed texts, see Bruno Blau, *Das Ausnahmerecht für die Juden in Deutschland 1933-1945* (2nd edition, Düsseldorf: Verlag Allgemeine Wochenzeitung der Juden in Deutschland, 1954), Items 12, 18, 21, 40, 45, 49, 84, 88, 108, 130, 169 (physicians); 21, 40, 62, 64 (dentists and dental technicians); 2, 4, 27, 37, 39, 44, 86, 175 (attorneys); 1, 17, 118 (notaries); 12, 18, 40, 49, 62, 64, 130, 139, 178 (sick funds); 28, 42 (newspapermen); 32, 72 (segregation of cultural activities).

286. See the chronological table in Wolfgang Scheffler, *op. cit.*, p. 234.

287. Session 17, testimony given by Moritz Fleischmann.

288. *Year Book I* of the Leo Baeck Institute (London, Jerusalem, New York, 1956), p. 377. In this context Miss Arendt writes (p. 60) that "Göring, probably on the initiative of Heydrich, decided to establish in Berlin a Reich Center for Jewish Emigration, and in the letter containing his directives Eichmann's Viennese office was specifically mentioned as the model to be used in the setting up of a central authority." The minutes of the Pogrom Conference of November 12, 1938 (IMT,

XXVII, pp. 532-533) clearly indicate that it *was* Heydrich who suggested this center. The Göring directive embodied in a letter to Heydrich, dated January 24, 1939 (Nuremberg Document NG-5764, pp. 10-11) does not, however, mention Eichmann's Viennese office.

289. Max Gruenewald, "The Beginning of the Reichsvertretung" in *Year Book I* of the Leo Baeck Institute, *loc. cit.*, pp. 57-67. See also Kurt Alexander, "Die Reichsvertretung der deutschen Juden" in *Festschrift zum 80. Geburtstag von Rabbiner Dr. Leo Baeck am 23. Mai 1953* (London: Council for the Protection of the Rights and Interests of Jews from Germany [1953]), pp. 76-84; K. J. Ball-Kaduri, "The National Representation of Jews in Germany—Obstacles and Accomplishments at its Establishment" in *Yad Washem Studies* (Jerusalem), Vol. II, 1958, pp. 159-178, and the same author's *Das Leben der Juden in Deutschland 1933; ein Zeitbericht* (Frankfurt a.M.: Europäische Verlagsanstalt, 1963), pp. 136-146; Hugo Hahn, "Die Gründung der Reichsvertretung" in *In zwei Welten. Siegfried Moses zum 75. Geburtstag* (Tel-Aviv: Bitaon, 1962), pp. 97-105; and Friedrich S. Brodnitz, "Die Reichsvertretung der deutschen Juden," *ibid.*, pp. 106-113. See also Dr. Ernst Herzfeld's statement on the establishment of the *Reichsvertretung*, a manuscript in the custody of *Yad Washem*. The same problems were discussed from a different angle by Philip Friedman in his article, "Aspects of the Jewish Communal Crisis in the Period of the Nazi Regime in Germany, Austria, and Czechoslovakia" in *Essays on Jewish Life and Thought, Presented in Honor of Salo Wittmayer Baron* (New York: Columbia Univ. Press, 1959), pp. 200-210. On the gradual increase of Gestapo control over the *Reichsvertretung* and *Reichsvereinigung*, see the study by K. J. Ball-Kaduri, "Von der 'Reichsvertretung' zur 'Reichsvereinigung,'" *Zeitschrift für die Geschichte der Juden* (Tel-Aviv), 1964, pp. 191-199.

290. In the paperback edition (p. 60) Miss Arendt writes: "A letter from a survivor of Theresienstadt, a German Jew, relates that all leading positions in the Nazi-appointed *Reichsvereinigung* were held by Zionists." In fact, the *Reichsvereinigung* up to the end included prominent non-Zionists, among whom were Leo Baeck, Otto Hirsch, Heinrich Stahl (president of the Jewish community of Berlin), Dr. Arthur Lilienthal, Hanna Karminski, and Cora Berliner. There was not one leading Zionist in the *Reichsvereinigung*, since most of them had left Germany before the beginning of the war. (Private communication from Dr. Max Kreutzberger, Secretary of the Leo Baeck Institute, dated March 19, 1965.)

291. Shaul Esh, *"Haavarah,* An Attempt at a Rescue Policy," *Studies in Contemporary Jewish Life* (Jerusalem: The Hebrew University, The Institute of Contemporary Jewry, 1964), pp. 330-349 (Hebrew).

292. *League of Nations: Records of the Fourteenth Ordinary Session*

(*1933*), p. 88. The resolution was called to a vote on October 11, 1933 and was not carried due to the German opposition. The text opposed by Germany obviously aimed at extending the *voeu* of September 21, 1922, to the Jews:

> The Assembly considers that the principles expounded in Resolution I, which reaffirms the recommendation of 1922, must be applied without exception to all classes of nationals of a State that differ from the majority of the population in race, language or religion.

293. Nathan Feinberg, *The Jewish Struggle Against Hitler in the League of Nations—The Bernheim Petition* (Jerusalem: Mosad Bialik, 1957), 186 pp. (Hebrew). Chapter III is published in English translation in *Yad Washem Studies* (Jerusalem), Vol. I, 1957, pp. 67-83. See also Georg Weissmann's memorandum: "Die Durchsetzung des jüdischen Minderheitsrechts in Oberschlesien 1933-1937" (with preface by Franz Meyer) in *Bulletin des Leo Baeck Institute* (Jerusalem), Vol. 6, 1963, pp. 154-198.

294. *League of Nations: Records of the Fourteenth Ordinary Session* (*1933*), *Plenary Meetings, loc. cit.*, pp. 89-90.

295. A list is given by Ball-Kaduri in *Yad Washem Studies* (Jerusalem), Vol. V, 1964, pp. 271-272.

296. Bruno Blau, *op. cit.*, item 348, §§1 and 2.

297. *Ibid.*, item 423.

298. Nuremberg Document 654-PS, reproduced in *Green Series,* III, pp. 504-506.

299. For full text of the law, see Blau, *op. cit.*, item 423.

300. See, for instance, Hans Lamm, *Über die innere und äussere Entwicklung des deutschen Judentums im Dritten Reich,* unpublished doctoral thesis, Erlangen, 1951 (mimeogr.), pp. 305-306.

301. Testimony of Hildegard Henschel (wife of the last chairman of the Jewish Community of Berlin, Moritz Henschel) at the Eichmann trial, Session 37: ". . . There were Jewish ushers to keep order and there were [German] policemen, as well as intelligence men . . ."

302. Report of Hildegard Henschel, dated 1947 (*Yad Washem* Archives 01/52). For more information on this stage in the history of German Jews, see Robert M. W. Kempner, *Eichmann und Komplizen* (Zurich, Stuttgart, Vienna: Europa Verlag, 1961), pp. 114-125.

nationale de Criminologie et de Police technique (Geneva), Vol. 16 (1962), pp. 19-60.

een, L. C. "Legal Issues of the Eichmann Trial," *Tulane Law Review* (New Orleans, La.), Vol. 37 (1962/1963), pp. 641-684.

——. "The Maxim *nullum crimen sine lege* and the Eichmann Trial," *British Yearbook of International Law, loc. cit.*, pp. 457-471.

——. "Aspects juridiques du procès Eichmann," *Annuaire français de Droit international* (Paris), Vol. IX (1963), pp. 150-190.

Ieazlett, Elizabeth. "Eichmann–International Law," *University of Pittsburgh Law Review*, Vol. 24 (1962/1963), pp. 116-132.

Ierzberg, Abel J. *Eichmann in Jeruzalem.* The Hague: Bert Bakker, Daamen, 1962. 204 pp. (Dutch.)

Iäger, Herbert. "Betrachtungen zum Eichmann-Prozess," *Monatsschrift für Kriminologie und Strafrechtsreform* (Cologne), Vol. 45 (1962), pp. 73-85. Also in *Freiburger Rundbrief*, Vol. XV (1963/1964), No. 57/60 (January 1964), pp. 47-52.

Jasper, G. "Eichmann," *Judaica* (Zurich), Vol. 19 (1962), pp. 65-104.

Jews and the Jewish People (London: Contemporary Jewish Library). Comments in the Soviet Press on the Eichmann trial. 7 (1.1.1962–31.3.1962), pp. 230-240; 8 (1.4.1962–30.6.1962), pp. 188-193; 9 (1.7.1962–30.9.1962), pp. 217-218; 10 (1.10.1962–31.12.1962), pp. 177-185 (Russian). See also *Yad Washem Bulletin* (Jerusalem), No. 11.

Kempner, Robert M. W. "Cross-examining War Criminals," *Yad Washem Studies* (Jerusalem), V (1963), pp. 43-68.

Kittrie, N. N. "A Post-Mortem of the Eichmann Case: The Lessons for International Law," *Journal of Criminal Law, Criminology, and Police Science* (Chicago), Vol. 55 (1964), pp. 16-28.

Leavy, Zad. "The Eichmann Trial and the Role of Law," *American Bar Association Journal* (Chicago), Vol. 48 (1962), pp. 820-825.

——. "The Eichmann Trial: Report from Jerusalem," *California Bar Journal* (San Francisco), Vol. 37 (1962), pp. 243-261.

Lippert, David I. "The Eichmann Case and the Nuremberg Trials," *American Bar Association Journal* (Chicago), Vol. 48 (1962), pp. 738-741.

Mulisch, Harry. *Strafsache 40/61. Eine Reportage.* Cologne: DuMont Schauberg, 1963, 177 pp. Translated from the Dutch original, *De zaak 40/61. Een reportage.* Amsterdam: De Bezige Bij, 1962. 194 pp.

Papadatos, Peter. "The Eichmann Trial," *Bulletin of the International Commission of Jurists* (Geneva), No. 14 (October 1962), pp. 13-19.

——. *The Eichmann Trial.* New York: Praeger, 1964. Also London: Stevens, 120 pp. French edition: *Le Procès Eichmann.* Geneva:

Bibliography

PART I. BOOKS AND ARTICLES ON THE EICHMA

Astor, David. *The Meaning of Eichmann.* Royston, En
    1961. 12 pp. (The Parkes Library Pamphlets, No. 5.)
"At Israel's Mercy," *The Economist* (London), Vol. 203 (A
    p. 17.
Baumann, Jürgen. "Gedanken zum Eichmann-Urteil," *Ju*
    (Tübingen), Vol. 18 (1963), pp. 110-121.
——. "Schuld und Verantwortung. Ein Beitrag zur juristisch
    gung des Falles Eichmann," *Freiburger Rundbrief*, Vol.
    53/56 (September 1962), pp. 29-32.
Bentwich, Norman. "The Trial of Adolf Eichmann," *The Solici*
    don), October 1962, pp. 303-308.
Bondy, François. " 'Ja mein lieber guter Storfer . . .' Eichmann v
    Der Monat (Berlin), Vol. 13 (1961), No. 153, pp. 58-61.
Cohen, Nathan. *Rechtliche Gesichtspunkte zum Eichmann-*
    Frankfurt am Main: Europäische Verlagsanstalt, 1963. 92 p
Draper, G. I. A. D. "The Eichmann Trial: A Judicial Precedent,"
    national Affairs (London), Vol. 38 (1962), pp. 485-500. A
    in *International Political Science Abstracts* (Oxford), Vol.
    (1963), p. 96.
Eban, Abba. "Lessons of the Eichmann Trial," *The Jewish Spec*
    (New York), Vol. XXVII (1962), Nos. 6-7.
Eisenberg, Alfred. "El caso Eichmann ante el derecho internacion
    Versión de una conferencia pronunciada en el Instituto Cultu
    Uruguayo-Israeli el día 26 de octubre de 1961. Montevideo: Com
    Central Israelita, 1962. 23 pp.
Fawcett, J. E. S. "Some Thoughts on the Eichmann Trial," *The Lawy*
    (Oxford), Vol. 4, No. 3 (1961), pp. 7-11.
——. "The Eichmann Case," *British Yearbook of International Lau*
    (London), Vol. 38 (1962), pp. 181-215.
Funaro, G. "Note sul caso Eichmann," *Giurisprudenza Italiana* (Turin),
    Vol. 113, IV (1962), pp. 41-52.
Graven, Jean. "Comment juger le jugement d'Eichmann," *Revue inter-*

Librairie Droz, 1964, 125 pp. (Travaux de droit, d'économie, de sociologie et de sciences politiques, No. 18.)

Peters, Karl. "Gedanken eines Juristen zum Eichmann-Prozess," *Eckart Jahrbuch 1961/1962*. Edited by Kurt Ihlenfeld. Berlin: Eckart-Verlag. Pp. 229-252.

Salgado, J. A. Cesar. *O caso Eichmann a luz da moral e do direito*. Saõ Paulo, Brazil: 1961. 61 pp.

Schüle, Erwin. "Die strafrechtliche Aufarbeitung des Verhaltens in totalitären Systemen: Der Eichmann-Prozess aus deutscher Sicht," *Studien und Berichte der Katholischen Akademie in Bayern* (Würzburg: Echter), Vol. 19 (1962), pp. 63-86.

Schwarzenberger, Georg. "The Eichmann Judgment," *Current Legal Problems* (London), Vol. 15 (1962), pp. 248-265. Spanish abstract in *Revista española de derecho internacional*, Vol. 16 (1963), pp. 328-329.

Schwelien, Joachim. *Jargon der Gewalt: Vom Gestern zum Morgen*. Frankfurt am Main: Ner-Tamid, 1961. 30 pp. (*Zeitgeschichtliche Schriftenreihe*, Vol. 14.)

Taylor, Telford. "Faces of Justice in Jerusalem," *The Spectator* (London), Vol. 208 (Jan. 5, 1962), pp. 9-10. See also the issues of April 21 and May 28, 1961.

Treves, Vanni E. "Jurisdictional Aspects of the Eichmann Case," *Minnesota Law Review* (Minneapolis), Vol. 47 (1962/1963), pp. 557-592.

Woetzel, Robert K. "The Eichmann Case in International Law," *Criminal Law Journal* (London), 1962, pp. 671-682.

———. "Postlude on the Eichmann Case," in his *The Nuremberg Trials in International Law*. London: Stevens. Also New York: Praeger, 1962. Pp. 245-272. (The London edition is listed in Miss Arendt's Bibliography.)

PART II. INSTITUTIONS

Detecting, cataloguing, and describing materials on the Jewish Catastrophe—and utilizing these materials for purposes of research, analysis, synthesis, and publication—are the central concern of the following Jewish research institutes:

1. Yad Washem Martyrs' and Heroes' Memorial Authority (Har Hazikaron, P.O.B. 84, Jerusalem, Israel). Field of interest: the Jewish Catastrophe in its entirety, including its background and setting. Maintains extensive archives and a specialized library. Publishes, in addition to books, a periodical *Bulletin* (Hebrew, Yiddish, and Eng-

lish) and *Studies* (Hebrew and English). (The name of this institution derives from Isaiah 56:5.) The "Bibliographical Series" is a joint undertaking of Yad Washem and YIVO Documentary Projects.

2. Documentary Projects at the YIVO Institute for Jewish Research (1048 Fifth Avenue, New York, N.Y.). Special field of interest: the history of the Nazi period in Eastern Europe, with emphasis on the Jewish Catastrophe. Has access to YIVO's archives and a specialized library within the framework of its collections. Publishes books (bibliographies, substantive studies). Current information in the bilingual *News of the YIVO*. Studies on the period of the Catastrophe are published in *YIVO Bleter* (Yiddish) and *YIVO Annual* (English).

3. Ghetto Fighters' House in Memory of Yitzhak Katznelson (Haifa, Israel). Special field of interest: the Jewish resistance.

4. The Wiener Library (4, Devonshire Street, London W. 1, England). Special field of interest: Germany, past and present; German-speaking Jewry. Maintains archives and a unique library in these fields. Publishes the *Wiener Library Bulletin*, now in its 18th year. (The title derives from the name of the founder, Dr. Alfred Wiener.)

5. Centre de Documentation Juive Contemporaine (15, Rue Geoffroy-l'Asnier, Paris 4, France). Field of interest: Jewish history under the Nazi regime, with emphasis on France. Maintains specialized archives and a library. Publishes books and *La Revue du Centre de Documentation Juive Contemporaine: Le Monde Juif*, now in its 19th year.

6. The Jewish Historical Institute in Warsaw (Ul. Gen. Świerczewskiego 79, Warsaw, Poland). Special interest: Eastern Europe, and Poland in particular. Rich archives and library. Publishes books and two periodicals: the Yiddish-language *Bleter far Geshikhte* (Historical Leaves), 1948 *et seq.*, and the Polish-language *Biuletyn* (Bulletin), 1951 *et seq.*

7. Centro di Documentazione Ebraica Contemporanea (Milan, Italy). Special field of interest: History of the Jews under the Fascist regime in Italy. Maintains archives and a library. Publishes at irregular intervals *Gli Ebrei in Italia durante il Fascismo*, 1961 *et seq.*

The following non-Jewish institutes have shown a special interest in materials on the Jewish Catastrophe:

1. The Central Commission for the Investigation of Hitlerian Crimes in Poland (Ministry of Justice, Warsaw, Poland). Publishes a Polish-language bulletin.

2. The Western Institute: Scientific Research Institute (Ul. Chełmońskiego 1, Poznań, Poland). Scope of interest: Germany, present and past. Publishes, *inter alia*, *Western Review* (in Polish and other languages).

3. Comité d'histoire de la deuxième guerre mondiale (22, Rue d'Athènes, Paris 9, France). Publishes *Revue d'Histoire de la Deuxième Guerre Mondiale*.

4. Netherlands State Institute for War Documentation (Herengracht 477, Amsterdam, The Netherlands). Publishes books on the history of the German occupation of The Netherlands.

5. Institut für Zeitgeschichte (Möhlstrasse 26, Munich, West Germany). Publishes *Vierteljahrshefte für Zeitgeschichte* and special series of books in its field.

6. Deutsches Institut für Zeitgeschichte (Hessische Strasse 12, East Berlin). Publishes *Dokumentation der Zeit* and *Beiträge zur Zeitgeschichte*.

PART III. REFERENCE WORKS

A BASIC REFERENCE WORK ON THE HISTORY OF THE JEWISH CATASTROPHE:
Robinson, Jacob, and Philip Friedman. *Guide to Jewish History under Nazi Impact*. New York: Yad Washem–YIVO, 1960. Detailed indexes (persons, places, subjects).

A SURVEY OF HEBREW-LANGUAGE LITERATURE:
Friedman, Philip. *Bibliography of Books in Hebrew on the Jewish Catastrophe and Heroism in Europe*. Jerusalem: Yad Washem–YIVO, 1960. Indexes also in English.

A SURVEY OF YIDDISH-LANGUAGE LITERATURE:
Friedman, Philip, and Joseph Gar. *Bibliography of Yiddish Books on the Catastrophe and Heroism*. New York: Yad Washem–YIVO, 1962. Indexes also in English.

A CATALOGUE OF PREDOMINANTLY GERMAN AND ENGLISH PUBLICATIONS:
Wolff, Ilse R. *Books on Persecution, Terror, and Resistance in Germany* (2nd ed.). London: Wiener Library, 1960. 208 pp.

A SURVEY OF LITERATURE ON THE BACKGROUND OF THE NAZI PERIOD:
Wolff, Ilse R. *From Weimar to Hitler: Germany 1918-1933*. London: Vallentine, Mitchell & Co. for the Wiener Library, 1964. 269 pp.

A SURVEY OF LITERATURE ON THE POST-HITLER PERIOD:
Wolff, Ilse R. *After Hitler: Germany 1945-1963*. London: Vallentine, Mitchell & Co. for the Wiener Library, 1963. 261 pp.

A SURVEY OF FRENCH-LANGUAGE LITERATURE:
La France: De l'Affaire Dreyfus à nos jours. Paris: Centre de Documentation Juive Contemporaine, 1964. Catalogue No. 1; in particular, pp. 71-183.

AN ANNOTATED POLISH-LANGUAGE BIBLIOGRAPHY:

Mark, Bernard. *The Martyrology and the Struggle of the Jews in the Years of Occupation.* Warsaw: Bibliographical Institute, 1963. 44 pp.

A MULTILINGUAL BIBLIOGRAPHY, MOSTLY HUNGARIAN:

Braham, Randolph L. *The Hungarian Jewish Catastrophe: A Selected and Annotated Bibliography.* New York: Yad Washem–YIVO, 1962.

WORKS DESCRIBING THE COURSE OF THE NAZI PERSECU-
TION AND EXTERMINATION OF EUROPEAN JEWRY:

Hilberg, Raul. *The Destruction of the European Jews.* Chicago: Quadrangle Books, 1961. 788 pp.

Poliakov, Leon. *Harvest of Hate: The Nazi Program for the Destruction of the Jews of Europe.* Syracuse, N.Y.: Syracuse Univ. Press, 1954. 388 pp.

Reitlinger, Gerald. *The Final Solution: The Attempt to Exterminate the Jews of Europe, 1939-1945.* New York: Beechhurst Press, 1953. 622 pp.

A BASIC SURVEY OF EUROPE UNDER THE NAZI REGIME:

Survey of International Affairs 1939-1946. Hitler's Europe. Edited by Arnold and Veronica Toynbee. London, New York, Toronto: Oxford Univ. Press, 1954. 730 pp. The companion volume of documents is *Documents on International Affairs 1939-1946,* Vol. II, *Hitler's Europe.* Edited by Margaret Carlyle. London, New York, Toronto: Oxford Univ. Press, 1954. 362 pp.

Index

Aaronson, Yehoshua Moshe, 221
Abduction: fact of Eichmann's 105-6; jurisdiction in cases of, 103-4, 310 (#3)
Act of State doctrine in international law, 61
Actus reus in Eichmann case, 130-31
Adler, H. G., 114, 179, 211, 229, 230, 232, 314 (#35, 36), 315 (#50), 327 (#77), 328 (#85), 334 (#135), 340 (#204), 350 (#5, 11, 18, 20), 351 (#24, 26, 32, 35, 36, 38, 39, 40, 41), 357 (#103)
Administrative Court (Cologne), 86
Adolph, Walter, 339 (#190)
Advisers on Jewish affairs, 235-36, 239, 241, 242, 249-50, 262, 267, 271, 292 (#139)
Ältestenrat. See Judenrat
Agatstein, Dora, 335 (#155)
Aggression. *See* Crimes
"Aiding and abetting," 132, 319 (#109)
Aizen, Abraham, 345 (#254)
Albania, 346 (#3)
Albrecht, Archduke of Hapsburg, 367, (#238)
Alcalay, David, 359 (#129, 131)
Alcalay, Ora, 361 (#165)
Alexander, Kurt, 373 (#289)
Alexandria, Va., 311 (#17), 316 (#64)
Alexianu, Gheorghe, 265
Aliya Beth ("illegal" immigration to Palestine), 118, 315 (#57)

Alliance Israélite Universelle, 349 (#3)
Allies, 30; protests and warnings by on war crimes, 52, 75, 76; and rescue of Jews, 210. *See also* United Nations
Altersghetto, 230
Amende, Ewald, 74
American Jewish Committee, 349 (#3)
American Jewish Congress, 349 (#3)
American Jewish Joint Distribution Committee. *See* Joint Distribution Committee
American Journal of International Law, 63, 106
Amihai, Yehuda, 138
Amsterdam, 241, 242, 341 (#212), 355 (#80); Central Office of Jewish Emigration, 242; Jewish Council, 240; Jewish Court of Honor, 172
Anders, Günther, 201
Anielewicz, Mordecai, 216
d'Annunzio, Gabriele, 247
Ansbacher, Mordecai, 230, 350 (#10)
Anschluss (annexation of Austria by Nazi Germany), 229, 277
Anti-Semitism, 38, 39, 44, 59, 102, 106, 227, 270. *See also* Legislation
Anticomintern Pact, 244
Antonescu, Ion, 259, 261, 262, 265, 362 (#188)
Antonescu, Mihai, 265
Antwerp, 239, 240

Geneva Convention (Polish-German) on Upper Silesia, 72-73
Geneva Red Cross Conventions, 64, 77
Genocide, 65, 70-72, 82, 297 (#23), 300-301 (#53-57), 307 (#126)
Gens, Jacob, 179, 186, 324 (#41)
Geography (political): unfit for history of the Catastrophe, 227, 345 (#1)
Gercke, Achim, 146
German Army, 16, 253-54
German Foreign Office, 3, 8, 22-23, 61, 107, 117, 168, 240, 246, 260, 272, 287-88 (#59, 61-67), 314 (#47)
Germany, 1, 14, 21-23, 27, 32, 36, 42, 45, 55, 69, 72-73, 76, 79-80, 91, 94, 96, 101, 104, 121, 127, 130, 135, 147-56, 163, 166, 204, 212, 214, 221, 227-28, 244-50, 255, 258-260, 264, 272-81, 286 (#43), 287 (#54), 289 (#75), 290 (#99), 292-93 (#142, 144, 145), 294 (#147, 149), 300 (#50), 302 (#66), 306 (#113, 114), 308 (#148), 310 (#16), 311 (#29), 313 (#30), 318 (#97), 319 (#113, 115, 116), 321 (#7), 329 (#88), 332 (#122, 123), 334 (#137), 337 (#171), 339 (#190), 341 (#208, 211), 345 (#1), 347 (#3), 350 (#17), 365 (#238), 370 (#266), 371 (#281), 372 (#283-88), 373 (#289-92), 374 (#300); character attributed to Nazi society in, 7-8; ethnic register in, 92; Jews of, 6, 53, 73-74, 276-80; judges of in international criminal court, 303 (#79); source material on the Catastrophe originating in, 150-51; trials and courts in, 70, 75, 300 (#45), 320-21 (#124-26). See also Bundesgerichtshof; Bundestag; Central Agency of the German Federal Republic; Ermächtigungsgesetz; Red Cross
Gerstein, Kurt, 210, 340 (#202)
Gestapo, 12, 17, 26, 44, 111, 116-17,

119, 121, 154, 155, 161, 164, 168, 170, 171, 187 ff., 204, 239
Ghetto Fighters House (Haifa), 221, 378
Ghettos, 10, 17, 123, 187 ff.
Gigurtu, Ion, 264
Gilbert, G. M., 25-26, 127, 145, 321 (#2-5), 322 (#8)
Glaser, Stefan, 66, 297 (#32)
Globke, Hans, 60, 111, 312 (#29)
Globocnik, Odilo, 19, 24
Glube, S., 334 (#144)
Goebbels, Josef, 26, 93, 364 (#220)
Göppinger, Horst, 372 (#283, 285)
Göring, Hermann, 25, 62, 296 (#12), 308 (#148), 313 (#30), 317 (#85), 370 (#265), 372 (#288)
Golden, Harry, 113
Goldstein, J., 305 (#111), 313 (#34)
Goldstein, Mordecai, 170
Gollert, Friedrich, 93-94
Government-General, 11, 16-20, 92-94, 130, 146, 147, 169, 206, 237, 252, 274, 293 (#142), 312 (#29), 313 (#29), 322 (#19), 329 (#92)
Governments-in-exile, 209
Grabner, Maximilian, 25
Grabow, Isaac, 170
Granatshtein, Yehiel, 342 (#220)
Graven, Jean, 66, 297 (#31), 375-76
Great Britain, 103, 209, 214, 347 (#3). See also England; United Kingdom
Greece, 75, 130, 158, 167, 224, 267, 326 (#64), 338 (#188), 346 (#3), 349 (#3)
Greek Orthodox Church (Bulgaria), 256
Green, L. C., 376
Green Series, 282
Greiser, Arthur (Gauleiter, Warthegau), 293 (#144)
Grell, Horst, 8, 36, 128, 318 (#98)
Grenoble, 221
Grimm, Georg, 302 (#76)
Grinberg, Nathan, 255, 360 (#149, 156, 157), 361 (#162)